Saving Our World

Volume Two

By

Randy Landry

Table Of Contents

Chapter Twenty–Is the Green New Deal Good or Bad?

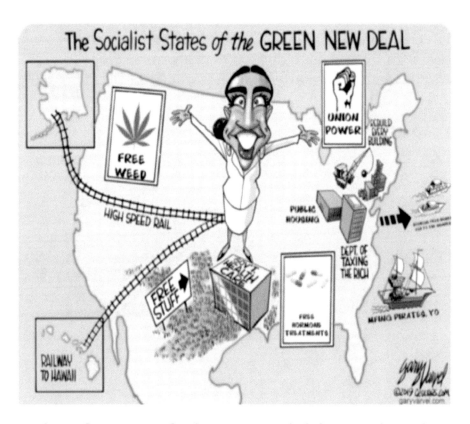

As if any of this would be a bad thing

The Green New Deal Explained

A call to end fossil fuels and build green jobs

The Green New Deal

The term *"Green New Deal"* has been used to describe various sets of policics that aim to make systemic change. For instance, the United Nations (UN) announced a Global Green New Deal in 2008.1 Former President Barack Obama added one to his platform when he ran for election in 2008, and Green Party candidates, such as Jill Stein and Howie Hawkins, did the same.

While it isn't a brand new concept, the Green New Deal has become a big part of policy debates in the country today, largely due to the remarkable ascent of Rep. Alexandria Ocasio-Cortez (D-NY), the youngest woman to be elected to the House of Representatives.

Her ambitious and wide-ranging proposal was a centerpiece of her campaign that addresses an issue that 60% of Americans say already affects their local community. As it stands, the deal promises to tackle economic inequality by creating high-quality union jobs. The Green New Deal has also been helped by a grassroots outfit called the Sunrise Movement, which organized a much-talked-about protest at Sen. Dianne Feinstein's office in February 2019.

KEY TAKEAWAYS

-The term *"Green New Deal"* has been used to describe various sets of policies that aim to make systemic change.

-The term was first used by Pulitzer Prize-winner Thomas Friedman in January 2007 and was made popular by the proposal made by Rep. Alexandria Ocasio-Cortez and Sen. Ed Markey in Congress in 2019.

-The deal, which failed to pass in the Senate, emphasizes environmental and social justice while calling for the creation of new jobs.

-Supporters say everyone is responsible to pay their fair share, which will result in tremendous cost savings.

-Critics say implementing the deal will cost as much as $93 trillion.

History of the Green New Deal

The term *"Green New Deal"* was first used by Pulitzer Prize-winner Thomas Friedman in January 2007. At that point, America experienced its hottest year on record (although there have been five hotter since). Friedman recognized the easy solution to climate change politicians hoped for wasn't possible. It was going to take money, effort, and upsetting an industry that is always generous with campaign contributions.

Transitioning away from fossil fuels, he argued in a New York Times column, would require the government to raise prices on them, introduce higher energy standards, and undertake a massive industrial project to scale up green technology.

"The right rallying call is for a 'Green New Deal,'" he wrote, referencing former President Franklin D. Roosevelt's domestic programs to rescue the country from the Great Depression.

"If you have put a windmill in your yard or some solar panels on your roof, bless your heart. But we will only green the world when we change the very nature of the electricity grid—moving it away from dirty coal or oil to clean coal and renewables."

The U.S. gets 80% of its energy from coal, petroleum, and natural gas.

Ocasio-Cortez's Green New Deal

Ocasio-Cortez and Sen. Ed Markey (D-Mass.) introduced a 14-page nonbinding resolution in Congress in February 2019 calling for the federal government to create a Green New Deal. The resolution had more than 100 co-sponsors in Congress and attracted a number of Democratic presidential candidates during the election.

On March 26, 2019, lawmakers in the Senate voted 57-0 against advancing the resolution with 43 out of 47 Democrats voting "present" in order to not take a formal position. The Democrats protested Senate Majority Leader Mitch McConnell (R-Ky.) bringing up the vote without scheduling hearings and expert testimonies first.

While politicians have known about climate change and the idea of a Green New Deal for years, this is the most detailed plan presented to the American people to transform the economy, even though it is extremely vague and acts as a set of principles and goals rather than of specific policies.

The text of the resolution details how climate change affects the economy, the environment, and national security, and outlines goals and projects for a 10-year national mobilization.

The plan emphasizes environmental and social justice. It acknowledges how historically oppressed groups (indigenous peoples, people of color, the poor, and migrants) are more likely to be affected by climate change and asks that they be included and consulted. Its progressive spirit is reflected in calls for the protection of workers' rights, community ownership, universal healthcare, and a job guarantee.

According to the resolution, the U.S. must lead the way to reduce emissions. That's because of its technological advancement and its historical contribution to the disproportionate amount of greenhouse gas emissions. The chart below, from the World Bank, illustrates how U.S. consumers account for an oversized share of global carbon emissions.

What's in the Green New Deal?

The main goal of the plan is to bring U.S. greenhouse gas emissions down to net zero and meet 100% of power demand in the country through clean, renewable, and zero-emission energy sources by 2030.

The Green New Deal also calls for the creation of millions of jobs to provide a job guarantee to all Americans, along with access to nature, clean air and water, healthy food, a sustainable environment, and community resiliency. These goals are to be accomplished through the following actions on the part of the federal government:

-Providing investments and leveraging funding to help communities affected by climate change

-Repairing and upgrading existing infrastructure to withstand extreme weather and ensuring all bills related to infrastructure in Congress address climate change

-Investing in renewable power sources

-Investing in manufacturing and industry to spur growth in the use of clean energy

-Building or upgrading to energy-efficient, distributed, and smart power grids that provide affordable electricity

-Upgrading all existing buildings and building new ones so that they achieve maximum energy efficiency, water efficiency, safety, affordability, comfort, and durability.

-Supporting family farming, investing in sustainable farming, and building a more sustainable and equitable food system

-Investing in transportation systems, namely zero-emission vehicle infrastructure and manufacturing, public transit, and high-speed rail

-Restoring ecosystems through land preservation, afforestation, and science-based projects

-Cleaning up existing hazardous waste and abandoned sites

-Identifying unknown sources of pollution and emissions

-Working with the international community on solutions and helping them achieve Green New Deals

Separate legislation would be needed to turn the Green New Deal into a reality if Congress passed the resolution.

The Green New Deal and the 2020 Election

The Green New Deal was one of the topics of the 2020 Presidential debates. Then-President Donald Trump disparaged rival Joe Biden's climate change plan, calling it a Green New Deal that would cost $100 trillion. Biden denied the charge saying, *"That is not my plan."*

During the Vice Presidential debate, Mike Pence claimed that the Biden-Harris team wanted *"to bury our economy under a $2 trillion Green New Deal. They want to abolish fossil fuels, and ban fracking, which would cost hundreds of thousands of American jobs all across the heartland."*

The resolution also factored into the campaign trail. Trump acknowledged that human activity contributes to climate change "to an extent." The Trump campaign wanted to keep fossil fuels in the energy conversation to appeal to those workers and to keep the U.S. relevant as a gas and oil exporter.

President Biden's Clean Energy Revolution

President Biden declined to endorse the Green New Deal but Vice President Harris was an original sponsor even though she says she fully supports the Biden climate plan. Called *"A Clean Energy Revolution,"* the plan has many of the same goals as the Green New Deal but with a less ambitious time frame and at a lower cost.

For example, the Green New Deal aspires to net-zero greenhouse gas emissions and 100% clean, renewable energy sources by 2030. Biden's plan, on the other hand, achieves that goal by 2050. The Green New Deal could cost between $51 and $93 trillion to implement, according to conservative think tanks. The Biden plan would involve a federal government investment of $1.7 trillion with a private sector, state, and local buy-in of about $5 trillion.

What's at Stake?

A common rebuttal to opponents from supporters of the Green New Deal is that although it will be expensive to implement, not doing so will be more expensive in the long run.

In order to stop temperatures from rising beyond 1.5 degrees Celsius—the target aimed for in the 2015 Paris Agreement—global emissions need to go to zero by 2050. This means that the window to avoid the most severe impact is rapidly closing.

The federal government spent $450 billion due to extreme weather and fire events between 2005 and 2018, according to a 2018 report by the U.S. Government Accounting Office. But experts warn that it will only get uglier.

Climate change will cause more than $500 billion in economic loss in the United States alone each year by 2090, according to a 2019 study. Independent research shows that about 10% could be wiped out in the global economy's value by 2050 if temperatures continue to rise by 3.2 degrees Celsius and the world doesn't meet the net-zero targets outlined by the Paris Agreement.

Support and Criticism of the Green New Deal

The Green New Deal resolution doesn't mention how the U.S. government, which has more than $30.4 trillion in debt, would pay for it. Ocasio-Cortez told CBS's 60 Minutes that *"people are going to have to start paying their fair share in taxes"* to pay for the Green New Deal and suggested tax rates of 60% to 70% for the very wealthy.

Regardless of where the money comes from, there is certainly a great deal of support for the proposal, not to mention a lot of criticism.

Support

Advocates of the Green New Deal who promote a heterodox macroeconomic framework called Modern Monetary Theory (MMT), including Ocasio-Cortez, believe the government shouldn't be too concerned about the cost.

"The federal government can spend money on public priorities without raising revenue, and it won't wreck the nation's economy to do so,"

a group of prominent MMT supporters wrote in an op-ed for The Huffington Post.

"The U.S. government can never run out of dollars, but humanity can run out of limited global resources. The climate crisis fundamentally threatens those resources and the very human livelihoods that depend on them."

Since its ascension in 2018, the Green New Deal has defined the terms of the global climate debate. Perhaps no other climate policy in history has been as successful. Democrats and Republicans alike have been judged by how closely they seem to hew to it. The Sunrise Movement, the highest-profile American climate-activism group, rallies for it. Abroad, the European Union has dubbed its 1-trillion-euro attempt to decarbonize its economy *"the EuropeanGreen Deal."* And on the histrionic fields of social media, progressives ask how society can afford flooded subways, horrific droughts, deadly heat waves, and uncontrollable wildfires but not pay for a Green New Deal.

The Green Party, whose plan also calls for America to move to 100% clean energy by 2030 and a job guarantee, says it will result in healthcare savings, (there will be fewer cases of disease linked to fossil fuels) and military savings (there will be no reason to safeguard fuel supplies abroad). The party's deal also advocates for a robust carbon fee program.

Healthcare and other savings were also touted in a 2015 study by a group of scientists from Stanford University and the University of California, Berkeley that said it is possible for the U.S. to replace 80% to 85% of the existing energy systems with ones powered entirely by wind, water, and sunlight by 2030 and 100% by 2050.

Criticism

The very real existential threat to the planet makes the Green New Deal a unique mission statement that is hard to ignore or dismiss. But critics call it too socialist, too extreme, or too impractical. Some are even warned that environmentalists *"want to take away your hamburgers."*

The kind of overhaul the deal calls for would be very expensive and require significant government intervention. The center-right American Action Forum pegs the maximum cost at $93 trillion, while Tax Policy Center senior fellow Howard Gleckman said the plan may slow the economy by adding to the debt and even drive jobs overseas.

"Instead of the Green New Deal, the federal government could adopt a revenue-neutral carbon tax to decrease emissions without exacerbating the fiscal imbalance,"

 said Jeffrey Miron, director of economic studies at the right-wing Cato Institute.

Edward B. Barbier, the American economics professor who wrote the report that formed the basis of the UN's Green New Deal, said that, instead of deficit funding, the government should use revenues that come from dismantled subsidies and environmental taxes.

Investing in a Green New Deal Economy

The passage of the Green New Deal is extremely unlikely in the current political climate. But it is worth looking at investing opportunities that may arise if it influences action at the state level or gets the green light in the future.

UBS says the Green New Deal is indicative of a longer-term trend towards more sustainable and green ways of producing and consuming. Justin Waring, the company's chief investment officer (CIO) strategist, recommends investing in environmentally oriented sustainable investments.

It feels a little odd to have to point this out as though it's some keen insight, but: US politics is pretty screwed up right now.

Waring added:

Oddly, one of few people to correctly grasp the stakes is New York Times columnist and longtime climate change bull-shitter Bret Stephens. In his latest column, he says:

"In addition to tapping into the themes' return potential, such an investment also represents a type of hedge against the possibility of more aggressive environmental legislation. It may seem counterintuitive, but if you are worried about environmental legislation, you might want to invest in environmentally-friendly investments."

Josh Price, an energy analyst at Height Capital Markets, told MarketWatch that while the resolution isn't *"a near-term catalyst for us by any means,"* the biofuels and renewables space is an interesting place to look for *"slow-money, long-time-horizon guys."* He mentioned NRG Energy (NRG), AES (AES), Xcel Energy (XEL) Renewable Energy Group (REGI), and Darling Ingredients (DAR) as stocks to watch.

So here it is: some people power, the most rare and precious commodity for anyone hoping to advance progressive goals.

While a Green New Deal doesn't explicitly call for eliminating fossil fuel usage, it would hit the industry hard. Nuclear energy stocks are best avoided as well in such a scenario since many don't consider it to be safe, renewable, or a clean source, and it isn't a part of the resolution. On the other hand, the semiconductor sector and electric vehicles industry would be among the winners.

How Much Would the Green New Deal Cost?

Opponents estimate a total cost between $51 and $93 trillion, based on upper-end estimates of the Green New Deal's policy objectives. While the cost may be high, supporters argue that the deal could lead to significant savings, by averting the worst consequences of climate change. Critics, on the other hand, say that implementing it could slow down the economy and will likely require a lot of overhaul and government oversight.

Who Wrote the Green New Deal?

The idea of a Green New Deal was first introduced by Thomas Friedman, who recognized there was no easy solution to climate change. He suggested it would take money, effort, and industry changes to make it a reality.

In 2019, Rep. Alexandria Ocasio-Cortez (D-NY) and Sen. Ed Markey (D-Mass) introduced a proposal for a Green New Deal in Congress, though it failed to pass in the Senate.

There have been a number of different versions of a Green New Deal, including one written by the Green Party.

How Would the Green New Deal Create Jobs?

The Green New Deal promises to create millions of jobs by tackling economic inequality. Americans would be guaranteed high-quality jobs backed by unions by shifting money from the fossil fuel industry to green technology. The deal supports the inclusion of traditionally marginalized individuals, such as migrant, indigenous, and racially diverse communities.

It's a vision that unites the left, from Joe Biden to John McDonnell. The trouble is, it's completely unworkable

Q: What binds together such disparate souls as Noam Chomsky and Keir Starmer, Yanis Varoufakis and Joe Biden, Alexandria Ocasio-Cortez and Caroline Lucas? A: They all want a green new deal. Right wingers pretend that today's left likes nothing better than to pull down statues for a laugh before disinviting speakers from student unions, but they are off by approximately 180 degrees. Only one project truly unifies the mainstream left across Europe and America today: trying to limit climate breakdown by overhauling a noxious economic model. Ask the individual parties how and a hundred flowers duly bloom, but all will be branded with those same three little words.

Promising a green new deal helped clinch the Labor leadership for Starmer. It's also how Biden keeps the Democrat base onside. It galvanizes activists and anchors progressive conversation. Measured from the start of 2018 until this week, the phrase *"Green New Deal"* appeared in this newspaper and on our website almost as many times as *"leveling up"* and far more than *"Narendra Modi"*. Seeing as one of those is Boris Johnson's signature policy and the other runs the world's second-most populous country, that is quite the showing. Such dominance should spur serious interrogation, yet what the green new deal has received so far is mostly explanation or celebration. So aren't I, as a gainfully employed Guardianista, coming to join the joyous party? Sorry, but no. I like and respect many of the people working on it, and a few I count as friends – at least until they read this. I certainly agree with their top-line argument that the planet cannot afford this kamikaze capitalism. I just don't see the green new deal as the answer.

The project itself – supposedly a stark, bold, urgent idea – is a conceptual fog. Like some kind of policy peasouper, it nestles densely around arguments of ecological limits, social justice and economic transformation, allowing only a glimpse of their outlines. That suits many on the left, as it serves to obscure all their disagreements and so keep the peace just a little longer. Rare is the bus that can keep on board both Sadiq Khan and John McDonnell, and take them to totally different destinations. But at some point the warm words and the broad coalitions lose their charm and you are left just as the delegates in Glasgow are: facing the grim reality of a planet on fire. Truth be told, the thing was born in a haze. In 2007, the New York Times columnist Thomas Friedman took a break from cheering on the Iraq war and crowing about corporate globalization to pen a demand for a green new deal. His gauntlet was picked up in London by a small group of environmentalists and economists (including Larry Elliott, of this parish), who spent the months after the collapse of Northern Rock writing a plan to tackle the *"triple crunch of financial meltdown, climate change and 'peak oil'"*.

No such radicalism was on Friedman's menu when he wrote:

"I am not proposing that we Americans radically alter our lifestyles. We are who we are – including a car culture. But if we want to continue to be who we are, enjoy the benefits and be able to pass them on to our children, we do need to fuel our future in a cleaner, greener way ... The next president will have to rally us with a green patriotism. Hence my motto: 'Green is the new red, white and blue.'"

Depending on which specs you had on, the green new deal either looked all-American and utterly painless – or it was internationalist and out for bankers' blood. And down the years, the contradictions have only multiplied. For AOC and today's US left, it is about jobs (albeit *"green"* ones, a term far easier to deploy than to define) and infrastructure; for Lucas, Labor's Clive Lewis and others currently pushing a green new deal through parliament, it includes citizens' assemblies and a shorter working week. It is both *"a green industrial revolution"* in the north of England and debt cancellation for the global south; both low-carbon Keynesianism and nationalization of the energy industry. It is, in other words, a big duffel bag stuffed with pent-up progressive demands and jumbled up with highly dubious history and tiresome war metaphors.

Why hark back to FDR, who entered the White House nearly a century ago, if you want to be a contemporary global movement? Why lean on Keynes as your crutch, when he set out to save capitalism not to scrap it? Most of all, why talk about a *"moonshot moment"* (an oft-deployed metaphor by green new dealers, invoking the space race)? The next few decades will not be about inventing entirely new things but substituting for what we already have. Installing heat pumps and ripping out boilers, using renewables rather than fossil fuels, relying on battery power over the internal combustion engine: moving to a lower-carbon future is not going to be a great, dramatic transformation – it will be slow and chronic, and frankly more expensive to societies reared on cheap food, cheap energy and the idea that the rest of the bill for both those things will be picked up by someone else, perhaps yet to be born. This isn't just a debate over words; it is a battle between rival visions of the future. When Ed Miliband enthuses in his recent (and good) book, Go Big, about moving to a wartime economy with a vast *"carbon army"* retrofitting draughty homes, he is talking about a green transition that is done to people rather than with them. And it turns voters off. Earlier this year, the polling firm Survation surveyed Britons on a scheme to employ a million people to insulate houses and asked: what should they call it? At the bottom of the list came green new deal. Almost as bad was green industrial revolution. Far and away the favorite was national recovery plan. A process not a product, common sense rather than radicalism.

At some point, the post-2016 left, radicalized by Trump and Brexit, will have to surrender its notions of a radical program executed through a vast state machinery. Zombie Johnsonism or revived Trumpism will see them off. I hope what comes next is a more focused, locally rooted and inclusive politics based around asking people what they actually need in their lives, and working out how to fit those things within an environmental framework. That can be done with universal desires such as housing and food, healthcare and education. This is not about green growth versus de-growth, and all those old dichotomies. It is about recognizing that large swaths of Britain are now effectively post-growth, and that the proceeds of whatever growth we have had has been very unfairly divided. So let us stop haring after *"British-owned turbine factories" and "dominating the industries of tomorrow"* and all the other boilerplate of politics. Let's get real.

The Green New Deal Does Not, Strictly Speaking, Exist

The idea has reshaped global climate policy, but is far less concrete than its supporters have been led to believe.

Even now, as Democrats in Congress and the White House wrangle over the terms of President Joe Biden's infrastructure bill, the Green New Deal leers from the sidelines. How does the bipartisan infrastructure deal differ from the Green New Deal? Will the partisan reconciliation bill amount to a Green New Deal?

With so much ballyhoo, it's become easy to miss the central, implacable fact about the Green New Deal: It does not exist.

By this, I don't mean that it hasn't passed. I mean something more fundamental: Nobody has written it down. Three years after the idea of a Green New Deal broke into the mainstream, you can't find an authoritative and detailed list of Green New Deal policies anywhere. There is no handbook, no draft legislation, no official report that articulates what belongs in a Green New Deal and what doesn't.

This is more than just an academic point. It means that tens of thousands of Americans want very badly to see Congress adopt a political program that definitionally cannot pass,because there is no "it" for lawmakers to vote on. It means that Biden's infrastructure package cannot be comparedwith the Green New Deal, because the contrast will not find purchase. It means that at a moment of historic possibility, American climate politics still has one leg stuck in the spectral and symbolic, when it should be knee-deep in the real.

I should clarify: We're not entirely ignorant about the Green New Deal's policy aims. To hear most supporters tell it, the core idea of a Green New Deal is that the federal government should be the author and finisher of America's climate transition. The government should decarbonize the country's energy system by 2030, if not sooner, and adapt American infrastructure to a hotter, angrier world. And it should do so while reducing material inequality and remedying racial injustice. So far, so good.

Onto these climate goals, the Green New Deal has tacked demands for good old-fashioned European social democracy: The original, 14-page Green New Deal resolution, which sketched broad goals and was introduced by Representative Alexandria Ocasio-Cortez and Senator Ed Markey in 2019, demanded universal health care, affordable and safe housing, and protections for workers' right to unionize. These goals made it into later versions of the Green New Deal: You could find them in Senator Bernie Sanders's climate platform during the 2020 presidential primary, and the Sunrise Movement still demands Medicare for All and student-debt forgiveness.

This bid to expand the welfare state has attracted nonstop criticism. But maybe surprisingly, it strikes me as one of the best-explained aspects of the Green New Deal's program. It rests (to my eye, at least) on the work of Naomi Klein, Alyssa Battistonti, and a handful of other leftist political theorists who have argued that climate change makes such intense demands of society that addressing it requires a full rewriting of the social contract between individuals and the state. Earth has too few resources to offer every human a life of private opulence; what it can sustain, instead, are communal luxuries—fewer Bugattis, more beautiful rapid-transit systems. The way to create buy-in for climate policy is by building those luxuries as the constraints of low carbon consumption start to bite.

That's a keen insight.But how to bring about that low carbon consumption? Here, the unifying thread starts to fray. For instance: The original Green New Deal resolution devoted a surprising amount of verbiage to *"de-industrialization"* and the decline of American manufacturing. It called for green tariffs, purchase guarantees, and beefy "buy American" rules to reinvigorate U.S. industry. When I wrote about the Green New Deal in February 2019, I dubbed this enthusiasm for industrial policy its *"big idea."*

That approach was championed by a think tank called New Consensus, which was supposed to write a summary report on the Green New Deal in 2019. Such a report would have clarified what, exactly, belonged in a Green New Deal and what didn't. But that report never came out, and no other group has tried to write it.

In the resulting vacuum, a series of more recent proposals has taken almost the opposite approach from New Consensus, arguing that the caregiving work of nurses, teachers, and child-care providers should dominate any Green New Deal. This approach sits uneasily at best with a demand for reindustrialization. And the closer one looks, the more one finds areas of silent but potent disagreement about what a Green New Deal even is.

Take these questions, for instance:

How much of a role should electric cars play in a Green New Deal?
Activists often talk about ubiquitous buses and high-speed rail. But Sanders's 2020 climate platform created a more or less direct $3.5 trillion

subsidy for the auto industry by helping Americans buy electric cars.

How much of a role should the government play? When Ocasio-Cortez spoke about the Green New Deal three years ago, she allowed for Tennessee Valley Authority–type institutions as well as public-private partnerships. *"It's not as though the federal government's going to wave a wand and say, 'We're going to do it all ourselves,'"* she said. Now the Sunrise Movement's main demand of the government is for a Civilian Climate Corps that will directly hire young people.

How should the Green New Deal be funded? Should the U.S. government push private capital into climate-friendly projects by establishing a new ratings agency for green finance? Or should it reject any role whatsoever for private capital in the energy transition, funding the whole affair through tax dollars?

And thorniest of all: What is the role of the American state in global decarbonization? Should the United States aim to play the same role in the energy transition that it played in World War II (whatever that means)? Can the Pentagon accelerate decarbonization, as Senator Elizabeth Warren has pitched? Or should the U.S. retreat from global affairs, seeking only to partner peacefully with China, or even going as far as defunding the military, as the Sunrise Movement has called for?

These questions matter because they shape how progressives think about climate policy now. Biden has championed both a new industrial policy and care work as infrastructure. How different are his plans from what a Green New Deal would do? The bipartisan infrastructure deal includes a $27 billion green financial accelerator, a sort of green bank. Is that good for progressives, because it is based off Sanders's plan for a state development bank; or bad, because it muddies a public process with private capital?

Perhaps I'm looking for too much specificity. Maybe no detailed plan is needed in advance. President Franklin D. Roosevelt's original New Deal was an improvisational response to a crisis; it was experimental and pragmatic, not foreordained and strategic. Yet if that's the case, then progressives should bring a sense of imagination, of possibility, to discussions of the Green New Deal. They should recognize that the Green New Deal is not a single policy to win, but a change in outlook and approach. It does not have a price tag, because it will never be a single thing at all.

This confusion, I think, points to perhaps the most ignored and most important aspect of the climate-policy debate: Nobody knows how to solve climate change. Nobody knows how to decarbonize the economy. Oh, people have ideas about what kind of technologies are important—the U.S. needs more wind, more solar, more electric vehicles, smarter electric grids—but on the fundamental question of how to make those changes happen quickly, we live in ignorance. What kind of political program will connect the prose to the passion, allowing climate-concerned policy makers and workers to build the infrastructure we need today, bank their successes tomorrow, and remake the economy in a decade? The answer is: We do not know. Nobody knows. The world remains open. That's what makes working on climate issues so enthralling, so terrifying, and such a privilege.

It's Not Just About Cost. The Green New Deal Is Bad Environmental Policy, Too

Nick is an economist who focused on energy, environmental, and regulatory issues as the Herbert and Joyce Morgan fellow. Sen. Bernie Sanders (I-VT) attends a news conference to introduce legislation to transform public housing as part of the Green New Deal outside the U.S. Capitol November 14, 2019.

KEY TAKEAWAYS

Researchers estimate it would take more than $5 trillion just to switch from coal, nuclear and natural gas to 100% renewables.

The Green New Deal would massively expand the size and scope of the federal government's control over activities best left to the private sector.

The reality is that environmental policies aren't good for the environment if they're so bad for people.

We're not hearing much about the *"Green New Deal"* these days, but it's still a priority for some candidates, as anyone who's attended a recent Bernie Sanders rally can attest.

Criticism of the GND tends to center on cost and rightly so. It would be extremely expensive. Researchers estimate it would take more than $5 trillion just to switch from coal, nuclear and natural gas to 100% renewables.

But even if you set economic concerns aside, an ironic fact remains: In the United States and around the world, the central-planning policies at the heart of the GND have a horrible track record for the environment.

Governments in countries such as Venezuela and China (or in the past like the Soviet Union and Cuba) either routinely mismanage and waste resources, or ramp up production with little to no accountability for environmental damage that comes with it. The absence of price signals reduces the incentive to be more efficient and do more with less.

In addition, the absence of property rights reduces the incentive to conserve and gives government-controlled industries a free pass to pollute without compensating or protecting its citizens.

The Green New Deal would massively expand the size and scope of the federal government's control over activities best left to the private sector.

It would empower the feds to change and control how people produce and consume energy, harvest crops, raise livestock, build homes, drive cars and manufacture goods.

Secondly, the Green New Deal would result in a number of unintended consequences. For instance, policies that limit coal, oil and natural gas production in the United States will not stop the global consumption of these natural resources. Production will merely shift to places where the environmental standards are not as rigorous, making the planet worse off.

Moreover, it's not as if wind, solar and battery technologies magically appear. Companies still have to mine the resources, manufacture the product and deal with the waste streams. There are challenges to disposing potentially toxic lithium-ion batteries and solar panels, or even wind turbine blades that are difficult and expensive to transport and crush at landfills. While these are solvable problems, they're seldom discussed by GND proponents.

There would also be massive land use changes required to expand renewable power. Ben Zycher at the American Enterprise Institute estimates that land use necessary to meet a 100% renewable target would require 115 million acres, which is 15% larger than the land area of California.

Two recent National Bureau of Economic Research papers underscore the unintended consequences of energy policy on human well-being. One found that cheaper home heating because of America's fracking revolution is averting more than 10,000 winter deaths per year. The Green New Deal would wipe all of that away, and reverse course by mandating pricier energy on families.

Another paper found that the Japanese government's decision to close safely operating nuclear power plants after Fukashima increased energy prices and reduced consumption, which consequently, increased mortalities from colder temperatures. In fact, the authors estimate that *"the decision to cease nuclear production has contributed to more deaths than the accident itself."* Unintended consequences.

Another hallmark of bad environmental policy is focusing on outputs, not outcomes. According to the frequently asked questions sheet released along with the Green New Deal, it is "*a massive investment in renewable energy production and would not include creating new nuclear plants.*"

One would think that if we only have 11 or 12 years to act on climate change, we'd want to grab the largest source of emissions-free electricity we can get. But that's not the case.

That's typical for most big-government environmental policies: they're so focused on prescriptive ways to control peoples' behaviors that they crowd out or ignore opportunities for innovative solutions.

The reality is that environmental policies aren't good for the environment if they're so bad for people. The costs of the GND would be devastatingly high for households. Government policies that drive up energy bills are not only very regressive, but they would also harm consumers multiple times as they pay more for food, clothes and all of the other goods that require energy to make.

By shrinking our economy by potentially tens of trillions of dollars, the Green New Deal will cause lower levels of prosperity and fewer resources to deal with whatever environmental challenges come our way. That's a bad deal for our economy and our environment.

THE GREEN NEW DEAL WOULD HARM AMERICANS, NOT HELP THEM

The Green New Deal (GND), a piece of legislation proposed by Rep. Alexandria Ocasio-Cortez, gained support from a large base of the younger generation.

The Green New Deal's goal is to solve America's environmental issues.

However, as a student and a young person who will receive the negative effects of this deal should it pass, I find this proposal concerning, as its main directive is to siege control and impose progressive laws override their desires to aid the "*climate crises.*"

Many support the GND because they want to solve climate change, but multiple studies have shown it wouldn't do much to help the issue. According to a study done by the American Enterprise Institute, the proposal would reduce global temperatures by "*0.083 to 0.173 degrees,*" a number "*barely distinguishable from zero.*"

The GND would also be astronomically expensive. In a study reported by Bloomberg News, the proposal could cost up to $93 trillion over the span of 10 years, or $65,000 per family, per year. That's more than three times the national debt. Between paying for my tuition and student loans, I can't afford to take on more financial burden and neither can the majority of other college students.

In addition, the Heritage Foundation reports that the GND would cause the average household's electricity cost to increase by about 12-14%. Economic recession or not, this is an additional hardship that struggling Americans cannot afford.

Another concern is that the initial goal of the GND was not to solve environmental issues, but rather to restructure the economy.

Rep. Ocasio-Cortez's former chief of staff, Saikat Chakrabarti, even said,

"The interesting thing about the Green New Deal is it wasn't originally a climate thing at all," and, *"...we really think of it as a how-do-you-change-the-entire-economy thing,"* according to the The Washington Post.

This legislation seems to be a proposal for economic change camouflaged as a piece of environmental legislation.

Environmental policies implemented by the government from the top-down, such as the GND, can lead to more pollution, which is contradictory to the solution this policy aims to provide. As reported by the journal Global Environmental Change, Russia (formerly the USSR when these policies were put into place) already implemented top-down policies like the GND, however, its air quality is 1.5 times dirtier than the USA's per unit of GDP in the 1980s.

The Green New Deal aims to restructure the economy under the guise of environmental solutions.

Lastly, the GND would largely expand the use of wind and solar energy, but in order to make this work on a national, industrial scale, it would mean the clearing of hundreds of thousands of square miles of forest and habitat to make way for those facilities, according to the Committee for a Constructive Tomorrow. In an effort to promote conservation, habitats for wildlife would be destroyed while making room for these facilities, such as solar panel farms.

The Green New Deal is a harmful environmental policy that aims to implement faulty solutions to the environmental problem that would harm the American people more than it
would help.

To be fair I will included a pro Green New Deal article here.

This is   an
emergency, damn it!

Green New Deal critics are missing the bigger picture.

Earlier this month, Sen. Ed Markey (D-MA) and Rep. Alexandria
Ocasio-Cortez (D-NY) introduced a Green New Deal resolution laying out
an ambitious set of goals and principles aimed at transforming and

decarbonizing the U.S. economy.

The release prompted a great deal of smart, insightful writing, but also a lot of knee-jerk and predictable cant. Conservatives called it socialist. Moderates called it extreme. Pundits called it unrealistic. Wonks scolded it over this or that omission. Political gossip columnists obsessed over missteps in the rollout.

What ties the latter reactions together, from my perspective, is that they seem oblivious to the historical moment, like thespians acting out an old, familiar play even as the theater goes up in flames around them.

To put it bluntly: This is not normal. We are not in an era of normal politics. There is no precedent for the climate crisis, its dangers or its opportunities. Above all, it calls for courage and fresh thinking.

Rather than jumping into individual responses, I want to take a step back and try to situate the Green New Deal in our current historical context, at least as I see it. Then it will be clearer why I think so many critics have missed the mark.

The context, part one: this is a fucking emergency

The earth's climate has already warmed 1 degree Celsius from preindustrial levels, unleashing a cascade of super-charged heat waves, wildfires, hurricanes, storms, water shortages, migrations, and conflicts. Climate change is not a threat; it's here. The climate has changed.

And it is changing more rapidly than at any time in millions of years. The human race is leaving behind the climatic conditions in which all of advanced civilization developed, going back to the beginning of agriculture. We have no certainty about what will happen next, mainly because we have no certainty about what we will do, but we know the changes are bad and going to get much worse, even with concerted global action.

Without concerted global action — and with a few bad breaks on climate sensitivity, population, and fossil fuel projections — the worst-case scenarios include civilization-threatening consequences that will be utterly disastrous for most of the planet.

At the moment, nobody is doing a better job of describing the tragic unfolding reality of climate change than author David Wallace-Wells, especially in his new book The Uninhabitable Earth, but also in this New York Times piece. Here's just a paragraph of coming attractions:

As temperatures rise, this could mean many of the biggest cities in the Middle East and South Asia would become lethally hot in summer, perhaps as soon as 2050. There would be ice-free summers in the Arctic and the unstoppable disintegration of the West Antarctic's ice sheet, which some scientists believe has already begun, threatening the world's coastal cities with inundation. Coral reefs would mostly disappear. And there would be tens of millions of climate refugees, perhaps many more, fleeing droughts, flooding and extreme heat, and the possibility of multiple climate-driven natural disasters striking simultaneously.

All of that is expected when the global average temperature rises 2 degrees Celsius.

New EPA Administrator Andrew Wheeler recently dismissed the latest IPCC report as being based on a *"worst-case scenario,"* which is darkly ironic, since the report is all about the dangers that lie between 1.5 and 2 degrees of warming.

But 2 degrees is not the worst-case scenario. It is among the best-case scenarios. The UN thinks we're headed for somewhere around 4 degrees by 2100. Believing that we can limit temperature rise to 2 degrees — a level of warming scientists view as catastrophic — now counts as wild-haired optimism, requiring heroic assumptions about technology development and political transformation.

The best-case scenario is very, very bad. And it gets much worse from there. From Wallace-Wells' book:

Two degrees would be terrible, but it's better than three, at which point Southern

Europe would be in permanent drought, African droughts would last five years on average, and the areas burned annually by wildfires in the United States could quadruple, or worse, from last year's million-plus acres. And three degrees is much better than four, at which point six natural disasters could strike a single community simultaneously; the number of climate refugees, already in the millions, could grow tenfold, or 20-fold, or more; and, globally, damages from warming could reach $600 trillion — about double all the wealth that exists in the world today.

The worst-case scenario, which, contra Wheeler, is virtually never discussed in polite political circles in the US, is, as Wallace-Wells quotes famed naturalist David Attenborough saying, *"the collapse of our civilizations and the extinction of much of the natural world."*

That is alarming and, if you must, *"alarmist,"* but as Wallace-Wells says, *"being alarmed is not a sign of being hysterical; when it comes to climate change, being alarmed is what the facts demand."*

The status quo — continuing along the same trajectory, doing the same things — leads to disaster on a scale that is genuinely difficult to comprehend, involving the fate of our species and thousands of others over centuries to come. (Remember, just because our models tend to stop at 2100 doesn't mean warming will stop then. It will just get worse.)

The crucial decisions that will shape our species' future will take place over the next decade. Dramatic change is the only hope of avoiding the worst.

Choosing to continue down our present path is madness. Nihilism. It is not *"moderation."*

The context, part two: US politics is a dumpster fire and there is no center

The conservative movement and the Republican Party have descended into unrestrained tribalism, rallying around what is effectively a crime boss who it now appears was elected with the help of a hostile foreign power. The media has calved in two, with an entire shadow right-wing media capturing the near-exclusive attention of movement conservatives, descending into increasingly baroque and lurid fantasies.

The president is now openly admitting to scheduling a "*national emergency*" because he wanted money for his wall, itself a lurid xenophobic fantasy. Meanwhile he is doing everything in his power to delay or shut down multiple federal investigations into his possible crimes. At every stage of his descent into paranoid lawlessness he has had the support of Republicans in Congress (because he lowered taxes on rich people) and the near-unanimous backing of Republican voters (because he owns the libs).

Basic norms of political conduct are crumbling on a daily basis. The country's core institutions are under intense stress. It plays out on television and social media like an exhausting spectacle, always turned to 11.

And it all takes place in the context of Americans' shrinking faith in their political system, which is ever-more-nakedly funneling wealth and power to the already wealthy and powerful (while protecting them from accountability) and heaping more risk and instability onto the most vulnerable.

The reactionary (largely older white male) backlash and the rising appeal of democratic socialism among the young are both, in their own ways, responses to a money-soaked, unresponsive political system.

The house is on fire. But an odd number of Democrats and pundits just seem to be whistling past it, acting out familiar roles and repeating familiar narratives, as though we're still in an era of normal politics, as though there are still two normal parties and some coherent "*center*" they are both attempting to capture.

One "*moderate*" critique of the GND, from Jason Grumet of the Bipartisan Policy Center, is that it overreaches, threatening bipartisan cooperation. But none of these allegedly moderate critics ever explains why, after more than a decade of openly stated, unapologetic, total opposition to anything

Democrats propose, the GOP would allow their opponents a victory on one of the most polarizing issues in public life.

For more than a decade, *"bipartisan cooperation"* has, with very few exceptions, meant inaction on climate change (and much else). And with every passing year, the Republican Party descends further into ethno-nationalism and plutocracy. Why are prospects better now?

There is nothing in 21st century American politics to suggest that Republicans will join with Democrats in a dramatic transformation of the economy along more sustainable lines. At this point, it is those who propose bipartisanship as an alternative who bear the burden of proof.

There are those who believe that the structure of US politics is such that bipartisanship is the only route to substantial progress. There's plenty of evidence and a good-faith argument to be made for that position.

But those who believe it should squarely grapple with the implications. Bipartisanship on any appreciable scale, at least based on reason and persuasion, is currently impossible in US federal politics. Republicans have made it so. If real progress is impossible without bipartisanship, then real progress is impossible, the US political system is doomed, and we will suffer the ravages of unabated climate change.

Let's assume the most dire predictions are right and we don't have a moment to lose in substantially decarbonizing the global economy, no matter what the financial cost or political pain. In that case, isn't Pelosi's incrementalist approach to climate absurdly inadequate?

Why yes. Yes it is.

Are we dealing with a problem so severe that it requires the political and economic equivalent of war socialism? Or should we think of climate change roughly the same way we think about global poverty — a serious problem we can work patiently to solve without resort to extreme measures like ending capitalism or depriving equally serious priorities of the attention they deserve?

One can quibble with whether it's accurate to characterize the New Deal as "*war socialism*" — it was, after all, run primarily in partnership with private industry.

One can also quibble with whether addressing climate change will deprive other issues of attention, as opposed to working in synchrony with them. (Water, agriculture, disease, economic development — climate overlaps with all of them.)

But Stephens gets the basic question right: Is climate change a priority-one emergency, threatening progress in all other areas, as the IPCC and America's own scientists say? Or is it a manageable problem, addressable with patient, meliorist policy?

Stephens chooses the latter. Tellingly, he offers absolutely no evidence, no reason to distrust the scientific consensus. He can't wrap his head around the implications of the science so he simply rejects them.

Nonetheless, it's clear that the US political status quo leads to morally unforgivable inaction. That is the baseline condition. Only something that jolts politics in a new direction, marshals some new force, tries some new strategy, has any chance of success (for the grim definitions of "success" still available).

Political change of that scale and speed is unlikely. It's a long shot. But it's either long shots or climate disaster at this point.

The context, part three: grassroots energy is not fungible

What can rescue American politics from its current swirl down the toilet bowl? What can give it a jolt of life?

It won't be a return to the late-Obama era status quo, wherein Democrats win, propose things, and Republicans block them, in a kind of politically numbing kabuki.

It won't be another scientific report or policy paper. It won't be another clever *"framing"* or promising poll result. It won't be any number or combination of words. It can only happen through power.

And the need for power is not symmetrical. Conservatives defend the status quo and the interests of incumbents. In all of politics, but especially in US politics, preserving the status quo is easier than changing it. It is easier to block and destroy things than to pass and build them. Conservatives have a lower bar for success and the reliable backing of those who benefit most from the status quo.

The left will never win the money game. The right's billionaires are united in advocating for their interest in lower taxes, less regulation, and less accountability. The left's are more likely to pick vanity causes or candidates. They love social causes but are far less likely than their counterparts on the right to focus on economic issues or redistribution, in part because many of them are quasi-libertarian tech bros who believe they are smarter than governments and better able to "change the world" if left to their billions.

And of course, government by the whims of the wealthy is problematic in and of itself.

That leaves people power.

Here's the only way any of this works: You develop a vision of politics that puts ordinary people at the center and gives them a tangible stake in the country's future, a share in its enormous wealth, and a role to play in its greater purpose. Then organize people around that vision and demand it from elected representatives. If elected representatives don't push for it, make sure they get primaried or defeated. If you want bipartisanship, get it because politicians in purple districts and states are scared to cross you, not because you led them to the sweet light of reason.

That's the only prospect I know of for climate action on a sufficient scale. (Seriously, if you know of another, email me.)

Into this milieu comes a youth movement that takes a Democratic Party disengaged and unambitious on climate change and smacks it upside the head. It puts the ultimate goal — to completely decarbonize the US economy in a just and equitable way — on the mainstream Democratic agenda for the first time ever. It accomplishes all this in the course of a few short months.

The conservative response, of course, was entirely predictable. The right reacted exactly as they have reacted to every proposal for social progress since the turn of the 20th century: they denounced it as socialism. You may remember that reaction from unions, Social Security, Medicare, air and water quality regulations, workplace safety standards, seat belts, labeling laws on cigarettes, or Obamacare.

And they lied about it, projecting a whole series of hyperbolic ideological fantasies — it will ban cows and airplanes and SUVs, oh my!

Again: as inevitable as the tides.

But what of people who share the goal of decarbonizing the US economy in a just and equitable way? How should they react?

Should they scold the young activists over ambiguous wording in the resolution? Over failures in the rollout, including the erroneous FAQ that was posted to AOC's site and then taken down? Over asking for too much — too much justice, too much equity, too many guarantees and promises for ordinary people? Over their failure to properly weight this or that favored technology or policy?

There was so much of this, a stale pageant of Very Serious gestures operating in bizarre indifference to the urgency of current circumstances.

These activists are people in their 20s and early 30s facing a looming catastrophe that previous generations — the very ones busy scolding them for their excess idealism — failed utterly to prevent or address. They are winging it, putting together a plan for economic transformation on the fly, like an overdue college project, because nobody else stepped up to do it.

As Wallace-Wells often points out, the majority of the carbon dioxide that is now in the atmosphere has been emitted since 1988, when climate scientist James Hansen first testified to Congress about climate change. This crisis has largely been created in the space of a generation, by people around the world who knew, or should have known, what they were doing.

These young people, the ones who will live with the snowballing damage, want the US to marshal its full resources to tackle the problem, to transform its economy without leaving anyone behind. It takes a lot of gall for the very people responsible for the current desperate situation to tell them they're asking for too much, that they should settle down and let the adults handle it.

And it's incredibly short-sighted. A wave of grassroots enthusiasm like this isn't fungible. It can't be returned to the kitchen in exchange for a new one with the perfect mix of policy and rhetorical ingredients. It is lightning in a bottle, easily squandered.

There isn't much time left to wait for another one. Smart leaders who share the broad goal of equitable decarbonization will amplify and deploy grassroots energy while it's available. The policy details can be worked out later.

Speaking of which, why not try to make sure the policy takes shape in a smart way? Why not be constructive?

The context, part four: the Green New Deal is not what people are saying it is

The GND resolution is not a policy or a series of policies. It is a set of goals, aspirations, and principles. It purposefully puts the vision up front and leaves the policymaking for later.

Nonetheless, many commentators have simply chosen to pretend it is policy, or project policy on it. *"The government would put sector after sector under partial or complete federal control,"* frets David Brooks in the New York Times, and *"oversee the renovation of every building in America."* None of this is in the resolution.

Nor is a prohibition on nuclear power. Nor is a prohibition on carbon taxes. All of these are things various critics have projected on it.

Neither, as even some sympathetic critics have charged, is it simply a *"laundry list"* of things progressives happen to like. As the Atlantic's Rob Meyer argues in this excellent piece, the GND is an expression of a coherent and very American economic philosophy: good old industrial policy.

Actively guiding the economy went out of fashion with the Reagan revolution. Since then, US policymakers have generally restrained themselves to correcting market failures (at least rhetorically — in practice, industrial policy never stopped, it just got buried in the tax code or omnibus bills).

The premise of industrial policy is that the market needs direction and that government should direct it, through public spending, tax policy, regulations, public-private partnerships, and the power of procurement, among other means. (Check out the reading list on the website of New Consensus, the think tank shaping GND policy, for a sense of the policy antecedents and rationales.)

Industrial policy has been the norm in the US, as in most developed countries, for most of its life. Most of the technological advances produced by the US economy have their roots in such policy. It is only in the last 40 years or so that the conservative movement, behind a well-funded media and advocacy apparatus, convinced Americans that the government is *"broke"* and that public intervention in the economy is presumptively illegitimate.

Part of good industrial policy is shielding ordinary people from the sometimes harsh consequences of economic transformation. The New Deal did that fairly well with land grants, bonds, and job programs, but all its programs were biased strongly in favor of white men.

The GND does not want to repeat those mistakes. So alongside the decarbonization targets for electricity, transportation, industry, and buildings are a series of provisions ensuring that everyone can get a job, that everyone can access health care regardless of their job situation, and that the benefits of public investment will be channeled toward the most vulnerable communities.

It says to Americans: we are going to do something really big, fast, disruptive, and ambitious, but during the transition, you will not be left behind or forgotten. You will be able to find a job and a role to play; you will be not be threatened with homelessness or lack of healthcare. We are going to do this big thing together, all of us, and through it we will lift each other up.

That message will not please America's oligarchs. It sounds entirely "unrealistic" given the narrow bounds of the possible in Washington, DC. But it can inspire ordinary people and get them invested in solving climate change. And if there's another way to get a broad swathe of Americans fired up about climate change, I haven't heard it, certainly not from the legion of GND armchair critics.

To be sure, many economists still oppose industrial policy, and perhaps some Democrats and pundits simply prefer those economists. Perhaps they really are ideologically devoted to market mechanisms and market mechanisms alone.

But to the extent Democrats and pundits are simply looking at the GND through the lens of recent US policy and political dynamics, they need to step back and think bigger. The whole point of this is to try something new, something different — because, again, the current trajectory leads to disaster.

Give the GND a chance

So that's the context here: a world tipping over into catastrophe, a political system under siege by reactionary plutocrats, a rare wave of well-organized grassroots enthusiasm, and a guiding document that does nothing but articulate goals that any climate-informed progressive ought to share.

Given all that, for those who acknowledge the importance of decarbonizing the economy and recognize how cosmically difficult it is going to be, maybe nitpicking and scolding isn't the way to go. Maybe the moment calls for a constructive and additive spirit.

The GND remains a statement of aspirations. All the concrete work of policymaking lies ahead. There will be room for carbon prices and R&D spending and performance standards and housing density and all the rest of the vast menu of options for reducing emissions. None of those policy debates have been preempted or silenced.

And yes, there are any number of ways it could go off the rails, politically or substantively. Everyone is free, nay, encouraged to use their critical judgment.

But the circumstances we find ourselves in are extraordinary and desperate. Above all, they call upon all of us to put aside our egos and our personal brands and strive for solidarity, to build the biggest and most powerful social force possible behind the only kind of rapid transition that can hope to inspire other countries and forestall the worst of climate change.

If there is to be swift, large-scale change in the US, a country with a political system practically built to prevent such things, it probably won't look exactly like any of us want. In fact, the odds are against it happening at all. So this doesn't seem like a time to be cavalier about the opportunities that do come along.

The kids are out there, organized, demanding a solution. Let's try to give them one.

Resources

Heritage.org, "It's Not Just About Cost. The Green New Deal is Bad Environment Policy, Too." BY Nicolas Loris; liberty.edu, "The Green New Deal Would Harm Americans, Not Help Them." BY Julia Heath. Investopedia.com, "The Green New Deal Explained." BY Deborah D'Souza; theatlantic.com, "The Green New Deal Does Not, Strictly Speaking, Exist." By Robinson Meyers; theguardian.com, "Muddled, top-down, technocratic: why the green new deal should be scraped." BY Aditya Chakrabortty; vox.com, "This is an emergency damnit: Green New Deal critics are missing the bigger picture." BY Davis Roberts;

Chapter Twenty-One–Saving Our Animal Life

Top 10 ways to save wildlife

There are more than 7 billion people on Earth. Imagine if every one of us committed to do one thing — no matter how small — to protect wildlife every day. Even minor actions can have a major impact when we all work together. Here are ways you can make a difference:

1. Adopt. From wild animals to wild places, there's an option for everyone. Get together with classmates to adopt an animal from a wildlife conservation organization such as the World Wildlife Fund (WWF). Symbolic adoptions help fund organizations.

2. Volunteer. If you don't have money to give, donate your time. Many organizations and zoos have volunteer programs. You can help clean beaches, rescue wild animals or teach visitors.

3. Visit. Zoos, aquariums, national parks and wildlife refuges are all home to wild animals. Learn more about our planet's species from experts. See Earth's most amazing creatures up close.

4. Donate. When you visit your local accredited zoos and nature reserves, pay the recommended entry fee. Your donations help maintain these vital conservation areas.

5. Speak Up. Share your passion for wildlife conservation with your family. Tell your friends how they can help. Ask everyone you know to pledge to do what they can to stop wildlife trafficking.

6. Buy Responsibly. By not purchasing products made from endangered animals or their parts, you can stop wildlife trafficking from being a profitable enterprise.

7. Pitch In. Trash isn't just ugly, it's harmful. Birds and other animals can trap their heads in plastic rings. Fish can get stuck in nets. Plus, trash pollutes everyone's natural resources. Do your part by putting trash in its place.

8. Recycle. Find new ways to use things you already own. If you can't reuse, recycle. The Minnesota Zoo encourages patrons to recycle mobile phones to reduce demand for the mineral coltan, which is mined from lowland gorillas' habitats.

9. Restore. Habitat destruction is the main threat to 85 percent of all threatened and endangered species, according to the International Union for Conservation of Nature. You can help reduce this threat by planting native trees, restoring wetlands or cleaning up beaches in your area.

10. Join. Whether you're into protecting natural habitats or preventing wildlife trafficking, find the organization that speaks to your passion and get involved. Become a member. Stay informed. Actively support the organization of your choice.

What You Can Do for Wildlife

STAND UP FOR WILDLIFE

-Your voice matters! Write to your federal and state elected officials encouraging them to support policies that protect wildlife.

–Sign up for action alerts from AWI, which keep you informed about urgent animal protection issues and provide quick and easy ways to get in touch with policymakers.

-Check out AWI's publications about various wildlife protection issues, and share the publications with others.

-Visit AWI's Action Center to take action on current action alerts.

MAKE YOUR YARD WILDLIFE FRIENDLY

-Plant native species of flowers, trees, and bushes in your yard. This gives wild animals food, shelter, and a place to raise families. Learn more about creating wildlife habitat in your yard.

+To attract birds to your yard, learn which native plant species are best for your location.

+To attract butterflies and moths to your yard, learn which native plant species are best for your location.

+To help imperiled monarch butterflies survive, plant native milkweed. Learn which species of milkweed are native to your region, and find milkweed suppliers in your area.

-Reduce the amount of lawn in your yard. Lawns offer minimal food and shelter for wildlife. -Try replacing part of your lawn with garden beds or native plants and flowers instead.

-Get crafty! Buy or build your own birdhouse or bat house. This can provide hours of fun for the whole family.

-No yard? No problem! Balconies and patios are great locations for container gardens.

-Do not use pesticides, insecticides, herbicides, or chemical fertilizers on your lawn or garden beds. These products are the leading cause of wildlife poisonings, and are also toxic to companion animals.

-**Reduce light pollution:** artificial light at night has severe negative effects on wildlife. To help, only use lighting when and where it is needed, properly shield all outdoor lights, keep your blinds drawn during the evening, and if safety is a concern, install motion detector lights and timers.

-**Rethink fall cleanup:** leaves, dead flower heads, and ornamental grasses provide critical food and shelter for birds, butterflies, bees, and other beneficial insects during the winter months. Learn more about how fall yard cleanup harms wildlife.

PROTECT THE ENVIRONMENT

-One of the easiest and most effective ways to help wildlife is to preserve the environment in which the animals live.

-Volunteer with organizations in your area to restore native forests, grasslands, and coastal ecosystems by planting native species, manually removing invasive plant species, and taking out old fences.

-Participate in or hold your own local trash clean-up to help protect the habitats of imperiled species and other wildlife.

-Reduce, reuse, recycle!

   -**Reduce:** Manufacturing consumer products uses energy and natural resources, and creates waste and pollution. When we consume less, we need fewer natural resources and produce less waste. Some waste, like plastic bags and bottles, can make its way into wildlands and oceans, with negative consequences for endangered species and other animals. Reduce or eliminate your use of single-use plastics, which are difficult to recycle and persist in the environment for decades.

   -**Reuse:** Do not throw it away if it still has a use! If you have unwanted books, toys, clothes or other items in good condition, consider giving them to charity instead of throwing them in the trash.

   -**Recycle:** Avoid disposable products and products with excessive packaging or packaging that cannot easily be recycled. Find out what is recyclable in your area and recycle everyday items such as aluminum cans, glass and plastic containers, and cardboard and paper products. Dispose of electronics, batteries, and other potentially hazardous materials at municipal collection centers that will handle them properly.

-**Save energy:** Driving less, using energy efficient vehicles and appliances, and simply turning off the lights when you leave a room reduce energy use. Many power plants rely on coal and other fossil fuels that damage wildlife habitat when they are extracted, and pollute the environment and contribute to climate change when burned. Unplug appliances and chargers when not in use to eliminate electricity bleeding. You can also consider joining a community solar program or adding solar technology to your home or business.

-Respect wild animals by keeping a safe distance away, not approaching them, and not removing them from their environment. If you find young animals, particularly in the spring, do not handle them. Mothers often leave young for extended periods to forage. Although the young may appear to be abandoned, the mother will almost certainly return within 24 hours, and handling the young puts them in danger. If you encounter an injured wild animal, contact a certified animal rescuer in your area.

BE AN EDUCATED CONSUMER

-**Think before you buy:** Choose products that are energy efficient, durable, made from sustainable sources, and sustainably packaged. Avoid products that harm animals and habitats, such as gas-guzzling vehicles, disposable plastics and plastic microbeads, paper products not made from recycled paper, products grown with pesticides, and products made with palm oil. Also avoid products that test on animals and contain animal parts or derivatives.

-Never buy exotic animals, particularly those who were wild-caught, and never purchase parts and products made from wildlife, including souvenirs.

-Do not buy clothing or other products that use fur or feathers.

-Support genuine efforts that keep wildlife in the wild, such as ecotourism, photo safaris, or community-based humane education programs.

-Eat less meat, particularly beef. Cattle ranching destroys native vegetation, requires enormous amounts of water, damages soil, often results in lethal control of native predators, contaminates waterways, and produces methane, a potent greenhouse gas. Globally, conversion of forest to rangeland for cattle is one of the leading causes of biodiversity loss.

-Learn more about where your food comes from and what food label claims such as *"sustainable," "humane,"* or *"all-natural"* really mean. If the product is rated or certified by an independent evaluator, find out what the rating/certification means and what animal and environmental advocates are saying about the certifier's standards.

LEARN ABOUT IMPERILED SPECIES AND THEIR HABITATS

–Learn about the threats faced by threatened and endangered species. Teach your friends and family about endangered species and other animals that live near you.

-For information on species imperiled by trade, visit the Convention on International Trade in Endangered Species of Flora and Fauna (CITES) database at www.cites.org, the US Fish and Wildlife Service Endangered Species website, or the more inclusive International Union for Conservation of Nature (IUCN) Red List at www.iucnredlist.org.

-Visit a national wildlife refuge, park, or other open space and learn about the threatened and endangered species and other animals who live there. Stay informed and support policies that keep these areas wild and protect native species.

–**Teachers:** Help spread awareness in your own classroom about endangered species with our educational poster.

PROTECT ENDANGERED SPECIES

-The Endangered Species Act is an effective safety net for imperiled species—extinction has been prevented for more than 98 percent of the animals under its care. Urge your elected officials to preserve the important safeguards in the Act.

HELP PUT AN END TO INHUMANE TRAPS AND SNARES

-Support proposed federal, state, or local legislation against the use of indiscriminate and inhumane traps and snares for commercial purposes or to "manage" wildlife. Let your legislators, as well as your state wildlife agency, know that you support a prohibition on the use of cruel traps and snares in your state and across the country.

-If you see a non-target species (such as a dog, cat, bird, or threatened/endangered species) caught in a trap, seek veterinary care for the animal immediately. Next, document and report your findings to your local humane society and AWI. Such information will aid our efforts to pass laws that ban inhumane traps and snares.

-If you or someone you know hires a nuisance wildlife control business to address a wildlife conflict situation, do not allow them to use cruel traps or snares. Ask for their trapping policies in writing before you hire them.

HELP PROTECT BIRDS

-Up to 1 billion birds in the United States die each year due to collisions with buildings. Learn how to reduce bird strikes by making windows more bird-friendly.

-Keep your cat indoors. Cats are one of the top causes of bird deaths in the United States. A study by scientists at the Smithsonian Conservation Biology Institute reported that between 1.4 billion and 3.7 billion birds are killed each year by cats roaming outdoors. Therefore, one of the most important things pet owners can do to reduce direct wildlife mortality is to keep their cat inside.

HELP PROTECT WILD HORSES

-Learn more about wild horse issues.

-Contact your US senators and representative and urge them to help reform the Bureau of Land Management (BLM) wild horse program.

-Write to Secretary of Interior Deb Haaland and tell her you oppose the BLM's overzealous wild horse roundup policy. The BLM admits it plans to round up far more horses than are adoptable—leaving many wild horses to remain indefinitely in long-term holding facilities. Urge the agency to act responsibly and stop removing these national treasures from the wild.

Saving the Animals Is More Important Than We Think

Animal conservation is a complicated issue, but it's a core part of addressing the climate crisis.

When it comes to climate change, we're inching dangerously close to the point of no return. This is what the world's climate scientists have been saying for more than a few years. But since the problem is so vast, it's easy to blow it off, burying your head in the sand and hoping it goes away on its own. So we wanted to offer some helpful tips on what you can do in your daily lives to put a dent in the climate change crisis. We hope to shed some light on the urgency of the problem through thoughtful deep dives that explore the systems and industry practices that exacerbate the problem and explore their social and ecological impacts. Within the series, you might also find some inspiring ways you can start to help make Earth more green and, hopefully, begin to turn back the clock on climate change.

Widespread animal extinction is one of the most dire consequences of the climate crisis, threatening the health of the planet and its ability to sustain all life, including those of humans.

Due to the instability of the climate crisis, one-third of all animal and plant species on the planet could face extinction by 2070, a February 2020 study warns. And a 2019 United Nations report said over one million species of plants and animals are at risk of being obliterated if we don't make drastic changes.

This rate of extinction is due to the Anthropocene — the current geological age in which human activity is jeopardizing the Earth's ability to sustain human life — which many climate scientists credit to the Industrial Revolution of the late 18th and early 19th century.

Zoologist and environmental studies scholar Malory Owen, a Masters of Science candidate at York University in Toronto, Canada, said,

"Extinction is a natural process. It's part of evolution, and it's how we get change in our ecosystems over time. But the problem is since the Industrial Revolution, we have seen an incredible spike in that rate…through the Anthropocene."

In 2019 alone, about two dozen species were declared extinct or nearly extinct, the Center for Biological Diversity reports. Among those lost included a tiny Hawaiian snail, one of the world's largest freshwater fishes, three bird species, a shark, two frogs, and several plants. Frighteningly, the number of plants lost is probably in the thousands, due to the fact that scientists sometimes wait years or decades searching to ensure that a species is completely extinct.

The IUCN Red List of Threatened Species also helps people learn more about global extinction risk status of animal, fungus and plant species. Their list is still not nearly comprehensive of every species, Owen points out, but their inclusion of fungi and plants is critical in the discussion of what species are most at risk.

Which species are most at risk?

Animal conservation is not just about animals, and it's not easy to determine what species we should focus on. When it comes to which species are most at risk, and therefore need most of our attention, the answer is complicated. *"Some wildlife that pop into our heads when we think of critically endangered species are orangutans or rhinos. But in reality, when we talk about animal conversation, it's tricky to try to simplify it like that,"* Owen says. *"For example, insects make up a huge portion of the biodiversity in our world. But it's the mammals, these large charismatic animals that get the most attention, as well as birds."*

This is a dynamic I saw myself when I briefly worked at the Smithsonian National Zoo and Biology Conservation Institute. Visitors were mostly interested in donating, lured in by the idea of helping to save majestic tigers or exotic birds or cute pandas. But the discussion about conservation rarely extended towards insects, plants, or more traditionally *"unsavory"* animals like bats.

Jon Flanders, Director of Endangered Species Interventions at Bat Conservation International, says that's why it can sometimes be difficult to engage the public on bat conservation. *"Sometimes people persecute and hunt bats for different reasons. They're nocturnal, found in dark places, and some people might be frightened. So there are lots of misunderstandings about them,"* he says. *"Bats are amazing, though. They're so engaging once you know more about them."*

Owen says the reason for this disparity is rooted in what we're drawn to. *"It represents what people are most vocal about, what they care the most about."*

She says a useful tool in thinking about this is the classic Lion King example. *"Lions depend on the gazelles, gazelles depend on grass, grass depends on the sun. That's a simplification though, because in real ecosystems, biodiversity is what gives flexibility to these ecosystems. So, if the gazelles aren't doing great, then the lions can shift to zebras or antelope."* But when there's no biodiversity because the rate of extinction is so high, those options dwindle and everything becomes infinitely more at risk.

This is why we can't afford to not care about all species — including plants and insects. Half of the one million species at risk are insects, and they provide crucial ecosystem services that we could not live without, especially pollination, nutrient cycling and pest control. The elimination of these ecosystem services would destroy our food supply, which would cause mass deaths from hunger and (further) global political instability due to the ensuing chaos.

Animal conservation can include hunting and fishing

While veganism is seen as a healthy choice for the environment — and in many ways it is, but it can also be very harmful — hunters and fishers are also part of the conservation movement. Hunter Morton, a Georgia-based outdoorsman, is enamored with the land and very much sees himself and his peers as part of animal conservation. Morton, who studied Agricultural Education in undergrad and is currently working on his masters in Wildlife Biology focusing on the history of African-American bird dog trainers in the South, argues that sportspeople play an important role in maintaining the environment.

"A lot of people see hunters and fishers as almost an enemy to wildlife, but hunters and fisherman are really the people that are on the ground helping efforts move forward for those endangered species and helping the ecosystem thrive," says Morton.

Indigenous practices of hunting are about managing animal populations and subsistence, not sport or mass production. For example, lionfish are an invasive species that is threatening the ocean biodiversity in the Caribbean. So eating them is actually incredibly good for the environment, although it must be done properly, since the fish contain toxins. In Australian's Western Desert, Aborginal hunters' method of using fire to clear patches of land actually increases the population of the animals they hunt by "creating a mosaic of regrowth that enhances habitat."

These methods could be adopted by more people, but the efforts should be led by those who have this ancestral connection to the land, because they have the deepest levels of knowledge. It's also important to consult scientists about sustainable food choices, because some items that you may think are good for the Earth — like almond milk or soybeans — may actually be contributing to conditions that make animal conservation difficult, and we should rethink how or whether we consume them.

What can we do to stop it?

"As much as humans can be destructive, we can be a force for positive change as well," Flanders said. For example, he says, in April 2017, partners in the U.S. and Mexico worked together to recover the lesser long-nosed bat, which was the first bat to ever be removed from the Endangered Species Act (ESA) protections. In addition to providing other

ecosystem services, this bat is also responsible for the production of tequila, since it is pretty much the sole pollinator of agave, Flanders says. The recovery of the lesser long-nosed bat is a success story of recovery.

Flanders also said that creating resilient ecosystems is key.

"Creating environments that are resilient for bats and other species is critical, because things are changing too quickly for these animals to adapt. It's not just the temperature changes but these sudden extreme events like monsoon, typhoons, droughts."

One of the best ways to do that is engaging in climate justice efforts that aim to dismantle the fossil fuel industry, he says. For Owen, climate justice activism is a key part of addressing animal conservation. She currently works with Fridays for Future Toronto, as well as some independent activism work.

"One of the biggest things we can do is listen to Black and Indigenous and other people for guidance. Indigenous people have been stewards of the land since time immemorial, they know what to do."

"If your passion is something in agriculture and wildlife, say 'Hey, this is what I want to do. I won't let anybody take it from me,'"

says Morton, as a mentor to others who want to get involved in this work.

Owen also says when it comes to personal action, it's crucial to *"investigate whether those actions are just reducing your footprint or changing the world that is forcing you to live unsustainably."*

Animal conservation is a complicated issue, but it's a core part of addressing the climate crisis and ensuring that the Earth is able to support all life, including human life. Animal conservation is also not limited to our favorite animals, like lions or giraffes. We have to care about all forms of life if we aim to protect it — from the largest elephants to the tiniest bacterium.

Experts say that we only have until 2030 to tackle the climate crisis before its worst effects consume us and make it pretty much impossible for human life to be sustained on this planet long-term. That sounds really terrifying because it is. But by fighting for animal conservation, we can make meaningful change, and ensure a place for our descendants on this beautiful planet.

We want to make life better for wild animals.

Although the natural world is a source of great beauty and happiness, vast numbers of animals routinely face serious challenges such as disease, hunger, or natural disasters. There is no *"one-size-fits-all"* solution to these threats. However, even as we recognize that improving the welfare of free-ranging wild animals is difficult, we believe that humans have a responsibility to help whenever we can.

Wild Animal Initiative currently focuses on helping scientists, grantors, and decision-makers investigate important and understudied questions about wild animal welfare. Our work catalyzes research and applied projects that will open the door to a clearer picture of wild animals' needs and how to enhance their well-being. Ultimately, we envision a world in which people actively choose to help wild animals — and have the knowledge they need to do so responsibly.

10 Easy Things You Can Do To Save Endangered Species

1. Learn about endangered species in your area. Teach your friends and family about the wonderful wildlife, birds, fish and plants that live near you. The first step to protecting endangered species is learning about how interesting and important they are. Our natural world provides us with many indispensable services including clean air and water, food and medicinal sources, commercial, aesthetic and recreational benefits.

2. Visit a national wildlife refuge, park or other open space. These protected lands provide habitat to many native wildlife, birds, fish and plants. Scientists tell us the best way to protect endangered species is to protect the places where they live. Get involved by volunteering at your local nature center or wildlife refuge. Go wildlife or bird watching in nearby parks. Wildlife related recreation creates millions of jobs and supports local businesses.

3. Make your home wildlife friendly. Secure garbage in shelters or cans with locking lids, feed pets indoors and lock pet doors at night to avoid attracting wild animals into your home. Reduce your use of water in your home and garden so that animals that live in or near water can have a better chance of survival. Disinfect bird baths often to avoid disease transmission. Place decals on windows to deter bird collisions. Millions of birds die every year because of collisions with windows. You can help reduce the number of collisions simply by placing decals on the windows in your home and office.

4. Native plants provide food and shelter for native wildlife. Attracting native insects like bees and butterflies can help pollinate your plants. The spread of non-native species has greatly impacted native populations around the world. Invasive species compete with native species for resources and habitat. They can even prey on native species directly, forcing native species towards extinction.

5. Herbicides and pesticides may keep yards looking nice but they are in fact hazardous pollutants that affect wildlife at many levels. Many herbicides and pesticides take a long time to degrade and build up in the soils or throughout the food chain. Predators such as hawks, owls and coyotes can be harmed if they eat poisoned animals. Some groups of animals such as amphibians are particularly vulnerable to these chemical pollutants and suffer greatly as a result of the high levels of herbicides and pesticides in their habitat.

6. Slow down when driving. Many animals live in developed areas and this means they must navigate a landscape full of human hazards. One of the biggest obstacles to wildlife living in developed areas is roads. Roads divide habitat and present a constant hazard to any animal attempting to cross from one side to the other. So when you're out and about, slow down and keep an eye out for wildlife.

7. Recycle and buy sustainable products. Buy recycled paper, sustainable products like bamboo and Forest Stewardship Council wood products to protect forest species. Never buy furniture made from wood from rainforests. Recycle your cell phones, because a mineral used in cell phones and other electronics is mined in gorilla habitat. Minimize your use of palm oil because forests where tigers live are being cut down to plant palm plantations.

8. Never purchase products made from threatened or endangered species. Overseas trips can be exciting and fun, and everyone wants a souvenir. But sometimes the souvenirs are made from species nearing extinction. Avoid supporting the market in illegal wildlife including: tortoise-shell, ivory, coral. Also, be careful of products including fur from tigers, polar bears, sea otters and other endangered wildlife, crocodile skin, live monkeys or apes, most live birds including parrots, macaws, cockatoos and finches, some live snakes, turtles and lizards, some orchids, cacti and cycads, medicinal products made from rhinos, tiger or Asiatic black bear.

9. Harassing wildlife is cruel and illegal. Shooting, trapping, or forcing a threatened or endangered animal into captivity is also illegal and can lead to their extinction. Don't participate in this activity, and report it as soon as you see it to your local state or federal wildlife enforcement office.

10. Protect wildlife habitat. Perhaps the greatest threat that faces many species is the widespread destruction of habitat. Scientists tell us the best way to protect endangered species is to protect the special places where they live. Wildlife must have places to find food, shelter and raise their young. Logging, oil and gas drilling, over-grazing and development all result habitat destruction. Endangered species habitat should be protected and these impacts minimized.

By protecting habitat, entire communities of animals and plants can be protected together. Parks, wildlife refuges, and other open space should be protected near your community. Open space also provides us with great places to visit and enjoy. Support wildlife habitat and open space protection in your community. When you are buying a house, consider your impact on wildlife habitat.

Understanding Conservation

Wildlife conservation is the preservation and protection of animals, plants, and their habitats. By conserving wildlife, we're ensuring that future generations can enjoy our natural world and the incredible species that live within it. To help protect wildlife, it's important to understand how species interact within their ecosystems, and how they're affected by environmental and human influences.

Phenology

Plants and animals have life events that seemingly occur like clockwork every year. Birds can migrate, mammals may hibernate, flowers bloom, and leaves change colors. The study of how the biological world times these natural events is called phenology. Scientists now understand that plants and animals take their cues from their local climate (long-term weather patterns). Climate is impacted by non-biological factors—temperature, precipitation, and available sunlight. Species use the predictable yearly changes in the climate to determine when they start natural events such as breeding or flowering.

Climate change is slowly increasing average annual temperatures. One of the most noticeable ways that climate change is impacting wildlife is by disrupting the timing of natural events. With warmer temperatures, flowering plants are blooming earlier in the year and migratory birds are returning from their wintering grounds earlier in the spring. Phenology is an important subject for conservationists to study because it helps us understand the patterns of specific species and overall ecosystem health. Every species has an impact on those in its food chain and community, and the timing of one species' phenological events can be very important to the survival of another species.

Food Webs and Bioaccumulation

The energy we receive from food can be traced back to the sun. As the sun shines, it radiates light energy. Plants absorb the light energy, convert it to sugars (photosynthesis), and produce energy for other wildlife. The energy from the sun moves its way through ecosystems by predators eating their prey. A food web breaks down how all the producers, consumers, and decomposers interact in an ecosystem and how energy is transferred between species.

When animals eat their prey, they consume more than just energy. They also absorb all the chemicals and nutrients inside the prey. Sometimes animals ingest pollutants that can become stored in their fat and tissues. Human-caused pollution has added heavy metals, oil, and industrial and pharmaceutical chemicals to the environment. Plants, fish, and other species absorb these toxins, and as they are eaten by predators, the toxins are then absorbed into the predators' tissues. As the chain of predator and prey continues up the food web, the toxins become more concentrated and move higher and higher up the food web. The process that causes the concentration of a substance to increase as it moves up the food web is called bioaccumulation. The pollutants can have a disastrous effect on the food web and potentially kill species.

Natural Disturbances

A natural disturbance is any event that causes a disruption to the current state of an ecosystem. Natural disturbances are caused by forces of nature, including weather, geology, and biological fluctuations. This may include fires, floods, earthquakes, diseases, and droughts. After a disturbance impacts an ecosystem, there can be devastation, but healthy ecosystems have an amazing ability to bounce back. Some ecosystems even depend on disturbances, such as the threatened longleaf pine ecosystem. Sometimes the ecosystem will go back to its former structure, with the same plant and animal species. Other times, the disturbance will create something new by allowing new species to populate the area.

Not all disturbances are natural. Human actions have contributed to many disturbances seen in ecosystems today. While natural disturbances happen on occasion, human disturbances are putting constant pressure on ecosystems and dramatically impacting species. Human disturbances, including clear-cutting, habitat fragmentation, and pollution, are continuously affecting ecosystems. The moment the ecosystem begins adjusting to one stress, another appears. Many ecosystems that we depend on are not given enough time to adapt to the new conditions. The natural cycle of disturbances—growth, dieback, and growth—cannot properly function because too many disturbances are putting pressure on the ecosystem at once.

Corridors and Flyways

Wild animals are always on the move. They move from place to place in search of food, mates, shelter, and water. Many animals do not have to move far in order to have all their needs met, but other animals—for example migratory birds, wolves, mountain lions, or butterflies—require much more space. Currently many species with large territories, including gray wolves, are threatened because habitat loss and fragmentation have limited their available space. Roads, fences, and buildings cut off habitat and force wildlife into smaller areas. Conservationists have to take into account the different spatial needs of wildlife when designing plans to protect them. They have to think about the territory size, different habitat types, and migration routes that wildlife need.

A wildlife corridor is a tract of land that connects different wildlife habitats (such as refuges, parks, or rivers) that might otherwise be separated by human development. Wildlife corridors provide many benefits to wildlife. With corridors, animals have a better opportunity of finding the basic necessities they need—food, water, shelter, and places to raise their young. Animals that require larger territories can access new habitats and maintain a healthy territory size. Wildlife corridors also promote genetic biodiversity. When more individuals of a species are interconnected, the gene pool becomes larger and more viable. Migratory wildlife benefit from corridors because they can move safely over long distances without having to come into contact with human developments or cars. Species are more likely to survive disturbances by having more undisturbed areas.

The National Wildlife Federation, in partnership with the Santa Monica Mountains Fund, is working to create a wildlife crossing for mountain lions in California. By linking protected habitat on either side of a freeway, mountain lions and other wildlife can the access to green space they need to survive. The Liberty Canyon Wildlife Crossing, when built, will be the largest such crossing in the world, and a model for urban wildlife conservation.

Unlike mammals, birds and butterflies travel from one place to another by flying, so they face different kinds of challenges. Not only do we have to protect their winter and summer habitat, but also key rest stops that migratory wildlife use along the way. Conservationists can help threatened bird and butterfly populations by protecting habitat along major migratory flyways—pathways used by migratory birds and insects. Birds tend to take predictable routes to get from the winter feeding grounds to the summer breeding grounds and back. Flyways usually occur along coastlines, major rivers, and near mountains. The United States has four main migratory flyways.

-**Pacific Flyway:** Along the Pacific coast, west of the Rocky Mountains

-**Central Flyway:** Over the Great Plains, east of the Rocky Mountains

-**Mississippi Flyway:** Along the Mississippi River

-**Atlantic Flyway:** Along the Atlantic coast

A great way to help birds and butterflies migrate is by building a Certified Wildlife Habitat® in your backyard or balcony. Learn how to provide a critical resting place and food source to help migratory birds reach their destination.

The Real Case for Saving Species: We Don't Need Them, But They Need Us

Conservationists argue that humans need to save species in order to save ourselves. The truth is we could survive without wild species — but they can't survive without us, and the moral argument for protecting them and the beauty they bring to the world is overwhelming.

There was a sign posted at a museum exhibit on big cats. A sign featuring a beautiful jaguar asked, *"Why should we care about wild cats?"* Its answer: *"Because in protecting big cats, we are protecting ourselves."*

Is that really true? That implies big cats are in trouble because "we" don't care to protect ourselves. And if it turns out that we don't really need jaguars in order to protect ourselves, have they lost their case for existence?

For decades, many conservationists have been trying to sell a clumsy, fumbling appeal to self-interest: the idea that human beings need wild nature, need wild animals, need the species on endangered lists. *"If they go extinct, we'll go extinct,"* is a common refrain. The only problem: it's false.

We drove the most abundant bird in the Americas — the passenger pigeon — to extinction. The most abundant large mammal — the American bison — to functional extinction. We gained: agriculture, and safety for cows, from sea to shining sea. Who misses the Eskimo curlew? Indeed, who knows they existed, their vast migrating flocks like smoke on the now-gone prairies? That experiment is done.

Billions of people want what you and I got in exchange: health and wealth and education. We now live the way most other people on the planet wish to live. Governments, institutions, and regular people have cheered the material expansion that has cost many species (and tribal peoples) everything. We have endangered species not because what is bad for them is bad for us, but because the opposite is true: what is bad for them has fueled the explosive growth and maintenance of human populations and technologies. We are losing many species along the way to humanity's only three apparent real goals: bigger, faster, more. Propelling the human juggernaut has entailed wiping many species out of the way. People live at high densities in places devoid of wild species and natural beauty. Human beings have thrived by destroying nature. When the animals and open spaces go, we have industrial-scale farms and factories, ball fields and strip malls and quick-lubes. How could saving this or that endangered species, that is following those whose oblivion brought fast food and sneakers, be a matter of — of all things — saving ourselves? Telling people that "we" need jaguars to *protect ourselves?*" That's a hard sell. We don't need them.

Can you name a single wild species whose total disappearance would be materially felt by, essentially, anyone?

There is no species whose disappearance has posed much of an inconvenience for civilization, not a single wild species that people couldn't do without, fewer whose erasure would be noticed by any but a handful of die-hard conservationists or scientists. The irrelevance of wild things to civil society is why endangered species never make it into polls of top public priorities. Can you name one wild species whose total disappearance would be materially felt by, essentially, anyone (you can easily function without having access to elephants, but if you misplace your phone for one whole day, it's personal chaos)? We can effortlessly list various species from tigers to mosquitoes whose annihilation has been diligently pursued. Annihilation comes easy to Homo sapiens. What's of little interest for us is coexistence.

Many of us have seen on TV, the role elephants have played as ecosystem engineers which effects all animals on the African savannas matters not at all to people converting bushland into vulnerable subsistence gardens or, more decisively, into large commercial farms raising flowers destined for vases on the tables of Europe. Think of your favorite species. Gorillas? Sperm whales? Hyacinth macaws? Karner blue butterflies? Billions of people never give them a thought.

Only a tiny minority of people actually work with wild creatures, as ecologists, conservation biologists, wildlife rehabilitators, falconers, or even fishermen (oddly and not coincidentally I've been all of those.) On an average day, animals and plants must put up or be pushed out. In most countries, few wild things can "*provide*" to humans anything more valued than their carcasses. Many major American tree species have disappeared or nearly so (American elm, American chestnut, eastern hemlock, for instance). Ash trees are now disappearing and the main pain-point for humanity is nothing more than angst for the future of baseball bats.

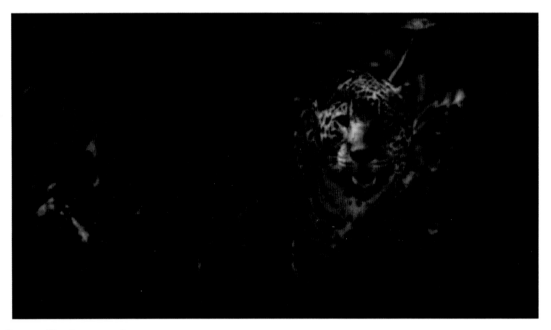

Jaguar (Panthera onca)

The predicament we are finding ourselves in is simply put, catastrophic.

It is of course true that the things that are bad for nature as a whole — degradation of land and soil, polluted water and air — are bad for people ultimately. A total breakdown of living systems would mean a breakdown of human economies, and indications are it likely will. But "ultimately" is very far down the line, long after we've lost all the big animals, wild lands, viable ocean habitats, and the world's living beauty. The human juggernaut can continue to blow through rhinos, parrots, elephants, lions, and apes and hardly feel a breeze. The most charismatic species all stand at or near historic lows and humans are at our historic high, two facts that are sides of the same coin. Claiming that people depend on wild nature is nice, but dependence on wild nature ended, and not well, generations ago. What keeps most people going is farming felling, pumping, and mining.

Far down the line when the land is exhausted and there's no water on an overheated planet, there may be a great reckoning. It's easy enough to hear the rumbles now. But even the recent hurricanes and fires that have left communities seemingly beyond recovery have not shaken the deniers. In this country, government disdain for natural places and species, and official ennui about the human health effects of environmental degradation, are worst-ever. And the current rollbacks remain too weakly opposed; most people don't feel affected. Most of wild nature could be gone long before the human species confronts an existential cliff.

What a grim world it will be by the time we're down to what humans need. Human need is a very poor metric for evaluating the existence of living things.

The natural services humans actually need to fuel modern living come from microbes of decay, a few main insect pollinators, the ocean's photosynthesizing plankton, and non-living things like water and the atmosphere. Eventually we may well simplify the world to the bare essentials, and it will still support billions more people. Indeed, that's the only way it can.

What a grim world it will be by the time we're down to what humans need. Which only shows that human need is a very poor metric for evaluating the existence of living things. Ask living creatures to justify their existence in terms of human need; they lose.

So, in what bleak terrain does this leave us? The law that has been called the gold standard of species protection, the U. S. Endangered Species Act, doesn't begin to get interested until after a species, considered in isolation, is already in dire straits. Then it sets a floor, measuring success as mere existence. A wiser law would target an aspirational ceiling of robust, resilient populations across broad, intact scapes of viable lands and productive waters.

Yet when applied in good faith it works. It works because of something many environmentalists have forgotten, most average people never think about, and most politicians are incapable of learning: it works because it doesn't ask a species to prove its usefulness, what they're good for, or how much money they're worth. The act doesn't say that we need them. It acknowledges that we harm them. In its first words,

"The Congress finds and declares that various species of fish, wildlife, and plants in the United States have been rendered extinct as a consequence of economic growth." It says that recovery plans shall *"give priority to… particularly those species that are, or may be in conflict with construction or other development projects or other forms of economic activity."*

Yet many conservationists continue trying to make the flimsy case that we need endangered species. And because the argument is false, it can be a counterproductive pandering to the self-interest of people who simply won't care. *"Prove that I need some endangered snail or whale."* You can't.

Sperm whales (Physeter macrocephalus).

Fortunately, you don't have to. The argument was decided decades ago, by Congress on behalf of all Americans, in favor of what you and I care about. The Endangered Species Act doesn't claim that our existence depends on the existence of wild species. It says that we, the people, don't let species go extinct, that this is who we are. It's not about practicality; it's about morality. The moral compass of species stewardship or loss is already mainstream — loss is bad. Conservationists and rank-and-file nature lovers should not pick that scab by trying to show that nature can and must serve us. The law says we need to serve nature. That's a lot to work with.

Of course, laws are only as strong as the support they have. Conservationists must not only remind themselves that the law guides policy based on moral principle; they must continue to make the wide case for that underlying moral principle. When people say, *What good are they. They're in the way!,*" conservation needs a stronger argument than an appeal to self interest. Self interest has already been considered and nature has lost. Oil palms make money; never mind orangutans. We don't need orangutans in order to "protect ourselves." Orangutans need us to protect them.

But how best to press the case for life on Earth?

Humans have considered ourselves the most moral of species. A moral species has moral obligations. Despite capitalism's appeal to self-interest, religions continue to assert the primacy of right and wrong. It may be that in our social species the only thing capable of standing up to pure self-interest is moral suasion. But what religions have underplayed — and indeed some have disdained — is seeing the physical world as sacred. On this planet where astrobiologists detect no other life in the galaxy, the rarity and perhaps even uniqueness of life in the universe makes Earth a sacred place. All known meaning in the universe is generated here, because this is the only living planet.

Winning the war against the natural in pursuit of accelerated material living, we lose the beauty that makes living worthwhile.

Although wild nature is not necessary for human survival, it is necessary for human dignity. Some of the grimmest places for human existence are those where nature has been scorched. People can lose their dignity in various ways, including oppressive governments. But oppressive surroundings are sufficient.

Zoom out from *"endangered species"* to the big picture. Abundant multitudes of species, wild things in wild places, anchor beauty to the face of this planet. What is true is this: Wild things create and live in the remaining beautiful places. As wild animals disappear, what is lost is the world's beauty. Winning the war against the natural in pursuit of accelerated material living, we lose the beauty that makes living worthwhile.

That is not trivial. It is the most profound thing on Earth.

Ecology — living relationships and reliances — may be the only concept containing sufficient scope for a future worth humanly living. Ecology is most easily perceived by this shorthand: natural beauty. Each of our senses has ways of informing us what is good and bad. Our sense of smell evolved to sense things good for us as smelling pleasant and bad as smelling putrid. Our mind evolved the ability to combine all our sense into one overall detector of what is good in the world, and that best overarching sense is what we call "beauty." As the beauty of the world drains away, we become less than human in the long run. And part of the long run is now.

Hyacinth macaw
(Anodorhynchus hyacinthinus).

Beauty is the single criterion that best captures all our deepest concerns and highest hopes. Beauty encompasses the continued existence of free-living things, adaptation, and human dignity. Really, beauty is simple litmus for the presence of things that matter.

If a future reckoning arrives for the human species, as seems likely, it will come because we asked life to prove its value compared to ever-more corn and shopping discounts, but could not hear the real answer. It will come because we did not see our planetary miracle as sacred.

Endangered species and wild things in the remaining wild places need us to care for them not selfishly but selflessly, for their sake, the sake of everything and everyone who is not us, for the sake of beauty and all it implies. As we make our habitual appeals to practicality, the argument we cannot afford to ignore, the one that must frequently be on our lips, is this: We live in a sacred miracle. We should act accordingly.

Meanwhile, a few things are right. Within the last few weeks, the long-endangered Kirtland's warbler came off the endangered species list. This didn't happen because we needed them. It happened because the Endangered Species Act determined that when species need us, we shall go to their aid. It happened, the U.S. Fish and Wildlife Service announced, because, *Kirtland's warbler has responded well to active management over the past 50 years.* Before the Endangered Species Act, the species was down to 200 singing males. The population has increased more than tenfold, not because we needed Kirtland's warbler, but because we understood that Kirtland's warbler needed us. We understood our moral responsibility and commitment to keep a tiny bird in the world with us. Many would say that the warbler doesn't matter to us. But the people who won the argument on behalf of the bird were those who argued and acted on the premise that we mattered to the warbler. Nothing elsc could have worked.

Oust species to save ecosystems

Network models might offer solution to cascading species loss.

Could you prevent nine local extinctions by hastening one extinction? It sounds completely counterintuitive, but a pair of ecosystem modellers are proposing that conservationists could sometimes prop up a troubled ecosystem by removing one or more of its species — and using models to determine the timing and order of those removals.

The species that make up an ecosystem are connected in complex 'food webs' of eater and eaten. When one species disappears, its predators can no longer eat it and its prey are no longer eaten by it. Changes in these populations affect others. Such impact 'cascades' can be unpredictable and sometimes catastrophic.

Sagar Sahasrabudhe and Adilson Motter of Northwestern University in Evanston, Illinois, have shown that in several model food webs, as well as in two webs modelled with data derived from real ecosystems — the Chesapeake Bay off Maryland and Virginia and the Coachella Valley in Southern California — removing or partially suppressing one or more species at key time points after one member has gone extinct saves other members of the web from local extinction.

The idea relies on the fact that ecosystem networks can often shift to a different stable arrangement after losing members. *"Ecological systems are quite robust, actually,"* says Motter. The famous *"balance of nature"* is perhaps better understood as the *"multiple possible balances of nature"*. But the order of removals matters.

Remove A and then B, for example, and a given web might change shape but retain all its other members; remove B and then A, however, and the cascade of changes drives many of the other members extinct.

Exit strategy

In very simple webs, the impacts can be easy to follow. For example, the removal of a large predator could allow a medium-sized predator to increase in numbers and eat its smaller mammal and bird prey into extinction. In this case, keeping a lid on the numbers of the medium-sized predator would prevent these extinctions.

Page 68

But even small webs can harbor complexities that can make the order of removals for ecosystem stability challenging to sort out. Motter likes the story of the island foxes (Urocyon littoralis) on the Channel Islands off the coast of California, which is recorded in the study. When feral pigs were introduced to the islands, they attracted golden eagles that preyed on both pigs and foxes. Fox numbers then dropped. Removing the pigs would have left the foxes as the sole diet of the eagles, and likely doomed them. So instead, conservationists captured and relocated the eagles and only then eradicated the pigs. The fox population is now recovering.

"The same actions at different times have very different consequences," says Motter.

In more complex webs, the key species that needs to be removed or suppressed to head off more serious collapse isn't intuitively clear. But, by modeling a variety of food webs using established ecological principles, the researchers were able to find such species and they hope that the algorithms that they created might eventually be able to identify target species in the real world.

Factoring in complexity

However, the results will only be accurate if the real ecosystem is well represented by the model. In their food-web modeling, Sahasrabudhe and Motter have used accepted ecological models of predator-prey relationships, but a more elaborate representation of an ecosystem would also include parasitism, seed dispersal, competition, mutualisms (in which species make life easier for each other), nutrient dynamics and more. And to include such complex detail in a model, scientists will first have to go out and gather that information in the field. Who is eating whom? Who is pollinating whom?

When the algorithms point to an exotic species as a target for removal or suppression, conservationists are likely to have little problem with the idea. But if a native species is the proposed target, that will go against many conservationists' impulses to protect rather than remove.

Page 69

Neo Martinez, director of the non-profit Pacific Ecoinformatics and Computational Ecology Lab in Berkeley, California, says that Sahasrabudhe and Motter's ideas are exciting, but the conservatism of conservation means that they won't be relied on in isolation, at least not right away.

"Because of the lack of realism — we don't include everything in these models — no one is going to make an important conservation decision solely on these models. That is a long time in the future."

But a long time in the future isn't never. Martinez says that whereas six or eight years ago ecologists generally considered ecosystems too complex to ever be productively modeled, not unlike the stock market, today modellers are gaining confidence.

Motter agrees. *"In the long run, I think we will have people in the field advocating for the suppression of native species."* He points out that land managers are already doing so, less systematically, by running regulated hunting of prey species in areas where top predators have been extirpated. Human impacts are just too great on most ecosystems, he says, for us to just hope they will sort themselves out. *"In the presence of perturbations, it is reasonable to consider compensatory perturbations,"* he says.

What Happens When Something in a Food Chain Goes Extinct?

All living organisms hold a place in the food chain, structured around the transfer of life-sustaining energy through an ecosystem: from sunlight to plant to rabbit to bobcat to maggot, to make a simple example. Because this energy transfer involves members of the food chain interacting with one another and their environment in a complex, interlocking ecological system, extinction of one species can have a cascading effect on others.

Increased Population of Prey

When a predatory species becomes threatened or extinct, this removes a check and balance in the food chain on the population of prey previously consumed by that predator. Consequently, the prey population can explode. For instance, the huge increase in white-tailed deer populations in the central and eastern U.S. in the latter half of the 20th century likely stemmed partly from reduced or altogether eliminated populations of deer predators, namely wolves and cougars. Over browsing as a result of such excessive deer numbers can transform the makeup of plant communities and negatively impact forest regeneration.

I think this concept is a little like playing God. Every time we think we know more than Mother Nature we end up messing things up royally. How many times have the Army Corps of Engineers tried to affect changes to our environment only to cause greater harm than good? There is an old saying *"two wrongs don't make a right."*

Ripple Effect on Other Species

Endangerment or extinction of one species can threaten the viability of another species. In Britain, for instance, the red ant population plummeted as the result of fewer sheep grazing in pastures; sheep had previously kept the grass short, the red ant's habitat preference. In turn, the paucity of red ants led to the extinction of a large butterfly species that eats red-ant eggs as part of its life cycle. Food chain disruptions from the loss of a single species can be ecosystem-wide, too: When sea otters decline, populations of sea urchins, a preferred otter food, can explode. The resulting overpopulation of kelp-munching urchins, meanwhile, can reduce kelp forests, threatening numerous marine species that rely on this habitat.

Reduced Biodiversity

Overall ecosystem instability due to reduced biodiversity ranks among the consequences of species extinctions. As the number of species in a food chain decreases, there are fewer sustainable alternatives for members of the food chain that had depended on the extinct species. Biodiversity also lends genetic variability to a population, helping it adapt to fluctuating environmental conditions. For instance, a study of tropical rain forests in

West Africa conducted by ecologists at Leeds University between 1990 and 2010 suggested that biodiversity mitigates the effects of climate change and helps tree species adapt to drought conditions.

Disrupted Habitat

Extinction of animal or bird species in the food chain may alter the physical environment as well. For instance, accidental introduction of the predatory brown tree snake to Guam wiped out 10 of the 12 native bird species on the island causing collateral damage to the forest, according to a University of Washington study. Biologists found that extinction of the birds had adversely impacted tree pollination, seed germination and seed dispersal. Without birds to spread seeds, there may only be a few clumps of mono-species trees in Guam's future, fundamentally changing forest habitat.

How would a species' extinction impact the food web, our ecosystems?

Every living thing plays a role in the food chain and Earth's ecosystems, and the extinction of certain species, whether predators or prey, can leave behind significant impacts.

"Since the origin of life on Earth, it's fair to say that more species have gone extinct than are currently alive now," said Dr. Anthony Giordano, president and chief conservation officer of the Society for the Preservation of Endangered Carnivores and their International Ecological Study (SPECIES). *"Extinction itself is part of the normal course of evolution."*

The effect a species would have if it were to fade from existence depends largely on its role in the ecosystem. Predators, for example, are often the first to be threatened by hunting or competition with people and resources, said Clemson University conservation biologist Dr. Robert Baldwin.

"Think about large animals like the grizzly bear," Baldwin said. "When a predator goes extinct, all of its prey are released from that predation pressure, and they may have big impacts on ecosystems."

The loss of a predator can result in what is called a trophic cascade, which is an ecological phenomenon triggered by a predator's extinction that can also impact populations of prey, which can cause dramatic ecosystem and food web changes.

"If there are too many deer, for example, they can really change the ecosystem because they can destroy forests, and they also carry disease," Baldwin said.

Scientists have noted the trophic cascade effect in parts of Africa where lion and leopard populations have dwindled, according to Smithsonian Magazine. It caused olive baboons to alter their behavior patterns and increase contact with nearby humans. The increased contact has led to a rise in intestinal parasites in both people and the baboons.

In the case of the northern white rhino, of which only two female rhinos now survive, the last male of the species was held in semi-captivity at the end of its life, and *"the damage was already done in the ecosystem by that point,"* Baldwin said.

However, in general, the loss of rhinos, which often face threats from humans, from the ecosystem can have wide-ranging effects, according to Baldwin, who noted that the rhino's eating pattern helps with seed dispersal.

"They eat grasses and vegetation in one place, and they move and defecate in another place," he said. *"That helps those plants to disperse throughout the ecosystem, and it also helps populate the ecosystem with rhino food."*

The loss of abundant organisms that provide food for a wide variety of species would also interrupt the food web, according to Baldwin.

"For instance, if krill in the ocean goes extinct or becomes depressed in numbers, then that's the bottom-up effect; predators that rely on krill will suffer," he said.

While not at the top of the food chain, sea otters are keystone predators in the kelp forests in which they reside.

"The presence of sea otters in marine near-shore communities and coastal communities, particularly on the West Coast, have been shown to be essential and critical to healthy kelp forests underwater," Giordano said.

North American whales face potential extinction as warming oceans force them into unsafe territory

Unchecked carbon emissions could jeopardize plants, animals in world's most vital habitats

These kelp forests provide habitat for many species.

"One of the ways sea otters help to maintain those kelp forests is by preying upon other species that would slowly start to eat or consume the kelp, which, if they were left unchecked, would then rattle the entire kelp bed and turn it into a rocky or barren wasteland,"

Giordano said.

Species like parrot fish, which graze on algae, are extremely important to coral reef ecosystems because they prevent algae growth from getting out of control and impacting those coral reefs, according to Giordano.

"As algae expands in those communities, it can lead to the expansion of coral dead zones," he added.

The loss of certain species can impact the ecosystem in a number of ways, Giordano said, but the issue is that researchers don't yet know about many of the species out there.

A 2011 study concluded that about 86 percent of the Earth's species have yet to be discovered, according to National Geographic.

"We know more about some of the larger ones, but for many species, especially the ones that are disappearing, we don't know the impact of their loss," he said.

Loss of large predators has caused widespread disruption of ecosystems Scientists say decimation of top consumers may be *"humankind's most pervasive influence on the natural world"* due to cascading effects on ecosystems

The decline of large predators and other *"apex consumers"* at the top of the food chain has disrupted ecosystems all over the planet, according to a review of recent findings conducted by an international team of scientists and published in the July 15 issue of Science. The study looked at research on a wide range of terrestrial, freshwater, and marine ecosystems and concluded that *"the loss of apex consumers is arguably humankind's most pervasive influence on the natural world."*

According to first author James Estes, a professor of ecology and evolutionary biology at the University of California, Santa Cruz, large animals were once ubiquitous across the globe, and they shaped the structure and dynamics of ecosystems. Their decline, largely caused by humans through hunting and habitat fragmentation, has had far-reaching and often surprising consequences, including changes in vegetation, wildfire frequency, infectious diseases, invasive species, water quality, and nutrient cycles.

The decline of apex consumers has been most pronounced among the big predators, such as wolves and lions on land, whales and sharks in the oceans, and large fish in freshwater ecosystems. But there have also been dramatic declines in populations of many large herbivores, such as elephants and bison. The loss of apex consumers from an ecosystem triggers an ecological phenomenon known as a *"trophic cascade,"* a chain of effects moving down through lower levels of the food chain.

"The top-down effects of apex consumers in an ecosystem are fundamentally important, but it is a complicated phenomenon," Estes said. *"They have diverse and powerful effects on the ways ecosystems work, and the loss of these large animals has widespread implications."*

Estes and his coauthors cite a wide range of examples in their review, including the following:

-The extirpation of wolves in Yellowstone National Park led to over-browsing of aspen and willows by elk, and restoration of wolves has allowed the vegetation to recover.

-The reduction of lions and leopards in parts of Africa has led to population outbreaks and changes in behavior of olive baboons, increasing their contact with people and causing higher rates of intestinal parasites in both people and baboons.

-A rinderpest epidemic decimated the populations of wildebeest and other ungulates in the Serengeti, resulting in more woody vegetation and increased extent and frequency of wildfires prior to rinderpest eradication in the 1960s.

-Dramatic changes in coastal ecosystems have followed the collapse and recovery of sea otter populations; sea otters maintain coastal kelp forests by controlling populations of kelp-grazing sea urchins.

-The decimation of sharks in an estuarine ecosystem caused an outbreak of cow-nosed rays and the collapse of shellfish populations.

Despite these and other well-known examples, the extent to which ecosystems are shaped by such interactions has not been widely appreciated. *"There's been a tendency to see it as idiosyncratic and specific to particular species and ecosystems,"* Estes said.

One reason for this is that the top-down effects of apex predators are difficult to observe and study. *"These interactions are invisible unless there is some perturbation that reveals them,"* Estes said.

"With these large animals, it's impossible to do the kinds of experiments that would be needed to show their effects, so the evidence has been acquired as a result of natural changes and long-term records."

Estes has been studying coastal ecosystems in the North Pacific for several decades, doing pioneering work on the ecological roles of sea otters and killer whales. In 2008, he and coauthor John Terborgh of Duke University organized a conference on trophic cascades, which brought together scientists studying a wide range of ecosystems. The recognition that similar top-down effects have been observed in many different systems was a catalyst for the new paper.

The study's findings have profound implications for conservation. *"To the extent that conservation aims toward restoring functional ecosystems, the reestablishment of large animals and their ecological effects is fundamental,"* Estes said. *"This has huge implications for the scale at which conservation can be done. You can't restore large apex consumers on an acre of land. These animals roam over large areas, so it's going to require large-scale approaches."*

Why Endangered Species Matter

The Trump administration has proposed to strip the gray wolf of its endangered status.

The Endangered Species Act (ESA) was established in 1973 to protect "imperiled species and the ecosystems upon which they depend" and help them recover.

The Trump administration has put forth a number of proposals that would weaken the ESA. These include measures to allow for the consideration of economic impacts when enforcing the ESA, ending the practice of automatically giving threatened species the same protection as endangered species, and making it easier to remove species from the endangered list.

In a way, this is nothing new because the ESA has been under attack for decades from construction, development, logging, water management, fossil fuel extraction and other industries that contend the act stifles economic development. But between 2016 and 2018 alone, there were almost 150 attempts to undercut the ESA; and last year, from July 8 to 22, Republicans in Congress or the Trump administration introduced 24 such measures and spending bill riders.

These bills included efforts to remove the gray wolf's protected status in Wyoming and the western Great Lakes; a plan to remove from the endangered list the American burying beetle that lives on oil-rich land; and a strategy to roll back protection of the sage-grouse, which also inhabits oil-rich land in the West and whose numbers have declined 90 percent since the West was first settled. The Trump Administration recently opened up nine million acres of sage-grouse habitat to drilling and mining.

Endangered species, if not protected, could eventually become extinct—and extinction has a myriad of implications for our food, water, environment and even health.

Extinction rates are accelerating

Ninety-nine percent of all species that have ever lived have gone extinct over the course of five mass extinctions, which, in the past, were largely a result of natural causes such as volcano eruptions and asteroid impacts. Today, the rate of extinction is occurring 1,000 to 10,000 times faster because of human activity. The main modern causes of extinction are the loss and degradation of habitat (mainly deforestation), over exploitation (hunting, overfishing), invasive species, climate change, and nitrogen pollution.

There are also other threats to species such as the pervasive plastic pollution in the ocean—a recent study found that 100 percent of sea turtles had plastic or microplastic in their systems.

Emerging diseases affecting more and more wildlife species such as bats, frogs and salamanders are the result of an increase in travel and trade, which allows pests and pathogens to hitch rides to new locations, and warming temperatures that enable more pests to survive and spread. Wildlife trafficking also continues to be a big problem because for some species, the fewer members there are, the more valuable they become to poachers and hunters.

How many species are endangered?

According to the International Union for Conservation of Nature's Red List of Threatened Species, over 26,500 species are in danger of extinction. This includes 40 percent of amphibians, 34 percent of conifers, 33 percent of reef-building corals, 25 percent of mammals and 14 percent of birds. In the U.S., over 1,600 species are listed as threatened or endangered.

A 2018 report by the Endangered Species Coalition found that ten species in particular are *"imperiled"* by the Trump administration's proposals: California condor, giraffe, Hellbender salamander, Humboldt marten, leatherback and loggerhead sea turtles, red wolf, rusty patched bumble bee,

The web of life

While it may seem unimportant if we lose one salamander or rat species, it matters because all species are connected through their interactions in a web of life. A balanced and biodiverse ecosystem is one in which each species plays an important role and relies on the services provided by other species to survive. Healthy ecosystems are more productive and resistant to disruptions.

A recent study found that extreme environmental change could trigger an *"extinction domino effect."* One of the study's authors said, *"Because all species are connected in the web of life, our paper demonstrates that even the most tolerant species ultimately succumb to extinction when the less-tolerant species on which they depend disappear."* So saving one species means saving its habitat and the other species that live there too.

"When you lose one species, it affects the ecosystem and everything around it gets a little bit more fragile while it adapts to change," said Kelsey Wooddell, assistant director of the Earth Institute Center for Environmental Sustainability.

"Even if it's not a keystone species a species that others in an ecosystem depend on, its loss will weaken the functionality of the entire ecosystem, which just makes it easier for that ecosystem to stop working."

What are the consequences of extinction?

Altering ecosystems through cascading effects

If a species has a unique function in its ecosystem, its loss can prompt cascading effects through the food chain (a "trophic cascade"), impacting other species and the ecosystem itself.

An often-cited example is the impact of the wolves in Yellowstone Park, which were hunted to near extinction by 1930. Without them, the elk and deer they had preyed upon thrived, and their grazing decimated streamside willows and aspens, which had provided habitat for songbirds. This left the stream banks susceptible to erosion, and a decline in songbirds allowed mosquitoes and other insects the birds would have eaten to multiply. When the wolves were reintroduced to the park in 1995, they once again preyed on the elk; plant life returned to the stream banks and along with it, birds, beavers, fish and other animals. (Note: David Bernhardt, acting secretary of the Department of the Interior, just announced a proposal to strip gray wolves of their endangered status in the Lower 48 states.)

Kelp forests are another classic example. They play an important role in coastal ecosystems because they provide habitat for other species, protect the coastline from storm surges and absorb carbon dioxide.

Otter in a kelp field.

Kelp forests are rapidly getting mowed down by exploding numbers of purple sea urchin. California sea otters eat the purple sea urchins that feed on giant kelp. These otters used to number in the hundreds of thousands to millions, but their population has been reduced to about 3,000 as a result of unchecked hunting in the 19th century and pollution. Moreover, in 2013 the sunflower starfish, which also eats purple sea urchins, began dying because of a virus that was likely exacerbated by warmer waters. Without the sea otter and the sunflower starfish predators, the purple sea urchin began feasting on the kelp forests, which declined 93 percent between 2013 and 2018. (A new study found that kelp forests are now also threatened by ocean heat waves.) The explosion of sea urchins not only damaged the kelp ecosystem, it also had serious impacts on Northern California's red urchins that are valued for sushi. Fish that need the kelp forests for spawning, such as sculpin, rock cod and red snapper may become vulnerable in the future as well.

As another example, Wooddell explained that on Guam, after the invasive brown tree snake was accidentally introduced to the island in the 1950s, 10 of the island's 12 endemic bird species went extinct. *"Typically birds eat seeds and spread seeds elsewhere on the island but that is no longer a functioning ecosystem,"* she said. *"So the forest and the trees have decreased a lot. And Guam is covered in spiders because the birds are not there to eat them."*

Losing apex species has multiple effects

Eliminating the large predators at the top of the food chain, the *"apex species,"* may be humans' most serious impact on nature, according to one study. These large species are more vulnerable because they live longer, reproduce more slowly, have small populations, and need more food and a greater habitat area. Scientists say their loss has played a role in pandemics, fires, the decline of valued species and the rise of invasive ones, the reduction of ecosystem services, and decreased carbon sequestration.

Elephants are an apex species that may go extinct in our lifetime, as a result of tourism, habitat loss and poaching for ivory. This could dramatically change ecosystems in Africa and Asia. Through consumption and digestion, elephants disperse more seeds farther than any other animals; this fosters the growth of plants and trees that birds, bats and other animals depend upon for food and shelter.

Elephants dig water holes that all animals share, and they fertilize the soil with their rich dung, which provides food for other animals.

The loss of apex species can also affect wildfires. After rinderpest, an infectious virus, wiped out many plant-cating wildebeest and buffalo in East Africa in the late 1800s, plants flourished. During the dry season, this over-abundance of vegetation spurred an increase in wildfires. In the 1960s, after rinderpest was eliminated through vaccinations, the wildebeest and buffalo returned. The ecosystem went from shrubbery to grasslands again, decreasing the amount of combustible vegetation, and the wildfires decreased.

Jeopardizing pollination

Seventy-five percent of the world's food crops are partially or completely pollinated by insects and other animals, and practically all flowering plants in the tropical rainforest are pollinated by animals. The loss of pollinators could result in a decrease in seed and fruit production, leading ultimately to the extinction of many important plants.

Flying foxes, also known as fruit bats, are the only pollinators of some rainforest plants. They have been over-hunted in tropical forests with several species going extinct. One study noted that 289 plant species, including eucalyptus and agave, rely on flying foxes to reproduce; in turn, these plants were responsible for producing 448 valuable products.

Bees pollinate over 250,000 species of plants, including most of the 87 crops that humans rely on for food, such as almonds, apples and cucumbers.
Honeybees are responsible for pollinating approximately $15 billion worth of crops in the U. S. each year.

But in recent years, large populations of bees have been wiped out by the mysterious "colony collapse disorder" wherein adult honeybees disappear from their hive, likely in response to numerous stressors.

Over the last 20 years in the U.S., monarch butterflies, which pollinate many wildflowers, have decreased 90 percent. The rusty-patched bumble bee, another important pollinator and the first bee species to be put on the endangered list, now only occupies one percent of its former range.

Insect populations overall are declining due to climate change, habitat degradation, herbicides and pesticides. A 2014 review of insect studies found that most monitored species had decreased by about 45 percent. And a German study found 75 percent fewer flying insects after just 27 years. As insect populations are reduced, the small animals, fish and birds that rely on them for food are being affected, and eventually the predators of fish and birds will feel the impacts as well. One entomologist who had studied insects in the rainforest in the 1970s returned in 2010 to find an up to 60-fold reduction. His study reported *"a bottom-up trophic cascade and consequent collapse of the forest food web."*

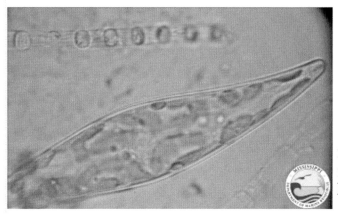

Endangering the food chain

Plankton, tiny plant and animal organisms that live in the ocean or fresh water, make up the foundation of the marine food chain.
Phytoplankton are critical

collapse of fisheries. She is concerned, however, that

"there could be changes in ocean ecosystems and we don't really know what those changes will be. What will the architecture of that ecosystem look like in the future? The problem is, the ocean is already changing and we don't understand the architecture of the ecosystem right now well enough to predict what will happen in the future."

Losing nature's therapeutic riches

More than a quarter of prescription medications contain chemicals that were discovered through plants or animals. Penicillin was derived from a fungus. Scientists are studying the venom of some tarantulas to see if one of its compounds could help cure diseases such as Parkinson's. One molecule from a rare marine bacterium could be the basis of a new way to treat to melanoma.

Scientists have so far identified about 1.7 million different types of organisms, but between 10 and 50 million species are thought to exist on Earth.

Twenty-five percent of Western medicines are derived from the rainforest.

Who knows what substances or capabilities some of these species might possess that could help treat diseases and make human lives easier?

Destroying livelihoods

According to a study for the U.N., the continued loss of species could cost the world 18 percent of global economic output by 2050.

Already, a number of industries have been economically impacted by species loss. The collapse of bee populations has hurt many in the $50 billion-a-year global honey industry. Atlantic cod in the waters off of Newfoundland formed the basis of the local economy since the 15th century — until overfishing the cod destroyed the livelihoods of local fishermen.

What you can do about extinction

Extinction is hard to see. We may not realize how much of the natural world has been lost because the *"baseline"* shifts with every generation. Past generations would regard what we see as natural today as terribly damaged, and what we see as damaged today, our children will view as natural.

Wooddell believes the most important thing one can do is to put pressure on Congress and elected leaders to create land management, pollution and other sustainable policies that will protect biodiversity and the environment. However, because it's unlikely that these kinds of top-down policies will be instituted in the current political climate, she recommends mobilizing grassroots community groups to create *"bottom-up"* policies.

Here are some other things you can do to protect endangered species and prevent extinction:

-**Eat less meat.** Soybean production is one of the main causes of deforestation, and most soybean meal is used for animal feed.

-**Buy organic food** because organic farmers use only non-synthetic or natural pesticides on their crops. Synthetic pesticides may be toxic for other organisms.

-**Choose sustainable seafood**. The Marine Stewardship Council provides a list of certified sustainable fish for responsible eating.

–**Compost food waste.** In New York City, the compost is used for urban farming and gardening, which provide habitat for pollinators.

-**Buy wood and paper products certified by the Forest Stewardship Council,** to ensure they're harvested from responsibly managed forests.

-**Don't buy products made from endangered or threatened species,** such as tortoise shell, ivory, coral, some animal skins, and "traditional" medicines.

-**Be aware of the source of palm oil used in countless food and cosmetic products**. Many tropical forests are being razed for palm oil plantations. If a product contains palm oil, make sure it's from a deforestation-free plantation.

–**Reduce your use of plastic.**

-**If you have a garden, plant native shrubs and flowers** that attract butterflies and other pollinators. Milkweed is particularly helpful for monarch butterflies.

–**Set up a beehive.**

-**Diversify your diet**. Eating these 50 foods will promote biodiversity and a healthier plant.

-Support and get involved with organizations that are helping endangered animals.

-Join the Center for Biological Diversity and use their Take-Action Toolboxes.

Resources

Share.america.gov, "Top 10 ways to save wildlife." BY Share America; awionline.org, "What You Can Do for Wildlife." By Deb Haaland; shondaland.com, "Saving the Animals Is More Important Than We Think: Animal conservation is a complicated issue, but it's a core part of addressing the climate crisis." By Nylah Burton; wildanimalinitiative.org, "We want to make life better for wild animals."; panthera.org, "Tiger Expert Answers Questions About Netflix's Tiger King." By John Goodrich Ph.D.; endangered.org, "10 Easy Things You Can Do To Save Endangered Species."; nwf.org, "Understanding Conservation."; e360.yale.edu, "The Real Case for Saving Species: We Don't Need Them, But They Need Us: Conservationists argue that humans need to save species in order to save ourselves. The truth is we could survive without wild species — but they can't survive without us, and the moral argument for protecting them and the beauty they bring to the world is overwhelming." BY CARL SAFINA;

nature.com, "Oust species to save ecosystems: Network models might offer solution to cascading species loss." By Emma Marris; sciencing.com, "What Happens When Something in a Food Chain Goes Extinct?" By Mary Dowd; sciencing.com, "The Effects of the Extinction of an Organism in a Desert Ecosystem Food Chain." By Jason Steele; accuweather.com, "How would a species' extinction impact the food web, our ecosystems?" By Ashley Williams; esajournals.onlinelibrary.wiley.com, "Effect of multiple disturbances on food web vulnerability to biodiversity loss in detritus-based systems." By Edoardo Calizza, M. Letizia Costantini and Loreto Rossi; news.ucsc.com, "Loss of large predators has caused widespread disruption of ecosystems: Scientists say decimation of top consumers may be "humankind's most pervasive influence on the natural world" due to cascading effects on ecosystems." By Tim Stephens; news.climate.columbia.com, "Why Endangered Species Matter." By Renee Cho;

Addendum

Tiger Expert Answers Questions About Netflix's Tiger King

With its larger-than-life characters, Netflix's docu-series "Tiger King" put a controversial spin on a real problem — breeding tigers for profit has created an animal welfare, public safety and law enforcement nightmare in the U.S. As this series and a number of investigative reports that preceded it have shown, America has a big and growing captive tiger crisis right in its own backyards, but it pales in comparison to the one facing endangered wild populations. In this blog, Panthera Chief Scientist and Tiger Program

Director Dr. John Goodrich talks about the threats facing wild tigers and why we need to advocate for them now more than ever.

What is the status of tigers in the wild?

Only about 4,000 tigers remain in the wild, as opposed to about 100,000 a century ago. To provide some context, by some estimates there are more than twice as many tigers living in roadside zoos in the U.S. than there are left in the wild.

What are the main reasons tigers are declining in the wild?

Their decline is the result of poaching and habitat loss, with poaching being the top threat today, driven by a very high black-market price for their parts, primarily for Traditional Asian Medicine. This poaching and the multi-billion dollar trade that drives it are illegal in every single tiger range state.

To help visualize the magnitude of the poaching problem, imagine an area roughly the size of France and Spain combined — around 1 million km of tiger habitat — sitting vacant, emptied of tigers and their prey. Due to poaching, tigers have gone extinct in Vietnam, Laos and Cambodia just in the past 15 years.

The second biggest threat to tigers is habitat loss. Tigers occupy some of the most densely populated countries in the world that are experiencing some of the greatest deforestation rates in the world.

What are the solutions?

The solutions are simple, at least conceptually. Tigers are a resilient species. They are generalists that can survive in a variety of conditions, from the frigid forests of the Russian Far East to the hot tropical forest in southern Asia. All they need to thrive is some decent forest — it doesn't have to be pristine old-growth —and protection from people. At the site-level — say a national park — tiger conservation involves patrolling to catch poachers and stop habitat degradation while working with local communities to improve their lives in ways that have a reduced impact on tigers and their habitat.

At larger scales, we need to ensure protected areas remain connected by tiger habitat, which is more complex and means planning and managing infrastructure development, agriculture and logging, in conjunction with local communities. These are usually the areas where tigers and people overlap, so we also need to manage human-tiger conflict to minimize and mitigate attacks on livestock and even people

COMMERCIALLY CAPTIVE-BRED TIGERS CANNOT BE USED TO RESTORE DWINDLING WILD TIGER POPULATIONS.

The Tiger King series shed light on the commercial exploitation of captive-bred tigers in the U.S. — as have several other investigative news pieces in recent months. What's going on?

When most people think of breeding tigers for profit, they think of Asia's tiger farms, where there are thousands of tigers in captivity. However, many countries breed and exhibit tigers for commercial purposes, either legally, or by skirting the law. In the U.S., there are an estimated 5,000-10,000 tigers in captivity, not including those in accredited zoos.

These tigers are bred for profit — not for conservation or education. In the U.S., 95% of captive tigers are privately owned. They are bred and kept primarily to entertain tourists who pay to pet and feed tiger cubs and have their photos taken with them.

"*Roadside zoos*" that exhibit wild cats often market themselves as having a conservation mission. Can tigers bred at these facilities ever be released in the wild?

Commercially captive-bred tigers cannot be used to restore dwindling wild tiger populations. Genetically, they are unfit for re-introduction; they are hybrids of the five extant wild tiger subspecies, or even bred with other cat species, like lions, and often have genetic defects. Further, generations in captivity and handling by people means they would be unlikely to survive in the wild. Most tigers in captivity are bred for human use and entertainment.

The concerns about the welfare of tigers in these places are pretty obvious. But do roadside zoos have any negative impacts on wild tigers?

The biggest threat from these backyard operations is the role they play in deflecting attention and dollars away from the plight of wild tigers and legitimate efforts to save them. Roadside zoo owners often engage in "greenwashing" to protect their image and attract visitors. They may make small donations to conservation organizations, or say they do, but there is no evidence that any of these operations are substantively funding wild tiger conservation. Also, the captive tiger cubs that age out of "pay-to-play" petting, or get too big for an owner to handle, have to go somewhere. This has created a need for big cat sanctuaries in the U.S. that raise funds from the public to house and maintain these cats for the rest of their lives. Meanwhile, funding for wild tiger conservation has been harder and harder to come by in recent years even as some populations in Southeast Asia teeter on the brink of extinction. It's a cruel irony that it will cost more to take care of America's glut of unwanted tigers than it would to secure a future for tigers in the wild.

Commercial breeding advocates make a case that increasing the supply of captive-bred tigers in the marketplace takes the pressure off of wild populations. Is that true?

Any trade in tiger parts, whether legal or illegal, perpetuates demand for tiger products and keeps poachers in business. Despite the increase in Asia's commercial captive breeding facilities in the past decade and the surplus of captive-bred tigers in the marketplace, poaching of wild tigers continues unabated. There is no evidence that farming tigers takes the pressure off of wild populations and it may actually be hurting them.

Does Panthera endorse big cat sanctuaries?

We would like to see a day when there is no need for big cat sanctuaries in the United States, but for now, rescue centers and sanctuaries are a necessary consequence of our captive tiger trade. They provide a home for unwanted cats, for example, when someone buys a tiger cub as a pet but abandons it when it gets too big. These operations should be certified by the Global Federation of Animal Sanctuaries, which requires, among other things, that the organization is non-profit, does not buy or sell cats, does not allow public contact with cats, and adheres to strict animal welfare standards.

Can captive breeding of big cats be beneficial to conservation?

Zoos accredited by the Association for Zoos and Aquariums (AZA) contribute to the conservation of wild species through the Species Survival Program (SSP). The SSP requires all AZA zoos to carefully manage the breeding of captive tigers to maintain pure genetic strains of subspecies and to minimize inbreeding so that if ever needed, animals from these zoos would be genetically suitable for release into the wild. These zoos do not breed for profit and do not allow public contact with
gers. They also contribute to conservation through funding, education and on-the-ground work in tiger range.

ANY TRADE IN TIGER PARTS, WHETHER LEGAL OR ILLEGAL, PERPETUATES DEMAND FOR TIGER PRODUCTS AND KEEPS POACHERS IN BUSINESS.

Does Panthera support the Big Cat Public Safety Act?

The Big Cat Public Safety Act is a step in the right direction to greatly limit who can own a big cat in the U.S. and under what circumstances. Enacting a federal law to restrict the unchecked breeding and exploitation of big cats is long overdue in this country. If rigorously enforced, the Big Cat Public Safety Act will not only protect captive-bred cats and people but will help to dismantle an industry with insidious implications for wild tigers by shrinking the availability of tiger parts for the global illegal wildlife trade.

We believe the law could be strengthened by requiring that existing privately held cats are spayed and neutered, and requiring that all animals are chipped and their fate tracked, to help ensure they are not traded illegally.

The Effects of the Extinction of an Organism in a Desert Ecosystem Food Chain

The desert is a harsh, dry environment, but plants and animals who have adapted to those conditions thrive in these ecosystems. From eagles to ants, there are a diverse range of plants and animals that live and interact with one another in deserts around the world. Like all ecosystems, the web of species interactions can be fragile, and species extinction can have a large effect. The identity of the organism that is lost and its role in the ecosystem determines how the food chain is affected.

Desert Food Chains

All ecosystems are composed of species that perform different roles in the food chain. In the desert, shrubs and cacti are the primary producers and form the base of the food chain. Next, there are small herbivores that eat the plants such as:

-mice

-prairie dogs

-ants

-grasshoppers

Above this trophic level there are mesopredators like foxes, snakes, and lizards that prey upon the small consumers. Finally, at the top of the food chain, animals like cougars and eagles will prey on all of the species below them. The role of the species that goes extinct plays a big role in how the food chain will be affected.

Functional Redundancy

Not all extinctions have big impacts on ecosystems. Sometimes there are a lot of different species that essentially perform the same job or function in an ecosystem. If one of these species goes extinct, the others will increase in number and perform the same job. Such a "replaceable" species is called functionally redundant. Since deserts are harsh environments, species are more similar to one another because they need similar adaptations to survive. For example, Guofang Liu at the Chinese Academy of Science found that plants in the desert steppe of Mongolia have less functional diversity than plants in the meadow and typical Mongolian. This may indicate that plant extinctions in the desert may not have as big an impact as extinctions in other ecosystems.

Keystone Species

Sometimes extinction can have a disproportionately large impact on an ecosystem. Such important species are called keystone species. Often keystone species are predators that maintain the stability of the entire ecosystem. The most well-known example is a species of seastar — Pisaster ochraceus — on the Washington Coast. When it's removed from the rocky intertidal, lots of other species go extinct as well. Top predators in the desert such as cougar and eagles are similarly important. Another keystone species in the American desert are hummingbirds. These are important pollinators of desert cacti that support a range of other species. When the hummingbirds are lost many desert plants and the species that depend on them disappear as well.

Domino Extinctions and Other Effects

Sometimes species are closely linked to another species. When one goes, the other one that depended on it goes as well just like dominoes knocking each other over. A great example in the desert is the relationship between prairie dogs and black footed ferrets. Black footed ferrets depend on prairie dogs for food. When prairie dogs were driven to low numbers due to poisoning, the black footed ferret went extinct in most places. Species extinctions can also alter the structure of desert food. For example, if large kangaroo rats go extinct in desert grasslands, the grassland turns into shrub land because the important seed predation job the kangaroo rats performed has been lost.

Effect of multiple disturbances on food web vulnerability to biodiversity loss in detritus-based systems

Global biodiversity is affected by human pressure and climate change, and the present rate of biodiversity loss is probably higher than ever before. Community composition is also changing, and interspecific interactions are under severe pressure. The extinction of one species within a food web can result in further secondary extinctions, due to bottom-up effects that can be even more intense and less predictable than the direct effects of disturbance, undermining our capacity for ecosystem management and conservation. Here we investigated a metric for assessing the structural stability of food webs in the face of species loss, referred to as "*Resistance*", based on two fundamental web properties: (1) the proportion of key species in the web, a "*key*" species being one whose deletion leads to at least one secondary extinction, and (2) the mean number of secondary extinctions observed per key species deletion. We compared web Resistance with web Robustness based on 12 detritus-based riverine food webs under four species extinction scenarios on various temporal and spatial scales. We investigated the effect of multiple disturbances (extreme flood and river basin urbanization) on community vulnerability to biodiversity loss, assessing the behavior of Robustness and Resistance under the applied species extinction scenarios and testing their dependence on web topology. We estimated the contribution of the rarest and the most dominant species, and that of the most and least connected species, to web Resistance.

Urbanization negatively affected community vulnerability to biodiversity loss. Only food web Resistance showed a significant flood effect and interaction between flood and urbanization. The most connected species contributed the most to food web resistance, whereas the rarest and the most abundant species had a similar, intermediate structural importance. Both food web Resistance and the role of selected key species varied across web description scales. Food web Resistance values were coherent across species extinction scenarios, demonstrating the suitability of the proposed approach for quantifying community vulnerability to species loss and the importance of considering food webs in monitoring and impact assessment programs. The approach is thus seen to be a promising research pathway supporting ecosystem management.

Page 98

Chapter Twenty-Two–Water Conservation and Desalination

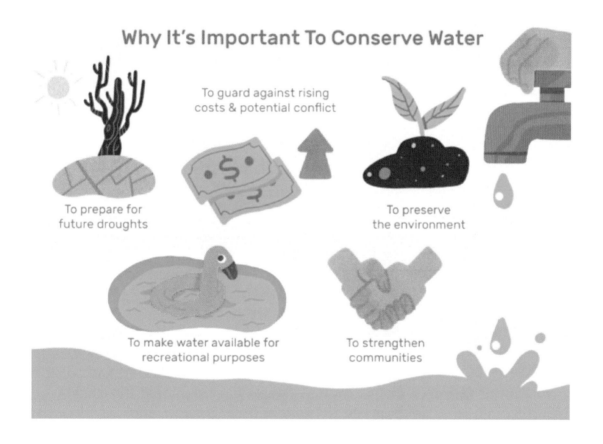

Why It's Important To Conserve Water

To prepare for future droughts

To guard against rising costs & potential conflict

To preserve the environment

To make water available for recreational purposes

To strengthen communities

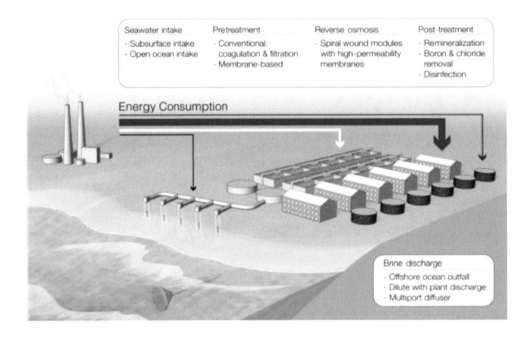

Seawater intake	Pretreatment	Reverse osmosis	Post-treatment

· Subsurface intake
· Open ocean intake
	· Conventional:
	  coagulation & filtration
	· Membrane-based
		· Spiral wound modules
		  with high-permeability
		  membranes
			· Remineralization
			· Boron & chloride
			  removal
			· Disinfection

Energy Consumption

Brine discharge
- Offshore ocean outfall
- Dilute with plant discharge
- Multiport diffuser

A Guide to Water Conservation - Saving Water and the Earth

Water conservation is the careful use and preservation of water supply, and it includes both the quantity and quality of water utilized. Water is an essential asset for the nourishment of all life. The fundamental demand for all activities appropriates local use to the agricultural industry.

With the regular expanding weight of the human population, there has been serious tension on water resources. Negligence of customary water bodies like tanks and lakes, unpredictable abuse of groundwater, and incorrect preservation of surface water systems have bothered the issue. Still further and is no doubt going to grow in the years to come.

There are various approaches to making your water last nowadays. One simple yet often disregarded strategy to cut your water bill is to use your water twice. Unlike electricity, you can reuse water again and again. That's the idea of water conservation.

Key Facts about our water:

Water is the most important natural resource that living things need. But at the same time, it has also been misused and wasted. To better grasp the full significance of water conservation, take a look at the few yet key facts about water:

-The average adult human body comprises 50-65 percent of water. They are averaging around 57-60 percent. With infants, they have a higher percentage. Often around 75-78% water, dropping to 65% by one year.

-The Earth has a limited amount of water. The water we have now is all we get, and it is recycled repeatedly. The water cycle can help you understand this condition.

-Water is the basic demand for every food. It grows our fruits and vegetable, and each livestock consumes it.

-A plant's life is dependent on water. Plants help the ecosystem and produce the oxygen necessary to keep us healthy. Additionally, trees are generally used for housing, paper, and a lot more.

-Ninety-seven percent (97%) of all water on Earth is saltwater- that is not suitable for drinking.

-Only three percent (3%) of water on Earth is freshwater. Only 0.5% is available is suitable for drinking.

-The other 2.5% of freshwater is found in glaciers, ice caps, the atmosphere, soil, or under the Earth's surface or is too polluted for consumption.

What is Water Conservation?

To point out, even more, Water Conservation is the practice of efficiently preserving, controlling, and managing water resources.

Water conservation has become an essential practice in every part of the world, even in regions where water appears to be enough. It is the most practical and environment-friendly approach to lessen our need for water. Likewise, using less water puts less weight on our sewage treatment facilities, which use an ample amount of energy for heating water.

Main reasons to conserve water:

-Conserving water saves energy. Energy is important to filter, heat, and pump water to your home, so lessening your water use likewise decreases your carbon traces.

-Consuming less water keeps more in our environments and aids with keeping wetland habitats best for creatures like otters, water voles, herons, and fish. This is particularly significant during dry season periods.

-Conserving water can save you money. If you have a water meter, the less water you use, the less you might be charged by your water company.

For the past 50 years, freshwater extraction from icebergs has expanded by three folds. Because of progression in life, a more significant amount of water is a need. This likewise implies a growth in the interest for the power supply with water.

Conserving water can likewise make the life of your septic system longer. This is by lessening soil immersion and reducing any contamination because of leaks. Overloading municipal sewer systems can also flow untreated sewage to lakes and rivers. The smaller the amount of water coursing through these systems, the lower the probability of contamination. Even the few groups like the community-wide domestic water preservation avoided the expensive sewage system development.

What are the Water-Related Problems?

The main problems with water are water shortage, shortages of clean water, and waterborne diseases. A lack of access to safe water caused 80% of all deaths worldwide. More than 5 million people die each year from water-related diseases such as hepatitis A, dysentery, and severe diarrhea.

Approximately 900 million to 1.1 billion people worldwide lack clean drinking water, and 2.4 billion lack basic sanitation. Water demand is increasing at a rate faster than population growth. Over the past 70 years, while the world's population has tripled, water demand has increased sixfold. The United Nations estimates that in 2025 that 5 billion of the world's 8 billion people will live in areas where water is scarce. Many of these people will have difficulty accessing enough water to meet their basic needs.

Increasing populations, growing agriculture, industrialization, and high living standards have boosted water demand. All this while drought, overuse, and pollution have decreased the supplies. To make up for this shortfall, water is often taken from lakes, rivers, and wetlands, causing serious environmental damage. According to a 2003 United Nations report, "*Across the globe, groundwater is being depleted by the demands of megacities and agriculture, while fertilizer runoff and pollution are threatening water quality and public health.*"

It seems there are alarming predictions every week related to water, such as disease, crop disasters, starvation, famines, and war. Safe drinking water and sanitation are major challenges in many developing countries, from shanty towns and areas to urban poor cities. At least in rural areas, the poor can dig wells and take care of the sanitation in their fields.

Water Pollution

The causes of much of the pollution in rural areas are untreated sewage resulting from a lack of toilets and sewers. Salts, fertilizers, and pesticides from irrigated land contaminate the flowing water and groundwater supplies and the saltwater entering overused aquifers. Places with sewers often have no wastewater treatment facilities while the sewage becomes dumped right into the water supplies, a source from which people draw.

Agriculture-related pollution such as fertilizer, pesticides, animal wastes, herbicides, salts from evaporated irrigation water, and silt from deforestation washes into the streams, rivers, lakes, ponds, and the sea. This agricultural runoff sometimes severs creating "dead zones" in coastal water zones.

Industry-related water pollution comes from mining and manufacturing toxic chemicals and heavy metals. Power plant emissions then create acid rain that contaminates the surface water.

People often bathe, wash their clothes, and swim in disgusting water. They also drink the water of uncertain quality from ponds and streams used by animals.

The water and air around the cities are polluted, and the water shortages and quality in rural areas are still rampant.

Water Shortages

Many countries worldwide face serious water shortages with its root not really about the shortage of water but of over population. The worse one to know is knowing people living in places where it is unfit for human habitation. Often, water shortages are local problems rather than national ones. Water shortages are worse in areas with little rain or water and lots of people.

Repeated drilling and well building caused the water table to drop in some places as much as six feet a year. This is the reason water tables are falling almost everywhere. Rich countries can compensate for these shortages in some areas by building dams, tapping deep water aquifers, importing food, recycling wastewater, or desalinating seawater. Unfortunately, developing countries are vulnerable to doing these things.

Water shortage is also a big problem in many cities. Water is only turned on a couple of times a day for about half an hour each time. People with money can have special storage tanks to collect water during those times. This can allow them to have water around the clock. People without storage tanks collect water in jugs and buckets and often take bucket baths when water is not turned on.

Global warming can worsen these water shortages in some places and create water shortages in other places.

Solutions to Water Problems

There are major disagreements between environmentalists and agriculturists on managing available water. But, water experts say that progress made in cleaning water and making it cheap has only encouraged people to waste it.

However, the goal of planners in solving water problems is to keep water cheap so poor people can get it but at the same time keep it expensive, so people don't waste it. In places where water is subsidized, people tend to waste it due to the low prices. The obvious solution was to end the subsidies.

The most practical solution is reusing and recycling water. Some cities can meet a fifth of their water needs by recycling water. Worldwide, two-thirds of urban water don't get treated. Systems that treat and reuse water are often the least costly. The most efficient way to clean water but have difficulty overcoming the aversion is to have drinking water derived from sewage.

Ultraviolet radiation is a popular means of disinfecting water but is less effective when the water contains sediments and sludge. For places where water is collected from dirty ponds and lakes, people have to clean it by folding clean clothes several times before placing them over a jug as the water pours through it. The cloth acts as a filter from all sorts of disease-causing organisms.

Women in Bangladesh have done the said process, not out of necessity but out of tradition. But instead of using cloth, they used cotton to remove the course debris. The best way to employ this method is to fold the cloth to four or eight thicknesses, wash, then sun dry the cloth after each filtering. At least in this method, it can remove the zooplankton that carries diseases such as cholera.

Water Conservation As A Solution

These old and tried and true methods are being brought back to conserve water through harvesting, transporting, and storing rainwater. These methods are brought back because modern technology can't solve problems in small communities. Systems that use catchments, gutters and other channels, storage tanks, and gravity or pump-driven delivery systems. These are cheaper or at least equal in cost to drilling and building a well.

Raised ridges to 10 meters wide alternate with shallow canals to channel water. They are either harvested rain or deviated river water. This helps water crops, stores heat, and keeps the fields warm on cold nights.

Saving WATER Really is IMPORTANT!

Since safe and clean water is limited, people have access to freshwater. They can take steps to control their water consumption to avoid waste and shortage. We know that the planet is mostly covered with saltwater. And can only be consumed after undergoing a desalination process, which is quite expensive. Saving water means a lot to humans and all the species on Earth.

Events such as droughts further limit access to clean and fresh water. This means that people need to take extra steps to reduce water use and save as much water as possible. In some areas of the world, access to water is limited due to contamination.

Water is Life!

Everything on Earth requires water to sustain itself. But abusing it means reducing its ability to provide us with this basic necessity. Water is a limited resource. While Earth is a self-contained ecosystem, the planet always has, and will always have, the same amount of water. The population growth puts a strain on water supplies. And clean water is reduced by the pollution, and contamination humankind creates.

People are particularly reducing the water supply due to pollution. So as other contaminants. On top of that, we are polluting the water for all of Earth's creatures, sending chemicals like oil and fertilizers through the rivers. These ultimately end up in the ocean.

Without freshwater, one will die in just a short period. It is a simple yet morbid fact that helps drive the point across, and water is life. Water conservation is the potential, most cost-effective, and environmentally sound way to reduce water demand.

The Why and How of Water Conservation

Using the limited water supply wisely and caring for it properly are just a few of the many keys to conserving water. Remember that we have limited availability of water supply. This means that we do not have an endless amount of water. Keep in mind that it is our responsibility to understand and learn more about water conservation. Even so, find ways to help keep the resources pure and safe for the coming generations.

Saving Water Saves Energy

A lot of energy is required to treat water and supply it to your home—the same as a tremendous amount of water expected to cool the power plants that produce electricity.

At home, heating water for showers, shaving, cooking, and cleaning likewise uses a lot of energy.

That is why it's imperative to recollect to save energy and water in your home. We tend to have longer, hotter showers as the climate gets colder. By placing a water-efficient shower and lessening the time spent in the shower, you can spare energy and water.

One of the best means to save energy across the region and in your own house is to use water more effectively.

Did you know that?

-Heated water utilizes 39% of energy in the typical home.

-Washing your garments in cold water can decrease energy use by up to 80% compared with a warm wash stack.

-Putting up a water-efficient showerhead can lessen your expenses by up to $100 every year.

Saving Water Saves Money

Using less water makes your money in your pocket. You may be able to save thousands of gallons of water every year by applying basic water conservation strategies.

For instance, you have your well and septic system, the extra gallons of water released each day will soak the soil in the septic system absorption field to a point where extensive repair or replacement is necessary.

Conserving water can extend the system's life and delay the need for repair. If you live in an area serviced by a municipal water system, the greater your water use, the more you pay for water.

Also, water conservation can help prevent water pollution. Overloading a septic system may cause nutrient and bacterial contamination. Of nearby lakes, streams, and drinking water, even the water from your well. The smaller the amount of water flowing through these systems, the lower the likelihood of pollution.

Pollution costs money, too. Excessive weed growth in a lake caused by mineral enrichment from poorly functioning septic systems often means costly weed control measures paid for by you and your neighbors. If they can be repaired at all, Polluted home water wells can cost thousands of dollars to fix.

Saving Water Saves Nature

Saving water likewise decreases the risk of natural disasters such as droughts. We have to reuse water in the same number as we're likely to save a more significant amount of it.

Saving water turns out to be critical for up-and-coming generations. They won't have enough water accessibility unless we wind up worried from this day at present.

We have to save water for plants as well. Earth's oxygen and a large portion of the food originate from plants. Plants require water for survival as well.

As the world modernizes, a greater amount of water is to be utilized to beautify urban communities and for recreational reasons. We have to consider it too.

What Can You Do?

We have first to understand that the preservation of water is the obligation of each person. It is to be done as a whole. No government authority or institution can help us save water unless we desire to. Right now is a high time to do so.

Reducing water use reduces the energy required to process and deliver it to homes, businesses, farms, and communities. Which in turn helps to reduce pollution and conserve fuel resources.

Cutting off the wastage of water will enable us to keep up the artistry of a city. Additionally, protecting our natural ecosystems from further damage is critical, especially for the survival of some endangered species. The great pacific garbage patch is a great example of the worst side of our wasteful practices.

There are many efficient approaches to preserve water in and around your home. Look through this rundown for ways that will work for you.

Here are demonstrated means to conserve more water:

In the Kitchen

-Don't leave the water running for rinsing whenever you wash the dishes by hand—it is the ideal way. If you have two sinks, fill one with rinse water. If you just have one sink, use a shower gadget instead of giving the water a chance to run. This saves 200 to 500 gallons every month.

-When washing the dishes by hand, use a minimal detergent as much as possible. This limits the rinse water needed. This saves 50 to 150 gallons every month.

-Make sure not to defrost frozen foods with running water. Either prepare in advance by putting frozen things in the icebox or refrigerator overnight. Or defrost them in the microwave. This saves 50 to 150 gallons every month.

-Make sure not to run the faucet while you clean vegetables. Wash them in a filled sink or container. This saves 150 to 250 gallons every month.

-Keep a container or bottle of drinking water in the fridge. This beats the inefficient tendency for running tap water to cool it for drinking. This saves 200 to 300 gallons every month.

-Cook foods in less water. This keeps the nutritional value of the food as well.

In the Bathroom

-When taking a shower, don't misuse the cold water while sitting tight for hot water to reach the showerhead. In a container/ pail, catch that water to water the plants outside or flush in your toilet. This saves 200 to 300 gallons every month.

-Examine the toilet for leaks. Place dye tablets or food coloring into the tank. If the color shows up in the bowl without flushing, there is certainly a leak that ought to be repaired. This saves 400 gallons per month.

-Make doubly sure your toilet is an ultra-low volume flush model which utilizes only one and a half gallons each flush.

-Make sure to turn off the water or faucet while brushing your teeth. This saves three gallons every day.

-Don't Use the Toilet as an Ashtray or Wastebasket. Every time you flush a cigarette butt, facial tissue, or other small bits of trash, you're wasting gallons of water. Put them in the proper garbage bin.

-Take Shorter Showers. One way to cut down on water use is to turn off the shower after soaping up, then turn it back on to rinse. A four-minute shower uses approximately 20 to 40 gallons of water.

In the Laundry Room

A high-efficiency washer is ideal for saving water in the laundry room. It uses less water than the traditional washer. Likewise, it will eliminate more water from the clothes before drying, bringing about shorter dry times. Here are a couple of different tips for saving water in the laundry room:

-Run the washer only when you have a full load.

-To cut your dry time, use wool dryer balls.

-Allow stained clothes to soak the sink in advance, so they don't have to be washed twice.

In the Yard or Garden

-Avoid watering the lawn on windy days. There's excessive evaporation. This can waste up to 300 gallons in a single watering.

-It is better to water during the cool parts of the day. Preferably in the early morning to keep from the development of an organism. This saves 300 gallons.

-If you have a pool, utilize a pool cover to eliminate evaporation. Likewise, it will keep your pool cleaner and lessen the need to include chemicals. This saves 1,000 gallons every month.

-Using a pail of soapy water, clean the car and make sure to drive it onto a lawn. The water used can help water the grass at the same time. Only use the hose for rinsing - this easy practice can save as much as 150 gallons when washing a car.

-Minimize watering on cool and cloudy days and not water in the rain. Change or deactivate automatic sprinklers. This can save up to 300 gallons each time.

-Put a layer of mulch around trees and plants. Pieces of bark, peat greenery, or rock gradually slow down evaporation. This saves 750 to 1,500 gallons every month.

For Kids

-Avoid toys that need constant running water. Rather, use a little pool to enjoy water outside, or use sports-related toys and remote-controlled gadgets.

-When washing hands, turn off the sink while kids are soaping up.

-Try not to let children flush tissues or other things down the toilet. In addition to the fact that this is inefficient, it can cause serious plumbing issues. Urge your children to use a wastebasket for tissues and other daily essentials they might be lured to flush.

-If your children have a pet fish, reuse the water from the tank as food for your houseplants instead of draining it.

-When washing the dog, ensure you wash them in an area of the yard that requires water so you can carry out two tasks at once. Be sure the soap you use is safe for plants.

-Train kids to consistently turn the faucets firmly to avoid drips and unnccessary water waste.

-Tell your kids not to play with the garden hose. This saves 10 gallons every moment.

-Whenever you allow your kids to play in the sprinklers, ensure it's just when you're watering the yard. Suppose it's not very cool around that time of day.

Saving Water in Special Conditions

At some point, it is necessary to use extra measures to reduce the amount of water you consume at home. Although suitable for any situation, these techniques may be especially helpful. When water levels are high around your house, your community water system temporarily loses the capacity to supply adequate amounts of water. You should consider these changes:

-Use much around trees and shrubs and in garden beds. They significantly reduce the amount of water lost through evaporation and reduce the need for watering.

-Consider using a drip irrigation system in your garden. It supplies water only to the root zones of plants and reduces weeding because it doesn't water areas between crop rows and hills.

-Use only plant varieties that are well adapted to your locality and soil conditions. Less suitable varieties may need more fertilizer or water to live.

-Use the water from your roof downspouts for watering your garden and flower beds.

Other Water Conservation Practices

Agricultural Water Conservation Practices

Water-saving irrigation system practices have three categories: field practices, management techniques, and system modifications. These practices include the chisel plow aeration of highly compacted soils, furrow diking to keep from uncontrolled overflow, and leveling of the land surface to distribute water equally.

Irrigation Scheduling

Improved irrigation scheduling can reduce the amount of water needed to irrigate a crop successfully by decreasing evaporative losses and providing water when generally required by the irrigated plants. And applying the water in a way most appropriate to the irrigated plants. A prudent decision of the irrigation rate and timing can help farmers keep up yields with less water. In settling on scheduling choices, irrigators ought to consider:

-The unpredictable rainfall and the timing of crop water demands.

-The restricted water storage limit of many irrigated soils.

-The limited pumping capacity of most irrigation systems.

-The cost of water and changes in water costs as extra operators increase water demand.

Irrigation Management

Management procedures include monitoring soil and water conditions and gathering water use and efficiency data. The techniques incorporate estimating rainfall, determining soil moisture levels, checking pumping plant productivity, and scheduling water systems. Usual system adjustments involve the expansion of drop tubes to a center pivot water system, upgrading wells with smaller pumps, installing a surge or demand water system, and building a tail-water or return flow recovery system.

Industrial and Commercial Consumers Water Conservation Practices

Water recycling is the reuse of water for a similar application for which it was initially used. Recycled water may require treatment before it tends to be reused. Cooling water distribution and washwater recycling are the most broadly used water recycling practices. The accompanying rules ought to be used when considering water reuse and recycling in industrial and commercial applications:

-Identification of water reuse possibilities: Are there zones inside the manufacturing plant or in the production process that presently use water just once that would be agreeable to reuse?

-Determination of the base water amount required for the given use: Are there areas inside the plant or in the production process where more water is being provided than is expected to achieve the purpose?

-Identification of wastewater sources that fulfill the water quality standards: Does the process require consumable water or water of lesser quality? Can a similar outcome be accomplished with lower-quality water?

-Determination of how the water can be shipped to the new use: What adjustments, assuming any, all the while or industrial facility might be expected to allow recovery and distribution/recycling of the water presently sent to waste? What might different treatment be important to reuse this water? What is the general cost of the necessary changes versus the cost of the raw water over the life of the adjustments?

Cooling Water Recirculation

Recycling water inside a recirculating cooling system can increase significantly less water usage by using similar water to play out a few cooling activities. The water savings are commonly adequately significant to bring about a general cost saving to the industry. Such savings can be considerably more prominent if the waste heat is used as a heat source somewhere else in the production process. Three cooling water protection approaches are ordinarily used to diminish water consumption: evaporative cooling, ozonation, and heat exchange.

Washwater Recycling.

Another usual usage of water by industry is using fresh or deionized water to eliminate contaminants from items and equipment. Deionized water can usually be reused after its first use, even though the reclamation treatment cost of reusing this water might be as extraordinary as or more noteworthy than the expense of buying raw water from a manufacturer and treating it. Similar processes needed to create deionized water from municipal water can be used to deliver deionized water from used washwater. It is also conceivable to mix used washwater with raw water, which would bring about overall water saving. The reuse of once-utilized deionized water for an alternate application inside a similar factory should likewise be considered a water conservation choice. For instance, used washwater might be worth washing vehicles or the factory premises.

Strategies to Support Water Conservation

Conserving water for individual use in urban areas (counting use by families and districts) needs an inspection—both the supply and demand for water.

A part of the strategies that can aid water preservation activities. And handle the water shortage issue include:

1. Rainwater harvesting

Rainwater harvesting is essentially a technique to store water and get it. This is for fair usage on the last day and period. The system has unique units that incorporate rainwater transportation, filtration, and storing processed water.

It will be more beneficial to install a rainwater storing unit in our homes to spare more water.

-Rooftop rainwater harvesting (PDF)

-Micro-catchment water harvesting

-Recharge structures for wells and bore wells

2. Sustainable water usage

Sustainable water supply includes an arrangement of joined activities and not disconnected strategies. It relies upon the person's ability to save water, administrative regulations, and changes in the building industry, industrial forms production, land occupation, and so forth. The challenge is to make components of direction. How reasonable it is to guarantee the sustainability of the system.

-Minimize domestic water consumption

-Recycling of wastewater

-Improved irrigation methods

3. Encourage natural regeneration of vegetation and supplementing with artificial regeneration

Regeneration is 'the renewal of a forest crop by natural or artificial means. Using crops by sowing, planting, and may it be through artificial methods. These have a greater impact on conserving water. The natural and artificial regeneration of vegetation is a dynamic procedure. Life recolonizes land when the vegetation has been somewhat or completely devastated. Life restores the lost ground through the instrument of the progression of species.

4. Maintain and improve the quality of water

Water quality in a waterway impacts how communities use the water for drinking, swimming, or business purposes. Particularly, the water might be utilized by the group to produce edible fish, shellfish and crustaceans, protect aquatic ecosystems wildlife habitats, supply drinking water, and the like.

-Collection and treatment of wastewater effluents (PDF)

-Pollution check

5. Raising awareness of water conservation

We all need to go hand in hand because water is a global priority. And it is imperative to save as much water we can get in any way possible. If it is not for us, then for the generations to come, and if not for the generation, for the world we live in, the Earth. Building awareness seems simple yet so hard to deliver to the human race. For sure, it is the easiest to start it in our home, with ourselves. Rather than sitting tight for another person to begin conserving, let us, as an individual, initiate in conserving.

Most importantly, we have to educate everyone about how essential water is. That is the very least way we can save water. The more we educate people, the more water we save. Every leakage ought to be fixed in the drainage system wherever available.

Wasting water has become a powerful environmental issue - both at consumer and industrial levels. It has turned out to be essential for people and organizations alike to discover approaches to decrease water wastage and conserve it.

There are various approaches to saving water. Conserving is one, and reusing it is another. Given that we live in a zone lying down to dry season, it shows well to save each. This means we can, and using water twice is one great approach to extend this valuable resource further.

Extend your Water Conservation Measures

-Recycle your water wherever, whenever you can. Collect the cold water you run before it's hot enough to shower and use it to water plants or flush the toilet. After, rinse water from dishes and food preparation can be collected and used to soak other dishes.

-Insulate your water pipes. It's convenient and low-cost to insulate your water pipes with pre-slit foam pipe insulation. You'll get hot water faster, plus avoid wasting water while it heats up.

-Eat less water-intensive foods. Our diets regime explains about half of all the water we consume. All food has a water footprint, but some are much larger than others. Eating less beef, one of the most water-intensive foods, is a smart place to start. Shifting away from animal products to a plant-based diet can shrink your water footprint.

-Buy less. Consumer products are an often-overlooked source of water use, accounting for up to a third of most people's water footprint and buying less of everything. It can dramatically decrease your water footprint from clothing to electronics to household goods.

Desalination can make saltwater drinkable — but it won't solve the U.S. water crisis

The water in the ocean is a tempting resource. Removing salt comes with environmental and economic costs, though.

Anybody with a 5-year-old's knowledge of geography might come up against this conundrum: There's a water shortage in the Western United States. Right next door, there's the Pacific Ocean. Why can't we take some of that big, blue body of water and move it into the increasingly parched territory that borders it?

The short answer, of course, is that there's salt in the ocean, which isn't good for people, plants and many other living creatures. But as shortages mount, there's increasing interest in the complicated process of desalination, or pulling out salt on a massive scale so that water can be put to use by the thirsty populations who live nearby.

Wells are drying up in California. The Colorado River is thinning to a dribble. The levels of Lake Mead and Lake Powell — the two biggest reservoirs in the United States — are at record lows.

There is precedent for large-scale desalination: Persian Gulf countries such as Qatar have precious little drinking water, and they have invested in the costly technology needed to filter the salt out of saltwater and pass the cleaned-up liquid to their entire society.

"Desalination can be a sustainable way to replenish our water cycle," wrote the authors of a European Commission-backed study last year that argued for wider use of desalination around the world, in partnership with efforts to minimize its environmental impact.

But the process is energy-intensive, costly and complicated to manage in an Earth-friendly way. Here's what you need to know.

So what is desalinated water, anyway?

Desalination is the process of getting salt out of saltwater so that it's drinkable and usable on land. There are two main techniques: You can boil the water, then catch the steam, leaving behind the salt. Or you can blast the water through filters that catch the salt but let the liquid through. The latter is the more modern process, but both methods use a lot of energy.

And is desalinated water safe to drink?

Generally, yes. Desalinated water, provided that it's clean, is perfectly fine to drink, and a lot of it is already being consumed both in the United States and abroad. San Diego inaugurated a vast new desalination plant about six years ago and is on the verge of approving another. Other plants dot the West Coast. Desalination has been in use in energy-rich, freshwater-poor parts of the world for decades — about half of global production is concentrated in the Middle East and North Africa. A United Nations-sponsored study from 2018 estimated that the world produces about 25 billion gallons of desalinated water

every day — enough to fill the taps of 25 New York Cities.

But cleaning up the water isn't challenge-free. Salt isn't the only thing that hangs out in seawater: There's also often a lot of boron, which isn't good for crops and in large concentrations might be unhealthy for humans. And it isn't always easy to clean saltwater. Other contaminants can also get in.

"There is an urgent need to make desalination technologies more affordable and extend them to low-income and lower-middle-income countries," Vladimir Smakhtin, director of the United Nations University Institute for Water, Environment and Health, wrote after he co-wrote the U.N. study on desalination. "At the same time, though, we have to address potentially severe downsides of desalination — the harm of brine and chemical pollution to the marine environment and human health."

Why do people get excited about desalination?

At its best, desalination is an attractive technology: It takes a relatively abundant but unusable resource, seawater, and turns it into something useful for freshwater-starved regions. And as time passes, it's becoming more efficient, less costly and more possible to fuel with renewable energy, easing the environmental impact. Eventually, backers hope, extracting the minerals from the high-salt leftovers will become economically viable, even though it's usually not right now.

At best, said the authors of the European Commission study, desalination can be "a far-reaching, climate change mitigating, water security solution."

Is desalination bad for the environment?

Opponents of desalination have long said that the technique isn't a panacea because it hurts the environment even as it cleans up water for human consumption. There are a few big challenges. Pulling saltwater into desalination plants can hurt fish and other marine life if it isn't done carefully. Then there's the energy needed to clean up the water, and the brackish, salty waste that is left after the clean water is filtered out.

Proponents of desalination "think it's table salt. They think the ocean can sustain the damage, but over 50 years, the ocean cannot sustain the damage, and neither can the atmosphere," said Susan Jordan, the executive director of the California Coastal Protection Network and a longtime critic of big desalination projects in her state.

There's no question that desalination is energy-intensive. And if that energy comes from dirty sources, desalination can lead to a paradoxical outcome: It can unleash greenhouse gases, worsening global warming, increasing droughts and therefore the need for more desalination.

The most modern desalination plants use significantly less energy than their predecessors. And proponents are looking for ways to use renewable energy to power the process.

A separate challenge is brine, the hyper-concentrated, salty fluid that is flushed away from the freshwater. If it is simply pumped straight back into the sea, the dense substance sinks to the bottom of the ocean floor and suffocates marine life. There are techniques to spread it over greater territory in the sea, diluting its impact.

"We call it the blanket of death because it settles on the floor, and it kills everything," Jordan said.

Can desalination solve the water crisis?

Alone, no. But it might help as part of a broader range of efforts to cut water use and increase water supplies. Its technologies are growing more energy-efficient, and there are new ways to reduce the environmental harm of the salty wastewater. And it could be used in especially parched parts of the world where water is desperately needed and where there are few alternatives.

"The benefits of desalination go beyond the single-use value of the water produced," the authors of the European Commission study argued last year, advocating for wider use of desalination in more-vulnerable and poorer regions of the globe. The technology can provide "plentiful water for human use, with all the benefits that entails, while helping preserve and restore ecosystems."

But in the United States, even proponents of the technology say desalination is likely to supply only a sliver of the American West's water needs in the coming years, leaving some of the biggest water users — notably the agriculture industry — to look for water elsewhere.

Los Angeles recently unveiled a $3.4 billion proposal to recycle and reuse its wastewater, for example, instead of treating the waste and pumping it into the ocean, as is currently done. Advocates say the change would significantly ease the pressure on the city's water sources farther north in California and the Colorado River — all without the need to lean more heavily on desalination.

"Conservation, recycling, all of those things are important first," Jordan said. *"And if you can't solve your water supply problem, then that's when we say, 'Do desalination, but do it right.'"*

Israel's desalination project is so successful that they will start refilling the Sea of Galilee in 2023. They get a majority of their water from desalination. Other middle eastern countries will soon be following their lead. Over 3/4 of the world is covered in water, over 98% of which is salt water, so it only makes sense to convert some of this to drinkable water. This process could turn all of the arid countries in Africa into flourishing paradises. I know it will cost a lot of money to do this, but just think of the trillions of dollars we wasted in fighting wars in Afghanistan and Iraq. Lets face it the only people who benefited from these wars were the stockholders in the armament companies and the independent contractors that supply troops and protection details. The money spent over the last twenty years on these two wars could have gone a long way towards accomplishing this goal. Not to mention that those countries can sell the salt.

You may ask how this helps the U.S.? Well many states in the U.S. are water poor, that goes for most of the western states. I live in one that is suffering a major water crisis and that is Nevada.

"Feds demand states cut water use"

The federal government has directed the states that share the Colorado River to reduce the use of the river by 2-4 million acre-feet by next year to help preserve sinking levels in Lake Powell and Mead. This mandate is in addition to 2021 federal shortage reductions. This is the largest reduction of water use ever ordered on the Colorado River and represents nearly one third of the water use of the entire river system. Southern Nevada shares the Colorado River with six other states and Mexico. Every state and every sector will have to reduce its water use. Lake Mead has dropped over 170 feet since 2000, and more than 24 feet so far in 2022, exposing the lake's first water intake, which is no longer operational.

The Southern Nevada Authority has built a low lake level pumping station and a third drinking water intake to ensure access to our water supply in Lake Mead should lake levels continue to fall. The intake also will address water quality challenges caused when warmer surface water draws closer to intake openings.

Water conservation efforts

Over the past two decades, the Authority established one of the nation's most comprehensive and aggressive water conservation programs in Southern Nevada. These efforts have been effective. The community used 24 billion gallons less water in 2020 than in 2002, despite a population increase of more than 780,000 residents during that time. This represents a 47-percent decline in the community's per capita water use since 2002.

However, continued declines in Lake Mead's water level are expected as Southern Nevada experiences a permanent transition to a more arid future, the result of ongoing climate change. For this reason, additional efforts are needed to ensure a reliable long-term water supply for our community.

This is just the dire circumstances that one state is experiencing. You will find similar stories in many other western states. The U.S. is fortunate to be bordered by three large bodies of salt water, so access to this resource is not an issue. What is standing in the way is liberal state governments. California has repeatedy refused to pass legislation for building desalination plants.

THE U.S. IS FACING A WATER CRISIS: COULD DESALINATION BE A SOLUTION?

The United States—like the rest of the world—has a water problem.

Water in the Colorado River is running low, Lake Mead recently reached record low levels, groundwater in Arizona and California is in jeopardy and the federal government is expected to declare a water shortage sometime this summer. An increased demand for water coupled with diminishing supplies leaves big questions: Where will our water come from? How will we ensure we have enough?

In the face of pressing water scarcity, some places in the U.S. in recent decades have looked to a specific type of technology to supply their drinking water: desalination.

Desalination—the process by which salty water is transformed into fresh water—can be a solution, especially in places where steady supplies of fresh water are scarce. This can be done by heating up salt water and collecting the pure water vapor, or by pumping salt water through a special membrane in a process called reverse osmosis.

Desalination has many uses. In addition to being a source of clean drinking water, the technology is also employed by industries that produce oil and gas and in power stations.

While more reliable than other water sources, desalination does have its drawbacks. The facilities needed to complete the process on a large scale can be expensive to build and operate and use a lot of energy. Plus, these plants can generate waste that can be difficult to dispose of and harmful to the environment.

There are nearly 17,000 operational desalination facilities worldwide, many of the largest of which are located overseas. Countries where water is scarce like Saudi Arabia, the United Arab Emirates and Israel employ desalination technology on large scales to generate reliable fresh water.

In the U.S., over 400 municipal desalination plants have been opened since 1971 and an estimated 200 or more are currently in operation, though the precise number is not known for certain. Most are in California, Florida and Texas.

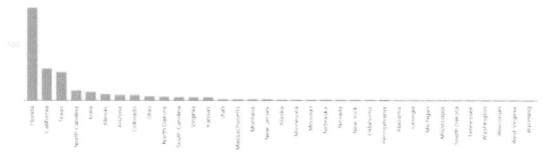

Facilities referenced here are municipal desalination plants with the capacity of 25,000 or more gallons per day of water. Older facilities included in this count may no longer be operational.

Source: U.S. Bureau of Reclamation • Get the data • Created with Datawrapper

Seawater Desalination

Sea water is abundant on Earth—the oceans, unlike other water sources, are always full. To be useful as a water source, it first must be transformed into fresh water.

Typically, of the water extracted from the ocean, only about half is converted to fresh water in the desalination process. This means that for every two gallons of sea water extracted, only one gallon of fresh water is created. Left over is a byproduct called brine, a concentrated salty mixture that needs to be disposed of.

The biggest seawater desalter in the western hemisphere is the Claude *"Bud"* Lewis Carlsbad Desalination Plant in San Diego County, California. Completed in 2015, the plant can produce up to 60 million gallons of desalted water in one day. In a region plagued with heat and drought, it's the only water supply in the county that is not dependent on snow or rainfall.

In 2016, California passed an amendment in support of using ocean water to supplement its traditional water supplies like river and groundwater. Called the "Desalination Amendment," the move provided a consistent method for permitting desalination plants statewide, prioritized protecting marine life, and required tighter regulations for how water is taken from the ocean and the brine is put back in.

Not everyone is convinced that desalinating ocean water is a smart investment. Critics of California's efforts say that expanding the state's use of the technology will only make it more challenging and expensive to reach the state's climate goals. In a 2016 issue brief from the National Resources Defense Council, the authors recommended that the state *"proceed with caution."*

"Given the significant energy, climate, and financial costs of desalination, California should prioritize water conservation, water use efficiency, stormwater capture, wastewater recycling, and renewably-powered groundwater desalination,"

they wrote. Only after these cheaper, lower impact alternatives have been pursued, the authors said, should seawater desalination be considered.

One of the major downsides of desalination is its price tag. Though the cost of running a desalination facility has dropped over time, the cost is still high, especially when compared to other water sources. The Carlsbad plant cost nearly $1 billion to build, and the water it generates is more expensive than water imported from other sources, costing between $2,125 to $2,368 per acre foot in 2017 (an acre foot is the amount of water needed to cover an acre one foot deep).

Approximate Cost of Water in California, 2015

The approximate cost to operate alternative water source facilities per acre foot of water.

Seawater Desalination	$1400	$4100
Indirect Potable Reuse	$1100	$2200
Brackish Water Desalination	$840	$1700
Stormwater Capture	$230	$1300

$500 $1000 $1500 $2000 $2500 $3000 $3500 $4000

All values are rounded to two significant figures. Costs reflect 2015 dollars. Low and high costs represent the 25th and 75th percentile of the estimated cost range. Values represent both large and small facility types. An acre foot is the amount of water required to cover an acre one foot deep.

Source: APM Research Lab analysis of Pacific Institute data • Get the data • Created with Datawrapper

Removing salt from sea water also requires a lot of energy—more than any other source of water—which contributes to its cost. According to the authors of the 2016 National Resources Defense Council issue brief, seawater desalination in California requires about twice the amount of energy required by water imported from the Colorado River, and about 50% more energy than desalinated brackish (less salty) water and water imported from the California State Water Project require.

An additional cost of seawater desalination is environmental. After the fresh water is removed from the sea water, concentrated brine is left over and deposited back into the ocean. The extra salty mixture doesn't mix well with the ocean water, so it can sink to the sea floor, lower oxygen levels and harm sea organisms if not managed properly. Not only is the brine salty, but it can also contain some of the chemicals used in the water treatment process.

The potential for negative environmental impacts has led some to oppose construction of the plants in the U.S. After plans for the Carlsbad plant were approved in 2006, the builders faced at least 14 legal challenges from environmental groups opposed to the project.

Despite the drawbacks, enthusiasm for seawater desalination hasn't completely waned. As of 2019, California has 12 seawater desalination plants, including the one in Carlsbad, and has proposals to build six more.

One of the newly proposed projects is in Huntington Beach. Once complete, the plant will produce 50 million gallons of fresh water a day, becoming one of the largest facilities in the country.

Brackish Water Desalination

Desalination doesn't just refer to de-salting sea water—it can also be used to transform water that's not as salty as the ocean, but still too salty to drink, into fresh water.

Known as *brackish water*," this water contains less salt in parts per million (or ppm) compared to sea water, which contains about 35,000 ppm of salt. Fresh water has less than 1,000 ppm of salt, and brackish water falls somewhere in between the two.

Brackish water appears in sources on the surface, like lakes and rivers, as well as in underground aquifers. According to research studies done in 2010, over 95% of the desalination facilities in the U.S. are located inland, away from the ocean, and most are designed to treat brackish groundwater.

In Texas, 27 of the state's 31 aquifers contain brackish groundwater. The state is also home to the largest inland desalination plant in the country. Located in El Paso, far from any ocean, the Kay Bailey Hutchison Desalination Plant transforms previously unusable groundwater into fresh water, and it's capable of making up to 27.5 million gallons of fresh water a day. To meet the growing demand for water, the plant plans to expand so it can produce up to 42 million gallons in a day.

Brackish water desalination poses a different set of challenges compared to seawater desalination. While there are fewer dissolved particles to remove from brackish

Source: APM Research Lab analysis of data from the U.S. Bureau of Reclamation, Mickley & Associates LLC • This map may be not an accurate representation of plants that are currently in operation. Many older, smaller facilities are no longer in operation and most of these closed plants were replaced with larger, centralized facilities serving the same locations. As far as we are aware, no comprehensive survey of existing desalination plants in the United States has been conducted. Some locations may have missing or incomplete data. Data were captured during four survey periods, represented in four colors above. Maximum facility capacity is shown in million gallons per day (MGD).

water, it can be harder to dispose of the leftover waste. And though less energy is required to pump the brackish water through filters than sea water, more energy is sometimes required to pump it from its source.

Is desalination a viable water solution in the U.S.?

In the face of water scarcity and the aridification of the U.S. the question remains: Is desalination a viable water solution?

"*Desalination is not a panacea*," Michael Kiparsky, director of the Wheeler Water Institute at the University of California Berkeley, told WIRED in an interview. The process is energy-intensive, he told the publication, speaking specifically about seawater desalination, and it will never be cheap.

But researchers are tackling these challenges and more now, making reverse osmosis membranes more efficient, turning the salty brine byproduct into useful chemicals and figuring out how to reliably power desalination facilities with renewable energy.

Page 131

States like California, Texas and Florida continue to invest in desalination technology. In Texas, regional groups in charge of water planning recommend desalination to meet at least part of their future water needs. If implemented, desalination in Texas could produce an extra 230,000 acre feet of water per year by 2070. And in coastal states, desalination could be used to help counteract the effects of seawater intrusion into fresh water.

In California, those in favor of desalination say the facilities act as a kind of insurance policy.

"The whole purpose of the desal plant is to diversify the water supply portfolio to reduce the need to import water from Northern California into Southern California," said Scott Maloni, vice president of project development at Poseidon Water, speaking to Yes! Magazine about the proposed Huntington Beach project. Poseidon Water has built several large desalination facilities around the world, including the one in Carlsbad.

While there is a consensus that diverse water supplies are needed, environmental advocates argue that desalination is not as good an option as increasing water conservation, efficiency and recycling through efforts like capturing stormwater.

"Desal should be the option of last resort," Newsha Ajami told Yes! Magazine in an interview. Ajami works with Stanford University's Water in the West program, where she is the director of urban water policy. *"There are so many other inefficiencies in the system that can be fixed to potentially harness more water."*

Even so, the tides appear to be moving such that desalination will be part of the country's water future. In 2018, the U.S. Department of Energy launched the Water Security Grand Challenge, an initiative designed to foster and fund innovation and new technologies to meet the global demand for water. Its first stated goal: To develop desalination technologies that generate clean water at more competitive prices by 2030.

Agency unanimously rejects California desalination project

HUNTINGTON BEACH, Calif. (AP) — A California coastal panel on Thursday rejected a long-standing proposal to build a $1.4 billion seawater desalination plant to turn Pacific Ocean water into drinking water as the state grapples with persistent drought that is expected to worsen in coming years with climate change.

The state's Coastal Commission voted unanimously to deny a permit for Poseidon Water to build a plant to produce 50 million gallons of water a day in Huntington Beach, southeast of Los Angeles.

Poseidon said it was disappointed in the decision.

"California continues to face a punishing drought, with no end in sight," a company statement said. "Every day, we see new calls for conservation as reservoir levels drop to dangerous lows. We firmly believe that this desalination project would have created a sustainable, drought-tolerant source of water."

The vote came after a heated meeting before the commission attended by dozens of supporters and critics of the plan. It was considered a crucial decision on the future of the plant after years of other hearings and delays. Poseidon's long-running proposal was supported by Gov. Gavin Newsom but faced ardent opposition from environmentalists who said drawing in large amounts of ocean water and releasing salty discharge back into the ocean would kill billions of tiny marine organisms that make up the base of the food chain along a large swath of the coast.

"The ocean is under attack" from climate change already, Commissioner Dayna Bochco said. "I cannot say in good conscience that this amount of damage is OK."

Other critics said the water would be too expensive and wasn't urgently needed in the area where it would be built, which is less dependent on state and federal water due to an ample aquifer and water recycling program.

Commissioners cited those issues in following a staff recommendation and rejecting the proposal. They also cited the energy cost of running the plant and the fact that it would sit in an earthquake fault zone.

Before voting, the 12-member commission heard hours of comments from scores of people packed into a hotel meeting room in the Orange County city of Costa Mesa in addition to those tuning in online.

At the meeting, supporters wore orange and yellow construction vests and toted signs saying *"support desal!"*

Opponents carried signs reading *"No Poseidon"* and *"Do not $ell our coast"* and included a woman who wore a plankton costume and held a sign reading *"I am a plankton — please do not kill me!"*

California has spent most of the last 15 years in drought conditions. Its normal wet season that runs from late fall to the end of winter was especially dry this year and as a result 95% of the state is classified as in severe drought.

Newsom last summer urged residents to cut consumption by 15%, but since then water usage has dropped by only about 3%. Some areas have begun instituting generally mild restrictions such as limiting how many days lawns can be watered. More stringent restrictions are likely later in the year.

Much of California's water comes from melting snow and with a far below normal snowpack, state officials have told water agencies they will receive only 5% of what they've requested from state water supplies beyond what's needed for critical activities like drinking and bathing.

Desalination takes ocean water and removes salt and other elements to make it drinkable. Those elements are discharged back into the sea, while the water can be channeled directly to consumers or used to replenish a groundwater basin. The country's largest seawater desalination plant is already operating in nearby San Diego County, and there are also coastal plants in Florida.

The idea of desalination has been debated for decades in Huntington Beach, a coastal community southeast of Los Angeles known as *"Surf City USA"* that relies on its sands and waves for tourism. Discussion of the project has also recently focused on the impact of climate change on regional water supplies and on sea level rise in the low-lying coastal area where the plant would be built.

More than two decades ago, Poseidon proposed building two desalination plants — the one in San Diego County, and one in Huntington Beach. The San Diego County plant was approved and built, and desalinated water now accounts for 10% of San Diego County Water District 's water supplies.

But the Huntington Beach project has faced numerous delays. In 2013, the Coastal Commission voiced concerns that the proposed use of intake structures to quickly draw in large volumes of water from the ocean would damage marine life. Poseidon, which is owned by Brookfield Infrastructure Partners, conducted additional studies and resubmitted the plan with a proposal to mitigate marine damage through restoration of nearby wetlands.

Last month, staff members for the panel issued a 200-page report opposing the project, arguing it fails to adhere to marine life protection policies and policies aimed at minimizing hazards from tsunamis and rising sea levels.

Some on Thursday also debated the extent of the local demand for the desalinated water. Orange County has an ample groundwater basin and recycles wastewater, making the region less dependent on imported water than San Diego. The Orange County Water District, which has said it intends to buy Poseidon's water, manages the basin that helps meet about 75% of the water demand in the northern and central parts of the county.

Poseidon contends the region would still benefit by locking in a drought-proof source of water and so would inland communities and states that could gain increased access to imported water supplies once the county can tap into desalinated water. Steve Sheldon, the Orange County Water District's president, said desalinated water is more expensive now, but he expects the cost of imported water to also rise over time.

Water restrictions show folly of California's rejection of large-scale

desalination projects

As the state continues to grapple with drought conditions, water restrictions are being placed on six million residents in Southern California. The latest restrictions are another reminder that the California Coastal Commission's recent rejection of the Orange County desalination plant, after 24 years of delay, reinforces the state's position as a laggard in adopting technology that could provide water security. While arid coastal countries worldwide are implementing desalination, the most obvious solution to water scarcity, the Coastal Commission unanimously voted against the Huntington Beach project.

Gov. Gavin Newsom, noting years of drought in the state, harshly criticized the rejection, saying, "We need more tools in the damn tool kit."

The commission claimed it was worried about higher water bills for the area's lower-income residents, impact on marine life near the facility, and reduced public access to the shoreline, especially during the construction period. It remains to be seen whether those objections will also defeat the proposed Doheny Beach desalination facility in southern Orange County despite its seemingly initially favorable reception from regulators. But even if the Doheny plant is approved, it would provide only 10% of the water that the Huntington Beach facility would've provided.

The Coastal Commission's objections to larger facilities are out of touch with numerous other countries pursuing desalination at scale. Australia has five major desalination plants with more under development. Spain has hundreds of smaller desalination plants providing water for industry, agriculture, and drinking. On El Hierro, in the Canary Islands, desalination plants are powered by wind energy and hydroelectric power, demonstrating how Spain is addressing climate change and water security.

Last year, Singapore opened its fifth desalination facility and now meets about 30% of its water requirements from purified seawater. Its government is also experimenting with new technologies that reduce desalination's energy consumption sharply.

Israel's success with desalination is well known. It has five operating plants and two more under construction. Once all seven plants are online, they will collectively provide enough fresh water to meet 85%-to-90% of Israel's municipal and industrial water requirements.

The world's largest desalination plants are in Saudi Arabia and the United Arab Emirates. The Ras Al Khair plant in Saudi Arabia can produce 228 million gallons of water daily—more than four times the volume processed by the facility in Carlsbad, which remains California's only major desalination plant.

These numerous examples suggest an overall pattern: countries with high per capita income, insufficient rainfall, and a seacoast are increasingly investing in desalination. But California, despite years of drought and its long-term water needs, is not following this global trend. And even within the United States, California is becoming an outlier.

This year, Arizona Gov. Doug Ducey proposed an ambitious plan to increase his state's water supply. Under Ducey's plan, Arizona would fund two desalination plants on the Sea of Cortez in northern Mexico. The desalinated water would be used in Mexico in exchange for Arizona being allowed to increase its use of Colorado River water, which is now limited by a binational agreement that reserves a portion of the water for Mexico.

If California officials cannot get comfortable with building more desalination plants in the state, they might consider participating in the Arizona project. Or, perhaps they could work a similar deal with the Mexican state of Baja California, which had to cancel its own desalination project in 2020 due to the declining value of the Mexican peso. If California agreed to buy a portion of the water purified by the proposed facility in Rosarito, about 15 miles south of the border, perhaps the economics would work for everyone.

While it is true that desalinated water is much more expensive than groundwater or snowmelt piped in from the Sierra, this cost needs to be put in perspective. The estimated cost of water from the Huntington Beach desalination plant would have been $2,900 per acre-foot, which works out to just under one cent per gallon. This is a tiny fraction of the cost of bottled water, recently estimated to average $9.60 per gallon.

With many of the state's politicians warning of worsening climate change and severe droughts, California shouldn't be rejecting a sustainable opportunity to buy water for a penny per gallon.

Desalination Is Booming as Cities Run out of Water

In California alone there are 11 desalination plants, with 10 more proposed. But there are big downsides to making seawater drinkable.

Some 30 miles north of San Diego, along the Pacific Coast, sits the Claude "Bud" Lewis Carlsbad Desalination Plant, the largest effort to turn salt water into fresh water in North America.

Each day 100 million gallons of seawater are pushed through semi-permeable membranes to create 50 million gallons of water that is piped to municipal users. Carlsbad, which became fully operational in 2015, creates about 10 percent of the fresh water the 3.1 million people in the region use, at about twice the cost of the other main source of water.

Expensive, yes, but vital for the fact that it is local and reliable. "Drought is a recurring condition here in California," said Jeremy Crutchfield, water resources manager at the San Diego County Water Authority. "We just came out of a five-year drought in 2017. The plant has reduced our reliance on imported supplies, which is challenging at times here in California. So it's a component for reliability."

A second plant, similar to Carlsbad, is being built in Huntington, California with the same 50-million-gallon-a-day capability. Currently there are 11 desalination plants in California, and 10 more are proposed.

It's been a long time coming for desalination—desal for short. For decades, we have been told it would one day turn oceans of salt water into fresh and quench the world's thirst. But progress has been slow.

That is now changing, as desalination is coming into play in many places around the world. Several factors are converging to bring new plants on line. Population has boomed in many water-stressed places, including parts of China, India, South Africa, and the United States, especially in Arizona and California. In addition, drought—some of it driven by a changing climate—is occurring in many regions that not that long ago thought their supplies were ample.

San Diego is one of those places. With just 12 inches of rain a year in the Mediterranean climate of Southern California and no groundwater, the region gets half of its water from the distant Colorado River. The amount of snow that falls in the Rocky Mountains and keeps that mighty river flowing, however, has greatly diminished over the last two decades, and according to some researchers may be part of a permanent aridification of the West. Climate change is a very real phenomenon for water managers throughout the Southwest and elsewhere.

I sent an email to the department of desalination in California. It addressed the issue of brackish water effluent from the desalination process.

Water.ca.gov:
I have recently read an article on desalination in California. Apparently you are pumping the left over brackish water back into the ocean. My question is why? The island of Bonaire pumps salt water in fields and once the water evaporates, they collect the salt and sell it. You could do the same thing, you could also use the brackish water for fracking. You could also make an inland sea with the brackish water, thereby creating a whole new ecosystem. The Bonneville Salt Flats used to be an inland sea. Why harm the ecosystem by pumping the brackish water back into the ocean?
The small amount of salt water taken out of the ocean would have little to no effect, especially if you are concerned about the sea levels rising. You would in essence eventually be offsetting this, if enough countries took up the practice. Think outside of the box.
Randy Landry

To this date I have not received a reply.

Meanwhile, the cost of desalinated water has been coming down as the technology evolves and the cost of other sources increases. In the last three decades, the cost of desalination has dropped by more than half.

A boom in desal, though, doesn't mean that everywhere with access to the sea has found a new source of fresh water. Circumstances play a large role. "As populations increase and existing surface water supplies are being tapped out or groundwater is depleted or polluted, then the problems are acute and there are choices to be made" about desal, said Michael Kiparsky of the Wheeler Water Institute at the UC Berkeley

School of Law. "There are places around the world where desal makes economic sense, where there is high pressure on the water resources plus a lot of available energy resources," such as the Middle East.

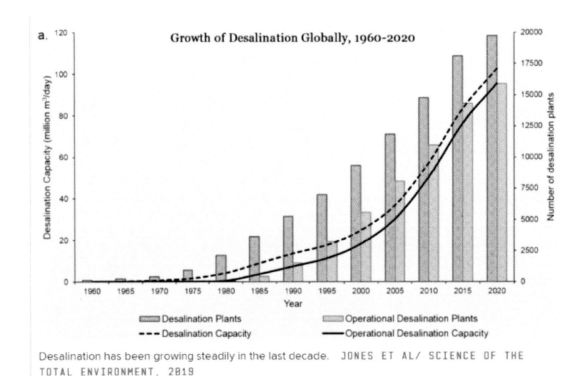

Desalination has been growing steadily in the last decade. JONES ET AL/ SCIENCE OF THE TOTAL ENVIRONMENT, 2019

Desal proponents acknowledge the industry must confront and solve some serious environmental issues if it is to continue to grow. Desalination requires vast amounts of energy, which in some places is currently provided by fossil fuels. Kiparsky warns of a feedback loop where more desal is needed as the planet warms, which leads to more greenhouse gas emissions. In addition, there are serious concerns about the damage to marine life from the plant's intake systems and extra-salty wastewater.

The first large-scale desal plants were built in the 1960s, and there are now some 20,000 facilities globally that turn sea water into fresh. The kingdom of Saudi Arabia, with very little fresh water and cheap energy costs for the fossil fuels it uses in its desal plants, produces the most fresh water of any nation, a fifth of the world's total.

Australia and Israel are also major players. When the Millennium Drought gripped southeastern Australia from the late 1990s until 2009 water systems in the region dropped to small fractions of their storage capacity. Facing a crisis, Perth, Melbourne, and other cities embarked on a large desalination plant spree. The plant in Melbourne, which provided its first water in 2017, cost $3.5 billion to build and provides a third of the city's supply. It's critical because the region has had below-average rainfall for 18 of the last 20 years.

Israel, too, is all in on desalination. It has five large plants in operation, and plans for five more. Chronic water shortages there are now a thing of the past, as more than half of the country's domestic needs are met with water from the Mediterranean.

Globally, more than 300 million people now get their water from desalination plants, according to the International Desalination Association.

But despite the need, desal plants will not be built on every coastline. Foremost among the barriers is the cost of constructing a plant and the cost of processing the water. The San Diego County Water Authority pays about $1,200 for an acre-foot of water sourced from the Colorado River and the Sacramento San Joaquin River Delta and pumped hundreds of miles to Southern California. The same amount from the Carlsbad plant—enough to supply a family of five for a year—costs about $2,200. As Lake Mead—the reservoir of Colorado River water on the Nevada-Arizona border that supplies San Diego—drops precipitously, it may someday, perhaps in the next several years, no longer be able to supply San Diego. Certainty is paramount.

Desal, however, is plagued by some serious environmental problems. There are two types of desalination—thermal, which heats up water and then captures the condensation, and reverse osmosis, which forces sea water through the pores of a membrane that are many times smaller than the diameter of a human hair. This traps salt molecules, but allows the smaller water molecules to go through. Both require a great deal of energy, and greenhouse gas emissions created by the power needed—especially in the Middle East, where fossil fuels generate electricity—are a significant contributor to global warming.

There are ecological impacts as well. It takes two gallons of sea water to make a gallon of fresh water, which means the gallon left behind is briny. It is disposed of by returning it to the ocean and—if not done properly by diffusing it over large areas—can deplete the ocean of oxygen and have negative impacts on sea life.

A study by the UN Institute for Water, Environment and Health published earlier this year contends that the problem of brine waste has been underestimated by 50 percent and that, when mixed with the chemicals meant to keep systems from fouling, the brine is toxic and causes serious pollution.

Another problem comes from the sucking in of sea water for processing. When a fish or other large organism gets stuck on the intake screen, it dies or is injured; in addition, fish larvae, eggs and plankton get sucked into the system and are killed.

"At our intake we [draw in] tiny little organisms, that amount to about a pound and a half of adult fish per day," said Jessica Jones, a spokesperson for Poseidon Water, which owns the Carlsbad plant. *"To mitigate that we are restoring 66 acres of wetlands in San Diego Bay. And we just got a new intake permitted which will lessen the impacts."*

According to Heather Cooley, research director at the Pacific Institute,

"There are a lot of unknowns around the impact on sea life. There hasn't been a lot of monitoring at the facilities." A strategy increasingly being used to obviate, or reduce, that problem is to bury the sea water intakes beneath the sea floor and use the sandy ocean bottom as a natural filter.

In 2016, California passed the Desalination Amendment, which tightened regulations for intake and brine disposal. Proponents of desalination contend the changes have been onerous and are slowing the march toward a desal future.

Because of the cost of seawater processing and the impacts on the ocean, much of the recent desalination growth has involved the use of brackish water. The solids in brackish water are one-tenth the amount in ocean water, and that makes the process much cheaper.

Arizona, perpetually short on water and facing a Colorado River supply shortage, is looking at both a seawater desal plant in partnership with Mexico—which has the ocean access that the state lacks—and at plants that can treat the 600 million acre-feet of brackish water deposits the state estimates it has.

Texas, meanwhile, now has 49 municipal desal plants that process brackish water, both surface and subsurface. San Antonio currently is building what will be the largest brackish water desal plant in the country. In its first phase, it produces 12 million gallons a day, enough for 40,000 families, but by 2026, the plant—known as H2Oaks—will produce 30 million gallons a day. Brackish water desal costs $1,000 to $2,000 per acre-foot.

The Pacific Institute's Cooley argues that before building desal plants, municipalities should fully implement conservation programs, promote potable re-use—the re-use of wastewater, also known as toilet-to-tap recycling—or treat storm water runoff. *"It makes sense to do the cheaper options first and leave the more expensive options down the road to be developed when you need them,"* she said.

Luckily for us other states have already started working on plans and in some cases have already implemented them. Florida is one of those forward thinking states.

What states in the US have desalination plants?

In the U.S., over 400 municipal desalination plants have been opened since 1971 and an estimated 200 or more are currently in operation, though the precise number is not known for certain.

Where Do We Get Our Water?

Until 1980, surface water was the largest source of fresh water in Florida. After 1980, ground water became the largest source of fresh water in Florida. In the future, ground water withdrawals are expected to level off as this source reaches its sustainable limit. New demand will increasingly be met by alternative water supplies.

What Do We Know About Future Demand?

The demand projections in the most recent water management district Regional Water Supply Plans indicate water use will continue to increase over the next 20 years. Between 2010 and 2030, public supply is expected to increase by about 29 percent and account for the majority of the increase in statewide demand. Agricultural irrigation will increase by about 7.4 percent and will represent the second largest water use. The other water use sectors show small increasing trends as well. Total water withdrawals for all uses are expected to increase by almost 21 percent to about 1.3 billion gallons per day.

Analyses conducted by the water management districts indicate that ground water resources are insufficient to fully meet future demands in large areas of the state. To do so would result in unacceptable environmental impacts including saltwater intrusion, reduction in spring flows, lowered lake levels and loss of wetlands. Consequently, steps are being taken now, and actions planned, to reduce the state's reliance on fresh ground water through the use of Alternative Water Supply.

What Are Alternative Water Supplies?

Alternative water supplies include seawater, brackish ground water, surface water, stormwater, reclaimed water, aquifer storage and recovery projects, and any other nontraditional supply source identified in a regional water supply plan. These sources are frequently more expensive to develop and operate than traditional sources.

Seawater and Brackish Ground Water

Brackish ground water and seawater can be converted to fresh water through a process called desalination. Water desalination can be accomplished by distillation, ion exchange, freezing, and use of membrane technology. In Florida, reverse osmosis, a membrane technology, is the most common method of desalination. Reverse osmosis uses pressure to force salty water through a semi-permeable membrane that keeps the salt on one side and allows pure water to pass through to the other side. This process creates a salty brine product that must be safely managed to protect the environment.

Reclaimed Water

Reclaimed water is domestic wastewater that has received advanced treatment and is reused for beneficial, nonpotable purposes. In some states, reclaimed water is called "recycled water." The use of reclaimed water is called "reuse." Reclaimed water is used for agricultural irrigation, ground water recharge, industrial processes, and irrigation of lawns, landscapes, cemeteries and golf courses. The use of reclaimed water is widely beneficial to Floridians because it preserves drinking water quality sources for potable uses; helps the environment by reducing treated wastewater discharges into our rivers and streams; and recharges our aquifers.

Aquifer Storage and Recovery

Aquifer storage and recovery involves the injection of potable water into the aquifer. The water is able to be stored in the aquifer and then be recovered as needed.

Development of alternative water sources has benefits beyond supplementing traditional water supplies. Source diversification creates a water supply system that is more reliable than a system that relies on a single source of supply. Diversification of water sources is an important tool in building drought resilience, increasing water supply reliability, and protecting Florida's natural environment.

Are Alternative Water Supplies Already Being Used In Florida?

Yes. During the past 20 years, Florida has been recognized as a national leader (along with California) in water reuse. In 2013, Florida used about 719 million gallons per day of reclaimed water for beneficial purposes. Florida leads the nation in the use of desalination technology. Florida's seawater desalination plant in the Tampa Bay area is the largest such facility in North America. In addition to the use of seawater, more than 140 facilities use desalination technology to treat brackish water. Florida also is increasing use of surface and stormwater as fresh water sources.

Still, these ongoing efforts alone will not meet the projected 2030 demand. More alternative supplies, as well as increased water conservation, are still needed.

Amid Scramble for Water, a Push for Desalination

SAN ANTONIO — Drilling rigs in the midst of cow pastures are hardly a novelty for Texans. But on a warm May day at a site about 30 miles south of San Antonio, a rig was not trying to reach oil or fresh water, but rather something unconventional: a salty aquifer. After a plant is built and begins operating in 2016, the site will become one of the state's largest water desalination facilities.

"This is another step in what we're trying to do to diversify our water

supply," said Anne Hayden, a spokeswoman for the San Antonio Water System.

More projects like San Antonio's could lace the Texas countryside as planners look to convert water from massive saline aquifers beneath the state's surface, as well as seawater from the Gulf of Mexico, into potable water. The continuing drought has made desalination a buzzword in water discussions around the state, amid the scramble for new water supplies to accommodate the rapid population and industry growth anticipated in Texas. But the technology remains energy-intensive and is already causing an increase in water rates in some communities.

"If you look around Texas and you look at the climate situation and the fact that the reservoirs are being drawn down, there just isn't much of an alternative," said Tom Pankratz, the Houston-based editor of the Water Desalination Report, who also does consulting for the industry.

Across the state, 44 desalination plants — none using seawater — have been built for public water supplies, according to the Texas Water Development Board. Ten more, including San Antonio's, have been approved for construction by the Texas Commission on Environmental Quality.

Most projects are small, capable of providing less than three million gallons per day, often for rural areas. The state's largest is in El Paso, where the $91 million Kay Bailey Hutchison Desalination Plant, completed in 2007, can supply up to 27.5 million gallons of water a day, though it rarely operates at full capacity because of the high energy costs associated with forcing water through a membrane resembling parchment to take out the salts. (Production of desalinated water costs 2.1 times more than fresh groundwater and 70 percent more than surface water, according to El Paso Water Utilities, which said that the plant's rate impact amounted to about 4 cents for every 750 gallons of the utility's overall supply.) Last year, the plant supplied 4 percent of El Paso's water.

Interest in desalination surged more than a decade ago, when the technology became more efficient and cost-competitive, according to

Page 147

Jorge Arroyo, a desalination specialist with the Texas Water Development Board. But the severe drought of the past two years has triggered extra calls to his office. Texas holds 2.7 billion acre-feet of brackish groundwater — which translates to roughly 150 times the amount of water the state uses annually — in addition to some brackish surface water. The state water plan finalized this year envisions Texas deriving 3.4 percent of its water supply from desalination in 2060. (It is less than 1 percent now.)

Environmentalists argue that desalination is not a silver bullet because it is energy-intensive and requires disposal of the concentrated salts in a way that avoids contaminating fresh water. Texas should first focus on conservation and the reuse of wastewater, said Amy Hardberger, a water specialist with the Environmental Defense Fund.

"What needs to be avoided is the, 'Oh, we'll just get more' mentality," she said.

But getting more is what many Texans want. Odessa, which draws water from dangerously low surface reservoirs, is considering a desalination plant that could ultimately become bigger than the one in El Paso. (Odessa's deadline for proposals is next week.)

Separately, a planned power plant near Odessa is studying prices for the technology. John Ragan, the head of Texas operations for NRG Energy, envisions natural gas power plants along the coast that desalinate water overnight when they are not needed for electricity. Residents near the half-full Highland Lakes in Central Texas say that desalination could reduce the water-supply burden on the lakes. Texas Tech University aims to begin wind-powered desalination research later this year, in the West Texas town of Seminole.

The San Antonio project is estimated to cost $145 million in its initial phase, with a daily production capacity of 10 million gallons, and $225 million assuming it is built out to a daily capacity of 25 million gallons (which is possible by 2026). The cost is significantly higher than El Paso's project, but San Antonio officials say that the figures reflect additional factors like acquiring land — and so far, the project is under budget. Local water rates, along with $59 million in low-interest loans from the Texas Water Development Board, are financing the project.

Desalination means *"you're going to have to spend some money,"* said state Rep. Lyle Larson, R-San Antonio. But it is worthwhile, he added, because *"our whole economic future could be up in the air."* Texans seeking a model, Larson said, should turn to Australia, where a major drought last decade spurred billions of dollars of investments in desalination.

Australia's focus has been desalinating seawater. That is an option for the Texas coast, but desalinating seawater generally costs more than twice as much as desalinating groundwater because seawater is saltier. Energy can account for 60 to 70 percent of the day-to-day operating costs of a seawater plant, estimated Pankratz, the Water Desalination Report editor.

The largest seawater desalination plant in the country, which is slightly larger than El Paso's brackish water plant, operates in Florida. Proposals are inching forward for a seawater plant in Texas. The Laguna Madre Water District, based in Port Isabel, completed a pilot seawater desalination project two years ago and is now looking for property on the north end of South Padre Island to locate a larger facility, said Carlos Galvan, the water district's director of operations. Desalination would reduce the utility's dependence on the often-diminished Rio Grande.

The Guadalupe-Blanco River Authority is also mulling seawater desalination, perhaps in the greater Victoria area. It has asked companies to submit project proposals by mid-September, and it may try to locate the water plant with a power plant, as is done in Saudi Arabia, to boost efficiency and cut costs.

Officials with both Laguna Madre and Guadalupe-Blanco hope to acquire some financing from private companies. But government at all levels, from water agencies on up, will be the key player. In El Paso, the federal government contributed $26 million in grants — more than a quarter of the cost — for the desalination plant.

The Texas Water Development Board has issued $7.1 million in grants for desalination projects since 2000, according to Arroyo, the desalination specialist.

But *"we don't have any more funds for desalination,"* he said. The board asked the Legislature for $9.5 million in financing for seawater desalination last session but did not get it.

Gov. Rick Perry has advocated for desalination in the past, but he has spoken little on it recently. Expanding the technology *"at a cost that is affordable to consumers will be an important part of any future water plans in the state,"* Lucy Nashed, a spokeswoman for the governor, said in an email.

Officials at the Texas Desalination Association, a new advocacy group, acknowledge that requests for money will probably fall on deaf ears. But they say that the state can help by easing regulations — for example, a requirement that every desalination project include a lengthy pilot study — and by doing more extensive mapping of Texas' brackish water resources.

"If we eliminate some of the red tape and some of the permitting issues," said Paul Choules, the group's president, *"it reduces a lot of the upfront cost."*

Conclusion

There is a concern about returning briny water back to the ocean. Why do it? There are plenty of areas that you can pump the water to inland, like the Sultan Sea for instance. Or you could just spread it over a large patch of the salt flats. Islands like Bonaire sell salt as an industry. Why waste it? We need to think outside of the box. There are always solutions to every problem. One thing we have no shortage out west is land. Inland Saltwater marshes could be a great reservoir for wildlife. I know one thing if we don't increase our utilization of saltwater we are going to find ourselves thirsty and hungry. Just one more thought, the brackish water can also be used for fracking. Why use fresh water when we have an unlimited supply of brackish water from the desalination plants. Like I said there are always solutions.

Resources

theberkley.com, "A Guide to Water Conservation - Saving Water and the Earth."; washingtonpost.com, "Desalination can make saltwater drinkable — but it won't solve the U.S. water crisis: The water in the ocean is a tempting resource. Removing salt comes with environmental and economic costs, though." By Michael Birnhaum; snwa.com; timesofisrael.com, "Israel to be 1st in world to pipe desalinated water into a natural lake, the Galilee: Underground channel set to start operating in spring; Sea of Galilee expert says tests indicate more pros than cons, but full effect on ecosystems will only emerge with monitoring." By Sue Surkes; apnews.com, "Agency unanimously rejects California desalination project." By AMY TAXIN; ocregister.com, "Water restrictions show folly of California's rejection of large-scale desalination projects." By Marc Joffe; floridaep.gov, " Alternative Water Supply."; texastribune.org. "Amid Scramble for Water, a Push for Desalination." By Kate Galbraith; apmresearchlab.org, "THE U.S. IS FACING A WATER CRISIS: COULD DESALINATION BE A SOLUTION?" By Katherine Sypher; wired.com. "Desalination Is Booming as Cities Run out of Water: In California alone there are 11 desalination plants, with 10 more proposed. But there are big downsides to making seawater drinkable."; waterless.com, "DESALINATION: THE GOOD, THE TROUBLESOME, AND THE FUTURE." By Klaus Reichardt;

Addendum

Water Facts and Trivia

-The overall number of water has continued for two billion years on our planet.

-Around 39,000 gallons of water are expected to create a vehicle.

-Around a billion people need stable access to clean water.

-It takes around 6 gallons of water to cultivate a sole portion of lettuce.

-More than 2,600 gallons are needed to deliver a single serving of steak.

-A typical shower utilizes around 25 gallons of water.

-Brushing your teeth utilizes around 10 gallons of water.

-The bathtub utilizes roughly 36 gallons of water.

-Shaving utilizes roughly 20 gallons of water.

-Dishwashing utilizes roughly 30 gallons of water.

-An automatic dishwasher utilizes roughly 16 gallons of water for every cycle.

-Washing your hands utilizes roughly 2 gallons of water.

-Flushing the toilet utilizes 5-7 gallons for each flush.

-A typical washing machine cycle utilizes 60 gallons of water.

-Watering outside utilizes around 10 gallons for every moment.

DESALINATION: THE GOOD, THE TROUBLESOME, AND THE FUTURE

Recently, an article revealed that Israel has 20 percent more water than it needs — quite an accomplishment. Israel is a desert country, just like all the other Middle Eastern countries. And in some ways, when it comes to water, it is geographically worse off than its neighbors.

Egypt, for instance, has the Nile, which has quenched the thirst of

Egyptians for centuries. Iranians depend on Lake Urmia, the largest lake in the Middle East, for much of their water.

Israel, on the other hand, has some streams but no major rivers. They have some lakes, such as the Dead Sea, but unlike Lake Urmia in Iran, the Dead Sea is a salt lake. The water is not potable.

Mentioning the salty Dead Sea is a good segue into what we want to discuss. Because it has no water, and what it does have is not potable, Israel has developed some of the most advanced technologies in the world to turn salt water into potable water — water that is safe to consume for humans and other living things.

Desalination is just one of the reasons Israel has 20 percent more water than it needs. Desalination plants are now being considered and constructed throughout the U.S. In California, they are virtually betting their future on desalination.

When discussing this technology, here are some issues we need to be aware of:

-Desalination is the process of removing salt and other minerals from water.

-It has been used as far back as the 1500s.

-The first significant desalination plant was not built in Israel but in Saudi Arabia in 1938

In the 1960s, then-President Kennedy started a small desalination program in the U.S. It was later dismantled in the 1980s.

-Several desalination technologies exist, such as solar distillation, natural evaporation systems, reverse osmosis, thermal, and others. Each method has its pros and cons.

-There are now more than 16,000 desalination plants in operation around the globe. Some are small, called micro desalination plants. Others are huge, with the largest in the United Arab Emirates, Saudi Arabia, and Israel.

-These 16,000 plants generate an estimated 780 million gallons of water per day — enough water to serve millions of people.

As more desalination plants are constructed in this country and around the world, it's clear that billions of gallons of water will soon be generated by these systems.

However, there is a downside. For example:

Desalinating plants are very energy demanding.

-At this time, most are operated using conventional energy sources such as electricity derived from petroleum and natural gas.

-These plants are very costly to construct and operate. The charges to run them are also high, which can make water costs prohibitive in some cases.

-Desalination plants are often constructed in remote areas, which means miles of power lines may need to be built to run them.

The effluent brine can be harmful to water ways and the sea environment

-The construction of some plants, especially here in the U.S., is being opposed by some environmentalists precisely because they are being developed in remote and sometimes environmentally sensitive areas of the country.

-While lower-cost renewable energy sources such as solar, wind, and geothermal are being used to power desalination plants, using these renewable resources increases total construction costs.

Even with these issues, the reality is that with a growing U.S. population and climate change leaving many parts of the country drier than ever before, desalination plants may prove to be lifesavers, just as they are in Israel and other parts of the Middle East. Further, there are signs that some of the construction costs are coming down.

However, in the meantime, we have one more way to reduce water consumption that has also proven its value. Water efficiency — reducing water consumption long term — is already saving billions of gallons of water per year worldwide. That's where waterless urinals come in. View waterless urinals as pioneers. They have helped lead the way for building owners, managers, and now, consumers, to use water wisely and certainly more efficiently.

Chapter Twenty-Three– Drought Tolerant Crops

What people fail to realize is that we are living in a closed loop system. We can't create water. We have the same amount of water on this earth as the dinosaurs had. The only difference is the percentage of salt to fresh water that exists now. Our world produces enough water for life to survive. The only problem is that it is not spread across the planet evenly. This is mainly due to weather patterns, and physical structures that exist on the planet, ie Mountains. Another issue is the temperature on the planet is not even everywhere. The closer you get to the equator the hotter it gets and the colser you get to the polar ice caps the colder it gets. Now these are just general rules of thumb, because there are always exceptions to the rule. In the previous chapter I discussed desalination and water conservation, in this chapter I am going to concentrate on a very important aspect of conservation and that is drought tolerant crops.

This is very important, mainly because a large portion of our planet is arid or semi arid, and whikle we do have plenty of water, bringing it to these areas is not only quite difficult but expensive as well. In many instances these regions are also quite poor, with the exception being the middle east which has large oil reserves.

Agriculture uses approximately 70% of the world's freshwater supply, and water managers are under mounting pressure to produce more food and fibre for a growing population while also reducing water waste and pollution and responding to a changing climate. In light of these challenges, more farmers are adopting innovative water management strategies, such as innovative irrigation systems and scheduling and methods to improve soil health. The Pacific Institute conducts research and works with innovative agricultural partners to identify and scale strategies to improve water management and ensure a vibrant agricultural system and global food security.

Drought tolerance is the ability to which a plant maintains its biomass production during arid or drought conditions. Some plants are naturally adapted to dry conditions, surviving with protection mechanisms such as desiccation tolerance, detoxification, or repair of xylem embolism. Other plants, specifically crops like corn, wheat, and rice, have become increasingly tolerant to drought with new varieties created via genetic engineering.

The plants behind drought tolerance are complex and involve many pathways which allows plants to respond to specific sets of conditions at any given time. Some of these interactions include stomatal conductance, carotenoid degradation and anthocyanin accumulation, the intervention of osmoprotectants (such as sucrose, glycine, and proline), ROS-scavenging enzymes. The molecular control of drought tolerance is also very complex and is influenced other factors such as environment and the developmental stage of the plant. This control consists mainly of transcriptional factors, such as dehydration-responsive element-binding protein (DREB), abscisic acid (ABA)-responsive element-binding factor (AREB), and NAM (no apical meristem).

Plants can be subjected to slowly developing water shortages (ie, taking days, weeks, or months), or they may face short-term deficits of water (ie, hours to days). In these situations, plants adapt by responding accordingly, minimizing water loss and maximizing water uptake. Plants are more susceptible to drought stress during the reproductive stages of growth, flowering and seed development. Therefore, the combination of short-term plus long-term responses allow for plants to produce a few viable seeds.

Natural drought tolerance adaptations

The scarlet globe mallow (Sphaeralcea coccinea) is a drought-escaping plant with natural drought tolerance. Some of its natural adaptations include silver-gray hairs that protect against drying; a deep root system;

and having seeds that only germinate when conditions are favorable.

Plants in naturally arid conditions retain large amounts of biomass due to drought tolerance and can be classified into 4 categories of adaptation:

Drought-escaping plants: annuals that germinate and grow only during times of sufficient times of moisture to complete their life cycle.

Drought-evading plants: non-succulent perennials which restrict their growth only to periods of moisture availability.

Drought-enduring plants: also known as xerophytes, these evergreen shrubs have extensive root systems along with morphological and physiological adaptations which enable them to maintain growth even in times of extreme drought conditions.

Drought-resisting plants: also known as succulent perennials, they have water stored in their leaves and stems for sparing uses.

Structural adaptations

Many adaptations for dry conditions are structural, including the following:

-Adaptations of the stomata to reduce water loss, such as reduced numbers, sunken pits, waxy surfaces.

-Reduced number of leaves and their surface area.

-Water storage in succulent above-ground parts or water-filled tubers.

-Crassulacean acid metabolism (CAM metabolism) allows plants to get carbon dioxide at night and store malic acid during the day, allowing photosynthesis to take place with minimized water loss.

-Adaptations in the root system to increase water absorption.

-Trichomes (small hairs) on the leaves to absorb atmospheric water.

Drought-Tolerant Crops to Plant Amid Water Scarcity

Water scarcity is a growing concern. Lack of water from long, recurring droughts is increasingly dominating the food and agriculture world. It's driven up the cost of groceries and put a dent in farmers' yields. According to NASA scientists, the past two decades have been some of the driest conditions on record. And recent data from the federal government shows that more than half of all states are suffering from moderate drought or worse.

For avid gardeners, especially in the West, the ongoing water crisis is a good time to reconsider which crops to put in the ground. There are some plants, such as rice, almonds and citrus, that require large amounts of water to thrive.

Others, categorized as drought-tolerant crops, require very little. So, if you're short on water, there's no need to let it stop you from growing. There are a number of crops you can plant that require minimal water input. Dive into our guide that lays out a variety of planting options.

In recent decades, research has increased to see how food crops cope with dry conditions, and scientists are breeding and crossing seeds to make them more drought-tolerant.

But major obstacles exist in scaling up their use.

"Getting new crop varieties into the hands of a large number of farmers quickly is the challenge," said Robert Asiedu, head of biotechnology and genetic improvement at the International Institute of Tropical Agriculture, a research center based in Nigeria.

"It can be five to 10 years before large quantities of new varieties reach farmers... That's the main bottleneck now."

It is crucial for farmers to grow drought-resistant crops as part of a range of pro-active measures, experts say.

For example, soil degradation and deforestation exacerbate the effects of drought because soil loses its ability to retain water, so farmers must improve soil fertility and irrigation practices.

Below are some of the drought-tolerant crops and methods farmers across the world are using to combat drought:

1. INTERCROPPING

Staple food crops like sorghum, cassava, sweet potato, pearl millet, cowpea and groundnut are naturally more drought-tolerant than maize.

For centuries, farmers in parts of West Africa have grown maize alongside cassava and sweet potatoes.

The practice known as intercropping - growing two or more crops together - means farmers have another crop to fall back on when maize harvests fail because of poor rainfall.

In recent decades, research has increased to see how food crops cope with dry conditions, and scientists are breeding and crossing seeds to make them more drought-tolerant.

But major obstacles exist in scaling up their use.

"Getting new crop varieties into the hands of a large number of farmers quickly is the challenge," said Robert Asiedu, head of biotechnology and genetic improvement at the International Institute of Tropical Agriculture, a research center based in Nigeria.

"It can be five to 10 years before large quantities of new varieties reach farmers... That's the main bottleneck now."

It is crucial for farmers to grow drought-resistant crops as part of a range of pro-active measures, experts say.

For example, soil degradation and deforestation exacerbate the effects of drought because soil loses its ability to retain water, so farmers must improve soil fertility and irrigation practices.

Below are some of the drought-tolerant crops and methods farmers across the world are using to combat drought:

INTERCROPPING

Staple food crops like sorghum, cassava, sweet potato, pearl millet, cowpea and groundnut are naturally more drought-tolerant than maize.

For centuries, farmers in parts of West Africa have grown maize alongside cassava and sweet potatoes.

The practice known as intercropping - growing two or more crops together - means farmers have another crop to fall back on when maize harvests fail because of poor rainfall.

COWPEA

Cowpea, also known as black-eyed pea, is mainly grown by small farmers in more than 80 countries, from Nigeria to Brazil.

Cowpea thrives in parched soils and drought-prone areas where its roots can grow with as little as 300 mm (11.8 inches) of rainfall per year. Once cowpea seeds have enough moisture to take root, the plants can survive drought.

The stems and stalks of the high protein grain can also be used as fodder for livestock.

Often intercropped with maize and cotton, cowpea plants provide shade and dense cover that help protect soil and preserve moisture.

Researchers are trying to map the genes found in cowpea to produce improved drought-resistant varieties.

CHICKPEA

Chickpea is one of the most important grain legume crops in the world. Thanks to its drought resistance, it is widely grown among small farmers in dryland areas of South Asia and in China.

Scientists in Australia are leading the way in research to enhance drought tolerance in chickpeas and to better understand how the food crop adapts to prolonged dry spells.

EARLY MATURING CROPS

Shifting rainfall patterns, often linked to climate change, have shortened the rainy season in many countries worldwide.

Hardest hit are small-scale and subsistence farmers as they largely depend on rain-fed crops for their livelihoods.

To adapt, farmers are increasingly planting new varieties of food crops that take less time to grow.

New varieties need 90 to 110 days to mature - against 120 days plus for traditional crops - and can survive without rain for three weeks.

In recent years, early-maturing food crops have been adopted by tens of millions of farmers in sub-Saharan Africa.

ANCIENT PLANTS

Chia, a flowering plant, is grown for its edible seeds and is known to thrive in hot and dry weather.

Once widely grown by the ancient Aztecs of Central America, chia is being rediscovered by small farmers across Latin America, including

Guatemala, Bolivia, Nicaragua and Ecuador.

High in protein, chia seeds can be eaten whole, ground into flour and pressed for oil.

TARWI

With its brilliant blue blossom, the tarwi pea plant stands out from the rest in the field.

Once grown centuries ago by the Incas, more Andean subsistence farming communities, particularly in Bolivia's highlands, are growing tarwi again.

The drought-resistant seeds are nutritious, high in protein and a source of cooking oil.

NEW MAIZE VARIETIES

Maize is one of the world's most important cereal crops.

In the past decade, farmers - especially in sub-Saharan Africa - have tried new strains that can withstand drought, allowing crops to grow when there is little or no rain.

Maize has also been genetically modified to include the desired DNA traits that thrive in drought conditions.

A 2010 study found that the widespread adoption of drought-tolerant varieties could boost maize harvests in 13 African countries by 10-34 percent.

NEW BEAN VARIETIES

Beans feature on any given plate in most of Latin America.

In drought-hit Central America - Guatemala, El Salvador and Honduras - prolonged dry spells since mid-2014, linked to the El Nino weather phenomenon, have decimated food harvests.

In 2015 alone, drought in these countries left 3.5 million people in need of food aid, prompting scientists to look for varieties of bean that can withstand drought.

"It is a priority in all the research centers to develop these new varieties of crops," said Tito Diaz, subregional coordinator for Mesoamerica at the U.N. Food and Agriculture Organization (FAO). Some have been successful, as in El Salvador.

Farmers there recently started to grow a new variety of drought-tolerant bean, named after the country's National Center for Agricultural and Forestry Technology (CENTA) where the research took place. The CENTA-EAC bean is a hybrid, made from crossing black and red beans after years of trial and error.

In Nicaragua, farmers are also growing a new variety of red bean, INTA-Tomabu, which can thrive with little rainfall.

Figs on a branch.

Figs

Fig trees need to be planted in a spot that has seven to eight hours of full sun. This plant also needs well-draining soil, with a pH anywhere from 6.0 to 6.5. Sandy soil is preferred over loamy or clay solutions.

Plant your trees in late fall to early spring. In addition to full sunlight, fig trees appreciate a lot of room. If you're planting more than one tree, make sure they have 15 to 20 feet between them. We suggest providing your figs with somewhere between 1 and 1½ inches of water per week—either from rainfall or irrigation. You will know if it needs to be watered if its foliage starts to turn yellow or its leaves drop off.

Improve a new tree's chance of survival by planting it so that its roots are two to four inches deeper than they were in the tree's nursery container. Fig trees planted in the ground may take eight to 10 years after planting before they begin fruit production. The common fig, Alma, Brown Turkey or Black Mission are all popular options.

Hardiness zones: 8-11

Grapevines are resilient plants.

Grapes

Once they have grown to establish long, deep root systems, grapevines can sustain prolonged periods of time without water. They should be planted in a spot that has six to eight hours of sun each day. Grapes prefer well-draining, sandy, loamy soil. Avoid planting anywhere near areas that collect water after it rains, as these plants don't tolerate wet conditions very well.

If there's no rainfall, saturate the soil at the base of each vine every seven to 10 days. If the leaves are wilting and the fruit is small, hard and dry, your vines need more water. If the leaves of your grapes are yellowing or if the tips of the leaves turn brown, this means you've watered it too much.

Read our guide to growing wine grapes for more information on planting and harvesting. On average, it can take two to three years for your crop to start bearing fruit.

Hardiness Zones: 7-10

Goji berries.

Goji berries

Good news: You can still plant a superfood with limited water needs. Pick a spot with full-day sun. Goji berries can tolerate many types of soil, but they prefer an environment that is well-draining with a pH ranging from 6.5 to 7.0.

If you have more than one plant, it should be spaced three to five feet apart within the row and at least six to eight feet apart between rows. This is to provide room for their root systems. It's also important to note that the sandier your soil is, the more likely it will need to be watered. A good general rule, however, is to apply approximately one inch of water per week.

Because goji is a member of the nightshade family, it will also need to be pruned after the first year. If growing from seed, sow them indoors about six to eight weeks before the last frost. If opting for a tree or shrub, plant in the early spring.

Goji plants will begin producing fruit when plants are two years old. Maximum production will not be reached until three to five years after planting. You can harvest them 35 days after full bloom. The two most popular varieties available to all growers are Crimson Star and Phoenix Tears.

Hardiness zones: 5-9

Mustard greens.

Mustard greens

Also known as curly or curled mustard, mustard spinach, Indian mustard or leaf mustard, mustard greens are known for their peppery taste that bites like that of a radish. Plant your mustard greens in loamy, rich and well-draining soil with a pH of 6.5 to 6.8. They also fare best in a spot that has full sun or partial shade. Mustard greens will require one to two inches of water each week.

If you're growing from seed, you can start them outdoors three weeks before your last frost date.

The Tendergreen or Southern Giant Curled are both varieties with low-maintenance water needs. On average, it takes anywhere from 35 to 70 days for mustard greens to be ready to harvest. You can cut the outer leaves, leaving the center in place to continue growing and produce more greens. Or you can treat the plant in a cut-and-come again fashion, cutting all the leaves to three to four inches from the ground and leaving the stub to re-grow.

Hardiness zone: 6-11

An okra plant.

Okra

As a staple in many southern dishes, it may not come as a surprise that okra can withstand the heat and will fare without copious amounts of water. For varieties that are extra tolerant to dryness, we suggest Hill Country Heirloom Red, Gold Coast or Jing Orange.

Okra grows best when planted in a spot with full sun. Plant it in sandy, well-draining soil that's high in organic matter. Provide one inch of water per square foot once a week. You can determine how to calculate that in gallons here. To improve the germination process, gently scratch the seeds with sandpaper and soak them in water for up to 24 hours before. You can plant your seeds with nine to 12 inches between them, so that seedling roots don't get tangled. On average, this vegetable is harvestable within 60 days after planting.

For the best yields, plant okra in the spring two to three weeks after all danger of frost has passed. For a good fall crop, plant at least three months before the first fall frost.

Hardiness Zones: 6-11A.

Japanese persimmon tree

Persimmon

At first glance, one might mistake a persimmon for an orange tomato, but this fruit is prized for its silky texture and sweet, tangy flavor. Persimmons can tolerate a wide range of soil types, but well-draining loamy soil that is neutral or slightly acidic with a pH of 6.0 to 7.5 is best.

For best results and to minimize immediate water needs, we suggest planting a tree over seedlings or seeds. If you do plant a tree, wait until the soil can be easily worked as you need to dig a hole as deep as the root ball and three times the width to accommodate its root system.

Choose a spot with full sun. If you leave a perimeter of mulch that stretches a few inches around the tree trunk, it will help avoid moisture accumulation. During the growing season, provide your tree with one inch of water each week. It can take trees anywhere from two to 10 years to bear fruit, depending on the variety. Eureka, Saijo or Texas persimmons are all good drought-tolerant choices.

Hardiness Zones: 5-11

Pitaya, also called dragon fruit.

Pitaya

Pitaya, also known as dragon fruit, is the fruit of cactus species native to the Americas. That makes it an attractive—and tasty—option.

This tropical crop should be planted in a spot with well-draining soil and full sunlight. Ideal pH level for its soil is between 6.0 and 7.0. Provide about one inch of water per square foot—or the first six inches of soil. A good rule of thumb would be to do this once a week or when the first two inches of soil are completely dry. Mulching around the base of the plant can help the soil retain its moisture.

You can grow pitaya by seed, cuttings or by purchasing it as a plant. Pitaya will not grow in cold climates, so make sure that the temperature is above 40°F year-round. The optimal temperature is 65-80°F. If grown from a seed, it takes up to seven years to bear fruit. If planted as a young plant, it typically takes two years. You will know your fruit is ready when the flaps on the outer skin begin to wither. Twist off each fruit from the stem to harvest.

Hardiness zones: 10-12

Pole beans.

Pole beans

Did you know that pole beans produce two to three times as much crop as bush beans would in the same amount of space? They rely on residual water found in the soil. They also prefer a spot with full sun and well-draining soil that has a pH level of 6.0 to 6.5.

For drought-hardy varieties, opt for the Rattlesnake or Preacher Bean. Willow Leaf, Louisiana Purple Pod, Worchester Indian Red, Ruth Bible and Garden of Eden Romano are all great options.

Upon planting, wait until the soil temperature is above 60°F. That could occur as early as April in southern climate zones and as late as June in cooler northern regions.

When it's time to plant, ensure that there are three inches of space between each seed. This vegetable needs one inch of water for every square foot once a week. And it takes about 65 to 75 days for the plant to mature.

Hardiness Zones: 3-11

A bounty of rhubarb.

Rhubarb

Rhubarb is drought-tolerant because of its fibrous root systems, but it's also cold-hardy, too! It thrives in soil with a pH level ranging from 5.0 to 6.8. When planting, find an area that has full sun with good drainage.

Many gardeners also plant them in raised beds.

Victoria, Macdonald or Valentine are popular variety choices. Rhubarb is typically grown from crowns, which look like root stubs. You can purchase these from your nursery or local seed company. Crowns can be planted in fall or spring. But if you want to start with seed, we suggest starting indoors eight to 10 weeks before the end of spring or the last frost.

When planting, place each crown upright in the planting hole with the buds one to two inches below the soil surface. Space the plants about three feet apart. After planting, water so that the top four inches of soil is soaked. It should watered every seven to 10 days.

After planting, it's best to wait two growing seasons before harvesting any stalks. The two-year establishment period allows the plants to become strong and productive. In its third year, rhubarb can be harvested over a four-week period. And in the weeks following, stalks can be harvested for eight to 10 weeks.

Hardiness zones: 3-8

Swiss chard

Swiss chard

Swiss chard is a good leafy green option for those either looking to cut back on their water use or needing to do so. Not only is it drought-tolerant, it's also cold-hardy. Your chard will prefer to be grown in a spot with full sun and rich, well-draining soil. Its pH level can be anywhere between 6.0 and 8.0.

When planting, ensure that seeds are two inches apart from each other. Its water needs are roughly one to 1½ inches of water each week. If hand watering, be sure not to get the plants wet. Wet foliage promotes disease or fungi, so apply water at the base of the plants, under the leaves instead.

On average, it takes about 50 to 70 days before harvest. The ideal time to plant is from early spring to mid-summer, and optimal soil temperature is 50-85°F. Bright Lights, Lucullus and Fordhook Giant are all great options, although most chard varieties are pretty drought-resistant.

Hardiness zones: 3-10

Water scarcity aggravates poverty and hunger

The heat wave in India and Pakistan is just one example of how extreme and less predictable weather conditions affect low-income communities. "As over 80 percent of our freshwater consumption is accounted for by agriculture, water scarcity directly impacts food security and exacerbates poverty and hunger," explains Dr. Suhas P. Wani, Former Director of the ICRISAT (International Crops Research Institute for the Semi-Arid Tropics) Development Center and consultant to the Asian Development Bank in Manila.

Without action, Suhas warns, the number of people suffering from hunger could increase by 10 million every year globally.

Livelihoods are also affected in more developed regions of the world. Severe drought in 2021 caused the California agriculture industry to shrink by an estimated 8,745 jobs and shoulder $1.2 billion in direct costs as water cutbacks forced growers to fallow farmland and pump more groundwater from wells, according to new research.

Formed by the Hoover Dam, Lake Mead is the largest reservoir in the United States. It is at an all-time low.

Since 2015, droughts in Europe have become more severe than any over the past 2,100 years, according to a study published in March 2021 in the Nature Geoscience. The recent series of summer droughts in Europe have also brought devastating ecological, agricultural, and economic impacts.

The European Environmental Agency EEA expects that droughts and water scarcity will aggravate during the remainder of the century and states in a report that the changing climatic conditions are already putting cultivation in Europe under pressure, especially for Mediterranean crops such as olives and grapes.

The worrying paradox: In 2050, our planet will need to provide food for an estimated 9 to 10 billion people. That's going to require a lot of water. Using water in a more sustainable manner and growing "more crops per drop" is the challenge we are facing globally. Technology and adapted farming practices could be part of the answer.

Fortunately, agriculture may be the sector with both the most to contribute and the most to gain in the fight against climate change and severe weather. Climate-adaptive farming offers a multitude of opportunities to reduce extreme weather events—and even to mitigate global warming itself. Along the way, transforming our agricultural system toward climate resilience will also significantly improve the lives of animals and the livelihoods of farmers while making healthier diets more accessible nationwide.

Achieving this vision will not be easy. But it is vital—both to ensure a secure the World food supply in the years ahead and to prevent the worst effects of global climate change.

Resources

modernfarmer.com, "10 Drought-Tolerant Crops to Plant Amid Water Scarcity: These fruits and vegetables will thrive even in the hottest conditions." By Lindsay Campbell; reuters.com, "From new beans to ancient plants, drought-busting crops take root." By Anastasia Moloney; enwikipedia.com, "Drought Tolerance." By Wikipedia Editors; bayer.com, "Severe Droughts Require Action to Avoid Future Food Crisis."By Stella Salvo; straydoginstitute.org, "Extreme Weather and US Agriculture." By Stray Dog Institute; news.yale.com, "Common weed may be 'super plant' that holds key to drought-resistant crops." By Bill Hathaway;

Addendum

Common weed may be 'super plant' that holds key to drought-resistant crops

A common weed harbors important clues about how to create drought resistant crops in a world beset by climate change.

Yale scientists describe how Portulaca oleracea, commonly known as purslane, integrates two distinct metabolic pathways to create a novel type of photosynthesis that enables the weed to endure drought while remaining highly productive, they report August 5 in the journal Science Advances.

"This is a very rare combination of traits and has created a kind of 'super plant' — one that could be potentially useful in endeavors such as crop engineering," said Yale's Erika Edwards, professor of ecology and evolutionary biology and senior author of the paper.

Plants have independently evolved a variety of distinct mechanisms to improve photosynthesis, the process by which green plants use sunlight to synthesize nutrients from carbon dioxide and water. For instance, corn and sugarcane evolved what is called C4 photosynthesis, which allows the plant to remain productive under high temperatures. Succulents such as cacti and agaves possess another type called CAM photosynthesis, which helps them survive in deserts and other areas with little water. Both C4 and CAM serve different functions but recruit the same biochemical pathway to act as *"add-ons"* to regular photosynthesis.

What makes the weed purslane unique is that it possesses both of these evolutionary adaptations — which allows it to be both highly productive and also very drought tolerant, an unlikely combination for a plant. Most scientists believed that C4 and CAM operated independently within leaves of purslane.

But the Yale team, led by co-corresponding authors and postdoctoral scholars Jose Moreno-Villena and Haoran Zhou, conducted a spatial analysis of gene expression within the leaves of purslane and found that C4 and CAM activity are totally integrated. They operate in the same cells, with products of CAM reactions being processed by the C4 pathway. This system provides unusual levels of protection for a C4 plant in times of drought.

The researchers also built metabolic flux models that predicted the emergence of an integrated C4+CAM system that mirrors their experimental results.

Understanding this novel metabolic pathway could help scientists devise new ways to engineer crops such as corn to help withstand prolonged drought, the authors say.

"In terms of engineering a CAM cycle into a C4 crop, such as maize, there is still a lot of work to do before that could become a reality," said Edwards.

"But what we've shown is that the two pathways can be efficiently integrated and share products. C4 and CAM are more compatible than we had thought, which leads us to suspect that there are many more C4+CAM species out there, waiting to be discovered."

Environmental Issues

-Extreme temperatures can disrupt crop growth and reduce yields. Heatwaves also threaten livestock—both directly with potentially lethal heat stress and indirectly with losses of fertility, milk production, and resilience to disease.

-Droughts will further dry out soils already depleted by industrial growing methods, threatening not only food crops but also animal feed crops, pastures, and the animals that rely on them. Satellite images have revealed increased browning of the land in the Southwest.

-Wildfires will become more likely in the context of high temperatures and extended drought conditions. Wildfires can leave severe impacts on agricultural land, killing crops through both burning and smoke damage.

-Floods and the damage they cause can be extremely costly. High water can devastate crops and livestock, accelerate soil erosion, pollute water sources, and damage the infrastructure of farms. The costs of recovery burden farming communities and disrupt food distribution.

Chapter Twenty-Four--New Super Foods, Soylent Green Anyone?

What are superfoods and why should you eat them?

The term "superfood" is a fairly new term referring to foods that offer maximum nutritional benefits for minimal calories. They are packed with vitamins, minerals, and antioxidants.

No standard criteria or legal definitions classify any food as a superfood at this time. However, most superfoods are plant-based.

In this article, we define what qualifies as a superfood, provide some common examples and their benefits, and provide tips on how to include them in the diet.

Açai berries are known to contain several different amino acids and antioxidants.

Superfoods are foods that have a very high nutritional density. This means that they provide a substantial amount of nutrients and very few calories.

They contain a high volume of minerals, vitamins, and antioxidants.

Antioxidants are natural molecules that occur in certain foods. They help neutralize free radicals in our bodies. Free radicals are natural byproducts of energy production that can wreak havoc on the body.

Antioxidant molecules decrease or reverse the effects of free radicals that have close links with the following health problems:

-heart disease

-cancer

-arthritis

-stroke

-respiratory diseases

-immune deficiency

-emphysema

-Parkinson's disease

Superfoods are not cure-all foods. Dietitian Penny Kris-Etherton explains:

"A lot of people have unrealistic expectations about these foods, thinking they'll be protected from chronic diseases and health problems. They may eat one or two of these nutrient-dense foods on top of a poor diet."

Including superfoods as part of daily nutritional intake is great but only when consuming a healthy, balanced diet overall. Eat a "super diet" rather than to concentrate on individual foods.

Common superfoods

Studies have demonstrated that superfoods high in antioxidants and flavonoids help prevent coronary heart disease and cancer, as well as improving immunity and decreasing inflammation.

Regularly eating fruits and vegetables also has strong associations with a lower risk of many lifestyle-related health conditions and overall mortality.

The nutrients they contain help promote a healthy complexion, nails, and hair and increase energy levels.

They can also help maintain a healthy weight.

2022 will be a year of health, wealth, and good sex (with triple-vaxxed partners, ofc). We all deserve it after the absolute sh*tshow that was the year 2021, aka 2020 the sequel. And although I can't promise that you will be seeing more commas in your bank account or anything of that nature, I can guarantee you will feel a *bit* healthier after stocking your fridge and entire pantry with this year's top superfoods. We have all the yummy secrets to eating the healthiest—and trendiest—foods in the new year.

But before you can take the official title of health goddess and culinary trendsetter, let's talk about what exactly makes a food ~super~. Merriam-Webster defines superfood as "a food that is rich in compounds such as antioxidants, fiber, or fatty acids, considered beneficial to a person's health." So basically, they're foods, ranging from broccoli and salmon to blueberries, that are full of nutrients and offer a multitude of health benefits. I guess this kind of makes superfoods the badass superheroes of any complete diet.

Now that we all know the deal with superfoods, let's get into what you clicked on this link for! Check out our superfoods list of 10 superstar ingredients that you will be reaching for in place of your beloved avocado, which didn't make the list this year. (Don't worry though, you are still totally allowed to order avo toast at New Year's brunch!)

1. Mankai

There is a good chance you haven't heard of Mankai, aka the world's

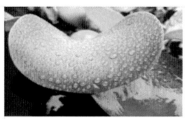 smallest veggie. I sure the hell didn't know about this tiny superfood until Samina Kalloo, RDN, CDN, nutrition communications lead for Pollock Communications, clued me in on its protein and vitamin-packing powers.

Despite its micro size, Mankai has all nine essential amino acids, vitamin B, iron and over 60 nutrients, says Kalloo. "Plus, with only one in 10 Americans getting enough vegetables, Mankai is an easy and impactful nutrition solution," Kalloo adds.

Eat it: Unlike a lot of other greens, Mankai has a neutral taste and texture, making it the perfect addition to your morning smoothie, your fave pasta dish, or guac recipe, says Kalloo. And for all the gorgeous, gorgeous girls who love soup out there, Kalloo recommends adding Mankai cubes to your broth for the heartiest of comfort meals.

2. Turmeric

You and your S.O.'s texts shouldn't be the only spicy thing in your life.

 Turmeric, a spice that you probably already have in your cupboard, can reduce inflammation, improve memory, lower the risk of some chronic diseases, and fight against free radicals (aka what contributes to aging), says Kalloo.

Eat it: Turmeric is super versatile and can be added to nearly anything and everything. Add a dash to your scrambled eggs in the a.m. Sprinkle on top of your yogurt for a midday snack. And for dinner, try sautéing your favorite veggies with turmeric or adding it to soup. Keep in mind that just a little bit of turmeric goes a long way, says Kalloo.

Pro tip from a dietitian: When cooking with turmeric, add a dash of black pepper to enhance the absorption of the curcumin (the active compound in turmeric), says Chelsea Golub, MS, RDN, CDN.

3. Tahini

You might be familiar with tahini if your late-night munchies include hummus and pita chips. Tahini, a main ingredient of hummus made from grounded sesame seeds, originates in the Middle East, but has made its way to the aisles of Trader Joe's and Whole Foods.

"It's a great source of polyunsaturated and monounsaturated fatty acids, which means there are lots of anti-inflammatory and heart protective benefits. Also, it provides protein, fiber, iron, copper, calcium, and other minerals that we need in our diet," says Golub.

Eat it: Give a more savory glow up to a classic, the PB&J, by swapping out peanut butter for tahini to make a T&J. To doctor up your jarred tahini for extra creaminess, Golub recommends mixing in lemon, water, and salt. Add in your favorite seasonings (did someone say Everything but the Bagel?) for a yummy veggie or pita dip.

4. Pomegranate Seeds

It can be a little bit perplexing figuring out what exactly to do with pomegranates or the seeds. But their health benefits def outweigh any lingering confusion you may have. As an antioxidant powerhouse, pomegranate seeds can protect your cells from damage and help prevent disease, says Golub. They are abundant in fiber which aids digestion, in addition to containing vitamin C, vitamin K, and folate, Golub says.

Eat it: Of course, you could always make some nature's cereal à la Lizzo's viral Tik Tok: fresh berries, coconut water, ice cubes, topped with pomegranate seeds, served in a bowl for an energizing breakfast. Crunchatize a cup of Greek yogurt, your Sweetgreen order, or a morning bowl of oatmeal by adding a small handful of pomegranate seeds, suggests Golub.

5. Moringa

I love matcha, but I think we can all agree it is time to give her a rest. Moringa (nicknamed the "miracle tree" for being drought resistant—how cool is nature!?) is predicted to have a major moment in 2022 as a popular alternative to matcha, says Rachel Bukowski, senior team leader of product Development at Whole Foods Market. Originating in Africa, the moringa leaf is one of the most nutrient-dense plants, packed with vitamin C, vitamin E, beta carotene, and protein, officially making it a superstar ingredient, adds Deane Falcone, PhD, chief scientific officer of sustainable agriculture group Crop One Holdings.

Eat it: Add a teaspoon of moringa powder to your go-to smoothie bowl recipe for a vibrant green color that is truly IG worthy. Moringa tea is also a great way to get nutrients first thing in the morning! And if you happen to have a sweet tooth next time you are strolling the aisles of Whole Foods, be on the lookout for moringa-infused desserts like Moringa Mint Chip Frozen Coconut Cream (perfect for all those who are lactose intolerant or vegan!) and Maple Toffee Crunch Chocolate with Moringa, says Bukowski.

6. Soy

Soybeans have a high concentration of isoflavones, a type of phytochemical. Phytochemicals are compounds that occur naturally in plants.

Some research demonstrates that isoflavones in soy help reduce the amount of low-density lipoprotein (LDL) or "bad" cholesterol in the blood.

A few studies have shown that soy may prevent age-related memory loss. Soy isoflavones might also reduce bone loss and increase bone mineral density during menopause, as well as decreasing menopausal symptoms.

7. Fermented Foods

Unlike the pair of skinny jeans that are now sitting in the back of your

closet, fermented foods will be trending yet again in 2022. Holding their title as the number one superfood trend for the fourth year in a row, according to a survey conducted by Pollock Communications and Today's Dietitian, fermented foods like kimchi, pickles, miso, and yogurt are not going anywhere. The reigning superfood category is linked to improved digestive health and reduced inflammation, Kalloo says. Fermented foods are probiotic-rich, meaning they contain good bacteria to keep your gut happy and healthy.

Eat it: Golub loves to dress up plain Greek yogurt with other superfoods like berries, hemp seeds, or tahini for the perfect protein-packed parfait. *"Dairy gets a bad rap...I always say that if you aren't lactose intolerant,* there's no need to eliminate dairy from your diet," says Golub.

If your body isn't a dairy-friendly zone, there are still a ton of other fermented foods you can incorporate into your day-to-day meals. "*Add kimchi to an egg scramble or serve it up in a burrito or taco. Toss sauerkraut into coleslaw or other chopped salads. And don't forget about pickles, which make a great addition to sandwiches and salads,*" recommends Kalloo.

8. Cruciferous Vegetables

Cruciferous (just a fancy word to describe plants within the cabbage family) vegetables are probably a part of your diet already. These veggies  include kale, cauliflower, brussels sprouts, broccoli, and arugula, among others. With plenty of antioxidants, vitamin K, folate, and fiber, these vegetables are pretty damn super. "*Increased consumption in these veggies may be related to decreased depression and improved cardiovascular conditions,*" says Golub. So I guess mom was right all along—eat your veggies to live a long and happy life!

Eat it, I know, it is so much easier to UberEats dinner after a hellish day of work, but you can make a delicious and good-for-you meal in no time using some cruciferous veggies and your preferred protein. On a baking sheet, add your protein and a couple handfuls of your vegetable of choice. Drizzle olive oil (adding a healthy fat like olive oil increases the vitamin and mineral absorption and makes digestion easier, says Golub), zhuzh it up with your fav seasonings, and pop it all in the oven for a yummy yet delivery-fee-free dinner.

9. Ancient Grains

Yes, ancient grains do not sound like the most appealing superfood, but they are actually so much cooler than you think. These grains (which include amaranth, teff, quinoa, and farro, among others) are not only

nutrient-dense and rich in phytochemicals that may help combat chronic disease, but they are also earth-friendly, says Kalloo. You can nourish your body and Mother Earth at the same time!

Eat it: Amaranth, quinoa, and farro are just a few ancient grains that you can likely find in your local supermarket. And they are actually pretty affordable (yes, superfoods can be super budget-friendly)! Quinoa is an especially versatile ancient grain with endless possibilities. Add it to your tacos or burrito bowls for a Taco Tuesday upgrade everyone will love. Oh, and don't forget the margs!

10. Hemp Seed

We are unlikely to see marijuana legalization throughout the country in

2022, but we will be seeing more hemp seeds in the new year. Hemp seeds, which come from the cannabis sativa plant, are the perfect addition to literally anything you eat. With an abundance of omega-3 fatty acids and vitamins, these little seeds support heart health, brain function, and keep your immune system in tip-top shape, which will also be essential, says Kalloo and Golub.

Eat it. Hemp seeds are an easy way to beef up the nutritional value of any meal, says Kalloo. Try sprinkling hemp seeds on your salad (bonus if your base is a cruciferous vegetable like arugula or brussels sprouts!), topping off a bowl of oatmeal for a fulfilling breakfast, or adding to your favorite baked goods for an omega-3 boost to a sweet treat, says Golub.

11. Avocados

Avocado is a key component to a modern-day brunch staple, avocado toast, and contains a bevy of nutrients worth celebrating. They offer Heart-Healthy Poly- and Monounsaturated Fat alternatives in your diet.

According to the U.S. Department of Agriculture (USDA), ½ an avocado provides 29 milligrams (mg) of magnesium, or about 7 percent of the DV. Magnesium plays a role in regulating blood pressure and blood sugar, and magnesium deficiency is associated with a higher risk for type 2 diabetes, according to the National Institutes of Health (NIH). Avocado also provides fiber (6.75 mg per ½ fruit, offering 24 percent of DV), along with heart-healthy polyunsaturated and monounsaturated fat. An advisory published by the American Heart Association in the June 2017 issue of Circulation noted that replacing saturated fat (from sources such as butter) with the fats found in foods such as avocado can help reduce the risk for heart disease.

12. Berries

Berries may help keep the brain healthy and may even fend off Alzheimer's Disease. Blueberries are at the top of almost every superfood list, but just about any edible berry is worthy of superfood status. While all differing in nutritional value, blackberries, blueberries, raspberries,

strawberries, cranberries, açai berries, Goji berries, and raspberries, to name a few, are low-calorie, high in fiber, and packed full of antioxidants that help fight against cancer-causing free radicals, notes a study published in March 2018 in Frontiers in Pharmacology.

Blueberries in particular have a high number of anthocyanin pigments, which not only give them their rich color, but also act as powerful antioxidants that may lower the risk of diabetes, heart disease, and degenerative diseases like Alzheimer's, according to a review published in July 2019 in Advances in Nutrition.

We've all been there: crying while chugging a bottle of Ocean Spray cranberry juice to help combat a painful UTI (IYKYK), but cranberries actually do so much more than just soothing symptoms of a urinary tract infection. On top of being loaded with antioxidants and vitamins C, E, and K, these little crimson-colored berries support gut health by making sure bacteria don't adhere to other cells, says Kalloo.

Eat it: Beyond the holiday season (#TeamHomemadeCranberrySauce) and the occasional UTI, you probably don't eat cranberries all that often. Next time you order a salad, ask for dried cranberries to be sprinkled on top for some added sweetness. Cranberries are a great addition to tuna and chicken salad too, says Kalloo. And if you are feeling inspired by your recent Netflix binge of The Great British Bake Off, preheat your oven and whip up a batch of white chocolate cranberry cookies.

13. Seafood

Seafood provides Omega-3 Fatty Acids for a healthy ticker. Unlike many animal products high in saturated fats, such as red meat and processed meats, that can raise the risk of heart disease, fish is full of protein and rich in healthy fats, Omega-3 fatty acids — namely the type you get from seafood including fish — are particularly beneficial to our bodies, notes the NIH. These types, eicosapentaenoic acid (EPA), and docosahexaenoic

acid (DHA), are used more efficiently than the third type of omega-3, alpha-linolenic acid (ALA), which comes from plant sources such as flaxseed and nuts, past research has shown. Overall, omega-3s can help play a role in reducing your risk of heart attack and stroke, alleviating depression, and aiding infant development, according to the NIH.

A study published in January 2019 in the journal Nutrients found omega-3 fatty acid intake across the United States was lower (and much lower in women and children) than the recommended amounts, which, the authors wrote, is "putting vulnerable populations at potential risk for adverse health outcomes." The AHA recommends consuming at least two servings (3.5 ounces) of fish per week, noting that fattier fish like salmon, sardines, mackerel, and herring are especially healthy.

14. Garlic and Onions

It has been shown that garlic and onions can contribute to the maintenance of healthy blood pressure levels. They may be pungent (some even bring us to tears), but allium vegetables — chives, onions, garlic, leeks, and the like— — deliver potent health benefits. Plus, they're delicious. Once used to ward off the evil eye,

garlic also has antibacterial and antiviral properties, according to an article published in April 2018 in Scientific Reports.

Studies have found allium vegetables may play a role in preventing cancer, and garlic in particular may benefit people living with diabetes, high cholesterol, and high blood pressure, according to an meta-analysis published in August 2019 in the journal Food Science and Nutrition.

15. Mushrooms

Mushrooms may complement breast cancer treatment, though more studies are still needed. For centuries, mushrooms have been considered a superfood and are still used in traditional Chinese medicine to cleanse the body and promote longevity. Researchers have long studied the antibacterial, antioxidant, and anti-inflammatory properties of mushrooms, and mycotherapy — the use of mushrooms as medicine — is used as a complementary treatment for breast cancer. While clinical research is lacking, lab and animal research has yielded promising data on the use of mushrooms to help prevent and treat breast cancer, according to a study published in May 2018 in the journal Oncotarget.

16. Nuts and Seed

Nuts and seeds supply a powerful punch of plant protein and can help regulate weight. Wellness gurus tout different superpowers for each nut — almonds for heart health, cashews for cognition, Brazil nuts for cancer — but all are a great source fat, fiber, and protein (ones encased in sugar or salt are on the less healthy side), notes the Harvard T.H. Chan School of Public Health. Seeds like flaxseeds, chia seeds, and hemp seeds are easy to incorporate into your diet and are packed with vitamins and minerals.

While nuts are high in fat, they also keep you feeling full longer, and studies, such as an October 2018 article published in the European Journal of Nutrition, have linked nuts to a lower risk of weight gain and obesity. Walnuts are at the top of the "supernut" list, with their antioxidant power helping to prevent diseases like certain types of cancer, according to a study published in November 2017 in the journal Critical Reviews in Food Science and Nutrition.

17. Dark, Leafy Greens

Dark, leafy greens may play a role in preventing colorectal cancer.

Generally, nutritionists like Wolfram say the darker the color of a vegetable, the more nutrients it contains. Dark, leafy greens like arugula, kale, collard greens, spinach, lettuce, and Swiss chard get their vibrant colors from chlorophyll, which keeps plants healthy, and the dietary fiber found in dark greens can decrease the risk of colorectal cancer, according to the American Institute for Cancer Research. Carotenoids, another type of plant pigment, also act as antioxidants that fight off potentially cancer-causing free radicals in the body, notes Harvard Medical School.

18. Citrus Fruits

Citrus fruits may help prevent age-related eye disease. Citrus fruits have been crowned as superfoods because of their fiber and vitamin C content. The sweet and sour bite of citrus fruits like grapefruit, oranges, lemons, and limes is also low in calories and high in water.

One study published in July 2018 in The American Journal of Clinical Nutrition found that adults ages 50 and older who ate oranges every day had a 60 percent less chance of developing macular degeneration compared with those who didn't eat oranges.

19. Dark Chocolate

Dark chocolate is a healthy dessert that may boost your mood. Unlike its sweeter milk and white chocolate counterparts, dark chocolate may offer health benefits. The cacao in dark chocolate is full of antioxidants, which may play a role in cancer prevention, heart health, and weight loss, according to a study published in December 2016 in the Journal of Neuroscience. A 1 or 2 ounce serving of dark chocolate (with a minimum of 70 percent cacao) a day may have other health benefits, such as improving cognition, preventing memory loss, and boosting mood, reported a study published in April 2018 in The FASEB Journal.

20. Sweet Potatoes

Sweet potatoes are a gluten-free, healthy source of carbs that help fight disease. Sweet potatoes have long been on the superfoods list, and for good reason. Carrots, beets, parsnips, potatoes, and yams are all types of root vegetables that have sustained human life for hundreds of years — and through many a harsh winter.

Nutritious, easy to grow, and with an exceptionally long life span (some can last months, if stored properly), root vegetables are packed with healthy carbs and starches that provide energy, according to the Harvard T.H. Chan School of Public Health.

A review of research on sweet potatoes published in November 2016 in Food Research International suggested that this root veggie may contribute to preventing diabetes, obesity, cancer, and other health conditions thanks to their anti-inflammatory, antioxidative, and antimicrobial properties.

As a bonus, root veggies including sweet potatoes are also gluten-free, making a great dietary alternative for those with celiac disease, noted a study published in May 2016 in the North Carolina Medical Journal.

21. Beans and Legumes

Beans and legumes may help reduce high cholesterol. As far as superfoods go, the beans and legume family possess the power of plant-based protein. Unlike food from many animal sources, beans and legumes are low in saturated fats — which can raise cholesterol levels and contribute to heart disease — and yield health benefits that animal products don't, according to the AHA.

Chickpeas, edamame, lentils, peas, and the thousands of other bean types are densely packed with nutrition, and research has found the high levels of fiber and vitamins in them can help with weight loss and regulating blood sugar levels, according to an study published in October 2015 in the journal Clinical Diabetes. Peanuts are also in the legume family as well, making this nut look-alike a great, low-carb snack, notes the Harvard Medical School.

22. Tea

Tea contains few calories, helps with hydration, and is a good source of antioxidants.

Catechins, potent antioxidants found primarily in green tea, have beneficial anti-inflammatory and anti-carcinogenic properties.

A study published in the Journal of Physiological Anthropology examined the effects of green tea, white tea, and water consumption on stress levels in 18 students.

The study suggestedTrusted Source that both green and white tea had reduced stress levels and that white tea had an even greater effect. Larger studies are necessary to confirm this possible health benefit.

Green tea may also have an anti-arthritic effect by suppressing overall inflammation.

23. Salmon

The high omega-3 fatty acid content in salmon and other fatty fish, such as trout and herring, can decrease the riskTrusted Source of abnormal heartbeats, reduce cholesterol and slow the growth of arterial plaque.

24. Wine and grapes

Resveratrol, the polyphenol found in wine that made it famously "heart healthy", is present in the skins of red grapes.

A few studies have shown promise that resveratrol can protect against diabetic neuropathy and retinopathy. These are conditions caused by poorly controlled diabetes where vision is severely affected.

One 2013 study found that it reduced the effects of neural changes and damage associated with diabetic neuropathy.

Researchers have also found resveratrol to be beneficial for treating Alzheimer's disease, relieving hot flashes and mood swings associated with menopause, and improving blood glucose control. However, large studies using human subjects are still needed to confirm these findings.

Another flavonoid that occurs in grapes, quercetin, is a natural anti-inflammatory that appears to reduce the risk of atherosclerosis and protect against the damage caused by LDL cholesterol in animal studies. Quercetin may also have effects that act against cancer.

However, more studies using human subjects are necessary before researchers can confirm the benefits beyond all doubt.

Although wine does contain antioxidants, keep in mind that eating grapes would provide the same benefit alongside additional fiber. The American Heart Association recommends that people limit alcoholic beverages to no more than two drinks per day for men and one drink per day for women.

25. Other Superfoods

-spirulina

-blue-green algae

-wheatgrass

Diet

A person can incorporate these foods into a varied healthy diet when available. However, do not overspend or search too widely trying to find them.

The secret is that any leafy green vegetable or berry in a grocery store will provide many of the same benefits an individual will find in the premium-priced superfoods.

Buy your produce in season and from local sources to ensure the highest nutrient content. Do not discount the humble apple or carrot either — all fruits and vegetables are essentially superfoods.

Replacing as many processed foods as possible with whole foods will drastically improve health.

Quick tips:

These tips can help you get more superfoods into your diet:

-Look at the colors on your plate. Is all of your food brown or beige? Then it is likely that antioxidant levels are low. Add in foods with rich color like kale, beets, and berries.

-Add shredded greens to soups and stir fries.

-Try replacing your beef or poultry with salmon or tofu.

-Add berries to oatmeal, cereal, salads or baked goods.

-Make sure you have a fruit or a vegetable every time you eat, including meals and snacks.

-Have a daily green or matcha tea.

-Make turmeric, cumin, oregano, ginger, clove, and cinnamon your go-to spices to amp up the antioxidant content of your meals.

-Snack on nuts, seeds (especially Brazil nuts and sunflower seeds) and dried fruit (with no sugar or salt added).

Try these healthy and delicious recipes developed by registered dietitians:

-Acai berry bowl

-Chocolate banana smoothie

-Spinach basil pesto

-Matcha vegetable curry

-Powered-up lasagna.

Risks

Taking superfoods in supplement form is not the same as getting the nutrients from the real foods.

Many supplements contain ingredients that can cause a strong biological effect on the body. Supplements might also interactTrusted Source with other medications. Taking supplements could result in vitamin or mineral toxicity, affect recovery after surgery, and trigger other side effects.

Tips for using supplements

The U.S. Food and Drug Administration (FDA) warns that combining or taking too many supplements can be hazardous. Only use supplements that the FDA has approved.

Tips for safe use include the following:

-Use non-commercial sites for information, such as the National Institutes of Health (NIH) and FDA.

-Beware of claims that a product "works better than a prescription drug" or "is totally safe."

-Remember that natural does not always mean safe.

-If using supplements, the FDA recommendsTrusted Source choosing high-quality products that have been tested by a third party.

Always check first with a health provider before starting to use a supplement.

Soylent Green Predicted 2022, Including Impossible Meat Substitutes

Charlton Heston paid for a cannibalistic cautionary tale set in 2022 with Soylent Green, now we can get fries with it.

Why settle for tacos when Tuesday can be Soylent Green Day? Far more nutritious than Soylent Red or Yellow, the green stuff is made with a secret ingredient that makes it a real delicacy. Of course the line "Soylent Green is people" is now an insta-spoiler meme and trope. But when Charlton Heston first uttered that anguished warning, it might as well have been a supermarket can-can sale promotion. Store shops in the 1973 science fiction classic **Soylent Green** were so mobbed on Tuesdays that riots started every week in this dystopian vision of 2022.

The historical montage which opens **Soylent Green**, based on real photographs from the 20th century, shows how industry and population colluded to form a dystopian future where too many people struggle for too little food, gag at the air, and wear masks on a daily basis. The face covering in the montage actually increases exponentially as the 20th century tumbles past into our own modern nightmares. Sludge and filth cover the perimeter of human existence in **Soylent Green**, and plague and famine eat humanity out from the inside.

There was a time once, says Sol Roth, played by the elegant Edward G. Robinson in his last cinematic role, when the world was beautiful. People were always rotten, but the world was beautiful. **Soylent Green** was set in the year 2022, and saw that beauty become faded, and the people jaded. While many of the predictions laid out in the opening montage have borne themselves out, other predictive promises have not been filled.

Directed by Richard Fleischer with a screenplay by Stanley R. Greenberg, **Soylent Green** was based on Harry Harrison's 1968 novel Harry Harrison Make Room! Make Room!, which is set in 1999. Soylent Green assumes the earth would be too overpopulated for sustainable coexistence by 2022, and put the world's population calculations at a then-frightening 7 billion people. We hit 7.9 billion in 2021, so hurray for our team, as we are already ahead of the curve!

Heston, who saw man as merely a superior monkeys' uncle in 1968's Planet of the Apes, and the earth go zombie in **The Omega Man in** 1971, had real concerns about overpopulation when he commissioned the script for **Soylent Green**. During the 1970s, fears of a "population bomb" were rampant, and warnings came from such disparate sources as Public Broadcasting System specials and songs like Jethro Tull's "Locomotive Breath." It was a common belief humanity was breeding too much for the natural world's ability to sustain it.

While **Soylent Green** underestimated the overall world population of today, it did inflate some of its numbers. In the beginning of the film, we learn that New York City's population is 40,000,000. Manhattan island might sink under the extra weight before this could happen. But the nightmare was also averted in the interim as fertility rates plummeted on a global scale, and China issued its national one-child policy to counter the growing birth rates which the world found so frightening at the time. Some of the eastern hemisphere is currently facing an aging population crisis because of the efforts to curb youthful sexual enthusiasm.

Soylent Green was one of the first mainstream films to bring climate change into public consciousness. Heston's character, NYPD detective Thorn, explains how a year-long heatwave created by the greenhouse effect poisoned the water, polluted the soil, decimated plant and animal life, and burned everything up. Only the wealthy can get their hands on real food, especially produce. It is, however, available on the black market. A jar of strawberry jam costs $150. In one very effective scene, Thorn and Sol savor a thin steak, an apple to the core, and a leaf of lettuce.

The food shortage prediction is actually true, depending on economic and geographic factors. Mass production means we make enough foodstuff to feed the entire world population, with a surplus. Yet some people starve and others suffer from obesity. The one-percenters don't shoot themselves off into the stratosphere in the film's 2022; they isolate themselves in luxury penthouses.

In the film, Det. Thorn is investigating the murder of Soylent Corporation executive William R. Simonson. The dead man's safe place includes not only the most deliciously decadent edibles, but it has the latest in post-post-modern "furniture." That's what sex slaves to the wealthy are called in the film; and the ever-dazed, tarot card-reading Shirl, played by Leigh Taylor-Young, could service parties in Stanley Kubrick's Eyes Wide Shut (or the most insane conspiracy theories of QAnon followers today).

Soylent is one giant corporation which has the power to exacerbate global hunger. It is like Amazon, Wal-Mart and probably Tyson Chicken combined, and the top earners live in protective custodial-ship to the starving masses. Half of New York City is unemployed and living in poverty, and when they take to the streets, it is only slightly more frightening than the militaristic police response to protestors we've seen in the past few years. The reason it is more frightening is artistic. It is because the scenario looks so commonplace. The cops don't mount tanks and urban assault vehicles in **Soylent Green**. They don't scoot activists into unmarked minivans. They come in with dump trucks and bulldozers and ship them off in "scoops."

While all of the footage and futuristic illusions were born of early 1970s cinematic imagination, some of the technological advances are surprisingly familiar. The video game Shirl is playing when we first see her looks remarkably like the Asteroid game Atari would introduce in 1979.

While we don't have government-sponsored euthanasia clinics, the immersive cinema of the 20-minute nature video Sol drifts off to before being ground up in Soylent Green can be had today in HD, 3D, and 5G. Immersive cinema has gotten smaller, not bigger. The earth, however, still turns on its own axis.

The scene where Tim Van Patten's character walks Robinson off to his final resting place was the very last scene the legendary actor would ever shoot. He died hours after filming it, according to Patten, of bladder cancer, age 79. His greatest regret was the loss of the world's natural beauty.

Long shots and aerial views in **Soylent Green** show a dense cover of smog, burning ash, and other visible airborne contaminants as Hollywood lost its golden sheen in the '70s. Fifty years later, the U.S. still gets more than 80 percent of its energy from fossil fuels, and on a clear day, you can see there have been less clear days. In the movie, smoke from forest fires is visible from miles away. The footage from 1973 echoes news clips we currently see every year as fires burn longer and larger in the American west. Science is still ignored. Conglomerates still profit from banking on the promise of soot yet to come.

At the start of the murder investigation in the film, Heston's detective comes across the top-secret *"Soylent Oceanographic Survey Report: 2015 to 2019,"* which finds the oceans are dying. This is the reason Soylent steaks are branded with new colors. The main ingredient of Soylent Green is plankton, just like Mr. Krabs' Krabby Patties on SpongeBob SquarePants. This is sadly coming to pass. Acidification in the ocean is endangering plankton, putting all fish life in peril.

The ominous words "*Soylent Green*" have appeared on the menu in The Simpsons, Family Guy, and South Park. It has become synonymous with the darkest solution to world hunger, in a world which averted the most dire predictions. This is because the prognosticators behind **Soylent Green** did not take into account the tech boom, and other advances.

A software engineer named Rob Rhinehart did indeed invent a protein bar called Soylent in 2013, but it didn't have the green. It was taken off the market three years later. Agricultural technology will make mass-produced lab-grown food available within a generation. It is important to note, however, that while the world has become politically cannibalistic, there are no government-sponsored human meat rendering plants currently waiting for suicidal volunteers.

But it's 2022, where can I get **Soylent Green** now?

Believe it or not, a version of **Soylent Green** is readily available. You can get **Soylent Green** at D'Agostino or Whole Foods. Harrison's book describes Soylent steaks as a meat substitute made from soy and lentils. This has not only become true blue American cuisine, it is a burgeoning business. The organic food market yields $61 billion in green every year, and with high-tech domestic vegetable gardens available to order online, you can make Soylent Green at home. You might not want to call it that though. People will think it is people, and people who eat people are not the luckiest people in the world.

Soylent, produced by Soylent Nutrition, Inc., is an American company that produces meal replacement products in powder, shake, and bar forms. The company was founded in 2013 and is headquartered in Los Angeles, California. Originally sold exclusively online in the United States, Soylent has expanded distribution to stores, such as CVS Pharmacy, 7-Eleven, Walgreens, Kroger, Target, and Walmart, and is available in Canada.

Soylent is named after a food in **Make Room! Make Room!**, a dystopian science fiction novel (which was the basis of the movie

Soylent Green) that explores themes of population growth and limited resources. Founder Rob Rhinehart promoted the product as part of global food security and providing a cheap means to consume necessary calories.

The company developed a following initially in Silicon Valley and received early financial backing from GV, the investment arm of Alphabet, Inc., and venture capital firm Andreessen Horowitz. In 2021, the company announced it had become profitable starting in 2020.

History

A Soylent package, along with the powder and resulting drink

In January 2013, American software engineer Rob Rhinehart purchased 35 chemical ingredients—including potassium gluconate, calcium carbonate, monosodium phosphate, maltodextrin, olive oil—all of which he deemed to be necessary for survival, based on his readings of biochemistry textbooks and U.S. government websites. Rhinehart used to view food as a time-consuming hassle and had resolved to treat it as an engineering problem. He blended the ingredients with water and consumed only this drink for the next thirty days. Over the course of the next two months, he adjusted the proportions of the ingredients to counter various health issues and further refined the formula. Rhinehart claimed a host of health benefits from the drink and noted that it had greatly reduced his monthly food bill, which fell from about US$470 to $155, and the time spent behind the preparation and consumption of food while providing him greater control over his nutrition.

Rhinehart's blog posts about his experiment attracted attention on Hacker News, eventually leading to a crowdfunding campaign on Tilt that raised about $1.5 million in preorders aimed at moving the powdered drink from concept into production. Media reports detailed how operations began for Soylent Nutrition, Inc. in April 2014, using a relatively small $500 system to ship the first $2.6 million worth of product. In January 2015, Soylent received $20 million in Series A round funding, led by venture capital firm Andreessen Horowitz.

Soylent is named after a food in Harry Harrison's 1966 science fiction novel Make Room! Make Room! In the novel, most types of soylent are made from soy and lentils, hence the name of the product, a combination of "soy" and "lent". The word also evokes the 1973 film adaptation **Soylent Green**, in which the eponymous food is made from human remains. Rhinehart also says he chose the name, with its morbid associations, to pique curiosity and deeper investigation, since the name was clearly not chosen with a traditionally "flashy" marketing scheme in mind.

Distribution

Soylent was only available for purchase and shipment within the United States until June 15, 2015, when the shipping to Canada began. In October 2017, Canada disallowed further shipments of Soylent due to a failure to meet Canadian food regulations on meal replacements. Shipments to Canada resumed in 2020.

In July 2017, Soylent was sold offline for the first time at 7-Eleven stores in and around Los Angeles. By April 2018, Soylent was sold in over 8,000 U.S. 7-Elevens and was available at Walmart, Target, Kroger, and Meijer.

Health effects

The makers of Soylent claim it contains the nutrients necessary for a healthy lifestyle.

Some people have experienced gastrointestinal problems from consumption of Soylent, particularly flatulence.

Lead and cadmium content

On August 13, 2015, As You Sow filed a notice of intent to pursue a lawsuit against the makers of Soylent, claiming that Soylent was in breach of California's Proposition 65 for not adequately labelling its product given the levels of lead and cadmium present in the drink.[citation needed] Although Soylent contains levels of lead and cadmium far below the national safety levels set by the FDA, it does contain 12 to 25 times the level of lead and 4 times the level of cadmium permitted in California without additional labeling. A lawyer who has worked on settlements of Proposition 65 suits described the case as "*alarmist*", as the levels are well below FDA limits of what is allowed in food products. However, as Soylent is marketed as a complete meal replacement, many customers consume the drinks three times a day, equating to 36 to 75 times the lead and 12 times the level of cadmium without the Prop 65 label.

Soylent's website displays the Proposition 65 warning required by California. Soylent Nutrition, Inc. published the position that the levels of heavy metal content in Soylent "*are in no way toxic, and Soylent remains completely safe and nutritious*". Soylent Nutrition, Inc. also published an infographic and spreadsheet based on an FDA study of heavy metal content in common foods, comparing two selected example meals to servings of Soylent with a similar amount of caloric intake. Both of the company's chosen comparison meals include high levels of cadmium and arsenic, along with levels of lead similar to those of Soylent; although one of them includes tuna and the other includes salmon, providing over 97% of the arsenic in each proposed meal, with spinach providing 74% of the cadmium in the higher-cadmium meal and fruit cocktail providing 71% of the lead in the higher-lead meal.

Product recalls

In 2016, the company announced it would halt sales of the Soylent Bar due to reports of gastrointestinal illness, including nausea, vomiting, and diarrhea. The company asked customers to discard any unconsumed bars and said it would offer full refunds. On October 21, 2016, the company triggered a product recall.

On October 27, 2016, the company also halted sales of Soylent Powder. The company said tests on the bar had not shown contamination but also said that some powder users had reported stomach-related symptoms from consuming the powder.

The company initially suspected soy or sucralose intolerance. However, on November 7, 2016, Soylent instead blamed algal flour for making people sick and said it planned to remove algal flour from future formulations of the powders and bars, which it did in the next formulation version 1.7 introduced on December 15, 2016. The drink-based products use algal oil, not algal flour, so were deemed to be safe for users.

Resources

cosmopolitan.com, "The Top 10 Superfoods of 2022 Have Officially Been Announced." By Olivia Wagner; everydayhealth.com, "15 Superfoods and the Scientific Reasons to Eat Them: 'Superfood' is a marketing term, and in reality, the best diet is one that is balanced. But some foods stand out more than others for their sterling nutritional profile." By Anna Brooks; medicalnewstoday.com, "What are superfoods and why should you eat them?" By Natalie Olsen and Megan Ware; denofgeek.com, "Soylent Green Predicted 2022, Including Impossible Meat Substitutes: Charlton Heston paid for a cannibalistic cautionary tale set in 2022 with Soylent Green, now we can get fries with it." By Tony Sokol; en.wikipedia.org, "Soylent (meal replacement)." By Wikipedia Editors;

Chapter Twenty-Five–
Population Control

Population Control

Population control is a policy of attempting to limit the growth in numbers of a population, esp in poor or densely populated parts of the world, by programs of contraception or sterilization.

The dangers of overpopulation cannot be exaggerated, because it amplifies all other problems. Being human-made, it lacks the checks and balances of the natural world to prevent its occurrence in this extreme form.

Concern as to human overpopulation is nothing new. Thomas Malthus' An Essay on the Principle of Population was first published in 1798 and went on to five further editions over the next thirty years. Despite his name, Malthus was a rural English clergyman. The publication of The Message coincided with the 250th Anniversary of his birth.

Although there have been a number of other, mainly scholarly, works on overpopulation since then the most significant recent contribution is probably The Population Bomb by Professor Paul Ehrlich (1968). This attracted heavy criticism for its, as it transpired, inaccurate prediction that hundreds of millions would die in the 1970s and 1980s through starvation due to overpopulation problems. The fact is that when Ehrlich wrote The Population Bomb in 1968 the human population was still under 4 billion and has nearly doubled since then.

It is arguable that Ehrlich's prediction only proved wrong because he underestimated the extent man could and would go to provide not just the extra food, but also all the other things necessary to support an ever increasing population.

This has been achieved by clearing more and more wild and forested areas (particularly tropical rain forests) for intensive agriculture; the ceaseless use of pesticides, artificial fertilizers and genetic engineering; and the plundering and industrialisation of the planet. 'The Message' is that it is the damage inflicted on our planet, a direct result of overpopulation, which is now the real and overwhelming threat to humans.

Over the years, a number of authors have used fiction to draw attention to social or political issues we would all prefer to ignore. Examples would be Oliver Twist, Uncle Tom's Cabin, Hard Times, The Grapes of Wrath, To Kill A Mockingbird, as well as Animal Farm.

"Two hundred years ago there were just one billion of us. Fifty years ago it was three billion. Now it's seven billion. If we go on like this there will be eleven billion of us within fifty years."

In The Message, Yan Vana cleverly uses a mix of fantasy and science fiction to make an otherwise unwelcome message palatable. Whether you agree with it or not, the message it is conveying will be clear to any reader without the need for explanation. In many ways, it can be said to combine some of the allegorical format of Orwell's Animal Farm with his grim factual reporting in A Road To Wigan Pier and the dystopian nature of his 1984.

It is arguable that, underneath the science fiction and fantasy, The Message is a serious philosophical study of the relationship between man and the rest of nature.

It questions many preconceived beliefs; in particular that technological advancement is a sign of superiority rather than simply an acceptance that, from an evolutionary standpoint, man is physically backward and has to rely on tools to do things which other species, ones we regard as inferior, can do naturally.

That is not to say that the plot is merely a platform for an undisguised moral message about overpopulation problems. To many it will also be a sad and moving love story, to some a study of humanity and for others a perspective view of twenty-first century environmental regulation.

It could be said that Malthus was warning what could happen as a result of human overpopulation, Ehrlich was predicting what was about to happen and Vana is telling us what is already happening.

Overpopulation has become a scientific fact

It exists when too many members of a species must compete for limited resources. We have reached that stage. Scientists have measured the impact that we are making on our planet. This measurement is called an ecological footprint. One footprint per person is sustainable, more are destructive. Our global average is more than 1.7, so at least 70% above sustainability.

Apologists for unlimited growth are quick to point out that there are flaws in the measurements. There undoubtedly are. But so far it is the best we have and serious critics nearly all agree that the present system underestimates rather than overestimates the size of our footprint. Besides this does not matter at all for comparisons of national footprints because any margin of error would be the same for all.

This means that to stay at our present level of development we would have to reduce the human population by more than one third or drastically reduce our standard of living. Both options are possible but extremely unlikely. That means that we are heading for steadily growing disasters, as more and more people consume steadily dwindling resources.

How excessive our numbers really are becomes clear when we examine how many people could survive in their natural state of hunter gatherers, something that might very well happen when we run out of the resources needed to maintain our high-tech society. Experts have calculated that in its present condition earth would not be able to sustain more than 300 million people, perhaps much less and that is a terrifying thought, bearing in mind that our current way of life is unsustainable. It took humanity 200,000 years to reach one billion and only 200 years to reach seven billion. We are still adding an extra 80 million each year and are headed towards 10 billion by mid-century.

"*It's coming home to roost over the next 50 years or so. It's not just climate change; it's sheer space, places to grow food for this enormous horde. Either we limit our population growth or the natural world will do it for us, and the natural world is doing it for us right now.*" "*All our environmental problems become easier to solve with fewer people, and harder — and ultimately impossible — to solve with ever more people."*

David Attenborough

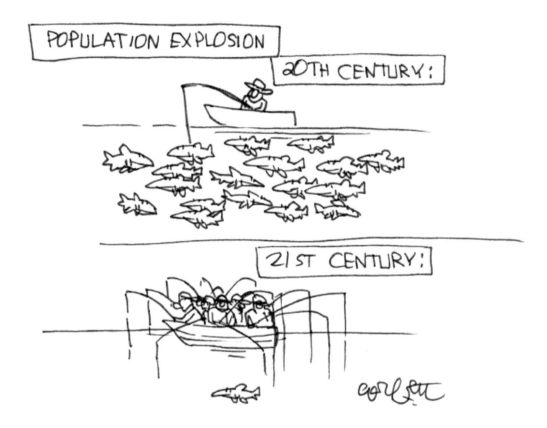

WE HAVE TO ADDRESS OVERPOPULATION

More people inevitably put more demands on the planet. More people require more food, water, sanitation, homes, public services, and amenities – but our Earth is struggling to cope. Populations of wild species have plummeted, global temperatures are rising, our seas are full of plastic and forests are disappearing.

Humans are directly responsible for the sixth mass extinction and the climate crisis, the most serious environmental threats our planet has ever faced.

In the rich world, we consume at astronomical and unsustainable levels. That cannot continue, and we must change our behaviour. Today, a child born in the US will produce 24 times more consumption carbon emissions per year than one born in Nigeria.

Addressing how people consume is not enough, however. We are already using the resources of more than one-and-a-half planets. Everyone has the right to a good quality of life and with increasing global affluence, the collective impact of billions more of us will increase even further. This is why we cannot ignore population.

TOGETHER, WE CAN DO SOMETHING ABOUT IT

The UN's projections show that very small changes in the size of families across the globe make an enormous difference - between a population of 7 billion and an unthinkable 16 billion by the end of the century.

We can achieve a sustainable global population when communities, governments and organisations take action to enable people to choose smaller families through women's empowerment and easy access to high quality education and family planning. By doing so, we can ensure that, in the future, everyone can have a decent standard of living on a healthy planet.

Here is what Jordan Peterson and Elon Musk have said so far:

"The idea of overpopulation kicked in in the 1960s, there were dire predictions for the year 2,000. Those were absolutely wrong. What happened was that everyone got way richer and the bottom section of the population got lifted out of poverty."

"There's going to be a terrible shortage of young people...there is nothing more implicitly genocidal than the idea that the planet has too many people on it. I've seen people shaming others out of having children. It's unbelievable."

— Jordan Peterson

"We need to watch out for population collapse. Some people think that the world has too many humans—but that's just because they live in a city. All humans on earth could fit in the city of New York on one floor. It's not exactly a secret, low birth rates and population collapse are a big risk. This is not a good way to end."

— Elon Musk

We've worried about overpopulation for centuries. And we've always been wrong.

Earth's population trends, explained.

For nearly all of human history, there haven't been that many of us. Around the year zero, Earth's population is estimated to have been 190 million. A thousand years later, it was probably around 250 million.

Then the Industrial Revolution happened, and human population went into overdrive. It took hundreds of thousands of years for humans to hit the 1 billion mark, in 1800. We added the next billion by 1928. In 1960, we hit 3 billion. In 1975, 4 billion.

That sounds like the route to an overpopulation apocalypse, right? To many midcentury demographers, futurists, and science fiction writers, it certainly predicted one. Extending the timeline, they saw a nightmarish future ahead for humanity: human civilizations constantly on the brink of starvation, desperately crowded under horrendous conditions, draconian population control laws imposed worldwide.

Stanford biologist Paul Ehrlich wrote in his best-selling 1968 book The Population Bomb, *"In the 1970's, hundreds of millions of people will starve to death"* because of overpopulation. (Later editions modified the sentence to read *"In the 1980's."*)

None of that ever came to pass.

The world we live in now, despite approaching a population of nearly 8 billion, looks almost nothing like the one doomsayers were anticipating. Starting in the 19th century in Britain and reaching most of the world by the end of the 20th century, birthrates plummeted — mostly because of women's education and access to contraception, not draconian population laws.

In wealthy societies where women have opportunities outside the home, the average family size is small; in fact, it's below replacement level (that is, on average, each set of two parents has fewer than two children, so the population shrinks over time). Called the demographic transition, it is one of the most important phenomena for understanding trends in global development.

There's still significant debate among population researchers about the extent of the sea change in population trends. Researchers disagree on whether global populations are currently on track to start declining by midcentury. There's also disagreement on what the ideal global population figure would be, or whether it's morally acceptable to aim for such a figure.

While academic research seeks to nail down these questions, it's important to be clear what is consensus among researchers. All around the world, birthrates are declining rapidly. Global population growth has been slowing since the 1960s, and global population will almost certainly start to decline. The world is absolutely not, as is sometimes claimed, on track to have 14 billion people by 2100.

Our projections around population are used to make global health and development policy. They're critical for planning, especially about climate change. Fears of overpopulation sometimes turn into hostility to immigrants, those who choose to have large families, and countries in an earlier stage of their population transition. Having an informed conversation about population is crucial if we are to get humanity's future right.

How we figure out population trends

There are about 7.7 billion people alive today. But that number's not as certain as you might think.

To understand why, you just have to think about the US census. The federal government is mandated by the Constitution to conduct a count of its population every 10 years. It is a big, industrialized country with modern technology and lots of resources. In 2010, it is estimated that our count of our nation of 300 million-plus was off by only about 36,000 people — or only 0.01 percent. That's pretty good (if researchers' estimate of the errors is reliable)! But that decent overall count masks some bigger errors: The same analysis estimates the black population was undercounted by 2 percent.

In many parts of the world, population data is much less reliable. Countries can have incentives both to overcount (in regions vying to demonstrate increased need for aid, say) and undercount their populations (perhaps to disfavor a disliked minority group). Even without any efforts to manipulate the numbers, it's expensive and challenging to accurately estimate populations.

If estimating populations is hard, estimating population trends is much harder. The demographers who estimated a ruinous, extremely fast growth trajectory were wrong, but how could they have known that the trend they were observing was about to reverse?

Today, it's still challenging to confidently estimate population sizes. But some organizations and institutions have done surprisingly well.

The United Nations publishes an estimate annually of the most likely population trend and then "high" and "low" fertility scenarios. These reports have turned out to be surprisingly accurate.

Since the UN has been making population projections since 1950, and since it publishes revisions and corrections to those projections over time, we can compare its initial estimates to the revisions and corrections. Researcher Nico Keilman did that, and found that the UN has an impressively accurate track record at population predictions. Their estimates of world population by 1990, published in 1950, were off by about 12 percent.

They quickly got better: By 1960, those estimates were off by only about 2 percent. Since then, the UN has pegged global population growth rates pretty precisely. Here's a graph of real population growth over time, compared to population growth as the UN projected it:

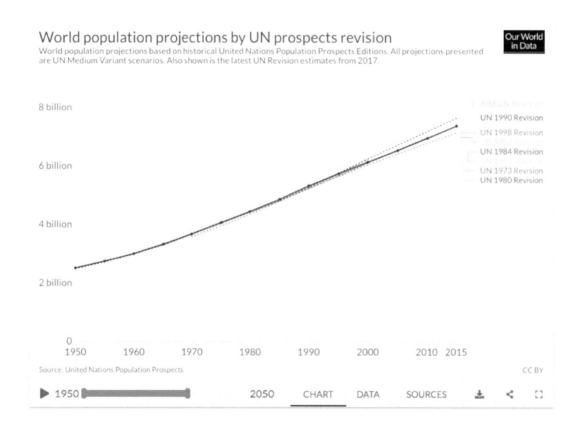

So up to the present day, the UN has been highly reliable in predicting global population trends. Its prediction now is that the world population will continue to increase until 2100, when it will peak at 11.2 billion and then start declining.

Some experts don't buy the UN's estimates

Nonetheless, they have their critics. Other analysts have argued that fertility will in fact fall more dramatically than the UN estimates even in its "low-fertility scenarios." One such critic is Norwegian academic Jorgan Randers, who studies climate strategy. "The world population will never reach nine billion people," he has claimed. "It will peak at 8 billion in 2040, and then decline."

Demographers at Vienna's International Institute for Applied Systems Analysis agree: They've estimated the population will stabilize by midcentury and then decline. These models expect fertility in low-income countries to fall faster than the UN projects it will.

Some of the differences are simply methodological. How the fastest-growing countries in the world are modeled has a huge impact on how global population models come out overall, so small differences in expectations in those countries can significantly shift overall results.

But much of the difference in projections may be rooted in disagreement over another question: how many people the world can handle. Adherents to lower-population models often call the UN projections "apocalyptic" — fearing that they'd make climate change impossible to manage. Demographer Wolfram Lutz has characterized the UN's model as the "population explosion" model (even though it projects a leveling off and declining population). Many of them have turned away from what they perceive as excessively "pessimistic" models toward ones that project a much faster-declining human population.

The challenges the pessimists anticipate aren't imaginary. With our current technology, of course, we don't know how to provide 11 billion people a good standard of living sustainably. But technology — including green and sustainable technology — has been rapidly improving for a long time. The year 2100 is more than 80 years from now, and almost all the technology that we have today to make civilization sustainable sounded like wild science fiction 80 years ago.

A global population peaking at 11 billion need not be an apocalypse or cause for pessimism, but it does pose challenges that we'll need to rise to.

While the UN deserves a lot of credit for how accurate they've been so far, past performance is obviously no guarantee of future accuracy. There's room for their estimates to be importantly wrong in the future — in either direction.

It's fairly straightforward to accurately predict the population in 20 years just by assuming that existing trends will continue. It's much harder to predict sea changes in habits around the world. If, for example, climate change drives currently developed countries back into poverty and drives their birthrates back up, the estimates are poorly equipped to account for that. On the other hand, if more reliable contraceptives are developed and virtually end unintended pregnancies the world over, birthrates could fall much faster than predicted.

Nonetheless, this disagreement obscures a lot of agreement. Randers might call the UN estimates "apocalyptic," but they're incredibly optimistic compared to estimates at midcentury. Everyone now agrees that without any totalitarian or coercive measures, populations will start declining; the big disagreement is simply when.

It was not at all obvious that the world would turn out this way, and it's tremendously significant that it has. It implies both good things — that coercive population controls will never be necessary — and concerning ones, like that societies will age and have a shrinking workforce. But on the whole, we are much better positioned for sustainable growth than it looked in 1950, and the fall in rich-country birthrates is why.

Demographic transition, explained

The big thing we know now about population that was unclear in the mid-20th century is something called the *"demographic transition."* In its simplest form, it's the principle that when societies get wealthy and child mortality falls, people tend to start having less children.

The connection between societies growing wealthier and people desiring smaller families is pretty straightforward. In richer societies, people do not need their kids to do labor and support the family, and they typically invest money and other resources in their kids, to give them the best shot possible at a decent life.

The connection between drops in child mortality and smaller desired family sizes is less obvious. Indeed, at first, when child mortality falls, the population shoots up, as people are still having lots of kids, but more of them survive to adulthood.

That produces a rapid increase in population. That was the state of the world in the 1960s, and some parts of the world are still in that state now. But then, overall growth rates started to fall.

Let's pull back here and get into the weeds a bit. Demographers think of this process as occurring in five stages. First, birthrates are high but so are death rates, and the population is low but stable (when child mortality is high, people have lots of children to reduce uncertainty). Then, in the second stage, technology helps more kids survive to adulthood. Birthrates remain high, and the population grows rapidly: for one or two generations.

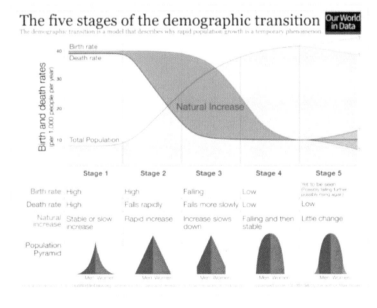

In the third stage, birthrates start to decline, driven by increased certainty about children's survival, women's rights, the dynamics of rich economies (where children are no longer an economic asset), and other factors. In the fourth stage, birthrates fall and the population stabilizes.

It's a little unclear where we'll go from there (in the fifth stage): Populations might shrink due to below-replacement reproduction, or stabilize, or slowly grow.

What does this demographic transition look like in action? In the US in 1900, the average woman had 3.85 children, and 0.89 children died before age 5 (the child mortality rate was 20 percent), leaving three surviving children on average. Today, the average woman has 1.9 children, with an 0.7 percent child mortality rate.

People used to think that ending child mortality would lead to a dramatic swell in global populations, and it does, in Stage 2 of the above chart, where death rates fall and birthrates remain high. But then in every country yet studied, birthrates eventually end up falling too.

Some of the best research into the demographic transition was published in 1989 by British researchers Anthony Wrigley and Roger Schofield. As the first country to have the Industrial Revolution, Britain was the first to have the demographic transition. Thanks to the state church, Britain also had unusually good birth and death records.

Here's how the demographic transition looked in Britain:

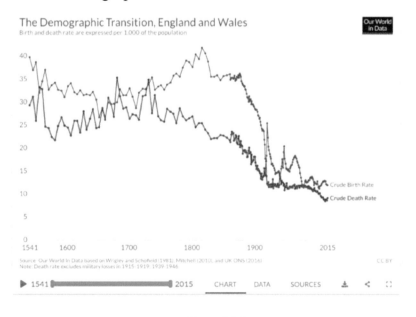

Today, most developed countries have joined Britain on the right end of that graph, with low birthrates and low death rates. Other countries, like Niger and Mali, are still in the middle stage, where death rates are falling but birthrates haven't yet followed suit.

That adds up to an overall global trend of a population that is still increasing, but it is increasing more slowly than ever.

It's a reality that hasn't quite penetrated public consciousness yet. Public conversations are often still consumed by fear that the population is spiraling beyond what the world can support.

The popular 2013 environmentalist book Ten Billion reports still-growing population numbers without discussing the underlying trends towards leveling off and then falling, and concludes, "Every which way you look at it, a planet of 10 billion looks like a nightmare." Widely published excerpts don't mention that the population is expected to start falling again either before or shortly after that "nightmare" milestone is reached.

Articles about population growth sometimes mention when we're expected to hit 9 billion or 10 billion, and then ask, "So is it time for all countries to turn to drastic population control in order to sustain life on Earth, or is it a violation of human rights, no matter what?" without mentioning that populations are expected to decline on their own, no coercion required.

It's a fear that sometimes has racial and xenophobic components: European white nationalists spread panic over declining white birthrates, while others express fears that poor populations, still growing, will crowd out rich ones. But birthrates are declining in poor countries, too, and look likely to continue to do so as they rapidly get richer. The trend that reached Europe first has since swept the rest of the world and shows no signs of stopping.

Calls to have few or no children to fight climate change are common, with prominent figures such as Miley Cyrus and Prince Harry endorsing them. The underlying assumption is often that we're on a runaway path to an exploding population. This misses a couple of key facts about population trends: First, the population will decline even if everyone who wants children has them.

Second, opposing children is not a good way to fight climate change. As Lyman Stone wrote for Vox, big changes in how the developed world produces power are what's needed, and they matter dramatically more than population does. "Lowering US carbon intensity by about a third, to around the level of manufacturing-superpower Germany today, has a bigger effect than preventing 100 million Americans from existing," Stone argued.

In other words, if we don't transition to better energy sources, we're doomed no matter how much we shrink our numbers, and if we do, we could actually sustain a significantly increased population.

What we think we know about population growth in the upcoming century

There's a lot of agreement between the UN and its critics when it comes to population forecasts. Both sides agree that fertility rates fall as countries get richer, and that even the poorest countries in the world are rapidly getting richer. Both agree that population will peak, and then start to decline.

Both agree that we're not yet at the peak, but that the Earth's population will never again double, barring some dramatic technological or cultural shift that fundamentally changes how humans live. Under a wide range of estimates, birthrates will remain below replacement in rich countries, and poor countries will continue to get wealthier and to have fertility patterns that are more similar to those in wealthy countries.

As for their disagreements, they'll be resolved by the real-world data soon enough. For the UN's mainline estimate of how these trends will continue into the future, it assumes that these trends will continue at approximately the pace they've kept through the past several decades.

Here is the 2019 UN
opulation forecast:

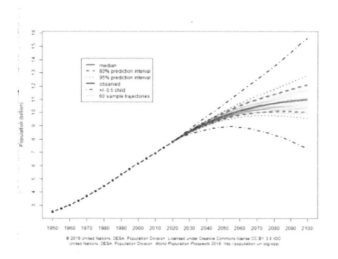

The red lines reflect the UN's predicted trajectories; the UN is 95 percent
confident that population will fall between the two dotted red lines. The
lower side of 95 percent confidence interval has global population peaking
in 2070 and falling slowly from there; the upper side has population
approaching 13 billion and still increasing in 2100.

The blue lines reflect the UN's projection of how population numbers
would shake out if birthrates were 0.5 children higher or lower. The total
global birthrate is 2.4 births per woman today. The lower blue line is
closest to the trajectory argued for by the European researchers who
consider the UN pessimistic; it shows population peaking around 2050
and falling from there.

Under the mainline UN estimates, global population will grow for the rest
of this century, but slowly, and this will be the last century with a growing
population. The UN has an impressive track record in this area, but some
European analysis groups think that the UN is estimating fertility that's
higher than realistic, and that population numbers will fall much sooner. It
should be clear by 2030 who is correct.

Conclusion

Rapid population growth in developing countries in the middle of the 20th century led to fears of a population explosion and motivated the inception of what effectively became a global population-control program. The initiative, propelled in its beginnings by intellectual elites in the United States, Sweden, and some developing countries, mobilized resources to enact policies aimed at reducing fertility by widening contraception provision and changing family-size norms. In the following five decades, fertility rates fell dramatically, with a majority of countries converging to a fertility rate just above two children per woman, despite large cross-country differences in economic variables such as GDP per capita, education levels, urbanization, and female labor force participation. The fast decline in fertility rates in developing economies stands in sharp contrast with the gradual decline experienced earlier by more mature economies. In this paper, we argue that population-control policies likely played a central role in the global decline in fertility rates in recent decades and can explain some patterns of that fertility decline that are not well accounted for by other socioeconomic factors.

Resources

aftermathmag.org, "Overpopulation has become a scientific fact."; yanvanathemessage.com, "HUMAN OVERPOPULATION."; populationmatters.org, "WHY POPULATION MATTERS."; vox.com, "We've worried about overpopulation for centuries. And we've always been wrong. Earth's population trends, explained." By Kelsey Piper

Part Four: Our Future

Chapter Twenty-Six--Where Does Our Future Lie?

Where does our future lie as a people: together or apart?

Rachel Clark considers the response to COVID-19 through the lens of collectivism and individualism and questions whether when this is all over we can be a more trusting nation.

I'm in the local park, running. My dog is with me, running, sniffing, and peeing. I hear a voice from halfway round the oval: "*You need a bag?*". I stop running momentarily, think, and call out my response: "*No thanks*". I continue running, and a couple of minutes later I'm parallel with the caller. She looks ready to speak. I continue to run; not a time to talk. As I pass her, she speaks loudly: "*You want a bag?*" "*No thanks*", I try to smile, running on. She continues, now at a yell: "*Good job you are doing the right thing then, using a dog bag for your dog*". She is now haranguing me. I continue running, affronted and confused in equal measure. Unfortunately for me this incident comes swiftly after another invasive dog-owner interrogation in the same park, only days earlier. I'm now thinking "don't we have more important things to worry about?"

And this gets to the nub of it all. The "*important things*" we are all trying to manage are beyond us individually, and collectively, and I sense that because of this, both of these encounters were about exerting individual control where they could. Not in my 17 years of being on this oval have I experienced what I now think was "*community policing*". And whilst not a terrible violation, it has shaken me because I sense an unravelling of the mores of our time; of trust in each other's actions being reasonable, safe, and ultimately pro-social. What was at play here, for me, was that I was not to be trusted.

When we need to trust each other – now more than ever – this is a huge, community-sized problem.

Thinking more deeply about my response, the news over recent weeks, and how COVID-19 has been managed in other countries around the world, I am drawn to an understanding of human actions based on the socio-political constructs of collectivism and individualism. For those of us who have worked in cross-cultural spaces, such notions hold insights into why people respond the way they do: people from broadly individualistic societies – Australia, The United States, Britain, to name a few – are socialised into desiring, and find in adulthood the perception that they do have, ultimate freedom of action. We are not used to the state announcing its presence – it is a fundamental tenet that we control the state, and not it us.

We are (generally) not monitored by state agencies, and when we are, we rebel against it. Back in 2015 there was civic opposition to the government's meta-data bill and further back, in 1986, of a proposed introduction of a national identity card – The Australia Card – which was subsequently defeated in the Senate.

Not so in societies where collectivism, in its different guises of communism, socialism, or more common today the developmental state, which guides rather than commands the forces of industry dominant party state capitalism, is the organising principle for human interaction; one where group needs are prioritised over those of individuals. This involves compromise and collective decision making at a family level, alongside technocratic and authoritarian style surveillance methods as a state response. This has been seen in action in various Asian countries through the use of mobile phones: China has an app called Health Code which collects personal health data, including user location and travel movements, whilst providing a personal colour coding from green to red to determine freedom of movement based on health status. South Korea has also been using a Singaporean developed app
called TraceTogether which shares information of people's movements

with other users.

Here in Australia, we may soon adopt similar tracing and monitoring methods using our personal devices in an attempt to reduce further community spread of COVID-19, despite our historical antithesis to such measures.

And we are seeing a community shift away from a tolerance and acceptance of individual freedom of movement and action, as witnessed in a huge uptake in community complaints – or *"community policing"* – through calls to the Covid-19 Hotline… and maybe my recent experiences in the park.

As I muse over all of these momentous changes over such a short time, including socialist-style provisions of state support to our citizens, I do wonder how Australia's cultural fabric will be changed as a result of these seismic societal shifts. Yes, we may have greater state intrusion into our personal lives in the name of our collective health. We may even see a radical alteration of the public-private healthcare landscape: a good thing in my book. We certainly will hold healthcare workers closer to our hearts and collective esteem. Wouldn't it also be magnificent if after all of this ceases, we truly recognize the heart of what I believe for us as people is critical: relationships built on trust.

For we truly are better together, when we connect on a human to human level, not based on where we live or how much we earn, but the *"staring into the eyes of another"* type connection that recognizes worth and strength and value and experience. Yes, we can do this as individuals, but I somehow feel that this misses the point. It is in a collective move towards really *"seeing"* each other for the gifts that we all can bring to the world regardless of economic background, ethnicity, age, gender, sexuality, health or disability, that provides us with a way forward.

Collectivist or individualist, countries worldwide fall somewhere along this continuum, with many influencing factors that means different societies operate as they do. Australia has a real chance at deciding how it wants to live, where it wants to inhabit on this continuum, in light of the

COVID-19 shakeup.

Do we really want to return to multimillionaires being rewarded further whilst many citizens can barely afford to pay rent each month?

Do we really want to return to valuing greed, over human need?

What if we returned to a community view of living which sees strength in many different human skills, and recognizes that we are only as strong as our weakest community members.

What if we were asked to consider our own personal needs less, and the needs of our collective communities, more?

Not only would we have flattened the curve, but also reduced the distance between those with more resources than any human ever needs, and those who have much less than any human deserves, in a fair society.

It's an inspiring thought that may just keep us all going, as we continue to live in isolation, for the collective good.

Does Our Future Lie in The Balance?

The greatest changes often take a leap of faith. A thinking that's outside the box.

When we learn, and encourage students to learn, in a regulated and regimented way, we tend to disregard thoughts that don't fit with mainstream thinking. We encourage the scientific investigation using the method, with its principles being laid down over 300 years ago, in the time of Isaac Newton. We use a standard model of enquiry, whereby we strengthen and build upon past endeavors. There is absolutely no doubt that both of these techniques have allowed us development to the lofty heights that we have so far reached. The lion's share of our progress in academic study and research has much to owe to these two techniques either separately or combined.

Yet some of the greatest leaps forward by mankind have demanded the use of something else, and possibly the ability to ignore or put aside conventional thought. Many of our greatest feats were brought about by accident: penicillin, x ray, microwaves – all of which came around when their inventors had their back turned and following conventional methods of scientific discovery.

Therefore there is a quandary. How do we both encourage the development of method and rigour, and yet still allow for the creative free-form thinking that is needed for the truly brilliant leaps forward?

It must start with our children. There is a real problem for both the individual and the wider world when we pigeon-hole ourselves and our students as either 'good at numbers' or 'creative'. We all know the children that seem to be brilliant at every subject at school, of course. But how much of this is down to raw talent and intelligence, and how much of it has perhaps been fostered and nurtured by parents and teachers alike? Some children will grow up to never have needed to question whether they are x, y, or z – they have been taught to believe that they in fact are capable in a huge variety of capacities. The creative and inventive exploration of thought must be given its space, and it may well come from the juxtaposition of the artistic and the scientific. We tend to split, divide and group people into simple sets but maybe we should encourage, as in a Venn diagram, the overlap of such traits. It is then we may encourage the thinker that does not limit themself to conventional or linear thought.

Why is it that we decide so early on that we are 'not creative' because our watercolor of the fruit bowl in art lessons went a little pear-shaped? Or that we are 'no good at numbers' because fractions got the better of us in maths? How sincere is it to grade a painting, the embodiment of individual expression, and how meaningful is it to dock marks in a maths paper because the child struggles to portray information in anything other than a pie chart? Is the information not still there, clear for us to understand?

Have we truly considered the longer-term impact this has on our students?

The dyslexic child with the brilliant communication skills may dream of becoming a University Lecturer, yet based on the constant poor grades they received for their inability to effectively communicate in the written format, the marking system of which is hugely inflexible, their confidence is destroyed, and they decide never to apply for the position for fear of marking and writing emails. Is it not time that we make adjustments from the beginning with our children, and maintain them in the adult world too? A typist is perfectly capable of transferring verbal speech to paper, after all, and is likely a worthy investment for a business in order to harness the talent of a brilliant and natural teacher.

We must foster both creative and regimented methods in every subject that we teach, and from the get go. This can be the only way to truly improve upon the world we see today, particularly when dealing with the bigger health, equality and environmental issues that threaten our existence today; these challenges need big, creative solutions, that must be managed rigorously and unerringly.

And of course it is not the teachers we take issue with here, but the system at large. To create the future that we need to survive the very real and very severe existential threats that humanity faces will require unique and 'unconventional' teaching methods to be brought into our classrooms. It is such a shame that, as it stands, any aspiration for rocking the educational boat may cost students their grades, and teachers their credibility.

The future lies in the past

To understand yourself and know your future better, a visit to your past self with all your early dreams, aspirations and motivators -is critical

Sometimes, in order to go ahead you need to take several steps backwards. Just as a tiger steps back and crouches to gather strength before making a giant leap, we need to be acquainted with our past and ourselves before making a leap of faith.

And since you need to lose some things in order to gain other, more precious treasures, it is critical to understand what is worth losing, and the risks that are worth taking. None of this is possible if we are uncertain about what we desire of life. In order to know that, we need to know ourselves and where we come from. Similarly, when we meet a stalemate in life, or a dead-end when we find no indication of where to go next, it helps to travel back in time to where we started off. It is there that we may find again what initially inspired and motivated us.

What was it that delighted you most in your young days? What dream gave you wings and lent stars to your eyes?

What angered you the most and made you want to lash back? And today - how far are you from those emotions, those motivators?

When I read Paulo Coelho's latest book, Adultery, I was disillusioned. But, not wanting to give up so easily on a writer who has captured the imagination of the world, I decided to visit his past, to go back to his first book, The Alchemist, in order to trace the genesis of the man and his thinking. And sure enough, it is there in the simplicity of the story and writing, and in the clarity of thinking, that I rediscovered the essential Coelho.

In The Alchemist, a crystal trader is watching life slip by in a deadening, repetitive pattern till Santiago reacquaints him with his first-ever dream, of becoming a rich businessman so that he can go on a holy pilgrimage to Mecca. This takes the man back in time to when dreams mattered and seemed real, and allows him to open his mind and heart to possibilities.And he is thus able to become a prosperous businessman - his initial aspiration! He is still not going to Mecca, but the dream of his youth has once again resurrected him.

Dreams and unfulfilled aspirations rooted in the past have that power.They keep you going. We all love to talk about what could have, but did not happen. Our regrets over unful filled dreams serve as a fuel to keep us going. The important thing is to remember the dreams. They connect our past to the present, and to a nebulous future. If you have fulfilled all dreams, met all aspirations, and have none other, what will hold you on to life?

The crystal trader confesses to Santiago that he will not really go to Mecca even if he can. "Because it is the thought of Mecca that keeps me alive... I'm afraid if my dream is realised, I'll have no reason to go on living!" He is scared to realise his dream.

Sometimes a connect with our own past and young dreams can be painful indeed, if we realise how far away we are from what we once considered an ideal life, and that brings about a certain restlessness that disturbs us. But that's no reason to lead half-lived lives.

Many people, especially those whose families relocated, have this deep desire to trace their roots and understand their origins. Placing yourself in the context of your origins helps give you an idea of who you are, which helps you understand the veracity and strength of your motivators, dreams and ambitions. Without knowing yourself, you cannot move ahead.

In order to build a worthwhile future, a visit to your past self is essential.

Welcome to 2030: Three visions of what the world could look like in ten years.

Pandemics have often proven turning points in history. The Black Death in the 1300s helped undermine feudalism, while some believe the Spanish flu tipped the balance in favor of the Allied cause in the final days of the First World War. Yet the current one has been less a disruptor than an accelerator of trends that were already fraying the fabric of the post-Cold War international system long before the outbreak of SARS-CoV-2.

Two grueling years into the pandemic, it feels like we've seen it all. But it may just be that we ain't seen nothing yet. Many of COVID-19's effects on twenty-first century human civilization, in fact, are not yet visible. Much of the non-Western world still awaits sufficient vaccines, and the fallout from pandemic-induced economic downturns will unfold over the course of years, just as the repercussions of the 2008 global financial crisis did. Meanwhile, Sino-US hostility exacerbated by the public-health crisis raises the specter of large-scale conflict after decades of relative peace among the world's most powerful states. Also suffering serious and hugely consequential setbacks: the march of globalization and the multilateralist architecture designed after World War II to maintain peace.

So what lies ahead? Well into the 2020s, COVID-19 will cast a long shadow over communities, workplaces, markets, battlefields, and negotiating rooms. But even as the centrifugal forces driving the world away from multilateralism and toward multipolarity accelerate, the future is not fixed. We humans have agency in shaping it.

Here, building on our work on strategic foresight and global trend analysis inside the US intelligence community and outside government, we envision three alternative worlds in 2030. The intention is not to predict what's coming next, but rather to highlight the factors that could lead the world in one direction or another—and thus provide insights that can spur strategists to prepare for possible challenges, plan for potential opportunities, and pursue a brighter future by making prudent decisions in the present. Instead of a crystal ball, what we offer are portals to different universes.

The scenarios in this ten-year forecast are informed by ten significant trends outlined below that are already transforming today's world and likely to shape the world a decade from now as well.

Ten trends shaping the current and future world

1. The Vaccine miracle--and cautionary message

The development of COVID-19 vaccines was remarkably rapid, with those most vulnerable to the virus in rich countries inoculated within a year of the pandemic breaking out. If vaccine development and distribution had been slower, the death toll from the disease would now be several times higher. The tragedy, however, is that poorer countries still lack enough vaccines; although a small majority of the world's population has now received at least one dose, coverage remains highly uneven; in Africa, for example, less than 12 percent of the population has received at least one dose as of December. The longer a substantial portion of the world's population remains unvaccinated, the higher the risk that more contagious variants like Delta and Omicron emerge.

Absent the vaccines, a much deeper global recession would have also ensued. Western countries would have gone into greater debt to cover health and unemployment costs, and struggled more to emerge from the crisis. The World Bank anticipates that economic growth in advanced economies will be almost twice as fast in 2021 as it was after the Great Recession. The fact that many Western policymakers were involved in or closely observed the response to the global financial crisis was an advantage: They pushed for higher stimulus than in 2008-09.

Will the current crisis yield similar wisdom for subsequent ones? The scale of this pandemic—only comparable to the Spanish flu a century ago—should not lull the world into thinking another one won't emerge in the near future. There is peril in wasting this opportunity to build more global resiliency, particularly for those without the means to weather such disasters. Will lessons be learned from the inequitable delivery of vaccines? Will the developing world gain the manufacturing capacity to ensure speedier distribution of vaccines next time? There should be no "losers" in a vaccine scramble. Yet who wants to bet that the developed world has learned this lesson—or that it grasps the long-term damage already done to its reputation in the rest of the world?

2. Technology's double-edged sword

If science came out of the pandemic a winner, technology was a close second. Without computers and connectivity, the lockdowns could have ground most economic activity to halt. Managers were surprised by the productivity of remote work. Some types of work, however, could not move online. Those in service jobs—including many ethnic and racial minorities—could not stay at home and were thus disproportionally affected by the COVID-19 crisis.

The future of work will be hybrid, with in-person and remote aspects. While telework has been around for decades, it took a transformative event to force the paradigm shift. To the extent that workers can benefit from a more flexible routine, this could be a positive development for keeping more people in the workforce—helping to persuade working mothers (who were disproportionately impacted by the economic fallout of the pandemic) to reenter and seniors to stay employed. But other challenges, including long-term job insecurity as automation progresses, will offer more tests but few easy solutions.

3. Here comes deglobalization

The developing world has lost many of the benefits of globalization—at least for the time being. A significant portion of the once-rising global middle class slid back into poverty as a result of the pandemic and its economic ramifications, reversing perhaps humanity's biggest achievement in recent decades. Without targeted policy interventions, the world is verging on return to a two-speed world of *"haves"* and *"have nots."* With the pandemic still raging in the developing world, the full extent of the damage to that new global middle class remains unknown. Some countries will gain strength from overcoming

Global exports of goods and services (% of global GDP)

The exports of goods and services as a percent of GDP are a good proxy for measuring trade openness and, with it, globalization. As the World Bank data shows, globalization has been stagnating since the end of the 2007-2008 financial crisis, prompting experts to warn of a "slowbalization" or even "deglobalization".

pandemic-related challenges, but the weakest will probably experience growing political instability and even state failure.

For many poor countries, recovery from the dislocations of deglobalization is further complicated by other challenges. The threat of food crises, for example, has increased for nations suffering endemic conflict plus the added strain of the pandemic and global economic slowdown. At least 155 million people in fifty-five countries and territories were estimated to be in danger of serious food deprivation or worse in 2020—an increase of around twenty million people since 2019—with catastrophic conditions in countries such as Afghanistan, Yemen, Burkina Faso, South Sudan, and the Democratic Republic of the Congo.

Another challenge in surmounting the consequences of deglobalization is climate change. Africa's gross domestic product, for example, could decline by 15 percent by 2030 as a result of climate-related disasters and spending on efforts to adapt to a warming world, according to the Economic Commission for Africa. African leaders aiming to overcome these challenges can look to trade and economic-reform opportunities. The African Continental Free Trade Area officially started trading on January 1, 2021, and estimates suggest that trade liberalization could increase African real income by $450 billion by 2035. Such a development could blunt the damage inflicted by COVID-19 and help boost the continent's post-pandemic economic recovery.

4. The deepening of domestic disorders

Today there is more inequality not just between developed and developing countries, but also within many of these countries themselves. This is the second major global economic crisis in a little more than a decade, battering those who had already suffered setbacks in establishing their careers or who had only recently picked up the pieces from the 2008 financial crisis. In the United States, for instance, many women left the workforce during the pandemic to take care of their kids when childcare centers closed and schools switched to remote learning, while ethnic and racial minorities have continued to suffer from higher unemployment than the working population as a whole.

In advanced economies, the relatively rapid recovery is a hopeful sign for those hurt economically by the pandemic. Yet the future of work will remain turbulent, particularly for the unskilled and semiskilled. The pandemic spurred employers in some industries to invest more in robotics and automation rather than recruiting and training workers. Even before the coronavirus crisis, in fact, there were numerous forecasts that greater automation was coming. That practice could now speed up, further increasing inequality and job insecurity.

Productivity growth and hourly compensation growth in the United States, 1948–2018

The Internet and social media—so vital in maintaining economic activity—have also unleashed forces that threaten democracy. On the one hand, new digital platforms support freedom of expression, offer new possibilities for democratic participation, and provide access to diverse information. For authoritarian leaders, the expansion of information and communications technology can be a menace in providing citizens with powerful tools to mobilize against the regime. On the other hand, new technology platforms give birth to information bubbles and polarization, increase the effectiveness of misinformation and disinformation, and promote a nonconsensual culture of debate. Hate speech and conspiracy theories pose an increasing danger to civic trust and democratic political order. In democracies, extremist and populist parties have been able to capitalize on these dynamics. These technologies also enable corporate and state entities to engage in potent new forms of surveillance and information manipulation.

Tech companies oppose government measures to address these concerns that go against their business models, while governments themselves worry about the impacts of such measures on innovation and national competitiveness. With more regulations increasingly likely in Western countries to guard against harm to children and better protect privacy, the burning question is how to balance these potentially conflicting objectives.

5. Meet the New World Order 2.0

The pandemic could have been a catalyst for a rebirth in global cooperation, but instead it revealed just how frayed the world's multilateral structures are. This largely proved to be a time for the nation-state to take charge, as countries closed borders, instituted lockdowns, and looked after their own interests.

Given how much mutual distrust the pandemic has sowed between China and the West, it will be hard for them to reach consensus on reforming the World Health Organization. That same distrust is evident in other international institutions. The United Nations Security Council has been paralyzed by Russia and China working together to wield their veto power. While the Biden administration has recommitted the United States to the Paris climate accord, it has yet to move ahead on an effort with European nations to reform the World Trade Organization, which is critical to the running of a rules-based trading system. We are living through an age of multipolarity without multilateralism.

Overall influence capacity of China and the United States, 1960-2020

Chinese influence has been increasing steadily around the world, at the same time as the United States' influence has been stagnant and even started declining in recent years.

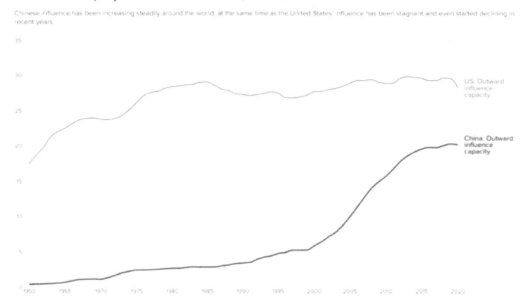

After the end of the Cold War, the George H.W. Bush administration talked about a *"new world order."* It envisioned a return to the original conception for a post-World War II multilateralist global order that never took shape due to divisions between the Soviet Union and United States. In such a world, so the thinking at the time went, countries would cooperate to solve common problems and strive for Western values such as democracy and liberal markets.

Three decades later, the pendulum has swung in the opposite direction. Sino-US tensions make military conflict between great powers conceivable again for the first time since the end of the Cold War. The Biden administration has chosen not to reverse or even temper the growing US hostility toward China that was a hallmark of the Trump administration. China, meanwhile, is rushing headlong to claim its perceived rights as a great power, determined to call into question any US pretense to unrivaled global leadership.

Just beneath the surface of US angst are fears of a world in which China displaces the United States as the dominant political and economic player.

Page 244

In the words of President Joe Biden, China has *"an overall goal to become the leading country in the world, the wealthiest country in the world, and the most powerful country in the world. That's not going to happen on my watch."*

China will probably overtake the United States later this decade or early in the next one to become the world's biggest economy as measured by market value. Most Europeans believe that China is already the dominant economic player, according to the Pew Research Center. But the US public is not ready to concede that preeminent position, which suggests that once the shift happens it will deal a psychological blow to Americans—having the effect of pulling the rug out from under the nation's *"exceptional"* destiny. Also striking in the Pew polling is that neither age nor political-party affiliation was a big factor in whether or not the American public had unfavorable views toward China, heightening the sense of a unified America engaged in a contest with China in which perceived defeat would be keenly felt. For Europeans who lost empires some time ago, the idea that the United States would be immune from relative economic decline seems unrealistic.

The United States and China may well find a pragmatic framework for cooperating on select mutual interests. Significant advances—the Helsinki Accords' human-rights agenda and arms-control agreements, for example—were made during the Cold War when it suited Washington and Moscow. One should not dismiss such possibilities. Yet the chances of US and Chinese leaders collaborating to build a more multilateralist world look dim, at least for the next decade.

Biden hopes to constitute a democratic order with US allies and partners, excluding China, Russia, and other authoritarian countries. On most global issues, this would be unworkable—and perhaps dangerous. The Versailles peace settlement after World War I ignored the Soviet Union and Germany, with disastrous consequences. No viable global order is possible without inclusion of all the major powers, including Russia and China.

China does not have any kind of multilateralist blueprint in mind for the global order and doesn't want Western-designed global institutions to set the rules for international relations. Chinese leaders know that the county's breakout as a global power on a par with the United States won't be frictionless. What China wants is a world that won't hinder its brand of state capitalism and authoritarian rule. As a rising power and former victim of colonial exploitation in the nineteenth and early twentieth centuries, China is sensitive to any perceived curbs on its sovereignty, believing that its great-power status gives it the right to regional, if not global, sway. Chinese leaders want to find ways to circumvent (and perhaps, over time, even supplant) the United States, which has used the web of multilateral institutions to anchor its global power.

6. Climate change: Where some Sino-US competition might actually be good

Even on issues like climate change, where China and the United States have obvious common interests, cooperation and competition will likely both occur. That may, in fact, be the best outcome.

Biden has talked about the United States producing the needed technology to fight climate change, yet as the Financial Times has noted China *"dominates the sourcing, production, and processing of key clean-energy minerals worldwide"* and is the global leader in clean-tech manufacturing. It controls around 70 percent of lithium-ion battery metals and processing along with 90 percent of the rare-earth elements used in high-tech weapons systems and offshore wind turbines, while making three-quarters of the planet's solar panels, according to the paper. If the United States deploys tariffs or sanctions against China's climate-related technology in a similar manner to how it has tried to combat the Chinese telecommunications company Huawei, then the global fight against climate change will suffer. At the same time, China is an egregious emitter of greenhouse gases and is having difficulty weaning itself off coal, despite its promises to do so. For all developing states, including China and India, the choice between growth fueled by cheap, dirty fuels and more expensive green-energy sources is a challenging one. The United States and European Union will need to use carrots and sticks to get China, other developing countries, and perhaps even some allied advanced economies like Australia to cut back on dirty fuels if the world is to achieve and accelerate its timetable for a carbon-neutral world.

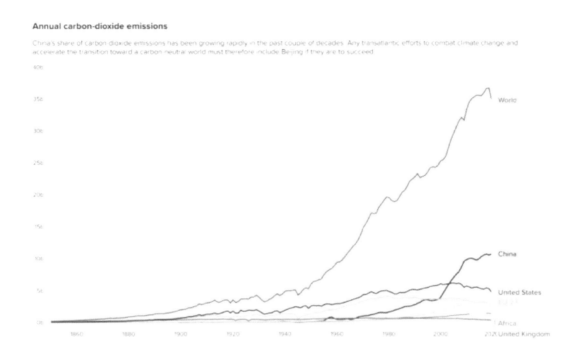

Annual carbon-dioxide emissions

China's share of carbon dioxide emissions has been growing rapidly in the past couple of decades. Any transatlantic efforts to combat climate change and accelerate the transition toward a carbon-neutral world must therefore include Beijing if they are to succeed.

Climate change is too important a global concern to be endangered by Sino-US competition, but it would be naïve to think that neither side will seize on the issue to gain advantage over the other. Some horse-trading between Beijing and Washington will inevitably have to happen if they are to reach their climate goals. Sino-US competition over which country is the global leader in the climate-change fight might even be a good thing as long as the rivalry stays does not swerve into military conflict.

7. A middle-power balancing act against a bipolar world

While the Sino-US relationship looms ever larger over the future of international relations, middle powers have nevertheless found ways to play critical roles (for good or ill) in a world in which power continues to diffuse. Despite the many predictions of its arrival, ours is not a bipolar world—not yet, at least. Even Asian nations that are highly dependent on China economically are hedging their bets, as many expand their security cooperation with the United States. European allies share US concerns about Chinese intellectual-property theft, forced technology transfers, and takeovers of businesses in strategic sectors with sensitive technologies. But they still want to cooperate with Beijing—not just compete—and are opposed to any economic decoupling between the West and China. These Asian and European partners seek to head off a military conflict between the United States and China, which could destroy the global system. They are pursuing their policy agendas independently of Washington and Beijing.

For the United States, this state of affairs has benefits and drawbacks. While Washington can't assume its allies and partners will automatically fall in line with its agenda, those allies and partners can take the lead on common objectives when the United States becomes preoccupied elsewhere. The European Union and Japan, for instance, sought to keep the flame of free trade alive when the United States disengaged from that effort during the Trump years. In just four years, the EU negotiated major trade deals with Japan and South Korea, reaching additional agreements with Canada, Singapore, Vietnam, and China. Japan's former Prime Minister Shinzo Abe didn't let the idea of the Trans-Pacific Partnership idea die when Donald Trump pulled the United States out of the trade agreement, remaking it as the Comprehensive and Progressive Agreement for Trans-Pacific Partnership (CPTPP) in hopes of getting a post-Trump America to join. Japan also joined the Regional Comprehensive Economic Partnership (RCEP). Other major Asian economies, including Australia, New Zealand, and Singapore, signed onto both CPTPP and RCEP.

8. Europe's quest for strategic autonomy

While *"strategic autonomy"* has long been a goal for many Europeans, the Trump presidency and the contempt that the former administration showed America's allies inspired a revival of European interest in being independent—not just from the United States but increasingly from the growing power of China as well. Protecting the European Union's digital sovereignty by enforcing regulatory standards on foreign tech companies operating in Europe has turned out to be one of the more promising ways for Europe to augment its strategic autonomy. Lacking tech behemoths comparable to those in the United States and China, the EU has aimed to use its power as one of the world's largest marketplaces to set regulatory standards for the rest of the planet. Brussels has spearheaded data-privacy protocols for the Internet, which have already influenced privacy standards or laws instituted by California and China. It is now trying to establish standards on artificial intelligence (AI). Along with trade deals, these efforts have boosted the EU's economic weight.

In the military realm, there have been renewed effort to develop a European defense identity alongside NATO. Without major new investments in defense, however, European leaders will still rely on the United States to deter Russia. Yet Europeans can take on more responsibility for other defensive tasks such as policing Europe's external borders for illegal migratory flows and criminal activity. Like the United States after its exit from Afghanistan, European governments are loath to engage in more nation-building. The reality is that EU member states would be dependent on Washington for intelligence and airlift capabilities even for a medium-scale intervention such as the counterterrorism mission that France is drawing down in the Sahel.

9. An emerging Asia-Pacific hedging strategy

Highly dependent on China as the economic motor for the region, some Asia-Pacific nations see the United States as a critical counterweight against Beijing. For them, Sino-US tensions escalating toward open conflict would be as alarming as a US exit from the region.

China's aggressiveness in recent years has revived and expanded the focus of the Quadrilateral Security Dialogue, or Quad, involving Australia, India, Japan, and the United States. While experts emphasize that the Quad is not an Asian NATO, US officials believe it can play an important coordinating role in diplomacy; maritime security; supply-chain security;

and technology design, development, governance, and use. The Quad, for example, recently set a joint goal of distributing one billion COVID-19 vaccine doses in Asia by the end of 2022. If and when that happens, such a provision of public goods would be hard for China to counter and represent a way for the United States and its partners to project leadership.

Collective efforts like these are necessary at a time when individually Asian countries are no match for Chinese power. That includes India, whose pandemic-pummeled economy, according to the Lowy Institute's Asia Power Index, is expected to be 13 percent smaller in 2030 than forecast prior to the COVID-19 outbreak—the only Indo-Pacific nation to suffer such a large economic setback. Even though India will eventually surpass China in gross domestic product, due to its still-burgeoning population, that moment is decades away. The Lowy Institute characterizes Japan as *the quintessential smart power*" in punching above its weight, but one that is nevertheless in decline. While others—such as Australia, Vietnam, and Taiwan—are gaining in power as measured by the index, none can hope to counter China alone. The United States still ranks as the preeminent power in the region but *registered the largest fall in relative power of any Indo–Pacific country in 2020,*" according to the Lowy Institute.

In an atmosphere in which neither of the superpowers has yet prevailed, the region's middle powers are better able to exert influence. While many Asian powers now appear more intent than they were in the past on countering an aggressive China, they worry that the United States will take an overly militarized approach to the endeavor. These nations would be apt to restrain Washington if the contest with Beijing heated up and risked breaking into open conflict.

10. The growing internationalization of conflict

The risk of conflict extends beyond growing Sino-US tensions. In today's multipolar order, governments see battlefields as fertile grounds to shape balances of power, advance their economic agendas, or aid parties to the conflict that are more aligned with their national-security interests.

Turkey, Russia, and Iran, for instance, are jockeying for expanded influence in such conflicts. In part because of this internationalization of intrastate conflicts, fighting is increasingly protracted, intense, and complex, to the detriment of civilians.

Battlefields are less traditional too. Since 2005, thirty-four states are believed to have sponsored cyber operations, with China, Russia, Iran, and North Korea thought to have instigated 77 percent of all suspected efforts. States can use cyberattacks both as an asymmetric tool to reduce a power imbalance in conventional military capabilities (e.g., North Korea), and as a symmetric one integrated across the entire spectrum of operations and domains (e.g., China). Whereas cyberattacks were previously mostly isolated incidents meant to disrupt particular systems, they are increasingly becoming a strategic tool. For example, the United States used offensive cyber operations to strike ISIS forces responsible for proselytizing, recruiting, and launching attacks.

Looking ahead, experts and policymakers alike are concerned that emerging technologies such as AI, biotechnology, and 5G, or new systems such as the Internet of Things (IoT) or cloud computing, will exacerbate Internet insecurity by revealing new vulnerabilities and providing additional tools to nefarious actors. For example, an Atlantic Council report considering alternative cyber futures mapped three potential universes: one in which cyber capabilities are mainstreamed and great-power competitors have the advantage; another in which the Internet is splintered across governmental, cultural, and business lines; and yet another in which new technologies such as AI lead to an arms race and generalized insecurity.

Three alternative worlds in 2030

Scenario 1: Cold War II, with a twist

European and Asian countries don't go along with splitting up the world again

Underlying drivers

Stung by criticism of his handling of the inflationary economy and messy US withdrawal from Afghanistan, Joe Biden compensates by getting tough on China and Russia. Future US administrations also consider the threat posed by China to be an existential one for American power in the world. Meanwhile, a lack of US coordination with allies on military, economic, and technological matters weakens transatlantic ties. As economic growth and tech innovation sputters momentarily in China in the mid-2020s, the country's middle class grows restive and the younger generation struggles to find good jobs.

Innovation

As part of its efforts in the mid-2020s to stunt Chinese tech advances, the United States sets immigration quotas on the number of Chinese students allowed to study science and technology and Chinese professors teaching at American universities. The United States forces universities receiving government research grants to prohibit their science faculty from getting grants from Chinese entities and to declare their Chinese contacts. All this leads to a decline in joint US-Chinese patents. The renewed vibrancy of Chinese innovation by the end of the 2020s despite these prohibitions surprises US officials. Chinese students seeking advanced studies start favoring Europe, and many US firms move their research labs to Europe to draw from available Chinese talent there.

Climate and energy

Innovation in climate-change technology slows as a result of US bans on imports of Chinese climate-related products. Early in the decade, China struggles to develop its own chip industry, which is critical to developing climate-related products such as high-powered sensors, but it overcomes these challenges by 2030. Beijing contemplates relaxing China's commitment to achieve carbon neutrality by 2060, out of fear that the country has been too slow to scale the needed technologies and that making good on its ambitious pledge will further slow economic growth. Geopolitical tensions between China and the United States take a toll on international efforts to achieve climate targets.

Trade and immigration

Even before the Taiwan crisis, the United States presses Asian partners to forestall negotiations on Beijing's bid to join the Comprehensive and Progressive Agreement for Trans-Pacific Partnership (CPTTP)—and to instead accelerate negotiations with Taiwan to enter into the pact. Throughout the 2020s, US leaders believe there is too much domestic political opposition for the United States itself to join the agreement. The United States slows EU and other efforts to reform the World Trade Organization, threatening the rules-based global trading system. Despite US pressure, the European Union pushes for strategic autonomy from Washington on economic and tech matters, resisting US secondary sanctions against China and Russia that would hurt EU businesses.

Domestic governance

Democracy continues to backslide. In former democracies, public faith in strong leaders grows, particularly amid slower economic growth. Washington is willing to turn a blind eye to allies that are adopting authoritarian approaches—as long as these leaders are prepared to join forces with the United States against China.

Page 252

Triggers

China meets many of its "Made in China 2025" goals but lags behind in developing domestic manufacturing of cutting-edge technologies. With Xi Jinping under pressure on the tech front, US administrations spot an opportunity to further undermine Chinese economic growth with more US tariffs against Chinese tech exports and restrictions on US chips and other exports that could aid Chinese tech companies. Perceiving China to be weaker than it once was, the United States also decides in 2025 to push its luck and officially recognize Taiwan, which sparks a Chinese nationalist outburst and increased popular support for Xi and the Communist Party. Beijing seizes the Pratas/Dongsha Islands in the South China Sea southwest of Taiwan, presenting the United States with a fait accompli. Washington calls on the United Kingdom and the European Union to implement stiff retaliatory economic sanctions against China, which the UK and EU water down as they call for the US and China to negotiate an agreement on Taiwan. On another front, Russia expands its control of territory in eastern Ukraine while the United States pushes Ukraine and Georgia toward NATO membership over Western European opposition.

Global cooperation

Global cooperation sinks to new lows. Russia joins China in blocking US actions at the United Nations and other multilateral institutions. European leaders strive to lower US-China tensions and rebuild global cooperation, but don't have sufficient influence with either Washington or Beijing to do so. Growing Russian aggression near Europe gives European leaders no alternative to backing Washington and NATO.

War and violence

Russian and Chinese cyberattacks on US critical infrastructure reach new heights, disabling the Washington and New York subway systems. Washington retaliates with a cyberattack against the Russian gas pipeline servicing China, halting natural-gas deliveries for over a month. As tensions escalate, Russia and China start planning a simultaneous invasion scheme: Russia will occupy a larger swath of Ukraine while China retakes Taiwan, stretching US resources. Acting on intelligence regarding Russia's plans, NATO forces mobilize on Ukraine's border. But the big European NATO members, such as France and Germany, refuse to go along with US desires to retake Russian-held territory and return it to Ukraine. Despite similar intelligence on Chinese scheming, most European and Asian allies won't engage in or actively support US-proposed preventive military strikes against Chinese invasion forces for fear of Chinese economic retaliation and military escalation. European and Asian countries call on both Washington and Beijing to stand down, as the European Union and the Association of Southeast Asian Nations organize a peace conference to settle all conflicts.

Europe

Western European governments position themselves between the United States and China, playing the role of mediators and facilitators of compromises. European countries nearer to Russia, meanwhile, seek continued US security guarantees—dimming the EU dream of "strategic defense autonomy" as regional leaders rally with NATO to deter Russian aggression. Western European governments oppose Central European efforts to offer NATO membership to Ukraine, splitting the European Union and paralyzing its foreign and security policy efforts. Some Central and Eastern European countries provide token military support for the US struggle against China, and Beijing retaliates with trade sanctions. US penalties for trading

North America

Under strong US pressure, Canada and Mexico go along with US measures to isolate China. The Mexican government, still fighting drug-related violence, responds by calling on Washington to police the border for arms trafficking, producing an agreement between the two countries to better secure the border by ending arms trafficking and regulating migrant flows.

Page 253

Eurasia

The region comes under a strong Sino-Russian grip. Following the US withdrawal from Afghanistan, Beijing and Moscow worry about instability and the spread of terrorism in Eurasia, and view Washington as sowing discord in their backyards. Moscow and Beijing back authoritarian regimes in the region seeking to quell dissident movements.

Asia-Pacific

As tensions mount with China over Taiwan, the United States' alliance-building efforts force countries in the region to choose a big power to align with. Australia, Japan, and Vietnam are easily persuaded to pick the United States. Others offer only small amounts of support to avoid angering China. At first, Beijing is heavy-handed in reaction to this realignment, levying economic sanctions against those who enter into security partnerships with Washington, but then it uses carrots (such as development assistance and infrastructure deals) in its bid to thwart encirclement. The exception is the Chinese government's punishment of those encouraging diplomatic recognition of Taiwan or Taiwanese independence.

South Asia

India pays an economic price for aligning with Washington, as Chinese investment in the country falls. Pakistan is racked by terrorism and insurgency, making its stability a common concern of New Delhi, Washington, and Beijing. Concern grows throughout the region about sea-level rise and water scarcity stemming from climate change, prompting calls from many South Asian countries for the United States and China to stop their bickering and cooperate on addressing the climate threat.

Middle East

Iranian nuclear-weapons development progresses to the point that Israel is planning unilateral military attacks against Iran. China and Russia mediate between Jerusalem and Tehran, hoping Israel will stand down and Iran will allow international nuclear inspections. When those efforts fail, Washington worries that a major regional conflict will stretch its forces just when its conflict with China is heating up. The United States strong-arms Israel into refraining from anything more than well-targeted strikes on Iran's nuclear facilities.

Africa

China's influence continues to spread in the region as Beijing draws needed commodities from African countries and offers unconditional assistance to help with post-pandemic recovery. European countries try to resist growing Chinese encroachment but expend most of their efforts on patrolling the southern Mediterranean coastline for immigrant boats, virtually stopping migration from Africa to Europe. Rapid population growth in the Sahel and elsewhere, combined with droughts caused by climate change, produce a major famine in the late 2020s.

South and Central America

The United States tries to get South and Central American countries to join its campaign to isolate China. With the closure of the US southern border, however, most don't go along with the campaign or provide only selective support. Washington cuts assistance to those that don't rally to that cause. The Organization of American States becomes moribund due to rising resentment between the United States and many Latin American countries, including over the level of US assistance to other member states during the pandemic. China, for its part, maintains most of its assistance programs to the region.

Scenario 2: A world transformed by climate shocks

Disasters reshuffle the geopolitical cards

Underlying drivers

Major powers procrastinate on measures that would rapidly cut carbon emissions for fear of causing economic distress. Developing countries wait on Western assistance to cut their emissions. Even when evidence mounts of more rapid climate change than scientists once assumed, decisionmakers think there is still time to act. The world's climate, however, begins to deteriorate rapidly, with the northern hemisphere hit harder than anticipated.

Triggers

As the northern polar jet stream weakens, the circulation of weather systems breaks down. High- and low-pressure systems move more slowly, lengthening heat waves and storms that unleash historic floods. Early indicators include flooding in northwestern Germany and the 2021 heat wave in the American West, which exacerbated droughts and brought unprecedented high temperatures. In the late 2020s, days of heavy rain in the New York City area and rising sea levels displace over a million people in the region; many residences are permanently condemned. Most of lower Manhattan becomes uninhabitable, with businesses closing for three to four months due to subway flooding and the destruction of utilities. London and Paris soon experience similar events. Shortly before these incidents, in China, a powerful typhoon tears through the Pearl River Delta, halting factory activity for four months. Rains and flooding build up, threatening the Yangtze River's massive Three Gorges Dam—a symbol of China's engineering prowess. While the dam holds, the crisis reminds Chinese leaders of the country's vulnerability to extreme-weather events.

Trade and immigration

Amid mounting public panic about climate change and pressure to combat it, the United States and other Western countries ease their restrictions on exports of highly sensitive climate-related technology to China and others. Scientific exchanges between the United States and China are stepped up, and Washington welcomes into the country students seeking new skills related to the climate-change fight.

Page 255

Innovation

As climate change takes on an urgency in the United States akin to George W. Bush's "war on terror" in the early 2000s, the US government stakes out a new top priority: to become the global center for climate innovation. Washington hosts a global summit on climate change and needed technologies to combat it. Washington declares select US technologies global public goods that will be shared with foreign manufacturers for the purpose of fighting climate change. The United States explores geoengineering, while China and Russia are suspected of conducting their own experiments at that new frontier as well, generating concern among many scientists and other governments about efforts to change the climate through man-made means; the European Union, for example, fears that such efforts will do more harm than good.

Climate and energy

The United States, Europe, and China agree to accelerate their timetables for achieving net-zero carbon emissions. Gulf countries and Russia oppose these moves and seek major fiscal assistance from the "Big Three." The United States, the European Union, and China establish a global investment fund to help low-income countries make the energy transition. But they are less generous toward the big oil producers who, they contend, ignored the writing on the wall for too long. With advances in battery storage in the early 2020s, the advanced economies (including China) are better positioned to move toward all electric vehicles. Still, supply constraints keep oil-guzzling vehicles on the roads into the early 2040s, particularly in developing countries.

Domestic governance

As in wartime, Western governments tell their people, extraordinary challenges require extraordinary measures. The Democratic US president begins mandating changes—from all-electric vehicles to new building codes and mandatory rehabilitation of existing structures to meet green energy standards. State governors, particularly in regions less affected by extreme weather, take the federal government to court, but the Supreme Court backs the new emergency powers. A significant minority of US citizens engage in civil disobedience to protest the government's new climate mandates. Some EU member states resist Brussels's growing federal powers but still require the European Union's assistance to make a more rapid energy transition. China and other authoritarian governments already have the executive powers to take climate action and face little public resistance to doing so. While it remains official US policy to call on China to liberalize, democracy promotion is now a lower priority for Washington.

Global cooperation

Most countries come to see the need for collaboration to counteract climate change. Low- to medium-income countries seize on the sudden panic over extreme-weather events to get richer countries to pay for their energy transition. US leaders opt for country-to-country cooperation rather than working through existing UN institutions they consider too slow or trying to establish new global institutions they fear will end up creating obstructionist bureaucracy or enabling China and other nations to dent US leadership. Although Brussels does not share the same concerns, the EU goes along with Washington to bolster the global campaign to save a warming planet.

Page 256

War and violence

With the threat of Sino-US conflict diminishing substantially as a result of expanding climate cooperation between the two powers, US leaders order the military to avoid any provocative actions against China. Each side beefs up its intelligence gathering on the other, anticipating that the contest will one day resume. And Chinese leaders do not let up on their military buildup. Pessimists see a parallel with the temporary US-Soviet cooperation against a common Nazi enemy during World War II, while others predict a generation or more of climate-change cooperation. Many US and EU policymakers worry about a Russia weakened by lower energy revenues becoming more aggressive. It proves politically difficult for the United States to lend a helping hand to Russia, but the European Union drops its economic sanctions against Moscow and invests in diversifying the Russian economy.

Europe

Germany, Europe's largest trader with China, welcomes the liberalized US-backed trade regime with Beijing. Europeans believe the United States has finally gotten on board the climate-change drive, and transatlantic ties reassume a closeness that has not existed since the Cold War. The biggest concern for Europe is accomplishing the costly energy transition without triggering a surge in unemployment and wage stagnation. EU leaders also worry about a brain drain of European scientific and tech talent to the United States due to Washington's resources (largely shifted out of the Pentagon's budget) for climate technology.

North America

US decisionmakers worry that the energy transition will benefit Chinese manufacturing as well as that of its trade partners in the United States-Mexico-Canada Agreement. While cooperating with China and supporting liberalized trade, they weave incentives for domestic manufacturing into their new energy-transition initiatives. It is a difficult balancing act. Some in Congress want to erect barriers against the flood of "cheap" Chinese climate imports. To avoid a populist backlash and a repeat of pandemic-era political divisions, the US federal government invests heavily in professional retraining and lifelong learning to better prepare the workforce for the green-energy era. Younger generations heavily back the needed changes and are better equipped to acquire new skills.

Eurasia

With prospects for its energy industry dimming due to China, the United States, and Europe accelerating their green agendas, the Russian economy begins to contract. With Sino-US tensions on the wane, Vladimir Putin is replaced by a leader who opens up the county to the West while still maintaining close ties with China.

South Asia

The Indian government is bitter about losing its privileged position with the United States vis-a-vis China. It calls for US, EU, and Chinese assistance to transition out of cheap coal.

Page 257

Asia-Pacific

Lower Sino-US tensions and trade liberalization fuel the growth of Asian economies. China and the United States both join the Comprehensive and Progressive Agreement for Trans-Pacific Partnership trade pact. Pressures build within China for more personal liberty. At first Xi Jinping tries to stoke nationalism, but ultimately he yields to others in the Communist Party who want limited political reform. It is unclear whether the reforms will suffice; Xi's supporters warn that China is on a slippery slope, pointing to the failures of the Soviet glasnost policy in the 1980s.

Middle East

Iran and the Gulf countries face diminishing returns from oil and gas. They pursue a policy of low production to maintain high prices. Over time, it proves impossible to maintain such quotas as oil producers try to maximize profit to finance economic diversification.

Africa

African governments point to growing climate-related ravages to their countries, such as droughts, and call for increased help as the United States and others put together a global investment fund to help the region adapt and become more resilient to the consequences of climate change. Food insecurity grows, resulting in famine in some countries. African leaders seek exemptions from limits on carbon emissions given Africa's limited role in causing climate change. Washington, Brussels, and Beijing are open to their position.

South and Central America

Latin America benefits from lower Sino-US tensions and the US government's new tech-sharing policy. Brazil calls on the international community to heavily fund the preservation of the Amazon rainforest.

Scenario 3: A democratic renaissance

Western governments get serious about tackling their governance crises

Underlying drivers

Initially hopes are high that the West will pull out of the pandemic, experience accelerated economic growth, and return to relative normalcy. After a spurt of growth in which most segments of the population see gains, however, pre-pandemic structural problems resurface—particularly the inequalities that had worsened during the COVID-19 crisis. It looks like Western societies could be pulled apart. Yet the pandemic has been an eye-opener for many about the deep divisions in their societies. For the more tech-savvy younger and coming-of-age generation, it is intolerable for the unskilled and semiskilled to be "losers" in the technological revolution. Older generations—increasingly victims of automation—also come to see the benefits of a better social-safety net. Over time, the fears fueling populism dissipate and centrist politics come back to the fore as the maintenance of social consensus becomes a popular expectation for political leaders. Western societies become a model for modernizing societies, balancing efficiency and productivity with social equities.

Triggers

Believing it best not to depend too much on the vagaries of human employment, in 2021-22 employers race to automate operations as much as possible. The wages of the unskilled and semiskilled, many of whom had provided crucial services during the pandemic, initially grow as employers try to attract workers. Soon, however, these workers learn they are expendable as firms begin to automate their operations. Pre-pandemic full employment does not return, despite monetary-easing policies of central banks. In advanced economies, worker-participation rates drop as low-skilled job seekers find few good-paying opportunities. Many drop out of the market or take early retirement. Meanwhile, in China, Xi Jinping's overreach with his economic and regulatory interventions sends China into a serious economic slowdown by the mid-2020s, buoying Western confidence in its democratic capitalist system despite that system's many evident challenges. Given China's growing structural problems, Western decisionmakers believe they have leverage to force Beijing to adopt market reforms. At home, Western leaders come to see some maneuvering room for crafting a new, more generous social contract with a stronger safety net, which counters the social fragmentation produced by new technologies.

Trade and immigration

Increased geopolitical tensions at first limit interaction between US and Chinese firms, resulting in the contraction of global supply chains. Some European businesses bow out of the Chinese market for fear of US secondary sanctions while others concentrate on doing business with China and sell off their US interests. Once China's economic crisis gives way to market reforms, overseas investment pours into the country, worrying some prescient Western policymakers who believe China may come out of the crisis stronger.

Climate and energy

The energy transition gets a boost from China's adoption of market reforms and a resulting decline in US-Sino tensions. Chinese and US collaboration on new battery-storage technologies, along with their sharing of those technologies with other countries, encourage the adoption of renewable energy. China, the United States, and the European Union agree on instituting a carbon tax to make progress against climate change. Nonetheless, the world is still unlikely to meet its 2030 emission-reduction targets.

Page 259

Domestic governance

In the post-pandemic era, and against the backdrop of the diminishing threat posed by China by mid-decade, those in the West who believe workers need more benefits and compensation have greater standing. Several CEOs of major companies take the lead by offering more benefits—paying educational and retraining expenses, for instance—and promising new employment to those whose jobs were eliminated through automation, resulting in greater productivity. Decreasing inequities and anger among publics produces healthier politics. As middle-class fortunes improve, democracy regains its allure as a system capable of securing its citizens' political and social rights.

Global cooperation

While differences remain over Taiwan and Chinese territorial claims in the South China Sea, Sino-US tensions decline in the mid- to late 2020s as China adopts market reforms to reboot its economy, encouraging more Western business involvement in the Chinese economy. Western collaboration with China includes efforts to reform the International Monetary Fund and World Bank so that they accelerate the distribution of development assistance. China even seeks closer collaboration with the World Bank on Beijing's Belt and Road Initiative. The Chinese government ends subsidies for many state-owned enterprises (a number of these go bankrupt), giving the United States sufficient confidence to try to reinvigorate the World Trade Organization.

War and violence

In Africa, Central America, and South Asia, civil war and insurgencies gather steam due to extensive economic problems in the wake of the pandemic. Western nations, despite their democratic renewal and rising self-confidence during the second half of the decade, are reluctant to intervene in these conflicts or engage in nation-building.

Europe

Automation, with its efficiencies and productivity gains, is seen as a godsend for European countries with low birth rates and rapidly aging populations. Smaller nations better stanch societal inequities stemming from rapid technological changes than larger ones do. Income disparities are not as high in many of these smaller countries, which have long invested in expensive social-welfare programs. Governments aim to incentivize unskilled citizens to learn new skills. That requires transforming educational systems and new measures such as creating the legal right to periodic sabbaticals to learn new skills over several months, which in turn provides businesses with highly skilled workers. Alongside existing rights to healthcare and retirement benefits, citizens are granted a new right to lifetime learning. Despite witnessing the democratic renewal of their smaller neighbors, larger European countries struggle with sufficiently reducing social inequities to replicate that revival. Businesses push back on expanding worker rights and shouldering the costs. In France, where the Macron government had been trying to lessen employers' burdens, cost concerns diminish interest in enhancing existing training programs and an already-generous social-welfare program. Critics cite low educational standards in economically deprived areas as the barrier to workers upgrading their skills.

Eurasia

Terrorist activity rises in Central Asia with Afghanistan's economic collapse and humanitarian crisis. After a decade of little to no growth, Russia is thrown into political crisis with mass protests in its big cities. Increasingly self-absorbed, the Kremlin trims security assistance to the former Soviet states. Amid mounting political opposition, Vladimir Putin is eased out of power to make way for a new regime that wants to re-energize the economy. Russia's new leaders seek to improve ties with the West in order to end sanctions and attract foreign investment. Given its problems at home, China cannot be the economic engine Central Asia counted on.

Asia-Pacific

Lessening Sino-US tensions and China's market reforms strengthen regional economic integration and make China appear less threatening to its neighbors. As its economic crisis recedes and it cuts subsidies for state-owned enterprises, China is welcomed into the CPTPP trade agreement, reinforcing its central role as the key trading partner for other Asian countries. With the exception of a few countries like Australia, India, Japan, and Vietnam, Asian nations are no longer interested in strengthening their security partnerships with the United States. By the end of the decade, as China recovers, Washington realizes that it needs to strengthen its economic hand in Asia but has no obvious lever to do so, having rejected membership in the CPTPP and its predecessor, the Trans-Pacific Partnership.

South Asia

India, scarred by the pandemic but facing a friendlier China, decides to join the Regional Comprehensive Economic Partnership, the trade agreement that includes China, Japan, and others. Seeing the revival of Western democracies, New Delhi postpones its military buildup to instead make similar investments in education.

Middle East

With tensions easing between Western powers and China and Russia due to the economic reforms in Beijing and change in political leadership in Moscow, cooperation at the UN Security Council springs back to life in the mid-2020s. Many wonder, however, whether it has come too late. Despite every effort by Israel, including aerial strikes and cyberattacks against Iran's nuclear facilities plus assassinations of its key nuclear scientists, Iran has the "bomb" and an intercontinental missile capability. Western intelligence reveals that other powers in the Middle East—Turkey and Saudi Arabia—are trying to develop or acquire nuclear weapons as well. The US government fends off Israeli pressure for a combined attack on Iran's nuclear facilities by delivering enhanced strategic missile defenses to protect Israel against any incoming attack, becoming an avowed nuclear guarantor of Israel's security. While Israel doesn't want to be beholden to the United States for its security, it doesn't have a choice. The United States also supports European, Russian, and Chinese efforts to organize regional negotiations on a framework for curbing nuclear proliferation and lowering tensions between Israel and Iran.

The Science of Sustainability

Can a unified path for development and conservation lead to a better future?

The Cerrado may not have the same name recognition as the Amazon, but this vast tropical savannah in Brazil has much in common with that perhaps better-known destination. The Cerrado is also a global biodiversity hotspot, home to thousands of species only found there, and it is also a critical area in the fight against climate change, acting as a large carbon pool.

But Brazil is one of the two largest soy producers in the world—the crop is one of the country's most important commodities and a staple in global food supplies—and that success is placing the Cerrado in precarious decline. To date, around 46% of the Cerrado has been deforested or converted for agriculture.

Producing more soy doesn't have to mean converting more native habitat, however. A new spatial data tool is helping identify the best places to expand soy without further encroachment on the native landscapes of the Cerrado. And with traders and bankers working together to offer preferable financing to farmers who expand onto already-converted land, Brazil can continue to produce this important crop, while protecting native habitat and providing more financial stability for farmers.

The Cerrado is just one region of a vast planet, of course, but these recent efforts to protect it are representative of a new way of thinking about the relationship between conservation and our growing human demands. It is part of an emerging model for cross-sector collaboration that aims to create a world prepared for the sustainability challenges ahead.

Is this world possible? Here, we present a new science-based view that says "Yes"—but it will require new forms of collaboration across traditionally disconnected sectors, and on a near unprecedented scale.

I. A False Choice

Many assume that economic interests and environmental interests are in conflict. But new research makes the case that this perception of development vs. conservation is not just unnecessary but actively counterproductive to both ends. Achieving a sustainable future will be dependent on our ability to secure both thriving human communities and abundant and healthy natural ecosystems.

The Nature Conservancy partnered with the University of Minnesota and 11 other organizations to ask whether it is possible to achieve a future where the needs of both people and nature are advanced. Can we actually meet people's needs for food, water and energy while doing more to protect nature?

To answer this question, we compared what the world will look like in 2050 if economic and human development progress in a "business-as-usual" fashion and what it would look like if instead we join forces to implement a "sustainable" path with a series of fair-minded and technologically viable solutions to the challenges that lie ahead.

In both options, we used leading projections of population growth and gross domestic product to estimate how demand for food, energy and water will evolve between 2010 and 2050. Under business-as-usual, we played out existing expectations and trends in how those changes will impact land use, water use, air quality, climate, protected habitat areas and ocean fisheries. In the more sustainable scenario, we proposed changes to how and where food and energy are produced, asking if these adjustments could result in better outcomes for the same elements of human well-being and nature. Our full findings are described in a peer-reviewed paper—"An Attainable Global Vision for Conservation and Human Well-Being"—published in Frontiers in Ecology and the Environment.

These scenarios let us ask, can we do better? Can we design a future that meets people's needs without further degrading nature in the process?

Our answer is "yes," but it comes with several big "ifs." There is a path to get there, but matters are urgent—if we want to accomplish these goals by mid-century, we'll have to dramatically ramp up our efforts now. The next decade is critical.

Furthermore, changing course in the next ten years will require global collaboration on a scale not seen perhaps since World War II. The widely held impression that economic and environmental goals are mutually exclusive has contributed to a lack of connection among key societal constituencies best equipped to solve interconnected problems—namely, the public health, development, financial and conservation communities. This has to change.

The good news is that protecting nature and providing water, food and energy to a growing world do not have to be either-or propositions. Our view, instead, calls for smart energy, water, air, health and ecosystem initiatives that balance the needs of economic growth and resource conservation equally. Rather than a zero-sum game, these elements are balanced sides of an equation, revealing the path to a future where people

and nature thrive together.
II. Two Paths to 2050

This vision is not a wholesale departure from what others have offered. A number of prominent scientists and organizations have put forward important and thoughtful views for a sustainable future; but often such plans consider the needs of people and nature in isolation from one another, use analyses confined to limited sectors or geographies, or assume that some hard tradeoffs must be made, such as slowing global population growth, taking a reduction in GDP growth or shifting diets off of meat. Our new research considers global economic development and conservation needs together, more holistically, in order to find a sustainable path forward.

What could a different future look like? We've used as our standard the United Nations' Sustainable Development Goals (SDGs), a set of 17 measures for "a world where all people are fed, healthy, employed, educated, empowered and thriving, but not at the expense of other life on Earth." Our analysis directly aligns with ten of those goals. Using the SDGs as our guideposts, we imagine a world in 2050 that looks very different than the one today—and drastically different from the one we will face if we continue in business-as-usual fashion.

A sustainable future is possible.

To create our assessment of business-as-usual versus a more sustainable path, we looked at 14 measurements including temperature change, carbon dioxide levels, air pollution, water consumption, food and energy footprints, and protected areas.

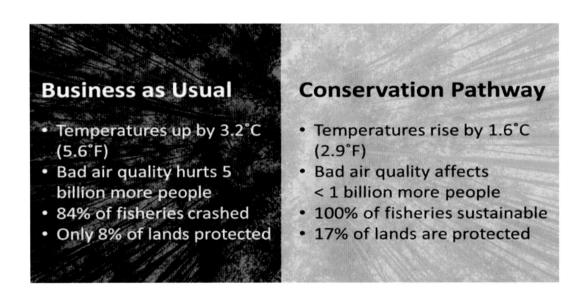

TWO PATHS TO 2050 TNC developed two scenarios for the future: one was business as usual, and the other was a conservation pathway. We learned that by 2050 we can support both conservation and economic growth.

Over the next 30 years, we know we'll face rapid population growth and greater pressures on our natural resources. The statistics are sobering—with 9.7 billion people on the planet by 2050, we can expect a

54 percent increase in global food demand and 56 percent increase in energy demand. While meetings these growing demands and achieving sustainability is possible, it is helpful to scrutinize where the status quo will get us.

The World Health Organization, World Economic Forum and other leading global development organizations now say that air pollution and water scarcity—environmental challenges—are among the biggest dangers to human health and prosperity. And our business-as-usual analysis makes clear what many already fear: that human development based on the same practices we use today will not prepare us for a world with nearly 10 billion people.

To put it simply, if we stay on today's current path, we risk being trapped in an intensifying cycle of scarcity—our growth opportunities severely capped and our natural landscapes severely degraded. Under this business-as-usual scenario, we can expect global temperature to increase 3.2°C; worsened air pollution affecting 4.9 billion more people; overfishing of 84 percent of fish stocks; and greater water stress affecting 2.75 billion people. Habitat loss continues, leaving less than 50 percent of native grasslands and several types of forests intact.

However, if we make changes in where and how we meet food, water and energy demands for the same growing global population and wealth, the picture can look markedly different by mid-century. This "sustainability" path includes global temperature increase limited to 1.6°C—meeting Paris Climate Accord goals—zero overfishing with greater fisheries yields, a 90 percent drop in exposure to dangerous air pollution, and fewer water-stressed people, rivers and agricultural fields. These goals can be met while natural habitats extend both inside and outside protected areas. All signatory countries to the Aichi Targets meet habitat protection goals, and more than 50 percent of all ecoregions' extents remain unconverted, except temperate grasslands (of which over 50 percent are already converted today).

III. What's Possible

Achieving this sustainable future for people and nature is possible with existing and expected technology and consumption, but only with major shifts in production patterns. Making these shifts will require overcoming substantial economic, social and political challenges. In short, it is not likely that the biophysical limits of the planet will determine our future, but rather our willingness to think and act differently by putting economic development and the environment on equal footing as central parts of the same equation.

Climate, Energy and Air Quality

Perhaps the most pressing need for change is in energy use. In order to both meet increased energy demand and keep the climate within safe boundaries, we'll need to alter the way we produce energy, curtailing emissions of carbon and other harmful chemicals.

Under a business-as-usual scenario, fossil fuels will still claim a 76 percent share of total energy in 2050. A more sustainable approach would reduce that share to 13 percent by 2050. While this is a sharp change, it is necessary to stanch the flow of harmful greenhouse gases into the atmosphere.

A Changing Energy Portfolio

In order to both meet increased energy demand and keep the climate in safe boundaries, we'll need to alter our energy makeup to curtail emissions of carbon and other harmful chemicals.

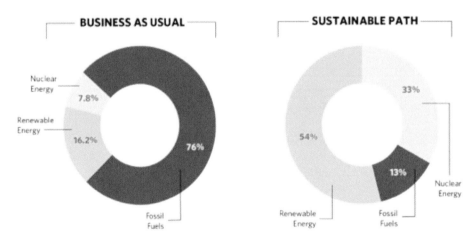

The reduction in carbon-based energy could be offset by increasing the share of energy from renewable sources to 54 percent and increasing nuclear energy to one third of total energy output—delivering a total of almost 85 percent of the world's energy demand from non-fossil-fuel sources.

Additionally, we will only achieve the full extent of reduced climate impacts if we draw down existing carbon from the atmosphere. This can be done through greater investment in carbon capture and storage efforts, including natural climate solutions—land management strategies such as avoiding forest loss, reforestation, investments in soil health and coastal ecosystem restoration.

The net benefit of these energy redistribution efforts is twofold. First, they lower the rate at which greenhouse gases are flowing into the air—taking atmospheric carbon projections down to 442 parts per million, compared to business-as-usual estimates that put the level closer to 520 ppm.

Second, these energy source shifts would create a marked decline in particulate air pollution. Our models show that the higher fossil fuel use in the business-as-usual scenario is likely to expose half the people on the planet to poorer air quality by 2050. Under the sustainable scenario, that figure drops to just 7 percent of the world's inhabitants, thanks to lower particulate emissions from renewable and nuclear energy sources.

Food, Habitat and City Growth

Meeting the sustainable targets we propose requires a second front on land to shift how we use available real estate and where we choose to conduct necessary activities. Overall, the changes we include in our more sustainable view allow the world to meet global food, water and energy demands with no additional conversion of natural habitat for those needs—an outcome that is not possible under business as usual.

While transitioning away from fossil fuels is essential to meet climate goals, new renewable energy infrastructure siting will present land-use challenges. Renewable energy production takes up space, and if not sited well it can cause its own negative impacts on nature and its services to people. In our more sustainable path, we address this challenge by preferencing the use of already converted land for renewables development, lessening the impact of new wind and solar on natural habitat. We also exclude expansion of biofuels, as they are known to require extensive land area to produce, causing conflicts with natural habitat and food security.

Perhaps most encouraging, we show that it is possible to meet future food demands on less agricultural land than is used today. Notably, our scenario keeps the mix of crops in each growing region the same, so as not to disrupt farmers' cultures, technologies, capacity or existing crop knowledge. Instead, we propose moving which crops are grown where within growing regions, putting more "thirsty" crops in areas with more water, and matching the nutrient needs of various crops to the soils available.

Unlike some projections used by others, for this scenario we left diet expectations alone, matching meat consumption with business-as-usual expectations. If we were able to reduce meat consumption, especially by middle- and high-income countries where nutritional needs are met, reducing future agricultural land, water and pollution footprints would be even easier.

Meanwhile, on the land protection front, our analysis is guided by the Convention on Biological Diversity, the leading global platform most countries have signed. Each signatory country has agreed to protect up to 17 percent of each habitat type within its borders. While many countries will fall short of this goal under business as usual, it can be achieved in our more sustainable option.

We acknowledge 17 percent is an imperfect number, and many believe more natural habitat is needed to allow the world's biodiversity to thrive. Looking beyond protected areas, we see additional differences in the possible futures we face. Our more sustainable option retains 577 million hectares more natural habitat than business as usual, much of it outside of protected areas. Conservation has long focused on representation—it is not only important to conserve large areas, but to represent different kinds of habitat. Under business as usual, we will lose more than half of several major habitat types by mid-century, including temperate broadleaf and mixed forests, Mediterranean forest, and temperate grassland. Flooded and tropical grasslands approach this level of loss as well.

But with the proposed shifts in food, water and energy use, we can do better for nearly all habitats in our more sustainable scenario. The one exception is temperate grasslands, a biome that has already lost more than 50 percent of its global extent today. In all, the more sustainable scenario shows a future that would be largely compatible with emerging views that suggest protecting half of the world's land system.

Drinking Water, River Basins and Fisheries

Water presents a complex set of challenges. Like land, it is both a resource and a habitat. Fresh water resources are dwindling while ocean ecosystems are overburdened by unregulated fishing and pollution. Business-as-usual projections estimate that 2.75 billion people will experience water scarcity by 2050 and

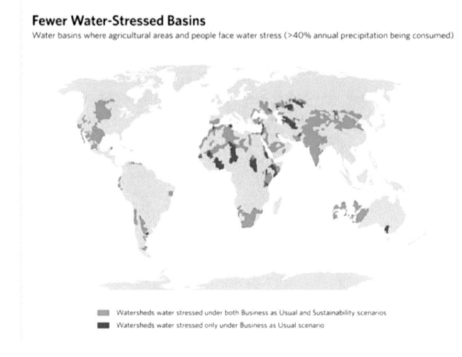

Fewer Water-Stressed Basins

Water basins where agricultural areas and people face water stress (>40% annual precipitation being consumed)

Watersheds water stressed under both Business as Usual and Sustainability scenarios

Watersheds water stressed only under Business as Usual scenario

770 water basins will experience water stress. Africa and Central Asia in particular would see fewer water stressed basins in the sustainable scenario.

Changes in energy sources and food production (see above sections) would lead to significant water savings by reducing use of water as a coolant in energy production and by moving crops to areas where they need less irrigation. Thanks to these changes, our more sustainable option for the future would relieve 104 million people and biodiversity in 25 major river basins from likely water stress.

Meanwhile, in the seas, we find an inspiring possibility for fisheries. Continuing business-as-usual fisheries management adds further stress to the oceans and the global food system as more stocks decline, further diminishing the food we rely on from the seas. But more sustainable fisheries management is possible, and our projections using a leading fisheries model shows that adopting sustainable management in all fisheries by mid-century would actually increase yield by over a quarter more than we saw in 2010.

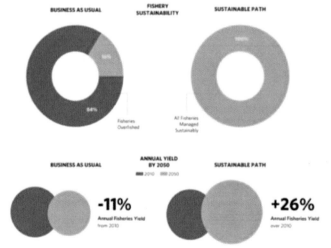

And, while we know that aquaculture is a certain element of the future of fish and food, many questions remain about precisely how this industry will grow, and how it can be shaped to be a low-impact part of the global food system. Given these unknowns, we kept aquaculture growth the same in both our views of the future.

IV. The Way Forward

This analysis does not represent a panacea for the growing need for economic development across the planet or for the environmental challenges that are ahead. But it does provide an optimistic viewpoint and an integrated picture that can serve as a starting point for discussion.

Our goal is to apply new questions—and ultimately new solutions—to our known problems. We present one of many possible paths to a different future, and we welcome like-minded partners and productive critics to share their perspectives with us. We encourage people from across society to join the conversation, to fill gaps where they exist, and to bring other important considerations to our attention. Most of all, we call on the development (e.g. energy, agriculture, infrastructure), health, and financial communities—among others—to work with us to find new ways of taking action together.

Ultimately, by illustrating a viable pathway to sustainability that serves both the needs of economic and environmental interests—goals that many have long assumed were mutually exclusive—we hope to inspire the global community to engage in the difficult but necessary social, economic and political dialogue that can make a sustainable future a reality.

Protecting nature and providing water, food and energy to the world can no longer be either-or propositions. Nature and human development are both central factors in the same equation. We have at our disposal the cross-sector expertise necessary to make informed decisions for the good of life on our planet, so let's use it wisely. Our science affirms there is a way.

Join us as we chart a new path to 2050 by helping people and nature thrive—together.

Opinion: What will the future of space travel look

like? And what does it mean for this planet?

We asked: SpaceX is planning its first orbital test flight of a starship that could one day take people to the moon or even Mars. What do you think about the future of space travel?

This dream is no longer out of this world

As a child, I remember spending late nights looking out of the window beside my bed, my warm breath fogging up the cold, reflective glass. I remember gazing wondrously at the sparkling stars above in the clear night sky, imagining that I was in a starship of my own. I remember imagining the loud hum of my house heater as the roar of my starship's engines as I was taken into the immense expanses of the universe. I remember dreaming about stepping foot onto the ground of foreign planets and exploring their alien environments, finding myself gazing into their vast horizons. Little did my young self know that may very well be possible in the near future.

With the development of next-generation spacecraft and technology, my dream of setting foot onto an unfamiliar planet these days may not be so impossible. Of course, I don't think we'd be setting foot on planets dozens of parsecs away anytime soon, but the future of space travel looks bright with SpaceX and NASA's recent advancements in spacecraft.

More specifically, SpaceX's recent developing spacecraft known as Starship has been in development for almost two decades and will reach orbit around Earth this year. This same spaceship is even capable of taking people to Mars on a planned mission in the future, as it can also refuel in orbit. These new developments in space technology, in my opinion, make space travel much more practical.

From what I think, at least, space travel may even one day enter the commercial field. Imagine this: You set foot into the cozy cabin of a starship after scanning your ticket, pulling your luggage inside and sighing as the air-conditioned cabin cools you down. After making your way farther into the cabin of the spaceship, you finally locate your seat beside a window. You place your luggage into the overhead bin and plop yourself onto the soft cushions of the seat, sighing as you look out the window and gaze into the vast expanse of the solar system and beyond. As you tune out the voices of nearby passengers and blend them into the peaceful lull of the spacecraft's engine, you observe the bright Moon in the distance. Maybe space travel for common people like you and me won't be so impractical soon!

Not getting much bang for our bucks

In the 1960s, I was an Apollo engineer at Cape Kennedy. We were going to land on the moon because President John F. Kennedy vaguely said it was a good idea. The money flowed freely. Some 50 years later, my grandson asked me why we went there. I was one of the people who worked to achieve that goal, and I could not find a good answer as to why.

I attended meetings at the cape in which the word was out — no questions permitted as to why, only discussions allowed as to how. It became clear — the corporations, the universities, the engineers — everyone wanted to share in the dollars. We brought back lots of moon rock samples to analyze. Still available to look at in Houston. More rocks would not be very useful.

The Challenger explosion in 1986 should remind us of how dangerous it is to try again to go back. The old phrase *"Been there, done that" is more than a cliché.* It is also a warning. **Fred Zarse, Alpine**

We should not fear the new frontier

Whenever humankind discovers a new technology, it's common for people to be afraid. Before modern science, when a woman liked to study botany or holistic practices, society might accuse her of witchcraft and put her on trial to be burned at the stake. Edgar Allan Poe wrote about his fear of modern technology and the future. At one point, reading books was criticized and considered strange.

Later, when the internet was invented, there was a lot of resistance. Older people used to be so out of touch, but now if you walk through an elderly facility, you'll see dozens of older people scrolling through the internet. My grandmother would stay up late into the night asking Siri questions about her childhood and past presidents. It was adorable.

People don't like to change. Although it can be scary to try new things, that's why we have so many wonderful inventions around the world. Who would have imagined that by studying genetics eventually scientists would be able to grow new hearts, livers and other organs for sick patients? (Although it's still a new science). Who would have imagined the prospect of growing our meat products in a lab instead of farming animals? The idea of space exploration is the same as all the other discoveries we've made.

"The unknown is scary, but it's also promising. Just as you never know what harm it could bring, you never know what good it could bring either. Therefore, I say, bring on the unknown!"

Cassidy Eiler, El Cajon

We must first save the planet we have

Matthew McConaughey redeemed himself on Super Bowl Sunday. In contrast with his suave Lincoln promotions, he turned out for Salesforce's *"Team Earth"* in a Super Bowl ad aimed at workers who would be happy for a benign commute on terra firma — honest Earthlings with no ambitions of being Joe the Plumber-turned-astronaut. It was refreshing.

In the last year, if we weren't reeling enough from the pretentious Donald Trump years and callous disregard for workers on the front lines of a pandemic, we were treated to the spectacle of billionaires flexing their intrepid astronaut wings, boldly bragging and spinning where none could have dreamed to do so before.

Some were honest not to dress it up as science, rather as a new consumer experience. Sir Richard Branson literally took a pen and pad to take notes on how to improve the guest experience. I suppose that merits a tax write off? Jeff Bezos won the feel-good moment by sponsoring our beloved Captain Kirk's initiation to actual space. Well played. Elon Musk surprised us by deferring his own travel in favor of sending a geologist along with a paying guest. That might offer a momentary counterbalance to his Scarlet A (arrogance), but it is hard to square his sustainability initiatives with this suspected objective to take his toys and slip the surly bonds of earth.

I can't sort out if he lacks confidence that humanity will solve the climate action imperative (and he would need a Planet B) or if he thinks his efforts will succeed so stunningly that his space exploits and all the carbon emissions and resource diversion they require will be a harmless investment?

Since none of these billionaires has shown how space travel could be affordable to the 99 percent, let alone environmentally benign, it feels a lot like our billionaire astronauts aren't content to simply squander Earth's resources for their own thrill rides They want adulation as well, as though Joe the Plumber now aspires to be a millionaire Martian, and dreaming will make it so.

Mothers like me watched NASA's missions as kids — Apollo missions, in my case. We have it in us to dream of new frontiers, and we want our children to carry forward and explore. SpaceX has helped this continue. But there is a clear and urgent threat we are facing now that makes our planetary explorations take a back seat to species health and sustenance. Further, even if we imagine earning a golden ticket, what kind of humans would emigrate from a populous planet in crisis without focusing their best efforts at saving it for all?

"Resources are finite. Our atmospheric carbon budget is non-negotiable. Carbon capture and sequestration, if it ever works out, will be a bandage, not a cure. We must not allow the 1 percent to delude the 99 percent on this. There is no Planet B for any of us, and certainly not the working class. I'm fighting for Team Earth!"

Darlene Garvais, Sabre Springs

Nothing close is really worth traveling to

The future of space flight will be the same as it is today: scientific robotic exploration and limited commercial missions, such as communication satellites. Meanwhile, the future of space travel for humans will still be a fantasy. These are just a few reasons why.

With current technology, the energy required to launch an Atlas D rocket into space with one person aboard could fuel some 3,000 cars. Basically, a person is sitting on top of high explosives, traveling hundreds of miles per hour into the massive debris field that shrouds the planet to be exposed to high levels of radiation. Despite the buy-in from various billionaire space moguls, getting people into space is expensive. While it's still murky what a commercial flight will cost, a ride in a Soyuz capsule was $20 million or more per seat. So space travel remains an impractical, dangerous and expensive proposition.

There is one other reason why human space flight is a fantasy. In 1969, I watched reruns of *"Star Trek"* with its rich tapestry of star bases and Class M worlds to explore. I had a scrapbook of news clippings of the NASA moon landing. Using the logic of a 7-year-old, the next step was for us to establish space stations and bases on the moon, Mars and other planets. Which presents the real problem with human space travel: There is nowhere for us to go.

Mike Stewart, Spring Valley

Too soon to tell what the future will hold

Space. The final frontier, or so they say. Many of us may have dreamt of being astronauts when we grew up one day, and some of us probably did. I frankly did not. But, I am always interested in hearing more about what the future of Space exploration holds, what was discovered, and simply looking at pictures of distant galaxies. When SpaceX came out saying they are developing a craft that could possibly take people to the moon or Mars, it was pretty exciting knowing what we may discover in the future.

I always used to say that I would go to the moon when I grew up, and I was going to find other life on planets we had yet to set foot on. First of all, training to go to space is significantly gruesome having to prepare your body for the mission. Secondly it is extremely expensive to get all the equipment needed, and faculty to ensure everything runs smoothly. That is not to mention all the debris that is left behind in Earth's orbit which is no longer of use to anyone. This was one of the main problems of space exploration before. The amount of money used to just no longer be of use to anyone and remain in Earth's orbit.

This is where the engineers at SpaceX revolutionized space travel. They finally achieved the ability to reuse what was once considered space junk, by returning stage one of the spacecraft back to the place of launch. This has opened new possibilities in terms of space as a whole. I am no scientist, but being able to consistently reuse the thruster of a spacecraft seems as if you would be able to send more spacecraft into or out of orbit within a much smaller time frame, and possibly even cost less in the long run.

If these rockets were to be mass produced and widely used, traveling to space would not take as long, and the price for someone to go into space should be lower as time goes on. We would not only be able to run more test experiments in space, but scientists would also be able to gather more information much more efficiently as well. I imagine a high end production line of scientist and groups waiting their turn to board the reusable rocket, or mounting their telescopes on other stages to explore the great unknown. It will all eventually trickle down to spacecraft becoming similar to airfare, where people will be boarding to fly to a colony on mars or the moon for a small getaway.

"This is a long process ahead of scientist and engineers, yet it is one that could change our way of life, and possibly lead to the evolution of mankind. Who knows, by that time we could be boarding our own Millennium Falcon or X-Wings that can take us into hyperdrive to other galaxies, and our current methods of transportation would become obsolete."

Daniel Martinez, San Ysidro

What is the future of space travel?

Discover the next giant leap in crewed spaceflight

In the 50 years since the Apollo 11 Moon landing, humans have made extraordinary progress in space exploration. But what is the next giant leap for crewed spaceflight – and could 'space tourism' soon become a reality?

Right now, unmanned space probes are exploring the universe far beyond our solar system, communicating with Earth from over 11 billion miles away. We have also developed technologies that allow humans to survive in space for lengthy durations, with Russian cosmonaut Valeri Polyakov holding the record for the longest single stay in space - a remarkable 437 days aboard the Mir space station.

What is the future of space exploration?

The Cold War 'Space Race' between the USA and Soviet Union ended in the 1970s. Today the landscape is very different, with multiple countries engaged in current and future space missions.

"Make no mistake about it: we're in a space race today, just as we were in the 1960s, and the stakes are even higher," US Vice President Mike Pence said during a speech in March 2019.

Currently there are over 70 different government and intergovernmental space agencies. Thirteen of these have space launch capabilities, including NASA, the European Space Agency (ESA), the Russian Federal Space Agency (Roscosmos) and the China National Space Administration (CNSA).

However, government space agencies are only part of the story when it comes to 21st century space travel. A number of commercial companies are also developing spaceflight capabilities, including SpaceX founded by Elon Musk, Blue Origin established by Amazon CEO Jeff Bezos, and Richard Branson's Virgin Galactic. By 2030, it has been estimated that the global space market could be worth £400 billion.

Both space agencies and commercial companies have a number of different objectives for the next 50 years, including:

-Automated and robotic exploration of the Solar System and beyond

-Telescopic exploration of deep space

-Development of innovative spacecraft

-Crewed spaceflight and settlements on planets

-Space tourism

-Mining of other planets.

Back to the Moon

As the closest celestial body to Earth, missions to the Moon are seen by many scientists and engineers as an essential starting point for voyages to more distant planets. The Moon may prove useful as a space station or testing ground for humans to learn how to replenish supplies, before looking to settle on distant planets such as Mars.

NASA has been set the ambitious goal of returning humans to the Moon by 2024 and establishing a sustainable human presence on the Moon by 2028. The US space agency is working with a number of international and commercial partners, including the European Space Agency, in order to achieve this. The mission is called Project Artemis: the goddess Artemis was the twin sister of Apollo in Greek mythology. Among the stated goals of the NASA mission is an aim to land the first woman on the Moon.

However, the United States is not the only country with lunar ambitions. China is planning a crewed mission to the Moon's south pole by 2030, and has already successfully landed a robotic rover on the Moon's far side.

India meanwhile launched a combined lunar orbiter, lander and rover on 22 July 2019, in a mission known as Chandrayaan-2. On 7 September 2019, the ISRO space station lost contact with the Vikram lunar lander, as it was just 2km from the lunar surface.

In September 2019 Elon Musk revealed a prototype of his Starship rocket, claiming it would be ready to take off in one to two months, reaching 19,800 metres before returning to Earth.

Future spacecraft

Organisations both public and private are looking to develop more sustainable ways of building and launching spacecraft for future missions, in order to overcome the major obstacle in space exploration: the astronomical costs involved.

One example of these innovations is the development of a new space capsule called Orion, managed by both NASA and the European Space Agency. The flexibility of the vehicle is designed to take astronauts to and from the International Space Station and also enable repeat landings on the Moon's surface. The Orion spacecraft was first launched in an uncrewed flight in December 2014, and it is intended to be the craft used during the Artemis missions to the Moon scheduled from 2020.

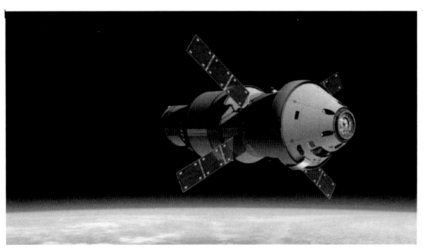

Artist depiction of the Orion module in space

Robotic exploration

As machines become increasingly capable of independently performing tasks, many organisations are looking to prioritise robotic over human spaceflight. These machines are designed for specific tasks and can withstand the extreme conditions of space.

NASA's Mars Curiosity Rover is a prime example of this. Launched on 26 November 2011, the robotic vehicle landed on the surface of Mars on 5 August 2012 and has been exploring the Martian landscape ever since. It even has its own Twitter account, keeping millions of followers up to date with its latest scientific observations.

Space tourism

In the last decade, companies such as Virgin Galactic, Airbus and Blue Origin have begun developing commercial spacecraft to send private customers into space. Currently, businesses are taking reservations for trips into the upper atmosphere, where patrons can experience zero-gravity and observe the curvature of the Earth. NASA has also announced plans to allow private individuals to visit the International Space Station, with the first flights scheduled for 2020.

Five future space missions

Name: Parker Solar Probe

Type: Probe

Launched: 12 August 2018

Operator: NASA

The Parker Solar Probe is named after astrophysicist Eugene Parker. While already launched, the probe won't reach its objective - the Sun - until

2025. Its mission is to obtain observations of the Sun and provide accurate data on solar winds (charged particles that escape from the Sun) and why they exist. The probe is built to withstand the 1377°C heat from the Sun at a distance of almost 95 million miles, seven times closer than any spacecraft before it.

Name: Mars Global Remote Sensing Orbiter and Small Rover (known as HX-1)

Type: Robotic rover

Launch: July 2020

Operator: CASC

This planned Chinese project aims to follow-up on its success of landing a probe on the far side of the Moon with its second mission to Mars in 2020. The stated objective of the HX-1 rover project is to land on Mars and search for the presence and potential for life on the Martian planet. It could also provide essential information as to the potential for crewed flights to Mars in the future.

Name: James Webb Space Telescope (JWST)

Type: Telescope

Launch: March 2021

Operator: NASA, ESA & CSA

Named after James Webb, the administrator at NASA during the Mercury and Gemini space programmes, this telescope will search for the first galaxies after the Big Bang. Furthermore, the use of infrared imaging will aid scientists in understanding the physical and chemical properties of these star systems, including the observation of some of the most distant events and objects in the universe.

Name: Starship

Type: Rocket

Launch: First commercial missions scheduled for 2021

Operator: SpaceX

The private company, SpaceX, is developing a powerful spacecraft and rocket system that could eventually be used to take humans to the Moon and Mars. With a potential carrying capacity of 100,000 kilograms, the rocket is designed to carry much larger payloads and crew numbers into space. Originally known as the Big Falcon Rocket, founder Elon Musk renamed the craft in November 2018, calling the transportation part of the vehicle 'Starship' and the rocket section 'Super Heavy'. Along with other SpaceX spacecraft and rocket systems, the project is aiming to be reusable, reducing the costs of future space exploration.

Name: Breakthrough Starshot

Type: Spacecraft

Operator: Breakthrough Initiatives

Breakthrough Starshot is a bold engineering project aiming to send 1000 tiny spacecraft to Alpha Centauri in a journey lasting 20 years. The mission intends to test the possibility of ultra-fast space travel (15-20 per cent of the speed of light), and achieve interstellar travel. However, the project is still very much in its infancy.

Why have we not been back to the Moon?

US astronaut Eugene Cernan is the last human to have walked on the Moon. He and fellow Apollo 17 astronaut Harrison Schmitt left the lunar surface on 14 December 1972. Since then, human crews have not returned.

Image showing SpaceX's Falcon Heavy demo mission at Cape Canaveral on 6 February 2018

However, many probes have been sent to the Moon in the decades since, including missions by Indian, Chinese and European space agencies.

One of the main reasons for the lack of crewed missions to the Moon is the cost. The Apollo missions cost roughly $200 billion (£160bn) in today's money. Even following a funding boost, NASA's annual budget for 2019 was $21.5 billion (£17.25bn).

Commercial space companies have changed the economics of space exploration, but for both private companies and national agencies the long-term objectives of future space missions need to be more innovative than simply repeating a historical mission. Current missions to the Moon are aiming to explore new regions of the lunar surface, including its far side and its south pole. Crewed missions are also designed to be part of a longer term process of exploring further into space, beginning with Mars.

How much does it cost to go into space?

The high cost of leaving the Earth is the major obstacle to further exploration of space. Currently for example, only the Russian Soyuz rocket is able to transport astronauts to the International Space Station, with NASA paying a reported $75 million per seat in 2017.

When NASA's space shuttle program was in operation between the 1980s and mid-2000s, it could carry a payload of 27,500 kilograms for an average cost per flight of $1.5 billion. This cost has reduced with the collaboration of private companies: a SpaceX Falcon 9 rocket can launch 22,800kg into low Earth orbit for a published cost of $62 million.

Once in space, the costs remain high. The International Space Station has been dubbed the most expensive machine ever constructed, with an estimated total cost since since its first launch in 1998 of $150 billion.

How much would a flight into space cost me?

Depending on where in space you're going, a ticket aboard a commercial spacecraft could cost from $250,000 to tens of millions of dollars.

Private company Virgin Galactic is offering 'space tourists' the chance to cross the boundary between the upper atmosphere and outer space (known as the Karman Line at 62 miles above the Earth). A place on the flight costs a reported $250,000, and more than 600 people are said to have bought tickets.

NASA announced in 2019 that it would be opening up the International Space Station to private individuals from 2020, with an estimated cost of $35,000 per day. However, this does not include the cost of the spaceflight itself, which is set to be run by private companies SpaceX and Boeing and could cost over $60 million per flight.

The world's first private astronaut Dennis Tito paid a reported $20 million to join the Soyuz TM-32 mission on 28 April 2001. The American businessman spent nearly eight days in space aboard the International Space Station. The trip was booked with a space tourism company called Space Adventures Ltd.

Dennis Tito, the world's first space tourist with pilots of the Soyuz TM-32, Talgat Musabayev and Yuri Baturin

Resources

probonoaustralia.com.au, "Where does our future lie as a people: together or apart?" By Rachel Clark; gaialearning.co.uk, "Does Our Future Lie in The Balance? The greatest changes often take a leap of faith. A thinking that's outside the box."; timesofindia.indiantimes.com, "The future lies in the past." By Vanita Dawra Nangia; atlantacouncil.org, "Welcome to 2030: Three visions of what the world could look like in ten years." By Mathew Burrows and Anca Agachi; iucn.org, "Nature's Future, Our Future - The World Speaks."; nature.org, "The Science of Sustainability: Can a unified path for development and conservation lead to a better future?"; sandiegouniontribune.com, "Opinion: What will the future of space travel look like? And what does it mean for this planet?" By U-T Letters; rmg.co.uk, "What is the future of space travel? Discover the next giant leap in crewed spaceflight." ;

Addenum

Nature's Future, Our Future - The World Speaks

The IUCN World Commission on Protected Areas has compiled the

voices of a range of global organisations and world leaders on the importance of protecting and conserving nature amidst the challenges of the COVID-19 pandemic. As the result of a global pandemic, we are witnessing an unprecedented call to transform human society and economies and thus reset the relationship between people and

nature. This compilation aims to capture a critical moment, as we work together to build the momentum for transformative action to address the major crises of our planet by maintaining nature and ecosystems.

Page 290

Antonio Guterres, Director General, United Nations

"Making peace with nature is the defining task of the 21st century, it must be the top, top priority for everyone, everywhere."

Kristalina Georgieva, Managing Director, International Monetary Fund

"The best memorial we can build for those who lost their lives in the pandemic is that greener, smarter, fairer world."

Carlos Manuel Rodríguez, CEO and Chairperson, Global Environment Facility

"When we look back in years to come, I truly believe that 2020, despite the suffering it unleashed on all of us, will be seen as the year where we took a decision, the proper decision, and a turning point happened."

"I believe that the only way forward is to invest in nature and focus on a green recovery to prevent not just future pandemics but as well to prepare ourselves to fight ongoing environmental threats such as climate change, and biodiversity collapse."

United Nations Decade of Restoration

"There has never been a more urgent need to restore damaged ecosystems than now.

Ecosystems support all life on Earth. The healthier our ecosystems are, the healthier the planet - and its people. The UN Decade on Ecosystem Restoration aims to prevent, halt and reverse the degradation of ecosystems on every continent and in every ocean. It can help to end poverty, combat climate change and prevent a mass extinction. It will only succeed if everyone plays a part."

HRH The Prince of Wales

"The current pandemic has brought unimaginable devastation to people's lives and livelihoods and national economies. At the same time, the green recovery offers an unprecedented opportunity to rethink and reset the ways in which we live and do business. I have long believed we need a shift in our economic model that places nature and the world's transition to net-zero at the heart of how we operate, prioritizing the pursuit of sustainable inclusive growth in the decades to come."

Dr Kathy MacKinnon

Chair, IUCN World Commission on Protected Areas (WCPA)

WCPA has pulled together this compilation of quotes and extracts from speeches of world leaders to capture a critical moment. As the result of a global pandemic we are witnessing an unprecedented call to transform human society and economies and reset the relationship between people and nature.

This collection is a contribution to the work of IUCN and the World Commission on Protected Areas. Please do what you can to amplify these messages by disseminating them to your networks, sharing with colleagues and influencers, distributing to students, sending to politicians or distributing through social media or any other means of communication. Change only happens when voices are raised: - by speaking together, we can be heard. We will try to keep the list evergreen and will set up a mechanism on the IUCN WCPA website to do so.

The calls for urgent transformative change have come from many quarters: major international institutions, politicians, business leaders, academics and religious thinkers - as well as from civil society. At a dark time for the world, this provides hope of a more rational and just future, based on science and respect for all life. We need to ensure that the inspirational quotes highlighted here will lead to positive action through ambitious conservation targets and a more sustainable future, with protected areas and other nature-based solutions at the heart of greener economic stimulus packages post- pandemic

The imperative to attain genuine sustainability is not new: it was heard nearly 50 years ago at the Stockholm Conference on the Human Environment, and is embedded in the UN Sustainable Development Goals and many other charters. The climate crisis, the catastrophic decline of ecosystems and species, and now the global pandemic show beyond doubt that humanity has no choice but to respond vigorously to these combined threats. That means moving rapidly to zero emissions, protecting and restoring earth's natural systems, and shaping all policies to secure a healthy planet.

Many of the quotes call for the better protection of natural ecosystems - through networks of protected and conserved areas. WCPA supports the calls for an international goal of protecting 30% of the oceans and land by 2030 under new targets for the Convention on Biological Diversity. Protected and conserved areas are key to maintaining healthy ecosystems, protecting diverse natural habitats and wild species. When governed and managed effectively, they also support human health and well-being, contributing to food and water security, disaster risk reduction, climate mitigation and adaptation and local livelihoods. And we now know that they can also help to protect us against the scourge of future pandemics.

This compendium was compiled by the WCPA Vice Chair for Oceania, Penelope Figgis with assistance from other WCPA members, including the WCPA Task Force on COVID-19 and Protected Areas. WCPA will publish a Special Issue of the journal PARKS at the end of February containing papers on the impact of the Covid pandemic on protected and conserved areas and how society can move forward to a greener nature-centred recovery.

United Nations

Antonio Guterres, Director General

"The State of the Planet" address Columbia University, December 2020

"Let's be clear: human activities are at the root of our descent towards chaos.

But that means human action can help solve it.

Making peace with nature is the defining task of the 21st century. It must be the top, top priority for everyone, everywhere.

In this context, the recovery from the pandemic is an opportunity. We can see rays of hope in the form of a vaccine. But there is no vaccine for the planet. Nature needs a bailout. In overcoming the pandemic, we can also avert climate cataclysm and restore our planet.

This is an epic policy test. But ultimately this is a moral test."

"But we must remember: there can be no separating climate action from the larger planetary picture. Everything is interlinked – the global commons and global well-being. That means we must act more broadly, more holistically, across many fronts, to secure the health of our planet on which all life depends. Nature feeds us, clothes us, quenches our thirst, generates our oxygen, shapes our culture and our faiths and forges our very identity.

2020 was supposed to have been a "super year" for nature but the pandemic has had other plans for us. Now we must use 2021 to address our planetary emergency... we must act more broadly, more holistically, across many fronts, to secure the health of our planet on which all life depends. Nature feeds us, clothes us, quenches our thirst, generates our oxygen, shapes our culture and our faiths and forges our very identity."

United Nations Congress on Trade and Development (UNCTAD)

September 2020

At the first ever global summit dedicated to biodiversity held virtually on 30 September, various leaders said the COVID-19 pandemic is an opportunity for countries to put bold and ambitious environmental action at the heart of their post coronavirus economic recovery strategies.

One of the tools at countries' disposal is BioTrade – the collection, production, transformation and commercialisation of goods and services derived from biodiversity under BioTrade Principles and Criteria, a set of guidelines that emphasise environmental, social and economic sustainability.

"Linking trade, biodiversity and sustainable development is a compulsory pathway towards more resilience at community, private sector and, ultimately, national levels in post-COVID-19 recovery efforts," said UNCTAD economic affairs officer Lorena Jaramillo.

Organization for Economic Co-operation and Development (OECD)

Angel Gurría, OECD Secretary-General, & Pedro Sanchez, President of Spain

OECD Opinion, December 2020

The third priority is to support a transformative recovery and develop a new narrative on economic growth. National recovery and resilience plans constitute unique opportunities not just to jump-start our economies, but also to undertake bold and transformative action to make them more equal, cohesive and environmentally sound, in line with the 2030 Agenda and the Sustainable Development Goals. The COVID-19 crisis has increased inequalities, while climate change, biodiversity loss and other environmental emergencies loom large. Analysis by the OECD shows that ambitious climate action to decarbonise our economies can be a source of growth, incomes and jobs.

The Climate COP26 in Glasgow and the UN Biodiversity Conference, both to be held in 2021, will be tests for our collective determination. Our single, most important intergenerational responsibility is to protect the planet. This new narrative also requires fostering an economic and productivity growth model based on fair wages, decent working conditions and enhanced social dialogue.

Over the last decade, the OECD has been a leading voice in promoting an approach to economic growth that combines inclusiveness and environmental sustainability. Building on solid evidence and data, we need to work together to develop this narrative further, measuring outcomes beyond GDP, and developing a consensus around a new economic framework that reconciles people, prosperity and the planet.

We are living in extraordinary times. The challenges ahead are too significant for any one country to tackle them alone. Only through collective action will we be able to address them and *"build back better"* towards more resilient, more inclusive and greener economies and societies. With a long-term vision, a strong ambition and an enlightened sense of mission, as we celebrate the OECD's 60th Anniversary, let us draw inspiration from its history and its accomplishments, to deliver better policies for better lives for the generations to come.

World Health Organisation (WHO)

June 2020

"On the occasion of World Environment Day, WHO calls for a healthy and green recovery from COVID-19 that places the protection and restoration of nature central.

A recently launched WHO Manifesto calls for decisive action to address the root causes of the COVID-19 pandemic by reducing social inequalities and ecosystem degradation, and transforming the way we relate to the environment in which we live."

WHO has published a set of Prescriptions for a healthy, green recovery from COVID-19, of which the first prescription is to "Protect and preserve the source of human health: Nature." An open letter to the G20 leaders from over 40 million health professionals also urged for a healthy recovery from COVID-19 where nature is thriving. A healthy recovery, the letter states, needs to double down on pollution, climate change and deforestation, in order to prevent "unleashing new health threats upon vulnerable populations".

World Economic Forum (WEF)

Akanksha Khatri, Head of the Nature Action Agenda

Future of Nature and Business Report, July 2020

The global COVID-19 pandemic has caused unprecedented job losses and economic uncertainty. As governments and businesses look to stimulate growth, a new study from the World Economic Forum found that 'nature-positive' solutions can create 395 million jobs by 2030.

The Future of Nature and Business Report provides blueprints for businesses to tap into a $10.1 trillion business opportunity, focusing on industry actions that are nature-positive, meaning that they add value to nature.

The report states there is *"no future for business as usual."* It finds that while fighting climate change is essential, it is *"not enough,"* and *"a fundamental transformation"* is needed across the socioeconomic systems of: food, land, and ocean use; infrastructure and the built environment; and extractives and energy.

"We can address the looming bio-diversity crisis and reset the economy in a way that creates and protects millions of jobs," said Akanksha Khatri, Head of the Nature Action Agenda, World Economic Forum. "Public calls are getting louder for businesses and government to do better. We can protect our food supplies, make better use of our infrastructure and tap into new energy sources by transitioning to nature-positive solutions."

Food and Agricultural Organization (FAO)

Qu Dongyu, Director General

World Environment Day Speech, June 2020

"The 2020 World Environment Day theme is "Time for nature" and it focuses on biodiversity. Biodiversity provides essential infrastructure to support all life on earth and it is also a key base of the ecosystem. More importantly, it is a base, genetic base for food diversity.

It is an excellent opportunity to rethink the relationship among humans, animals, and the environment. The recent events, from the locust infestations across East Africa, to the fall army worm, and now the global disease pandemic, demonstrates the interdependency of humans, animals and the environment."

FAO launched its flagship report on the State of World Biodiversity for Food and Agriculture. This report highlights the need to protect our natural resources including biodiversity and the need to conserve and use genetic resources to increase productivity.

We know that we can produce enough food to feed the world and protect the environment at the same time. Eradicating hunger is essential.

The FAO adopted its Strategy on Mainstreaming Biodiversity across agriculture sectors, a strategy that automatically aims at reducing the negative impact of agriculture practices on biodiversity, to promote sustainable agriculture practices and to conserve, enhance, preserve and restore biodiversity as a whole.

United Nations Development Program (UNDP)

Achim Steiner, Administrator

Launch of the 2020 Human Development Report, December 2020

"Scientists call this emerging era, the Anthropocene – or the age of humans. And in it, as the 2020 Human Development Report (HDR) sets out, humanity is waging a war against itself.

Consider this: the total mass of the things humans have made - like buildings, roads and bottle tops — now exceeds the total mass of all living things on the planet, from tiny bacteria to giant whales, according to new research.

Today, humans literally have the power to alter the atmosphere and the biosphere in which we live. The power to destroy, and the power to repair. No species has ever had that kind of power before. With it, we humans have achieved incredible things, but we have also taken the Earth and all the people on it to the brink."

This year, constrained by mostly pre-pandemic data, we decided to try something new. We added countries' consumption and carbon footprints to the Human Development Index (HDI). The result is a less rosy but clearer analysis of human progress.

Plotting out the data on a graph reveals a profound insight: there are countries that leave a minimal imprint on the planet. There are countries with prosperous populations. But not one nation in the world sits in both camps. In the graphs used to illustrate this data in the report we have, quite literally, an 'empty box'. Filling this empty box is the next frontier for human development.

This may sound daunting. But the way forward is not rocket science. It comes down to the incentives, social norms, and nature-based solutions that will reset how people and planet interact. And the choices leaders make today as they build forward better from COVID-19 will be fundamental.

United Nations Educational, Scientific and Cultural Organisation (UNESCO) Audrey Azoulay, Director-General

Launch of Strategic Direction for UNESCO, December 2020

If we are to build sustainable societies, the environment must be preserved through the promotion of science, technology, and natural heritage. Respondents to the World in 2030 survey named climate change and biodiversity loss the greatest challenge to peaceful societies this decade – and also called for the relationship between humans and nature to be rethought… the second great challenge of our time lies in the imperative need for humanity to find a sustainable way of interacting with nature.

"Through our new strategy, we must respond to this challenge, mobilising knowledge, but also education and culture, and disseminating information, to achieve a decisive change in humanity's relationship with its environment."

One way of achieving this – one with growing global consensus – will be to protect 30% of the planet for nature. UNESCO's networks of biosphere reserves, geoparks and natural World Heritage sights, says Azoulay, are tried and tested tools to this end. Recently, 25 new sites have been designated as biosphere reserves. Other important UNESCO projects that help improve the relationship between humans and nature include a new agreement with Italy to establish a network of international experts for nature preservation, and the UN Decade of Ocean Science, for which UNESCO has a leading role.

UN Human Rights Council

Right to a healthy environment: good practices: Report of the Special Rapporteur on the issue of human rights obligations relating to the enjoyment of a safe, clean, healthy and sustainable environment, December 2019

"In the present report, the Special Rapporteur highlights good practices in the recognition and implementation of the human right to a safe, clean, healthy and sustainable environment. The term "good practice" is defined broadly to include laws, policies, jurisprudence, strategies, programmes, projects and other measures that contribute to reducing adverse impacts on the environment, improving environmental quality and fulfilling human rights. The good practices address both the procedural and substantive elements of the right to a safe, clean, healthy and sustainable environment. The procedural elements are access to information, public participation, and access to justice and effective remedies. The substantive elements include clean air, a safe climate, access to safe water and adequate sanitation, healthy and sustainably produced food, non-toxic environments in which to live, work, study and play, and healthy biodiversity and ecosystems."

European Central Bank

Christine Lagarde, President, with Sir David Attenborough, natural historian

International Monetary Fund Podcasts, May 2019

In nature, everything is connected. This is equally true of a healthy environment and a healthy economy. We cannot hope to sustain life without taking care of nature. And we need healthy economies to lift people out of poverty and achieve the United Nations Sustainable Development Goals.

In our current model these goals sometimes seem to collide, and our economic pursuits encroach too closely on nature. But nature—a stable climate, reliable freshwater, forests, and other natural resources—is what makes industry possible. It is not one or the other. We cannot have long-term human development without a steady climate and a healthy natural world.

The bottom line is that when we damage the natural world, we damage ourselves. The impact of our growing economic footprint threatens our own future directly. By some estimates, more than 50 percent of the world's population is now urbanised, increasing the likelihood of people losing touch with nature.

With the projected rise in ocean levels and increase in the average temperature of the planet, large swaths of land, even whole countries, will become uninhabitable, triggering mass climate-induced migration. Never has it been more important to understand how the natural world works and what we must do to preserve it.

European Commission

Ursula von der Leyen, President

May 2020

"The recovery plan turns the immense challenge we face into an opportunity, not only by supporting the recovery but also by investing in our future: the European Green Deal and digitalisation will boost jobs and growth, the resilience of our societies and the health of our environment. This is Europe's moment. Our willingness to act must live up to the challenges we are all facing. With Next Generation EU we are providing an ambitious answer."

We Mean Business Coalition

May 2020

150 global companies with a combined market capitalisation of over US$ 2.4 trillion and representing over 5 million employees signed a

statement urging governments around the world to align their COVID-19 economic aid and recovery efforts with the latest climate science. They reaffirmed their own science-based commitments to achieving zero carbon economy and call on governments to match their ambition.

Ignacio Galán, Chairman and CEO, Iberdrola, said: "The world must be united to tackle the current health crisis. And, as we emerge from this crisis, we must focus economic recovery on activities aligned with key priorities, such as the fight against climate change, and reactivating economic activity and employment quickly and sustainably. Companies like ours remain committed to investing billions in clean energy, creating jobs and long-term economic and environmental benefits. Pursuing environmental sustainability will be essential for long-term economic recovery."

The business voices are convened by the Science Based Targets initiative (SBTi) and its Business Ambition for 1.5 C campaign partners, the UN Global Compact and the We Mean Business coalition.

World Resources Institute

Charles Barber, Senior Biodiversity Advisor

Report Chair, COVID-19 Response and Recovery: Nature-Based Solutions for People, Planet & Prosperity, October 2020

CEOs from 22 leading conservation and sustainable development organisations, including the World Resources Institute, have come together in unparalleled consensus to urge policymakers to integrate nature into COVID-19 response and recovery efforts. The group preleased a set of recommendations for policymakers, COVID-19 Response and Recovery: Nature-Based Solutions for People, Planet and Prosperity.

"The COVID-19 pandemic has shown the world that the destruction of our natural environment has a profound impact on human wellbeing – these issues are interconnected.

Our community of experts agrees that taking a nature-based approach is absolutely essential for nature and is often the most effective way of tackling the corresponding public health and economic crises.

"The Nature-Based recommendations for policymakers provide a concise and practical roadmap for governments and other stakeholders to confront the intertwined challenges of COVID-19, biodiversity loss, climate change and sustainable development."

April 2020

"In the midst of our global response to COVID-19, the world is in need of an economic transformation, one that promotes both the sustainable wellbeing of individuals as well as the environment in tandem. We have arrived at a turning point. The challenges we face now, together, are tremendous. But in the face of current adversity, and the near halt of our global economy, we have a collective opportunity to join together for a brighter, more sustainable future. The decisions that policymakers, businesses and individuals choose now will determine if we prosper and accelerate a more sustainable world, or not."

INTERNATIONAL LEADERS

Joseph Biden

President, United States of America

On signing an Executive order calling for the reversal of many negative environmental policies and for a renewed commitment to environmental and human health 20 January 2021

"Our Nation has an abiding commitment to empower our workers and communities; promote and protect our public health and the environment; and conserve our national treasures and monuments, places that secure our national memory. Where the Federal Government has failed to meet that commitment in the past, it must advance environmental justice. In carrying out this charge, the Federal Government must be guided by the best science and be protected by processes that ensure the integrity of Federal decision-making. It is, therefore, the policy of my Administration to listen to the science; to improve public health and protect our environment; to ensure access to clean air and water; to limit exposure to dangerous chemicals and pesticides; to hold polluters accountable, including those who disproportionately harm communities of

colour and low-income communities; to reduce greenhouse gas emissions; to bolster resilience to the impacts of climate change; to restore and expand our national treasures and monuments; and to prioritise both environmental justice and the creation of the well-paying union jobs necessary to deliver on these goals.

To that end, this order directs all executive departments and agencies (agencies) to immediately review and, as appropriate and consistent with applicable law, take action to address the promulgation of Federal regulations and other actions during the last 4 years that conflict with these important national objectives, and to immediately commence work to confront the climate crisis."

Angela Merkel

Federal Chancellor, Germany

One Planet Summit, January 2021

"Natural habitats are being destroyed every day. We risk losing around a quarter of most plant and animal species. These drastic losses have a grave impact on life and quality of life, including for us humans. And so, we must step up our efforts to protect biodiversity and natural habitats – not some time or other, but now, and not somehow or other, but monumentally. If we do not, the consequences will soon be irreversible."

"We humans can only truly flourish on a healthy planet with a rich and healthy tapestry of animals and plants. This is the core of the One Health approach. We have worked with France to launch the One Health High-Level Expert Panel. This panel aims to facilitate cooperation between the WHO, the FAO, World Organization for Animal Health and the UN Environment Program."

Justin Trudeau

Prime Minister, Canada

World Environment Day, June 2020

"Biodiversity and healthy ecosystems are vital to our health and continued prosperity. This year, as we practice physical distancing and spend more time than usual in our homes to keep our families and communities safe during COVID-19, we are reminded of how important nature is to our well-being and everyday lives. As we look toward restarting our economy, we need to continue investing in the protection of our natural

surroundings and the fight against climate change—because if you do not have a plan for the environment, you cannot have a plan for the economy. I encourage Canadians to do their part in creating a more equitable and sustainable world, and to take action to protect our environment. To take care of ourselves, we must take care of nature.

"Together, we can build a world that is cleaner, healthier, and more sustainable – today and for future generations."

One Planet Summit, January 2021

"If we do not act, the ecosystems on which we depend for our water, air, and food could collapse. .... We must work together to prevent future global health crises. By adopting measures to protect nature, fight climate change, and promote scientific knowledge, we will make 2021 a defining year in our collective efforts to save the planet."

Greta Thunberg

Youth Advocate for Action Climate Change

World Economic Forum, January 2021,

"For me, hope is the feeling that keeps you going, even though all odds may be against you. For me hope comes from action not just words. For me, hope is telling it like it is. No matter how difficult or uncomfortable that may be.

And again, I'm not here to tell you what to do. After all, safeguarding the future living conditions and preserving life on earth as we know it is voluntary. The choice is yours to make.

But I can assure you this. You can't negotiate with physics. And your children and grandchildren will hold you accountable for the choices that you make. How's that for a deal?"

"Planting trees is good, of course, but it's nowhere near enough of what needs to be done, and it cannot replace real mitigation or rewilding nature."

Sir David Attenborough

International filmmaker and conservation icon

From the film 'A life on our Planet', September 2020

"To restore stability to our planet, we must restore its biodiversity, the very thing that we've removed. It's the only way out of this crisis we've created – we must rewild the world."

Xi Jinping

President, China

United Nations (UN) Summit on Biodiversity. September 2020

"The loss of biodiversity and the degradation of the ecosystem pose a major risk to human survival and development. COVID-19 reminds us of the interdependence between man and Nature. It falls to all of us to act together and urgently to advance protection and development in parallel, so that we can turn Earth into a beautiful homeland for all creatures to live in harmony."

"At present, there exists an acceleration of the global extinction of species. The loss of biodiversity and the degradation of the ecosystem pose a major risk to human survival and development. COVID-19 reminds us of the interdependence between man and Nature. It falls to all of us to act together and urgently to advance protection and development in parallel, so that we can turn Earth into a beautiful homeland for all creatures to live in harmony."

"The industrial civilisation, while creating vast material wealth, has caused ecological crises as manifested in biodiversity loss and environmental damage. A sound ecosystem is essential for the prosperity of civilisation. We need to take up our lofty responsibility for the entire human civilisation, and we need to respect Nature, follow its laws and protect it."

Larry Fink

CEO of BlackRock

Annual letter to company leaders, January 2021

The CEO of the world's largest asset manager, BlackRock, which manages some $7 trillion for investors has urged global companies to publicly disclose their plans for how they will operate in a world with net-zero emissions by 2050. The CEO highlighted climate change as a business and investing priority in his annual letter to company leaders. He also called for a single global standard for sustainability disclosures, saying it would *"enable investors to make more informed decisions about how to achieve durable long-term returns"*.

"We know that climate risk is investment risk" "But we also believe the climate transition presents a historic investment opportunity."

"I have great optimism about the future of capitalism and the future health of the economy -- not in spite of the energy transition, but because of it."

Volkan Bozkir (Turkey)

President, UN General Assembly

Opening the United Nations Summit on Biodiversity, 30 September 2020

"Humanity's existence on Earth depends entirely on its ability to protect the natural world around it. Yet every year, 13 million hectares of forest are lost, while 1 million species are at risk of extinction. Meanwhile, species of vertebrates have declined by 68 per cent in the past 50 years. "Clearly, we must heed the lessons we have learned and respect the world in which we live," he said, describing COVID 19 as an opportunity to do just that through a post pandemic green recovery that emphasises the protection of biodiversity can lead to a more sustainable and resilient world."

United Nations Summit on Biodiversity

Leaders Pledge for Nature

Political leaders participating in the UN Summit on Biodiversity, representing 82 countries from all regions and the European Union, September 2020

"We are in a state of planetary emergency: the interdependent crises of biodiversity loss and ecosystem degradation and climate change - driven in large part by

unsustainable production and consumption - require urgent and immediate global action. Science clearly shows that biodiversity loss, land and ocean degradation, pollution, resource depletion and climate change are accelerating at an unprecedented rate. This acceleration is causing irreversible harm to our life support systems and aggravating poverty and inequalities as well as hunger and malnutrition. Unless halted and reversed with immediate effect, it will cause significant damage to global economic, social and political resilience and stability and will render achieving the Sustainable Development Goals impossible. Biodiversity loss is both accelerated by climate change and at the same time exacerbates it, by debilitating nature's ability to sequester or store carbon and to adapt to climate change impacts. Ecosystem degradation, human encroachment in ecosystems, loss of natural habitats and biodiversity and the illegal wildlife trade can also increase the risk of emergence and spread of infectious diseases. COVID-19 shows that these diseases have dramatic impacts not only on loss of life and health but across all spheres of society."*

His Excellency Dr Mohamed Irfaan Ali

President, Guyana

Statement on behalf of The Group of 77 and China at the virtual UN Summit on Biodiversity, September 2020

"*This Summit should galvanise the necessary political will for the post-2020 global biodiversity framework in line with the 2030 Agenda and energise stakeholders for the fifteenth meeting of the Conference of the Parties to the Convention on Biological Diversity under the theme "Ecological civilisation: building a shared future for all life on Earth."*

Relaying the concerns of the G77, President Ali stated that "our development challenges have been exacerbated by the COVID-19 pandemic and its impact will continue to be felt well into the future. The pandemic is also jarring reminder of the important relationship between people and nature. There must be urgent and significant actions to reduce the degradation of natural habitats, halt biodiversity loss, protect and prevent the extinction of threatened species. The international community must strengthen efforts to counter these trends and protect the ecosystems, on both land and water."

Speaking in his national capacity President Ali reminded of the important ecosystem services provided by Guyana's forest and Guyana's commitment to low carbon development. Since 1929, Guyana has used protected areas as models for sustainable livelihoods and living in harmony with nature.

Mary Robinson

Former President of Ireland

July 2020

"We will not reach the goals of the Paris Climate Agreement without fully embracing nature-based solutions and protecting at least 30 percent of the world's land and ocean by 2030."

H.E. Barbara Creecy

Minister of Environment of South Africa & President of the African Ministerial Conference on the Environment

8th special session of the African Ministerial Conference on the Environment, December 2020

"Whilst this Pandemic is having a profound negative impact on sustainable development and our efforts to combat environmental degradation and eradicate poverty, it also presents opportunities to set our recovery on a path of transformative sustainable development. Many governments and regions are prioritising a green recovery as part of their stimulus packages to address the crisis."

"Now more than ever, it is imperative to work together as Africa and take collective and resolute action to deal with the socio-economic and environmental fallout from this crisis, for the benefit of the Continent. There is indeed a compelling case for the environment and rich natural resources of the African Continent, if utilised in a sustainable manner, to contribute significantly to the Continent's recovery from the impacts of the Pandemic."

Pacific Island Nations

Protected Areas and Conservation Conference Major Statement November 2020

The 10th Pacific Islands Conference on Protected Areas and Conservation was held online in November 2020. As part of the high-level segment of the Conference Ministers and heads of organizations of the Pacific Island Roundtable (PIRT) endorsed the Vemoore Declaration committing to urgent action for nature conservation. This Declaration aligns to the Conference Action Tracks and also essentially endorses the new Framework for Nature Conservation in the Pacific Islands region.

"We, representatives of the governments of Pacific Island countries and territories, our partner countries, and the Heads of Organizations of members of the Pacific Islands Round Table for Nature Conservation, gathered for the High-Level Session of the 10th Pacific Islands Conference on Nature Conservation and Protected Areas, declare that the global biodiversity crisis is urgent, and that transformative action must not be delayed.

This crisis is an existential threat to our Pacific Ocean, our Pacific Islands, and to ourselves as Pacific peoples. We join world leaders that met at the UN Summit on Biodiversity 2020 and recognized the current planetary emergency of interdependent crises of biodiversity loss and ecosystem degradation and climate change that requires urgent and immediate global action. We note with grave concern that none of the global 2011-2020 Aichi Biodiversity Targets have been fully met.

The Blue Pacific collectively calls for all countries to adopt a strong deal for nature and people, to reverse or halt the loss of our natural ecosystems and put nature on a path to recovery by 2030. The COVID-19 pandemic is a stark reminder of the dependency of all our societies on healthy and resilient natural ecosystems. Our necessary social and economic recovery from the pandemic is a regional and global opportunity to transform our collective relationship with the natural world, and to build back better. We recognise the potential of our Pacific Islands to lead the world in ecological stewardship, drawing on our rich indigenous heritage and the close relationship of our communities with the land, sea and sky."

Boris Johnson

Prime Minister, United Kingdom

Announcing Covid Green Recovery Plan, November 2020

"We will use science to rout the virus, and we must use the same extraordinary powers

of invention to repair the economic damage from Covid-19, and to build back better. Now is the time to plan for a green recovery with high-skilled jobs that give people the satisfaction of knowing they are helping to make the country cleaner, greener and more beautiful."

"Green and growth can go hand-in-hand. So let us meet the most enduring threat to our planet with one of the most innovative and ambitious programmes of job-creation we have known."

Ban Ki-Moon

Former UN Secretary General

Quoted in BCG article 'How Government Can Fuel a Green Recovery', September 2020

"World leaders are committing unprecedented funds to recovery packages. Their choices will shape our economies and societies for decades, and determine whether we breathe clean air, create a sustainable low-carbon future and possibly even survive as a species."

Helen Clark

Former Prime Minister of New Zealand

Former Administrator of the United Nations Development Program

"Although biodiversity loss continues globally, many countries are significantly slowing the rate of loss by shoring up protected natural areas and the services they provide, and in expanding national park systems with tighter management and more secure funding."

Johnson Cerda

Indigenous Kichwa of the Ecuadorian Amazon

"Many Indigenous communities rely on nature for everything — from food and water to their livelihoods and culture. Though they account for only 5 percent of the world's population, Indigenous peoples use or manage more than a quarter of Earth's surface

and protect 80 percent of global biodiversity. Indigenous peoples manage 35 percent of intact forests and at least a quarter of above-ground carbon in tropical forests.

Because of this intimate relationship with nature, we are the first ones to feel the impact of the climate crisis."

"Rather than trying to take over lands or make all of the decisions of how to protect a certain area, governments and environmental organisations must instead work with Indigenous peoples to ensure that everyone's interests are taken into account. Indigenous peoples have centuries' worth of traditional knowledge to contribute to the fight to stop climate change and biodiversity loss. We all want to achieve the same goal — and the first step is making sure our voices are heard."

Svenja Schulze

Federal Environment Minister, Germany

June 2020

"I am committed to an ambitious strategy for the international conservation of biodiversity in line with the One Health approach to protect nature and our health.

The IPBES Global Assessment on Biodiversity and Ecosystem Services shows that the global loss of biodiversity is dramatic. Natural habitats are being altered and destroyed. People are encroaching on these habitats, and biodiversity is declining drastically in many regions of the world.

The current situation in particular shows that these kinds of crises can only be contained or prevented through international coordination together with global partners. This can be achieved through bilateral and multilateral cooperation, for example, in the context of major campaigns such as the UN Decade for Ecosystem Restoration. Or by establishing binding international laws. The 15th Conference of the Parties to the Convention on Biological Diversity next year represents an opportunity.

The international community can show that it has learned from the coronavirus pandemic. It can adopt a new global biodiversity strategy that includes the necessary measures for the global conservation of biodiversity, which will also reduce the risk of future pandemics.

The focus is reconciling economic activities with nature conservation, preserving ecosystems and protecting habitats."

High Ambition Coalition

Statement on Resilient Recovery, June 2020

"The COVID-19 crisis has shown the intrinsic linkages between planetary and human health, and the urgent need to strengthen our global response to systemic threats. As we continue our efforts to address the ongoing climate crisis, an ambitious recovery from the COVID-19 pandemic that supports the vulnerable, creates jobs, and sets us on track to limit global warming to 1.5 °C is both possible and necessary."

"The COVID-19 pandemic has also created an unprecedented moment for countries to reset their economies with climate-conscious recovery policies – and the HAC has once again heeded a call for ambitious action. At a June 2020 HAC virtual ministerial meeting, leaders endorsed the UN Secretary General's six climate related principles for COVID recovery and called for solidarity measures in support of developing countries and encourages a target of 60% of recovery spending to focus on "the green economy and low-carbon professions."

C40 Mayors' Statement for a Green and Just Recovery

July 2020

"Around the world, C40 Cities connects 97 of the world's greatest cities to take bold climate action, leading the way towards a healthier and more sustainable future. Representing 700+ million citizens and one quarter of the global economy, mayors of the C40 cities are committed to delivering on the most ambitious goals of the Paris Agreement at the local level, as well as to cleaning the air we breathe."

"In July we released the C40 Mayors' Agenda for a Green and Just Recovery defining our vision, putting forward concrete policies and initiatives and calling for action by all governments and institutions to support our efforts. In less than four months, we have made crucial progress, showing what can be achieved when we act quickly, unlock funds and shift to a new green and just paradigm. Since then, we have taken bold action in our cities, including: the launch of the first city-led Green New Deal in Asia, funding programs supporting green start-ups and entrepreneurs, additional investments worth millions of dollars in zero emissions mobility, more liveable and affordable housing and resilient infrastructure. We are developing new programs to create thousands of new green jobs, upskill and train workers and have passed temporary protections for gig and essential workers. We have created dozens of kilometres of new, permanent walking and cycling lanes and have accelerated planting

Page 313

new trees and increasing greening in our cities."

In addition, 12 cities with 36 million residents are calling on city and pension funds with over US$295 billion in total assets to divest from fossil fuels. As mayors and representatives of many of the world's leading cities representing over 700 million people and 25% GDP worldwide, we know we cannot achieve ambitious climate change goals alone. Therefore, we are committed to working with every citizen, company, government agency and international institution to deliver real outcomes. Our collective prize will be returning to a safer and healthier climate, achieving a more equitable economy, and recovering faster from the pandemic.

INTERNATIONAL ENVIRONMENTAL INSTITUTIONS

International Union for Conservation of Nature (IUCN)

Extracts IUCN Statement on Covid 19, April 2020

A crisis, especially one of this intensity, inspires reflection and evokes difficult questions. Beyond the human tragedy, much attention has turned towards humanity's relationship with the natural world and the impact of our activities. With an economic catastrophe resulting from the sudden and drastic halt of activity, many have observed that, beyond the human tragedy, our footprint on the planet has temporarily become lighter.

No doubt, this is a sign that we are capable of doing things differently, but to look on this as a positive outcome would be a grave mistake. The cost has been and will be enormous in terms of lost jobs, hardship and suffering. Furthermore, it is clear that the COVID-19 outbreak is also bringing new threats to indigenous peoples and rural communities, as well as exacerbated violence, in particular against women and girls as quarantine conditions make unsafe homes even more dangerous.

We can rebuild, but let us rebuild smarter. As a community we have been speaking of the need for transformational change – let us work together now to ensure we follow a thoughtful sustainable path. IUCN will continue to engage with women and men across communities to build and implement safe and gender-equitable solutions.

To draw a lesson from this ongoing tragedy, we should all vow to revisit the way we work. We must look at how we can reduce our footprint on the natural world by continuing to use the tools we are using now.

Convention on Biological Diversity (CBD)

Elizabeth Mrema, Executive Director

Speaking at the launch UN's Global Biodiversity Outlook report, September 2020

"As nature degrades new opportunities emerge for the spread to humans and animals of devastating diseases like this year's coronavirus. The window of time available is short, but the pandemic has also demonstrated that transformative changes are possible when they must be made."

"Earth's living systems as a whole are being compromised, and the more humanity exploits nature in unsustainable ways and undermines its contributions to people, the more we undermine our own well-being, security and prosperity."

The report amplifies the UN's support for nature-based solutions, hailed as one of the most effective ways of combatting climate change. Alongside a rapid phase-out of fossil fuel use, they can provide positive benefits for biodiversity and other sustainability goals.

And, in relation to health concerns, and the spread of diseases from animals to humans, the report calls for a *"One Health"* transition, in which agriculture, the urban environment and wildlife are managed in a way that promotes healthy ecosystems and healthy people.

United Nations Environment Program (UNEP)

UNEP and FAO briefing of UN Member Countries on the Decade of Ecosystem Restoration, December 2020

"There has never been a more urgent need to restore damaged ecosystems than now due to the rising impacts of climate change and the COVID-19 pandemic. It is a monumental task and everyone has a role to play. Ecosystems support all life on Earth,

and their restoration can create jobs, build up resilience, and address climate change and biodiversity loss, all at the same time.

"Now, more than ever and over the next ten years, every action counts. The United Nations (UN) General Assembly has proclaimed the UN Decade of Ecosystem Restoration following a proposal for action by over 70 countries from around the world. The Decade runs from 2021 through 2030, coinciding with the deadline for the Sustainable Development Goals and with the timeline scientists have identified as the last chance to prevent catastrophic climate change."

Wildlife Conservation 20 (WC20),

Recommendations to Global Leaders at the G20 Summit in response to the impact of the COVID-19 pandemic, November 2020

Political and financial commitments to avert environmental crises that negatively impact people and our planet have yet to be translated into effective action. Government sectors need to be coordinated and engage wider society to ensure effective implementation of strategies that promote a realignment of our relationship with nature. There is an urgent need for partnerships and unified policy and strategy among institutions dealing in ecology and wildlife conservation, zoonotic diseases, animal and human health, food safety, trade, finance and relevant regulatory and enforcement agencies.

Intergovernmental Science-Policy Platform on Biodiversity and Ecosystem Services (IPBES)

Robert Watson, Chair

On release IPBES Global Assessment Report on Biodiversity and Ecosystem Services, May 2020

"The overwhelming evidence of the IPBES Global Assessment, from a wide range of different fields of knowledge, presents an ominous picture. "The health of ecosystems on which we and all other species depend is deteriorating more rapidly than ever. We are eroding the very foundations of our economies, livelihoods, food security, health and quality of life worldwide."

"Despite progress to conserve nature and implement policies, the Report also finds that global goals for conserving and sustainably using nature and achieving sustainability cannot be met by current trajectories, and goals for 2030 and beyond may only be achieved through transformative changes across economic, social, political and technological factors."

Extracts from Media Release IPBES Workshop on Biodiversity and Pandemics, October 2020

"The same human activities that drive climate change and biodiversity loss also drive pandemic risk through their impacts on our environment. Changes in the way we use land; the expansion and intensification of agriculture; and unsustainable trade, production and consumption disrupt nature and increase contact between wildlife, livestock, pathogens and people. This is the path to pandemics."

"Pandemic risk can be significantly lowered by reducing the human activities that drive the loss of biodiversity, by greater conservation of protected areas, and through measures that reduce unsustainable exploitation of high biodiversity regions. This will reduce wildlife-livestock-human contact and help prevent the spillover of new diseases"
The Nature Conservancy

"One of the many things we've learned from the global shock of COVID-19 is just how intertwined humanity is with nature. A wildlife-borne pathogen has infected more than 70 million people, disrupted global supply chains, spotlighted inequities and exposed new vulnerabilities in our financial systems: the costs of our broken relationship with nature are startlingly clear.

"As we set our collective vision toward global recovery in 2021, recognising and making decisions based on nature's value will be essential for building a better world. Whether it's for our physical health or our fiscal health, it's clear that we need nature now."

Recent analyses suggest that the cost of preventing further pandemics over the next decade by protecting wildlife and ecosystems would equate to just two per cent of the estimated financial damage caused thus far by COVID-19. The profits – legal and illegal – that are generated from the commercial trade in wildlife are negligible in comparison to the tens of trillions of dollars of economic devastation that we are now witnessing, and are even more negligible when limited to wildlife trade and markets for human consumption.

United Nations Environment Programme (UNEP)

Inger Anderson, Under-Secretary-General and Executive Director of UNEP

Foreword to CBD Global Outlook Report 2020

"Now, we must accelerate and scale-up collaboration for nature-positive outcomes – conserving, restoring and using biodiversity fairly and sustainably. If we do not, biodiversity will continue to buckle under the weight of land- and sea-use change,

overexploitation, climate change, pollution and invasive alien species. This will further damage human health, economies and societies – with particularly detrimental effects on indigenous peoples and local communities.

"We know what needs to be done, what works and how we can achieve good results. If we build on what has already been achieved, and place biodiversity at the heart of all our policies and decisions – including in COVID-19 recovery packages – we can ensure a better future for our societies and the planet."

WWF-International

Marco Lambertini, Director-General

January 2020

"The initiatives and funding announced at the One Planet Summit provide critical momentum on nature ahead of major global environmental agreements to be made later this year and, crucially, start the process of turning commitments into action. However, a step change in both ambition and urgency is still needed if we are to secure a sustainable future for both people and the planet.

"Science tells us that our broken relationship with nature is increasing our vulnerability to pandemics, threatening our economies, and undermining our efforts to tackle the climate crisis. Never has the need for urgent action been clearer, but world leaders are yet to demonstrate that they have grasped the scale of the crisis at hand. We urge them to take the necessary steps to deliver a transformative biodiversity agreement in Kunming that secures a nature-positive world this decade while supporting climate action."

14 Leaders of the High Level Panel for a Sustainable Ocean Economy

The Ocean Panel represents nations of highly diverse oceanic, economic and political perspectives. It is supported by the UN Secretary-General's Special Envoy for the Ocean.

"We, the 14 members of the High Level Panel for a Sustainable Ocean Economy (the Ocean Panel), are heads of state and government representing people from across all ocean basins, nearly 40% of the world's coastlines and 30% of exclusive economic zones. We recognise that the ocean is the life source of our planet and is vital for human well-being and a thriving global economy."

"The ocean is home to many complex ecosystems facing significant threats. The actions we take now can safeguard the ocean's capacity to regenerate, in order to deliver

substantial economic, environmental and social value and offer powerful solutions to global challenges. Rapid action must be taken today to address climate change, acidification, ocean warming, marine pollution, overfishing, and loss of habitat and biodiversity. Failure to act will jeopardise global health, well-being, and economic vitality and exacerbate inequalities."

Conservation International

Herbert Lust, Vice President, Managing Director for Europe

Statement on the 11th Petersburg Climate Dialogue Commitments, April 2020

"We know public and economic health are linked to the health of our planet. Not only will balanced ecosystems help prevent the future spread of disease, they will help prevent other global crises like climate change. Thus, it is urgent that we rethink our relationship with nature and invest in smart solutions as we navigate an uncertain economic future and recover from the current pandemic."

"It is very positive to see biodiversity prioritised alongside climate change at the top of the global agenda during the Petersburg conference. It is important to acknowledge the challenges we face in advancing these priorities in what we hoped would be a 'super year for nature.' A green recovery will not always be easy but challenging does not mean impossible. Together, we can chart a course that keeps nature at the forefront of the global economic recovery."

The High Ambition Coalition (HAC) for Nature and People

HSH Prince Albert II of Monaco at launch of the coalition of over 50 governments from across six continents aiming to secure a global agreement to protect the lands and oceans of the planet.

"The ecosystems we rely on for our water, our air, our food are at risk of collapse. Our survival depends on nature's survival. Scientists say we must act boldly and urgently.

That is why Monaco has joined forces with many countries across the world to form the High Ambition Coalition. Together we are championing a global deal to save the planet and ourselves - Lets Act now!"

WWF Global Biodiversity Framework

WWF and major conservation bodies releasing Nature Positive by 2030, August 2020

"We are causing a catastrophic loss of species and exacerbating already dangerous

levels of climate change. In the next year Parties to the United Nations Convention on Biological Diversity (CBD) can deliver the change needed by securing an ambitious new global biodiversity framework that will transform our world to become nature-positive by 2030, for people and the planet. With high level commitment and action on biodiversity we can achieve all Sustainable Development Goals by 2030 and transition to a more prosperous, safe and healthy world now and in the future."

"To create a global biodiversity framework that is a tool for transformative change, we need leadership at the highest level of state or government in both its development and implementation, through a whole-of-government approach. All government ministries, not just the Ministry of Environment, need to unite behind an ambitious mission, goals and targets that remove the sectoral drivers of biodiversity loss and decrease our ecological footprint."

Global Steering Committee of the Campaign for Nature

Report launch: A Key Sector Forgotten in the Stimulus Debate: The Nature-Based Economy, July 2020

"We have formed this group with the overarching purpose of calling on world leaders to support a new global goal to protect at least 30 percent of the planet's land and ocean by 2030. Scientists are telling us that this is the minimum amount needed to halt global biodiversity loss, which threatens up to one million species with extinction and is considered by the World Economic Forum to be one of the top five risks facing the global economy.

We believe that the issue of land and marine conservation is timelier than ever. The coronavirus pandemic has further underscored the need to protect more of the natural world, as studies have shown that the destruction of nature increases the risk of infectious disease outbreaks.

We also believe that nature conservation must both be a core element of the economic rescue plans that global leaders are developing to respond to the emerging global recession, and a cornerstone of creating a resilient new economy."

WWF Living Planet Report

September 2020

"At a time when the world is reeling from the deepest global disruption and health crisis of a lifetime, this year's Living Planet Report provides unequivocal and alarming evidence that nature is unravelling and that our planet is flashing red warning signs of vital natural systems failure. The Living Planet Report 2020 clearly outlines how

Page 320

humanity's increasing destruction of nature is having catastrophic impacts not only on wildlife populations but also on human health and all aspects of our lives."

"It is time we answer nature's SOS. Not just to secure the future of tigers, rhinos, whales, bees, trees and all the amazing diversity of life we love and have the moral duty to coexist with, but because ignoring it also puts the health, well-being and prosperity, indeed the future, of nearly 8 billion people at stake".

Covid-19 Response and Recovery Nature-Based Solutions for People, Planet and Prosperity

Recommendations for Policymakers November by 22 major environmental organisations, November 2020

"COVID-19 highlights the critical connection between the health of nature and human health. This connection must be better reflected in our priorities, policies and actions. The root causes of this pandemic are common to many root causes of the climate change and biodiversity crises. Confronting these intertwined crises requires an integrated approach and unprecedented cooperation to achieve an equitable carbon-neutral, nature-positive economic recovery and a sustainable future. Our organisations' recommendations to policymakers for meeting this challenge are offered below (recommendation 1).

I. Halt degradation and loss of natural ecosystems as a public health priority. Human activities are destroying, degrading and fragmenting nature at an unprecedented rate, directly affecting our resilience to future pandemics. By throwing ecosystems off balance, human activities have turned natural areas from our first line of defence into hot spots for disease emergence. Reversing this trend is critical for preventing the next pandemic long before it can enter human communities."

Mark Willuhn, Director, Alianza Mesoamericana de Ecoturismo

"We are learning how to unlearn"

Syed Hasnain Raza, Independent Wildlife & Conservation Filmmaker

"Our Ecosystems are under severe threat from human intervention, its better we understand this sooner that we draw our bread and butter from our Ecosystems. In other words it's right to say Healthy Ecosystems are equal to Healthy Economies. In this anthroprocene we must realise the importance of healthy Ecosystems and survival of species that keep them healthy. We need to move forward with Nature Based Solutions, Climate Change Adaptation and Ecosystems Based Adaptation but this all needs awareness first at every possible level."

Chapter Twenty-Seven–Does Intelligent Life Exist Elsewhere?

Intelligent life probably exists on distant planets — even if we can't make contact, astrophysicist says

Recently released Navy videos of what the U.S. government now classifies as *"unidentified aerial phenomena"* have set off another round of speculative musings on the possibility of aliens visiting our planet. Like

other astrophysicists who have weighed in on these sightings, I'm skeptical of their extraterrestrial origins. I am confident, however, that intelligent life-forms inhabit planets elsewhere in the universe. Math and physics point to this likely conclusion. But I think we're unlikely to be able to communicate or interact with them — at least in our lifetimes.

Wanting to understand what's "*out there*" is a timeless human drive, one that I understand well. Growing up in poorer and rougher neighborhoods of Watts, Houston's Third Ward and the Ninth Ward of New Orleans, I was always intrigued by the night sky even if I couldn't see it very easily given big-city lights and smog. And for the sake of my survival, I didn't want to be caught staring off into space. Celestial navigation wasn't going to help me find my way home without getting beaten up or shaken down.

From early childhood, I compulsively and continuously counted the objects in my environment — partly to soothe my anxieties and partly to unlock the mysteries inside things by enumerating them. This habit earned me nothing but taunts and bullying in my hood where, as a bookish kid, I was already a soft target. But whenever I looked up at a moonless night sky, I wondered how I might one day count the stars.

By age 10, I'd become fascinated, even obsessed, with Einstein's theory of relativity and the quantum possibilities for the multiple dimensions of the universe it opened up in my mind. By high school, I was winning statewide science fairs by plotting the effects of special relativity on a first-generation desktop computer.

So perhaps it's not surprising that I have gone on to spend much of my career working with other astrophysicists to develop telescopes and detectors that peer into the remote reaches of space and measure the structure and evolution of our universe. The international Dark Energy Survey collaboration has been mapping hundreds of millions of galaxies, detecting thousands of supernovae, and finding patterns of cosmic structure that reveal the nature of dark energy that is accelerating the expansion of our universe. Meanwhile, the Legacy Survey of Space and Time will make trillions of observations of 20 billion stars in the Milky Way.

What we're discovering is that the cosmos is much vaster than we ever imagined. According to our best estimate, the universe is home to a hundred billion trillion stars — most of which have planets revolving around them. This newly revealed trove of orbiting exoplanets greatly improves the odds of our discovering advanced extraterrestrial life.

Scientific evidence from astrobiology suggests that simple life — composed of individual cells, or small multicellular organisms — is ubiquitous in the universe. It has probably occurred multiple times in our own solar system. But the presence of humanlike, technologically advanced life-forms is a much tougher proposition to prove. It's all a matter of solar energy. The first simple life on Earth probably began underwater and in the absence of oxygen and light — conditions that are not that difficult to achieve. But what enabled the evolution of advanced, complex life on Earth was its adaptation to the energy of the sun's light for photosynthesis. Photosynthesis created the abundant oxygen on which high life-forms rely.

It helps that Earth's atmosphere is transparent to visible light. On most planets, atmospheres are thick, absorbing light before it reaches the surface — like on Venus. Or, like Mercury, they have no atmosphere at all. Earth maintains its thin atmosphere because it spins quickly and has a liquid iron core, conditions that lead to our strong and protective magnetic field. This magnetosphere, in the region above the ionosphere, shields all life on Earth, and its atmosphere, from damaging solar winds and the corrosive effects of solar radiation. That combination of planetary conditions is difficult to replicate.

Still, I'm optimistic that there have been Cambrian explosions of life on other planets similar to what occurred on Earth some 541 million years ago, spawning a cornucopia of biodiversity that is preserved in the fossil record. The more expert we become in observing and calculating the outer reaches of the cosmos, and the more we understand about how many galaxies, stars and exoplanets exist, the greater the possibility of there being intelligent life on one of those planets.

For millennia, humans have gazed in wonder at the stars, trying to understand their nature and import. We developed telescopes only a few hundred years ago, and since then the dimensions of our observable universe have expanded exponentially with technological advances and the insights of quantum physics and relativity. Beginning in the early 1960s, scientists have tried to calculate the odds of advanced extraterrestrial life. In 1961, researchers at the NASA-funded search for extraterrestrial intelligence (SETI) developed the "Drake Equation" to estimate how many civilizations in the Milky Way might evolve to develop the technology to emit detectable radio waves.

Those estimates have been updated over the decades, most recently by Sara Seager's group at MIT, based on observations of exoplanets outside our solar system by successive generations of advanced space-based telescopes — such as the Kepler Space Telescope, launched in 2009, and NASA's MIT-led Transiting Exoplanet Survey Satellite, launched in 2018. Detecting the presence of life on exoplanets requires large telescopes outfitted with advanced spectroscopy instruments, which is what the James Webb Space Telescope will deliver when it launches in November.

In 1995 the first exoplanet was discovered orbiting Pegasus 51, 50 light-years distant from Earth. Since then, there have been more than 4,000 confirmed discoveries of exoplanets in our galaxy. More important, astronomers agree that almost all stars have planets, which radically improves the odds of our discovering intelligent life in the universe.

At the low end of consensus estimates among astrophysicists, there may be only one or two planets hospitable to the evolution of technologically advanced civilizations in a typical galaxy of hundreds of billions of stars. But with 2 trillion galaxies in the observable universe, that adds up to a lot of possible intelligent, although distant, neighbors.

If only one in a hundred billion stars can support advanced life, that means that our own Milky Way galaxy — home to 400 billion stars — would have four likely candidates. Of course, the likelihood of intelligent life in the universe is much greater if you multiply by the 2 trillion galaxies beyond the Milky Way.

Unfortunately, we're unlikely to ever make contact with life in other galaxies. Travel by spaceship to our closest intergalactic neighbor, the Canis Major Dwarf, would take almost 750,000,000 years with current technology. Even a radio signal, which moves at close to the speed of light, would take 25,000 years.

The enormity of the cosmos confronts us with an existential dilemma: There's a high statistical likelihood of intelligent life-forms having evolved elsewhere in the universe, but a very low probability that we'll be able to communicate or interact with them.

Regardless of the odds, the existence of intelligent life in the universe matters deeply to me, and to most other humans on this planet. Why? I believe it's because we humans are fundamentally social creatures who thrive on connection and wither in isolation. In the past year, many of us felt the hardship of isolation as deeply as the threat of a potentially fatal infectious disease. Enforced seclusion during the pandemic tested the limits of our tolerance for separation and made us acutely aware of our interdependence with all life on Earth. So, it's no wonder that the idea of a trackless universe devoid of intelligent life fills us with the dread of cosmic solitary confinement.

For a hundred years, we've been emitting radio signals into space. For the past 60 years, we've been listening — and so far, in vain — for the beginning of a celestial conversation. The prospect of life on other planets remains a profound one, regardless of our ability to contact and interact with them. As we await evidence of extraterrestrial intelligence, I draw comfort from the knowledge that there are many powerful forces in the universe more abstract than the idea of alien intelligence. Love, friendship and faith, for example, are impossible to measure or calculate, yet they remain central to our fulfillment and sense of purpose.

As I head into my mid-50s, I look forward with an infinity of hope to the moment when humans will finally make contact with extraterrestrial intelligence — in whatever far-flung star system they may live, and in whatever century or millennium moment that momentous meeting may occur. Until that day, I have no doubt that generations of young humans around the globe will continue to stand watch, looking skyward with the same sense of amazement and wonder that intoxicated me as a young boy.

Hakeem Oluseyi, president-elect of the National Society of Black Physicists, has taught and conducted research at MIT, University of California at Berkeley and the University of Cape Town. His memoir, *"A Quantum Life: My Unlikely Journey from the Street to the Stars,"* co-written with Joshua Horwitz, was published last week.

Do we really want to know if we're not alone in the universe?

It was near Green Bank, W.Va., in 1960 that a young radio astronomer named Frank Drake conducted the first extensive search for alien civilizations in deep space. He aimed the 85-foot dish of a radio telescope at two nearby, sun-like stars, tuning to a frequency he thought an alien civilization might use for interstellar communication.

But the stars had nothing to say.

So began SETI, the Search for Extraterrestrial Intelligence, a form of astronomical inquiry that has captured the imaginations of people around the planet but has so far failed to detect a single *"hello."* Pick your explanation: They're not there; they're too far away; they're insular and aloof; they're zoned out on computer games; they're watching us in mild bemusement and wondering when we'll grow up.

Now some SETI researchers are pushing a more aggressive agenda: Instead of just listening, we would transmit messages, targeting newly discovered planets orbiting distant stars. Through *"active SETI,"* we'd boldly announce our presence and try to get the conversation started.

Naturally, this is controversial, because of . . . well, the Klingons. The bad aliens.

"ETI's reaction to a message from Earth cannot presently be known,"

states a petition signed by 28 scientists, researchers and thought leaders, among them SpaceX founder Elon Musk. *"We know nothing of ETI's intentions and capabilities, and it is impossible to predict whether ETI will be benign or hostile."*

This objection is moot, however, according to the proponents of active SETI. They argue that even if there are unfriendlies out there, they already know about us. That's because *"I Love Lucy"* and other TV and radio broadcasts are radiating from Earth at the speed of light. Aliens with advanced instruments could also detect our navigational radar beacons and would see that we've illuminated our cities.

"We have already sent signals into space that will alert the aliens to our presence with the transmissions and street lighting of the last 70 years," Seth Shostak, an astronomer at the SETI Institute in California and a supporter of the more aggressive approach, has written. *"These emissions cannot be recalled."*

That's true only to a point, say the critics of active SETI. They argue that unintentional planetary leakage, such as *"I Love Lucy,"* is omnidirectional and faint, and much harder to detect than an intentional, narrowly focused signal transmitted at a known planet.

These critics add that it's bad form for scientists to attempt such interstellar communication without getting permission from the rest of humanity. Plus there's the question of what, exactly, a message to the stars ought to say.

Thus one of the greatest scientific mysteries — Are we alone in the universe? — leads to a thorny political and cultural question: Who speaks for Earth?

'A waste of time'

This discussion about the proper protocols of communicating with aliens is not the most mainstream scientific debate ever concocted. But it got a lot of attention here in San Jose at the annual meeting of the ultra-mainstream American Association for the Advancement of Science.

Page 328

Astronomer Jill Tarter, a pioneer of SETI who is neutral about the more active approach, organized a symposium on the topic. Before the symposium, two advocates of the idea, Shostak and Douglas Vakoch, appeared at a press briefing alongside science-fiction writer David Brin and planetary scientist David Grinspoon.

"Active SETI is a reflection of SETI growing up as a discipline," said Vakoch, a clinical psychologist who is the SETI Institute's director of Interstellar Message Composition. "It may just be the approach that lets us make contact with life beyond Earth."

But Brin, a signer of the petition protesting the campaign for active SETI, said we don't know what's out there and shouldn't presume that aliens are benign. He said there are roughly 100 scenarios to explain why we haven't heard from the aliens so far. About a dozen of those scenarios are unpleasant, he said.

The zodiacal light, left, and the Milky Way, right, are seen from the region of Salgotarjan, northeast of Budapest, on Feb. 17, 2015.

Vakoch countered that Brin was being inconsistent, because he collaborated on a message that will be carried into space by NASA's New Horizons spacecraft after its fly-by of Pluto later this year.

"No one is going to get it!" Brin interjected. (The spacecraft is very slow in the galactic scheme of things and will journey for eons into the void of interstellar space.)

As the scientists debated one another, a white-haired, bespectacled man in the back of the room listened quietly: Frank Drake.

He is 84 years old, the beloved dean of the SETI field. He is the Drake of the famous Drake Equation, the formula he scribbled down in 1961 in advance of a meeting in Green Bank. His equation offers a technique for estimating the abundance of communicative civilizations.

He parked himself on a bench in a corridor and, bracketed by a clutch of reporters, held forth for 30 minutes. He said he thinks it's too soon to engage in active SETI. We don't know enough.

"I think it's a waste of time at the present. It's like somebody trying to send an e-mail to somebody whose e-mail address they don't know, and whose name they don't know."

Odds of someone out there

When Drake plugs his estimates into the Drake Equation (and who is more entitled to do so?), he comes up with 10,000 alien civilizations that we could detect if we looked in the right places with the right techniques.

"It's 10,000 that we can detect. There are a lot more," Drake clarifies. "A lot more young ones that can't be detected because they don't have the technology, and there are older ones that have technology that is so good that they don't waste any energy."

The Drake Equation has endured despite being rather ungainly at first glance:

$$N = R^* \cdot fp \cdot ne \cdot fl \cdot fi \cdot fc \cdot L$$

Drake also created the Arecibo Message, a simple binary encoded message broadcast into space by the Arecibo radio telescope in Puerto Rico in 1974. The message encodes several things: the numbers 1 to 10, the basic chemistry of life on Earth, the double helix structure of DNA, Earth's population, a graphic of the solar system, a human figure, and a graphic of the Arecibo radio telescope and its dish's dimensions. (Ramin Rahimian for The Washington Post)

It's not as complicated as it looks. The number (N) of detectable civilizations is the product of seven factors: the rate of star formation (R*), the fraction of stars with planetary systems (f p), the average number of habitable planets per planetary system (n e), the fraction that actually have life (f l), the fraction that have intelligent life (f i), the fraction with communicative civilizations (f c) and the average longevity of the communicating phase of such civilizations (L).

Exoplanets — outside our solar system — were first discovered in 1995. NASA's Kepler Space Telescope and other observatories in space and on the ground have found more than 1,000 planets in the years since. Astronomers say it's likely that our galaxy has tens of billions of "habitable zone" planets. And of course (channeling Carl Sagan) our galaxy is just one of billions and billions of galaxies.

But after the first three factors in the Drake Equation, we enter the murk. How many of those potentially habitable planets out there actually have life? No one knows, because we don't yet know how life began on Earth. How likely is it that simple, microbial life will evolve into complex, multicellular organisms and eventually into creatures with large brains? We don't know, because we have only the one data point of life on Earth.

Do intelligent creatures tend to be communicative and potentially detectable? No idea. And finally, there's that ominous "L" at the end of the equation: Do technological civilizations tend to survive a long time?

"Those factors are just completely unknown. It's a great way to organize our ignorance," Tarter says.

Why, a reporter asked Tarter, should we try to pick up signals from an alien civilization?

"We're curious how many different ways there are to do this thing called life," she said. *"And we're curious if it's possible for us to have a long future."*

That's because we'd most likely find a very old civilization, not a young one. It's a matter of statistical probabilities. The universe is 13.8 billion years old. If we pick up a signal, it is unlikely to be from a civilization that has only recently become communicative.

Tarter isn't discouraged by SETI's null result to date. She says our ability to detect signals, though much improved since 1960, remains limited.

An artist's illustration of Kepler-186f, the first validated Earth-size planet to orbit a distant star in the habitable zone, a range of distance from a star where liquid water might pool on the planet's surface.

"We've explored one eight-ounce glass of water out of the ocean," she says.

"We've explored one eight-ounce glass of water out of the ocean," she says.

But you hear something different from Geoff Marcy, an astronomer who has found many of those exoplanets, and who also came to San Jose to discuss results from the Kepler mission. Marcy — who, like David Brin and Elon Musk, signed the petition to protest efforts in active SETI — said it is striking that we have found all these distant planets but no evidence at all of intelligent civilizations.

"The absence of strong radio beacons, television broadcasts, robotic spacecraft, obelisks on the moon — all of those absences add up to give us the suggestion that our galaxy is not teeming with technological life,"

Marcy said.

Planetwide decisions

After the active SETI symposium at the AAAS convention in San Jose, the interested parties reconvened for a Valentine's Day workshop at the SETI Institute up the road in Mountain View. Bottom line: No one's going to be beaming signals to the aliens anytime soon.

"We need tools to enable true global deliberation and then action," Tarter said in an e-mail summarizing the workshop. She pointed out that this active SETI issue echoes another debate that got a lot of attention at the AAAS meeting: whether to inject aerosols into the upper atmosphere to reflect sunlight and combat global warming. No one's going to do that, either, in the near future, but suddenly people are discussing these basic issues of planetary management and global decision-making.

Rogue alien-hunters can always go it alone, of course — and they have. For example, a Russian astronomer, Alexander Zaitsev, has repeatedly beamed messages to nearby stars. Even NASA has gotten into the act, beaming the Beatles song *"Across the Universe"* toward the star Polaris in 2008 ("I see that this is the beginning of the new age in which we will communicate with billions of planets across the universe," Yoko Ono said, according to the NASA news release).

Frank Drake has dabbled in active SETI himself. It was just a stunt, a proof-of-concept, on April 16, 1974, at the dedication ceremony of the rebuilt Arecibo Observatory in Puerto Rico. He transmitted an encoded message — one that described the elements that make up DNA, the planets in our solar system, the size of a human being, etc. — toward a star cluster in the constellation Hercules. The star cluster is about 25,000 light-years away.

The odds that anyone will get that message are vanishingly small, but Drake did catch grief from Britain's Astronomer Royal at the time, Sir Martin Ryle, who thought it was reckless. Drake shrugs and says, *"Anyone who's even 100 years ahead of us in technology could detect our run-of-the-mill transmission."*

Drake said he doesn't worry, as some do, that we would become depressed by contact with a superior civilization. Children aren't depressed by the company of adults, he says. He compared SETI to doing research on ancient civilizations on Earth, such as the Greeks and the Romans.

"We're going to do the archaeology of the future," Drake says. "We're going to find out what we're going to become."

Intelligent Alien Life Is Rare In The Universe, Study Concludes

You might be forgiven for getting excited whenever NASA announces a finding that has to do with the possibility of alien life.

Whether it's water spurting from the icy moons Europa or Enceladus, or the possibility of microbes living on Earth-like planets like those of TRAPPIST-1, we have a host of exciting possibilities all over the universe for life. But remember, this discussion is mostly limited to microbial or bacterial life, not intelligent life as we know it.

Is E.T. actually out there? There are numerous discussions calculating the probabilities of intelligent life, the most famous being the Drake Equation that estimates the number of active and communicating intelligent civilizations in our own galaxy, the Milky Way. But a new study says it is quite unlikely that intelligent life exists.

The study in large part looks at the history of our own Earth, which had a number of unique evolutionary events (such as the asteroid that killed off the dinosaurs some 66 million years ago, allowing mammals and humans to occupy the dinosaurs' niche.)

"Intelligent life in the Universe is exceptionally rare, assuming that intelligent life elsewhere requires analogous evolutionary transitions to Earth," reads the new study in the scientific journal Astrobiology.

Our culture has numerous movies and science fiction series about aliens, such as the 1982 movie "E.T.: The Extraterrestrial", whose starring character is shown here.

The study points out that on Earth, intelligent life emerged "*on a timescale similar to that of Earth's lifetime.*" The Earth is about 4.5 billion years old and it was only about 5 million years ago (or 0.5 billion years ago) that intelligent life arose, the study authors say. And the window of intelligent life's existence here appears to be narrow, as in less than 1 billion more years from now, the sun will become so luminous that surface temperatures on Earth will increase beyond what could support life on our planet.

The authors also pay attention to transition times between key evolutionary markers of Earthly life, such as the origin of life (or abiogenesis) and markers of increasingly complex life forms such as eukaryotic (a type of cell used by mammals), multicellular and intelligent life. Some of these transitions may be quite unusual, especially the eukaryotic cells that emerged on Earth a billion years after their more simple precursors, called prokaryotic cells. Others may be more common, such as multicellular life that may have originated independently more than 40 times.

But what the authors say we must pay attention to is the chain of events that led from the simplest forms of life to the intelligent forms of life we have today. The sequence of evolution alone appears to be unlikely, leading to an oft-quoted passage from Stephen Jay Gould that the chances of intelligent life are "*vanishingly small*" if we were to rerun the sequence of Earth's evolution from the start, over and over again.

But there are limitations in making these estimates, the authors note. "The timings are subject to a sample bias," they said, meaning the bias that we only know of one planet — our own — with intelligent life. "In particular, we can only observe evolutionary transitions that occurred rapidly enough to fit within Earth's habitable lifetime," they added, noting that these transitions may take even more time on other planets.

Another limitation is how unpromising other solar systems may be to any life at all. M-dwarf stars, previously thought to be promising candidates to host life-friendly planets, turn out to be flaring stars that may spew deadly radiation often enough to kill any chances of life on rocky planets.

While this story only captures some of the arguments the authors put forth, their overall conclusions do point to an unlikelihood for intelligent life overall. So while Earth-sized planets appear to make up a noticeable fraction of planets in the universe, it is unclear how many of them are hosted in solar systems that allow water and stable conditions on their surface for billions of years, just like our own planet.

That said, the universe is big. And to paraphrase the movie Contact from 1997, which discussed intelligent alien life, we live in a big universe and it seems that only having a single instance of intelligent life would be an awful waste of space.

Life in the Universe: What are the Odds?

As humanity casts an ever-wider net across the cosmos, capturing evidence of thousands of worlds, an ancient question haunts us: Is anybody out there?

The good news: We know vastly more than any previous generation. Our galaxy is crowded with exoplanets – planets around other stars. A healthy percentage of them are small, rocky worlds, of a similar size and likely similar composition to our home planet.

The ingredients in the recipe for earthly life – water, elements associated with life, available sources of energy – appear to be almost everywhere we've looked.

Now the bad news. We have yet to find another "*Earth*" with life, intelligent or not. Observing signs of possible microbial life in exoplanet atmospheres is currently just out of reach. No convincing evidence of advanced technology – artificial signals by radio or other means, or the telltale sign of, say, massive extraterrestrial engineering projects –– has yet crossed our formidable arrays of telescopes in space or on the ground.

And finding non-intelligent life is far more likely; Earth existed for most of its history, 4.25 billion years, without a whisper of technological life, and human civilization is a very late-breaking development.

Is there life beyond Earth? So far, the silence is deafening.

"I hope it's there," said Shawn Domagal-Goldman, a research astronomer at NASA's Goddard Space Flight Center in Greenbelt, Maryland. "I want it to be there. I'll be planning a party if we find it."

Domagal-Goldman co-leads a team of exoplanet hunters who, in the years and decades ahead, are planning to do just that. Working with scientists across NASA, as well as academic and international partners, his team and others are helping to design and build the next generation of instruments to sift through light from other worlds, and other suns. The goal: unambiguous evidence of another living, breathing world.

While the chances of finding life elsewhere remain unknown, the odds can be said to be improving. A well-known list of the data needed to determine the likely abundance of life-bearing worlds, though highly conjectural, is known as the *"Drake equation."*

Put forward in 1961 by astronomer Frank Drake, the list remains mostly blank. It begins with the rate of star formation in the galaxy and the fraction of stars that have planets, leading step-by-step through the portion of planets that support life and – most speculatively – to the existence and durability of detectable, technological civilizations.

When Drake introduced this roadmap to life beyond Earth, all the terms – the signposts along the way – were blank.

Some of the first few items are now known, including the potential presence of habitable worlds, said researcher Ravi Kopparapu from Goddard, also a co-leader of Domagal-Goldman's team. He studies the habitability and potential for life on exoplanets.

If we develop and launch a powerful enough space telescope, *"we could figure out if we have advanced life or biological life,"* he said.

Finding a planet that's 'just right'

Drake's list can be a good conversation starter, and a useful way to frame the complex questions around the possibility of other life. But these days, scientists don't spend a great deal of time discussing it, Domagal-Goldman said.

Instead, they use a narrower yardstick: the habitable zone.

Every star, like every campfire, has a definable zone of radiated warmth. Too close, and your marshmallow – or your planet – might end up as nothing more than a charred cinder. Too far away, and its surface remains cold and unappetizing.

In both cases, "just right" is more likely to be somewhere in between.

For a planet, the habitable zone is the distance from a star that allows liquid water to persist on its surface – as long as that planet has a suitable atmosphere.

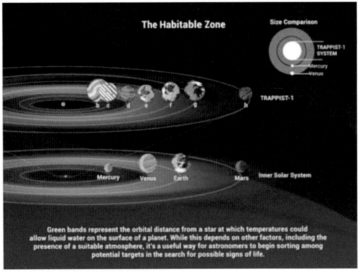

In our solar system, Earth sits comfortably inside the Sun's habitable zone. Broiling planet Venus is within the inner edge, while refrigerated Mars is near the outer boundary.

Determine the distance of an exoplanet from the star itself, as well as the star's size and energy output, and you can estimate whether the planet falls within the habitable zone.

For larger, hotter stars, the zone is farther away; for smaller, cooler stars, it can be very close indeed. Finding these *"just right"* planets in the habitable zone is one of the keys to finding signs of life.

"If they fit within these parameters, they could potentially support a temperate environment," said Natasha Batalha, a research scientist at the NASA Ames Research Center. *"Therefore it would be incredibly interesting to study their atmospheres."*

Batalha's specialty, in fact, is finding ways to read exoplanet atmospheres – and building computer models to better understand them.

"That is the next step, the next frontier," she said.

The habitable zone concept is not yet definitive. Small, rocky worlds like ours that orbit other stars are too far away to determine whether they have atmospheres, at least using present-day technology.

That's where teams like the one co-led by Kopparapu and Domagal-Goldman come in. The space telescopes and instruments now on their drawing boards are meant to be powerful enough to peer into these atmospheres and identify the molecules present. That will tell us which gases dominate.

We could find a small, rocky, watery world around a Sun-like star with an atmosphere of nitrogen, oxygen, and carbon dioxide: a little like looking in a mirror.

"To search for life anywhere, we have this 'follow the water' approach," Domagal-Goldman said. *"Anywhere you find water on Earth, you find life. Whether it's life on Mars, ocean worlds, or exoplanets, water is the first signpost we're looking for."*

For now, the habitable zone remains a kind of first cut in the search for life-bearing worlds.

"The habitable zone is a very useful tool for mission design," said Rhonda Morgan of NASA's Jet Propulsion Laboratory in Southern California.

She studies how to use the data gathered so far on exoplanets to refine designs for future space telescopes.

Over the past quarter century, thousands of exoplanets have been confirmed in a Milky Way galaxy that likely holds trillions. Thousands more will come to light in the years ahead. Tools like the habitable zone will help planet hunters sort through these growing ranks to pick the most likely candidates for supporting life.

"We are in a position now where we can propose a potential, future mission that would be capable of directly imaging an Earth-like planet around a nearby, Sun-like star," she said. *"This is the first time in history that the technology has been this close, probably less than 10 years from launch."*

Still, we might need something beyond the habitable-zone concept for more extreme cases. It won't help much, for instance, with "weird" life – life as we don't know it. Living things on other worlds might use vastly different chemistry and molecular compounds, or even a solvent other than water.

"This is one of the questions we get from the public often: If there are aliens, how are we going to recognize them if they're really weird?" Domagal-Goldman said. *"How do we find what we would consider to be weird life? And how do we make sure not to be tricked by strange, dead planets that look alive – mirages in the desert?"*

Life on planets around other stars also might be hidden in a subsurface ocean encased in ice, invisible even to our most powerful space telescopes. Moons of Jupiter and Saturn are known to harbor such oceans, some revealing through remote sensing at least a few of the characteristics we expect for habitable worlds.

Some *"exo-moons"* also might be habitable worlds, as in the film, *"Avatar."* But even proposed, future instruments are unlikely to have sufficient power to detect atmospheres of moons around giant exoplanets.

Still, the habitable zone is a good start, a way to zero in on signs of life made familiar by our fellow organisms here on planet Earth.

Cosmic eavesdropping

A shortcut to finding lifeforms like ourselves, of course, would be to intercept tech-savvy communications. Searches for signs of intelligent life have been underway for decades.

In recent years, among NASA scientists, such potential signs have acquired an intriguing new name: technosignatures.

Evidence of a communicative, technological species somewhere among the endless fields of stars could come in the traditional form: signals by radio or optical light waves, or from some other slice of the electromagnetic spectrum.

But scientists imagine many other forms. An exoplanet atmosphere might show signs of synthetic gases, such as CFCs, revealing an industrial species like us.

Or maybe we'll see the glimmer of something like a *"Dyson sphere,"* popularized by physicist Freeman Dyson: an epic-scale structure built around a star to capture the lion's share of its energy.

Such possibilities remain speculative. For now, we have no real answer to a disturbing question from another 20th century physicist, Enrico Fermi.

Where is everybody?

The question has fueled more than 70 years of debate, but boils down to a simple observation. Our Milky Way galaxy has plenty of stars, plenty of planets, and plenty of time to develop intelligent lifeforms – some of whom might well have had billions of years to develop interstellar travel.

Yet so far, we've seen no sign of such technology, nor heard a peep of conversation. Why is the cosmos so profoundly silent?

"If life had so much time to evolve, why haven't we found it?" Batalha asks, to summarize the question. *"Why isn't life just crawling everywhere*

in the galaxy, or the universe? It could be a combination of a lot of things. Space travel is very difficult for us."

Vast amounts of energy would be needed just to get us to our nearest neighboring star, Proxima Centauri, she said. *"It would just be incredibly expensive, and require a lot of resources."*

And once we – or some other civilization – reached such a distant destination, she said, another problem would be perpetuating the travelers' existence into future generations.

Experts offer many reasons why somebody, or something, might be out there, yet beyond our detection. On the other hand, the ultra-cautious might remind us that, while a lifeless cosmos seems unlikely, we have exactly zero information one way or the other.

Still, scientists like Kopparapu say they like our chances of finding some form of life, and are hard at work on the telescopes and instruments that could make that future, party-starting epiphany a reality.

"It's not a question of 'if,' it's a question of 'when' we find life on other planets," he said. *"I'm sure in my lifetime, in our lifetime, we will know if there is life on other worlds."*

Resources

washingtonpost.com, "Intelligent life probably exists on distant planets — even if we can't make contact, astrophysicist says." by Hakeem Oluseyi; washingtonpost.com, "Do we really want to know if we're not alone in the universe?" By Joel Achenbach; forbes.com, "Intelligent Alien Life Is Rare In The Universe, Study Concludes." By Elizabeth Howell; exoplanets.nasa.gov, "Life in the Universe: What are the Odds?";

Chapter Twenty-Eight--Is Interstellar Travel Possible?

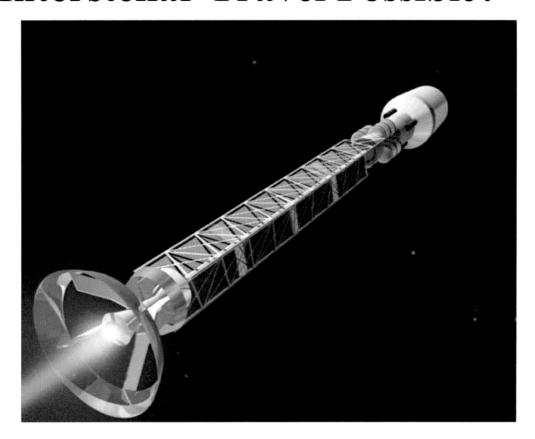

Listen folks, I love a good sci-fi movie as much as anyone. Cruising around the galaxy, finding weird stuff, and blowing up aliens--it's all good. But just because a writer can come up with something, it doesn't make it possible. I'm sorry to say that we're going to be bound to our solar system for a really, really long time. As in, probably forever.

Interstellar space travel is the fantasy of every five-year-old kid within us. It is the staple of science fiction serials. Boldly going where nobody has gone before in a really fantastic way. As we grow ever more advanced with our rockets and space probes, the question arises: could we ever hope to colonize the stars? Or, barring that far-flung dream, can we at least send space probes to alien planets, letting them tell us what they see?

The truth is that interstellar travel and exploration is technically possible. There's no law of physics that outright forbids it. But that doesn't necessarily make it easy, and it certainly doesn't mean we'll achieve it in our lifetimes, let alone this century. Interstellar space travel is a real pain in the neck.

Let's get some perspective. The nearest star to Earth (which is also home to a small rocky world!) is Proxima Centauri, which sits a little less than 4 light-years away. Four. That's doesn't sound like a lot, does it? Imagine making a scale model of our solar system. Let's say in that scale model you put the Earth three feet away from the Sun. In that scale model, Proxima Centauri would sit about 200 miles away.

It took one of our fastest spacecraft, New Horizons, traveling 36,000 miles per hour nearly a decade just to reach Pluto. If it were pointed at Proxima Centuari (and it's not), cruising at that speed it would get to visit our nearest neighbor in about 25,000 years.

That's a long trip.

If you want to visit another star system in any reasonable amount of time, you need to go fast. To go fast, you need a lot of energy. And that's what makes interstellar travel so dang hard.

One proposed for an interstellar spacecraft is called the Starshot Initiative, which aims to shoot a super-powerful laser on a lightsail (a giant nearly perfectly reflecting membrane), using the energy from the light to propel the spacecraft to a tenth the speed of light. That would enable it to reach Proxima in less than half a century.

To make this work, the laser would have to use all the energy from every single nuclear reactor in the United States at once. And it would have to operate for 10 minutes, which is about a quadrillion times longer than we've ever operated our most powerful lasers).

Oh, right, and the spacecraft could weigh no more than a paperclip.

Nothing about the Starshot is physically impossible. Just really, really difficult and expensive…and using technology that is decades, if not centuries, away from coming to fruition (assuming we even want to develop that kind of technology in the first place).

Sure, there are more fanciful ideas out there, like building wormholes or warp drives. And while those concepts do have their roots in legit physics (most notably, general relativity, our modern understanding of the force of gravity), the reality of their near impossibility is also rooted in physics. If you ever want to build a wormhole or warp drive, you first need to find yourself a healthy amount of negative mass. By which I mean matter that has negative weight. If that sound weird, it's because it is: we have no evidence that anything with negative mass actually exists in our universe, and we have very good reasons to suspect it can't.

Voyage outward

If you're sufficiently patient, then we've already achieved interstellar exploration status. We have several spacecraft on escape trajectories, meaning they're leaving the solar system and they are never coming back. NASA's Pioneer missions, the Voyager missions, and most recently New Horizons have all started their long outward journeys. The Voyagers especially are now considered outside the solar system, as defined as the region where the solar wind emanating from the sun gives way to general galactic background particles and dust.

So, great; we have interstellar space probes currently in operation. Except the problem is that they're going nowhere really fast. Each one of these intrepid interstellar explorers is traveling at tens of thousands of miles per hour, which sounds pretty fast. They're not headed in the direction of any particular star, because their missions were designed to explore planets inside the solar system. But if any of these spacecraft were headed to our nearest neighbor, Proxima Centauri, just barely 4 light-years away, they would reach it in about 80,000 years.

I don't know about you, but I don't think NASA budgets for those kinds of timelines. Also, by the time these probes reach anywhere halfway interesting, their nuclear batteries will be long dead, and just be useless hunks of metal hurtling through the void. Which is a sort of success, if you think about it: It's not like our ancestors were able to accomplish such feats as tossing random junk between the stars, but it's probably also not exactly what you imagined interstellar space travel to be like.

Speed racer

To make interstellar spaceflight more reasonable, a probe has to go really fast. On the order of at least one-tenth the speed of light. At that speed, spacecraft could reach Proxima Centauri in a handful of decades, and send back pictures a few years later, well within a human lifetime. Is it really so unreasonable to ask that the same person who starts the mission gets to finish it?

Going these speeds requires a tremendous amount of energy. One option is to contain that energy onboard the spacecraft as fuel. But if that's the case, the extra fuel adds mass, which makes it even harder to propel it up to those speeds. There are designs and sketches for nuclear-powered spacecraft that try to accomplish just this, but unless we want to start building thousands upon thousands of nuclear bombs just to put inside a rocket, we need to come up with other ideas.

Perhaps one of the most promising ideas is to keep the energy source of the spacecraft fixed and somehow transport that energy to the spacecraft as it travels. One way to do this is with lasers. Radiation is good at transporting energy from one place to another, especially over the vast distances of space. The spacecraft can then capture this energy and propel itself forward.

This is the basic idea behind the Breakthrough Starshot project, which aims to design a spacecraft capable of reaching the nearest stars in a matter of decades. In the simplest outline of this project, a giant laser on the order of 100 gigawatts shoots at an Earth-orbiting spacecraft. That spacecraft has a large solar sail that is incredibly reflective. The laser bounces off of that sail, giving momentum to the spacecraft. The thing is, a 100-gigawatt laser only has the force of a heavy backpack. You didn't read that incorrectly. If we were to shoot this laser at the spacecraft for about 10 minutes, in order to reach one-tenth the speed of light, the spacecraft can weigh no more than a gram.

That's the mass of a paper clip.

A spaceship for ants

This is where the rubber meets the interstellar road when it comes to making spacecraft travel the required speeds. The laser itself, at 100 gigawatts, is more powerful than any laser we've ever designed by many orders of magnitude. To give you a sense of scale, 100 gigawatts is the entire capacity of every single nuclear power plant operating in the United States combined.

And the spacecraft, which has to have a mass no more than a paper clip, must include a camera, computer, power source, circuitry, a shell, an antenna for communicating back home and the entire lightsail itself.

That lightsail must be almost perfectly reflective. If it absorbs even a tiny fraction of that incoming laser radiation it will convert that energy to heat instead of momentum. At 100 gigawatts, that means straight-up melting, which is generally considered not good for spacecraft.

Once accelerated to one-tenth the speed of light, the real journey begins. For 40 years, this little spacecraft will have to withstand the trials and travails of interstellar space. It will be impacted by dust grains at that enormous velocity. And while the dust is very tiny, at those speeds motes can do incredible damage. Cosmic rays, which are high-energy particles emitted by everything from the sun to distant supernova, can mess with the delicate circuitry inside. The spacecraft will be bombarded by these cosmic rays non-stop as soon as the journey begins.

Is Breakthrough Starshot possible? In principle, yes. Like I said above, there's no law of physics that prevents any of this from becoming reality. But that doesn't make it easy or even probable or plausible or even feasible using our current levels of technology (or reasonable projections into the near future of our technology). Can we really make a spacecraft that small and light? Can we really make a laser that powerful? Can a mission like this actually survive the challenges of deep space?

The answer isn't yes or no. The real question is this: are we willing to spend enough money to find out if it's possible?

Interstellar Travel Could Be Possible Even Without Spaceships, Scientist Says

In about 5 billion years, the Sun will leave the main sequence and become a red giant. It'll expand and transform into a glowering, malevolent ball and consume and destroy Mercury, Venus, Earth, and probably Mars.

Can humanity survive the Sun's red giant phase? Extraterrestrial Civilizations (ETCs) may have already faced this existential threat.

Could they have survived it by migrating to another star system without the use of spaceships?

Universe Today readers are well-versed in the difficulties of interstellar travel. Our nearest neighboring solar system is the Alpha Centauri system.

If humanity had to flee an existential threat in our Solar System, and if we could identify a planetary home in Alpha Centauri, it would still take us over four years to get there – if we could travel at the speed of light!

It still takes us five years to get an orbiter to Jupiter at our technological stage. There's lots of talk about generation starships, where humans could live for generations while en route to a distant habitable planet.

Those ships don't need to reach anywhere near the speed of light; instead, entire generations of humans would live and die on a journey to another star that takes hundreds or thousands of years. It's fun to think about but pure fantasy at this point.

Is there another way we, or other civilizations, could escape our doomed homes?

The author of a new research article in the International Journal of Astrobiology says that ETCs may not need starships to escape existential threats and travel to another star system.

They could instead use free-floating planets, also known as rogue planets. The article is "*Migrating extraterrestrial civilizations and interstellar colonization: implications for SETI and SETA*". The author is Irina Romanovskaya. Romanovskaya is a Professor of Physics and Astronomy at Houston Community College.

"I propose that extraterrestrial civilizations may use free-floating planets as interstellar transportation to reach, explore, and colonize planetary systems," Romanovskaya writes. And when it comes to the search for other civilizations, these efforts could leave technosignatures and artifacts.

"*I propose possible technosignatures and artifacts that may be produced by extraterrestrial civilizations using free-floating planets for interstellar migration and interstellar colonization, as well as strategies for the search for their technosignatures and artifacts,*" she said.

It's possible that rogue planets, either in the Milky Way or some of the other hundreds of billions of galaxies, carry their own life with them in subsurface oceans kept warm by radiogenic decay.

Then if they meet a star and become gravitationally bound, that life has effectively used a rogue planet to transport itself, hopefully, to somewhere more hospitable. So why couldn't a civilization mimic that?

We think of free-floating planets as dark, cold, and inhospitable. And they are unless they have warm subsurface oceans. But they also offer some advantages.

"*Free-floating planets can provide constant surface gravity, large amounts of space and resources," Romanovskaya writes. "Free-floating planets with surface and subsurface oceans can provide water as a consumable resource and for protection from space radiation.*"

An advanced civilization could also engineer the planet for an even greater advantage by steering it and developing energy sources. Romanovskaya suggests that if we're on the verge of using controlled fusion, then advanced civilizations might already be using it, which could change a frigid rogue planet into something that could support life.

The author outlines four scenarios where ETCs could take advantage of rogue planets.

The first scenario involves a rogue planet that happens to pass by the home world of an ETC. How often that might occur is tied to the number of rogue planets in general.

So far, we don't know how many there are, but there are certainly some. In 2021, a team of researchers announced the discovery of between 70 and 170 rogue planets, each the size of Jupiter, in one region of the Milky Way. And in 2020, one study suggested there could be as many as 50 billion of them in our galaxy.

Where do they all come from? Most are likely ejected from their solar systems due to gravitational events, but some may form via accretion as stars do.

Another source of rogue planets is our Solar System's Oort Cloud. If other systems also have a cloud of objects like this, they can be an abundant source of rogue planets ejected by stellar activity.

Romanovskaya writes: "*Stars with 1–7 times solar mass undergoing the post-main-sequence evolution, as well as a supernova from a 7–20 times solar mass progenitor, can eject Oort-cloud objects from their systems so that such objects become unbound from their host stars.*"

But how often can an ETC, or our civilization, expect a rogue planet to come close enough to hitchhike on? A 2015 study showed that the binary star W0720 (Scholz's star) passed through our Solar System's Oort Cloud about 70,000 years ago.

While that was a star and not a planet, it shows that objects pass relatively close by. If the studies that predict billions of free-floating planets are correct, then some of them likely passed close by, or right through, the Oort Cloud long before we had the means to detect them.

The Oort Cloud is a long way away, but a sufficiently advanced civilization could have the capability to see a rogue planet approaching and go out and meet it.

The second scenario involves using technology to steer a rogue planet closer to a civilization's home. With sufficient technology, they could choose an object from their own Oort Cloud – assuming they have one – and use a propulsion system to direct it towards a safe orbit near their planet.

With sufficient lead time, they could adapt the object to their needs, for example, by building underground shelters and other infrastructure. Maybe, with adequate technology, they could alter or create an atmosphere.

The third scenario is similar to the second one. It also involves an object from the civilization's outer Solar System. Romanovskaya uses the dwarf planet Sedna in our Solar System as an example.

Sedna has a highly eccentric orbit that takes it from 76 AUs from the Sun to 937 AU in about 11,000 years. With sufficient technology and lead time, an object like Sedna could be turned into an escape ship.

The author notes that "*Civilizations capable of doing so would be advanced civilizations that already have their planetary systems explored to the distances of at least 60 AU from their host stars*".

There are lots of potential problems. Bringing a dwarf planet from the distant reaches of the Solar System into the inner Solar System could disrupt the orbits of other planets, leading to all sorts of hazards.

But the dangers are mitigated if a civilization around a post-main sequence star has already migrated outward with the changing habitable zone. Romanovskaya discusses the energy needed and the timing required in more detail in her article.

The fourth scenario also involves objects like Sedna. When a star leaves the main sequence and expands, there's a critical distance where objects will be ejected from the system rather than remain gravitationally bound to the dying star.

If an ETC could accurately determine when these objects would be ejected as rogue planets, they could prepare it beforehand and ride it out of the dying solar system. That could be extraordinarily perilous, as periods of violent mass loss from the star creates an enormous hazard.

In all of these scenarios, the rogue planet or other body isn't a permanent home; it's a lifeboat.

"For all the above scenarios, free-floating planets may not serve as a permanent means of escape from existential threats," the author explains. "Because of the waning heat production in their interior, such planets eventually fail to sustain oceans of liquid water (if such oceans exist)."

Free-floating planets are also isolated and have fewer resources than planets in a solar system. There are no asteroids to mine, for example, and no free solar energy. There are no seasons and no night and day. There are no plants, animals, or even bacteria. They're simply a means to an end.

"Therefore, instead of making free-floating planets their permanent homes, extraterrestrial civilizations would use the free-floating planets as interstellar transportation to reach and colonize other planetary systems,"

writes Romanovskaya.

In her article, Professor Romanovskaya speculates where this could lead. She envisions a civilization that does this more than once, not to escape a dying star but to spread throughout a galaxy and colonize it.

"In this way, the parent-civilization may create unique and autonomous daughter-civilizations inhabiting different planets, moons, or regions of space.

"A civilization of Cosmic Hitchhikers would act as a 'parent-civilization' spreading the seeds of 'daughter-civilizations' in the form of its colonies in planetary systems," she writes. "This applies to both biological and post-biological species."

Humanity is only in the early stages of protecting ourselves from catastrophic asteroid impacts, and we can't yet manage our planet's climate with any degree of stability. So thinking about using rogue planets to keep humanity alive seems pretty far-fetched. But Romanovskaya's research isn't about us; it's about detecting other civilizations.

All of this activity could create technosignatures and artifacts that signified the presence of an ETC. The research article outlines what they might be and how we could detect them. Rogue planets used as lifeboats could create technosignatures like electromagnetic emissions or other phenomena.

An ETC could use solar sails to control a rogue planet or use them on a spaceship launched from a rogue planet once they have reached their destination. In either case, solar sails produce a technosignature: cyclotron radiation.

Maneuvering either a spacecraft or a rogue planet with solar sails would produce *"... cyclotron radiation caused by the interaction of the interstellar medium with the magnetic sail"*.

Infrared emissions could be another technosignature emitted as waste heat by an ETC on a rogue planet. An excessive amount of infrared or unnatural changes in the amount of infrared could be detected as a technosignature.

Infrared could be emitted unevenly across the planet's surface, indicating underlying engineering or technology. An unusual mix of different wavelengths of electromagnetic energy could also be a technosignature.

The atmosphere itself, if one existed, could also hold technosignatures. Depending on what was observed, it could contain evidence of terraforming.

For now, astronomers don't know how many rogue planets there are or if they're concentrated in some areas of the galaxy. We're at the starting line when it comes to figuring these things out. But soon, we may get a better idea.

The Vera Rubin Observatory should see first light by 2023. This powerful observatory will image the entire available sky every few nights, and it'll do it in fine detail. It houses the largest digital camera ever made: a 3.2 gigabyte CCD.

The Vera Rubin will be especially good at detecting transients, that is, anything that changes position or brightness in a couple of days. It'll have a good chance of spotting any interlopers like rogue planets that might approach our Solar System.

There's a strong possibility that some of those rogue planets will exhibit unusual emissions or puzzling phenomena. Scientists will probably puzzle over them as they did over Oumuamua.

Maybe another civilization more advanced than us has already faced an existential threat from their dying star. Maybe they made a Herculean effort to capture a rogue planet and engineer it to suit their needs.

Maybe they've already boarded it and launched it towards a distant, stable, long-lived yellow star, with rocky planets in its habitable zone. Maybe they're wondering if there's any life at their destination and how they might be received after their long journey.

Will Humanity Achieve Interstellar Travel And Find Alien Life?

Although our
dreams of making
contact with an
alien civilization
have traditionally
been rooted in
either a direct
visitation or the
picking up of an
intelligent signal
transmitted
throughout the
galaxy, these
remain long-shot
possibilities. But
real technology
may enable us to
find worlds where
life is abundant
and ubiquitous far
sooner than we
might have
expected based on
playing this cosmic
lottery.

Page 358

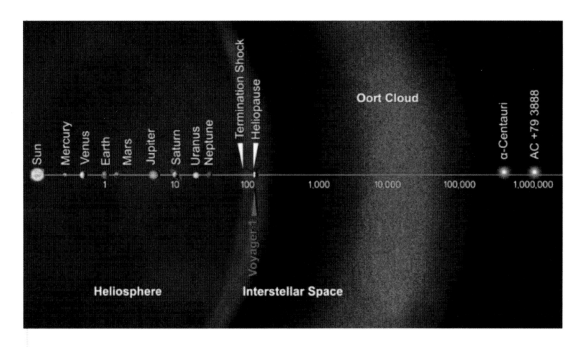

A logarithmic chart of distances, showing the Voyager spacecraft, our Solar System and our nearest star, for comparison. If we ever hope to travel across the great interstellar distances, it will require a technology that's superior to chemical-based rockets.

The biggest problem with the idea of interstellar travel is scale. The distances to even the nearest stars are measured in light-years, with Proxima Centauri being our nearest neighbor at 4.24 light-years away, where one light-year is approximately 9 trillion kilometers: some 60,000 times the Earth-Sun distance. At the speed of the fastest space probes humanity has ever sent on their way out of the Solar System (the Voyager 1 and 2 spacecraft), covering the distance to the nearest star would take approximately 80,000 years.

But all of this is based on current technology, which uses chemical-based rocket fuel for propulsion. The biggest downside of rocket fuel is its inefficiency: one kilogram of fuel is capable of generating just milligrams' worth of energy, as measured by Einstein's $E = mc2$. Having to carry that fuel on board with you — and requiring that you accelerate both your payload and the remaining fuel with that energy — is what's hamstringing us right now.

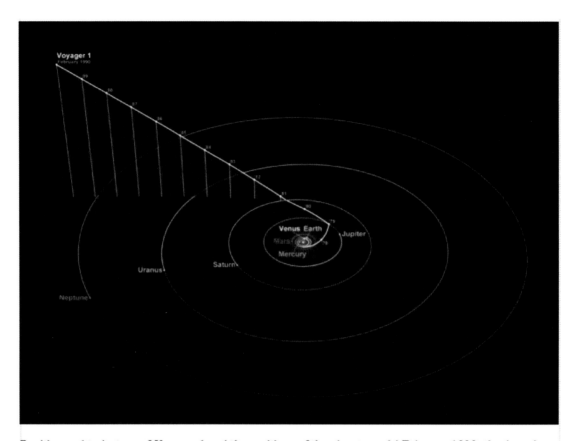

Position and trajectory of Voyager 1 and the positions of the planets on 14 February 1990, the day when Pale Blue Dot and Family Portrait were taken. Note that it is only Voyager 1's position out of the plane of the Solar System that enabled the unique views we retrieved, and that Voyager remains the farthest object ever launched by humanity, but still has thousands of times farther to go until it travels ~4 light-years.

But there are two independent possibilities that don't require us to dream up Warp Drive-like technologies that would rely on new physics. Instead, we can pursue the routes of either using a more efficient fuel to power our journey, which could increase our range and speeds tremendously, or we can explore technologies where the thrust-providing source is independent of the payload that's going to be accelerated.

In terms of efficiency, there are three technologies that could vastly outperform chemical-based rocket fuel:

nuclear fission,

nuclear fusion,

and matter-antimatter propulsion.

Whereas chemical-based fuels convert a mere 0.0001% of their mass into energy that can be used for thrust, all of these ideas are far more efficient.

Fission converts approximately 0.1% of the mass of fissile materials into energy; approximately one kilogram of fissionable fuel yields about one gram's worth of energy, via $E = mc^2$. Nuclear fusion does a superior job; fusing hydrogen into helium, for example, is 0.7% efficient: one kilogram of fuel would yield 7 grams' worth of usable energy. But far-and-away the most efficient solution is matter-antimatter annihilation.

If we could create and control 0.5 kilograms of antimatter, we could annihilate it at will with 0.5 kilograms of normal matter, creating a 100% efficient reaction that produced a full kilogram's worth of energy. We could conceivably extract thousands or even a million times as much energy from the same amount of fuel, which could propel us to the stars on timescales of centuries (with fission) or even just decades (with fusion or antimatter).

On the other hand, we could work to achieve interstellar travel via a completely different route: by placing a large power source capable of accelerating a spacecraft in space. Recent advances in laser technology have led many to suggest that an enormous, sufficiently collimated array of lasers in space could be used to accelerate a spacecraft from low-Earth orbit to tremendous speeds. A highly reflective laser-sail, like a solar sail except specifically designed for lasers, could do the job.

If a large-enough, powerful-enough array of in-phase lasers were constructed, potentially reaching gigawatt power levels, it could not only impart momentum to a target spacecraft, but could do so for a long period of time. Based on calculations performed by Dr. Phil Lubin a few years ago, it's possible that speeds up to 20% the speed of light could be reached. While we don't yet have a plan for decelerating such a spacecraft, reaching the nearest star in a single human lifetime is within the realm of possibility.

By the same token, the search for extraterrestrial life is no longer restricted to either waiting for an alien visit or searching the Universe with radio signals for intelligent aliens, although the latter is certainly still an active scientific field spearheaded by SETI. Although no signals have been found, this remains a stunning example of high-risk, high-reward science. If a positive detection is ever made, it will be a civilization-transforming event.

However, as exoplanet astronomy continues to advance, two techniques that have already been demonstrated could bring us our first signatures of life on other worlds: transit spectroscopy and direct imaging. Both of these involve using the light from a planet itself, with transit spectroscopy leveraging the light that filters through a planet's atmosphere and direct imaging taking advantage of the sunlight directly reflected off of the planet itself.

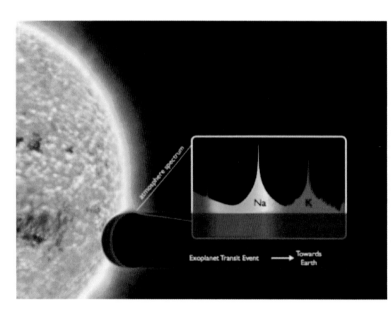

When a planet transits in front of its parent star, some of the light is not only blocked, but if an atmosphere is present, filters through it, creating absorption or emission lines that a sophisticated enough observatory could detect. If there are organic molecules or large amounts of molecular oxygen, we might be able to find that too, at some point in the future. It's important that we consider not only the signatures of life we know of, but of possible life that we don't find there on Earth.

Transit spectroscopy relies on us having a serendipitous alignment of our observatory with both a target exoplanet and its parent star, but these alignments do occur. Whereas a small fraction of the star's light will get blocked by the transiting planet, an even smaller fraction of starlight will transmit through the planet's atmosphere, similar to the sunlight that gets transmitted through Earth's atmosphere and lights up the Moon (in red) during a total lunar eclipse.

This enables us, if our measurements are good enough, to decode what elements and molecules are present in the target planet's atmosphere. If we could discover biological signatures or even technosignatures which could be an oxygen-nitrogen atmosphere, complex biomolecules, or even something like a chlorofluorocarbon (CFC) molecule we would immediately have a strong hint of a living world that would tantalizingly await confirmation.

Above is an image of Earth from the DSCOV-EPIC camera. To the right of the image is the same photo degraded to a resolution of 3 x 3 pixels, similar to what researchers will see in future exoplanet observations.

Direct imaging could provide exactly that sort of confirmation. Although our first image of an Earth-sized exoplanet likely won't be very visually impressive, it will contain a ton of information that can be used to reveal indicators of life. Even if the planet itself is just one pixel in a detector, we could not only break its light apart into individual wavelengths, but can look for time-varying signatures that could reveal:

-clouds,

-continents,

-oceans,

-plant life greening with the seasons,

-icecaps,

-rotation rates,

and much more. If there are light-emitting signatures at night, just as planet Earth has our light that illuminate the world at night, we could conceivably even detect those as well. If there's a civilization out there on a nearby Earth-like planet, the next generation of telescopes might be able to find them.

The Earth at night emits electromagnetic signals, but it wouldtake a telescope of incredible resolution to create an image like this from light years away. Humans have become intelligent, technologically advanced species here on Earth, but even if this signal were smeared out it might still be detectable by next generation direct imaging.

All of this, together, points to a picture where a spacecraft or even a crewed journey to the stars is technologically within our reach, and where the discovery of our first world beyond the solar system with possible life on it could occur in a decade or two. What was once solely in the realm of science-fiction is quickly becoming possible due to both technical and scientific advances and the thousands of scientists and engineers who work to apply these new technologies in practical ways.

How close is humanity to achieving this dream that's spanned innumerable generations? The first thing you might be wondering is about whether warp drive itself is really feasible or not. And the answer, believe it or not, is maybe, but not unless we figure out a source of energy that goes well beyond anything we've got so far, including antimatter.

The reason is simple: to achieve warp drive, you need to bend the space in front of you so that it contracts, and that can only occur at the expense of expanding the space behind you. This takes an enormous amount of energy all localized in one spot, and you need to do it while still keeping the space where your spaceship will be not too severely bent, or you'll wind up destroying it with terrific gravitational tidal forces.

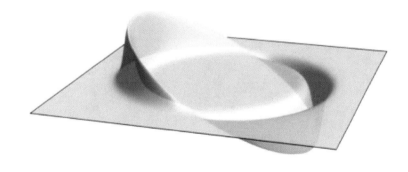

The Alcubierre soluing motion similar to warp drive. This solution requires negative gravitational mass, which could be exactly what antimatter might provide.

But if you can do it, and it is something allowed in General Relativity, this requires not only the matter-and-energy we know, but also some form of negative energy: either matter with negative mass or a form of anti-energy itself. If we could harness this, it would mean we could travel through the contracted space (slower than light), but we could do something like contract a 40 light-year journey down to 6 light-months.

Even if we only traveled through that now-contracted space at half the speed of light, we'd get there in 1 year, rather than 40. That's pretty impressive!

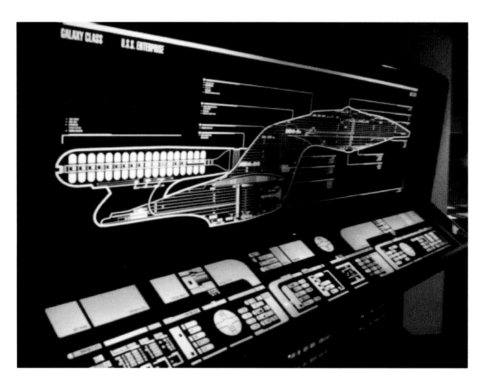

The warp drive system on the Star Trek starships was what made travel from star to star possible. If we had this technology, we could easily bridge the distance to the stars, but this remains in the realm of science fiction for today. Star Trek Discovery's Spore Drive opens up a new possible mechanism for faster-than-light travel that may be even superior to Warp Drive.

That doesn't mean, however, that the plot devices or treknobabble cooked up by Star Trek's writers, which includes things like:

-dilithium crystals,

-warp nacelles,

-Bussard ramjets

-warp cores,

or anything else we might immediately refer to has any relevance. Science fiction provides us with possible outcomes, but only very rarely gets the path to that technological solution correct. We know enough about physics, today, to be certain that Star Trek's "*solution*" to this problem is not feasible. But, then again, that's part of what makes science so wonderful: it can take a fictional idea and make it a reality. Or, if we're really lucky, surpass our sci-fi dreams!

Aliens, on the other hand, are likely ubiquitous, based on what we know about the ingredients for life in the Universe, the workings of chemistry, and our measurements of exoplanets with the right conditions for life around other stars. We have literally billions and billions of potentially habitable planets in our galaxy alone, with similar conditions to early Earth. In many models, early Venus and Mars were similar to early Earth.

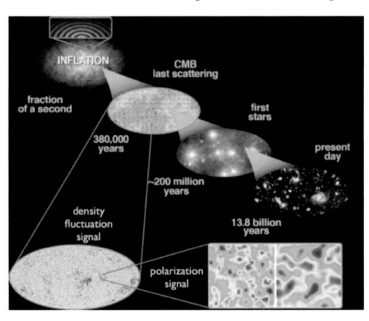

From inflation to the hot Big Bang, to the birth and death of stars, galaxies, and black holes, all the way to our ultimate dark energy fate, we know that entropy never decreases with time. But we still don't understand why time itself flows forward. However, were pretty certain that entropy is not the answer.

Are we supposed to believe that Earth, where life arose within the first ~3% of our planet's history, is somehow unique in that regard? Although winding up with something like human beings is a difficult proposition, winding up with no life at all, across billions and billions of other instances with similar initial conditions, seems far more unlikely, at least from a scientific perspective.

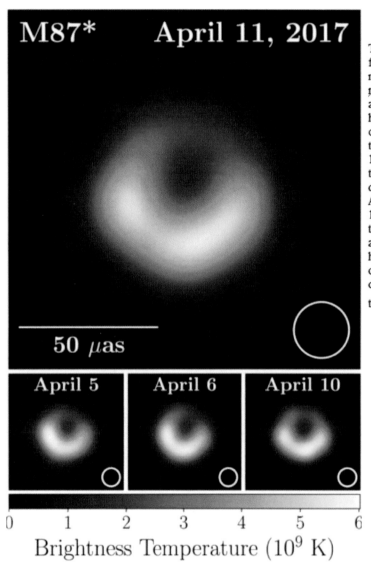

The Event Horizon Telescope's first released image achieved resolutions of 22.5 microarseconds, enabling the array to resolve the ancient horizon of the black hole at the center of M87. A single-dish telescope would have to be 12,000 km in diameter to achieve this same sharpness. Note the differing appearances between the April 5/6 images and the April 10/11 images, which show that the features around the black hole are changing over time. This helps demonstrate the importance of syncing the different observations, rather than just time-averaging them.

In the 1920s, we didn't know the Universe was expanding, but its discovery led to the idea of the Big Bang. In the 1960s, we didn't know that the Big Bang was true, but its confirmation led to questions about what came before it and what our Universe's ultimate fate would be.

And now, as you can see, we're talking about the mysteries of cosmic inflation and dark energy, which are where those frontiers now lie. And in any field, this is how it works: discovering an answer only reveals a deeper frontier that we haven't yet explored.

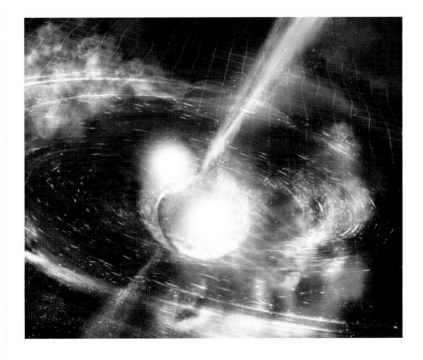

Artist's illustration of two merging neutron stars. Binary neutron star systems inspiral and merge as well, but the closest orbiting pair we've found within our galaxy won't merge until nearly 100 million years have passed. LIGO will likely find many others before that.

Science is all about discovering and following the rules; science-fiction is about breaking those rules. I haven't explicitly thought about it in those terms, and I agree that this is pretty much how it usually works. I don't know that this is why I, personally, like or don't like various forms of science-fiction, but it's a new perspective to think about for me.

We constantly have advancing technology, and science-fiction asks the question of how advancing technology will change our lives.

Visualizations, based on a mix of science and artistic license, have been around for as long as we've even known enough about science to imagine what could realistically be. Also, side note, the "interstellar" black hole is probably not very likely to be what we see when we examine our realistic black holes in supreme accuracy; there's a lot of artistic license and some likely unphysical assumptions that were made for Interstellar.

Do you know why things like rockets and space shuttles have the shapes they do? That elongated, narrow-cone shape you're familiar with? It's because of atmospheric drag.

If you're going to build your ship in space, and fly it only in space, you don't need to factor in aerodynamic considerations at all! You'd be much, much smarter to build a structure with a good volume-to-surface-area ratio: a sphere. The Death Star, not the Millennium Falcon or an X-Wing, is going to be much more practical for structures we build in space!

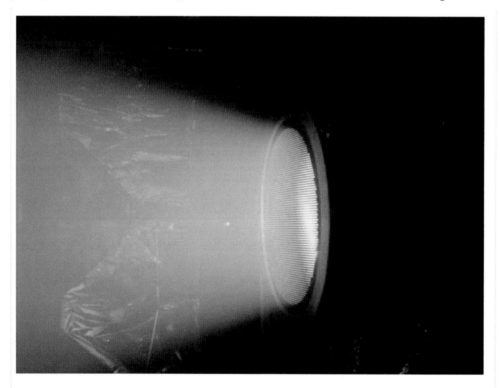

The NEXIS Ion Thruster, at Jet Propulsion Laboratories, is a prototype for a long-term thruster that could move large-mass ongects over very long timescales.

Ion drives are real, and they're very cool. But if you want to power a journey across large distances in a reasonable amount of time, ion drives won't get you far at all. They can take you ~6 billion kilometers over 11 years, as Bryan said, and can do so pretty efficiently. But if you factor that distance over that time as a "*mean acceleration*," you get something truly atrocious: 100 nanometers/second.

You're... not going to go very far very fast. ~100,000 years to the nearest star, same as conventional fuel. Obviously not a viable option.

Normally, structures like IKAROS, shown here, are viewed as potential sails in space. However, if a Large-area object were placed between the Earth and the Sun, it could reduce the total irradiance received at the top of our atmosphere, potentially combating global warming.

Solar Sails

You can accelerate with a solar sail and you can also decelerate with a solar sail as well. The "fuel" is simply radiation provided by a star, so as long as you visit a star comparable to the Sun, you could decelerate the same way you accelerated.

Unfortunately, this technology is inferior to ion drives not only in terms of distance reached, but in terms of acceleration and control over your spacecraft. It's a nice idea, but it's an idea that's in its infancy, at best, despite being proposed more than 400 years ago by Johannes Kepler!

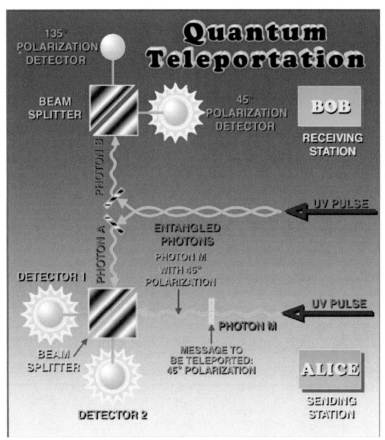

Quantum Teleportation, an effect (erroneously) touted as faster-than-light-travenformation is being exchanged faster than light. However, the phenomenon is real, and in line with the predictions of all viable interpretations of quantum mechanics.

Quantum Teleportation doesn't involve teleporting a particle, it involves teleporting the quantum state of a particle. This doesn't solve the problem of teleporting an inanimate object, much less a person.

You need a lot of information to encode a human being. Remember that there are around ~10^28 atoms in the human body, and that means something like 10^29 or 10^30 quantum bits of information. As Bryan says, *"I don't think we'll be teleporting anytime soon."*

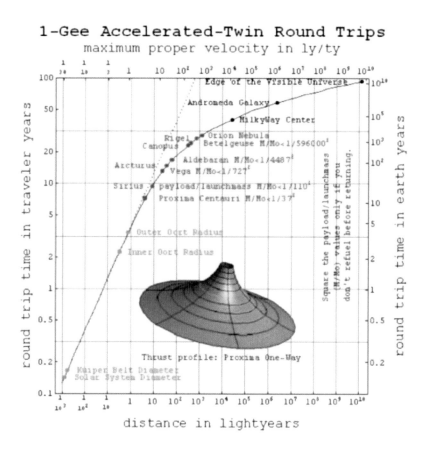

The travel time for a spacecraft to reach a destination if it accelerates at a constant rate of Earth's surface gravity. Note that, given enough time, you can go anywhere.

Time dilation could be a viable option for interstellar travel. If you wanted to go more than ~100 light-years, it would always take you more than

~100 years (a human lifetime, at the far end) to get there from the frame-of-reference of a person remaining on Earth.

But if you continue to accelerate at 1 g, or 9.8 m/s^2, you'll get to wherever you want to go in a much shorter timescale from your frame of reference, as you travel close to the speed of light.

An artist's conception of a starship making use of the Alcubierre drive to travel at apparently faster-than-light speeds. By combining warp technology with the mycelium drive and the ship's shields, Stamets and Tilly devise a plan to get Discovery home while keeping the mycelium network intact.

The DEEP laser-sail concept relie: on a large laser array striking and accelerating a relatively large-area low-mass spacecraft. This has the potential to accelerate non-living objects to speeds approaching the speed of light, making an interstellar journey possible withir a single human lifetime. The work done by the laser, applying a force as an object moves a certain distance, is an example of energy transfer from one form into another.

Using the transit method, we can find out properties of the planets that orbit around the stars, and they come in enormous varieties, just like we'd expect if we didn't assume the rest of the Universe was just like our little corner. We've found the planets that are easiest to find, and that means the largest planets relative to their star in close-in orbits. This, unsurprisingly, has skewed the population of planets that we've found.

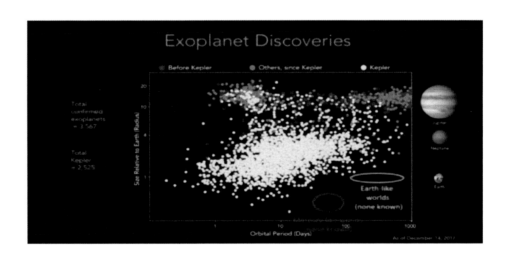

Although more than 4,000 confirmed exoplanets are known, with more than half of them uncovered by Kepler, finding a Mercury-like world around a star like our Sun is well beyond the capabilities of our current planet finding technology. As viewed by Kepler, Mercury would appear to be 1/285th the size of the Sun, making it even more difficult than the 1/194th size we see from the Earth's point of view.

Resources

space.com, "Is Interstellar Travel Really Possible?" By Paul Sutter; sciencealert.com, "Interstellar Travel Could Be Possible Even Without Spaceships, Scientist Says." By Evan Gough; forbes.com, "Will Humanity Achieve Interstellar Travel And Find Alien Life?" By Ethan Siegel;

Chapter Twenty-Nine--What Does It All Mean?

If you have read this book from cover to cover, your head must now be chockfull of all kinds of information. You probably also feel like your head is going to burst. I promise you the pain will go away with time. Haha! Once it does, you will probably start asking yourself what does it all mean? You may also ask what yourself what can we do to save our planet? Unfortunately we cannot control everything that affects our world. There are things that are just beyond our control.

When you come to this realization it will probably make you feel a quite powerless and perhaps even fatalistic. Relax...it is only human to feel this way. Since we are at the top of the food chain, it is only natural that we should believe that we have complete control of our world and our destinies. Unfortunately this is just a lot of wishful thinking on our part.

Even our moon plays a very important role in our very existence. The moon gives our planet stability, kind of like the axis of a gyroscope which allows it to spin smoothly. Without the moon, our rotation would be erratic and unstable and totally unsuitable for the existence of life. The magnetic core also plays a role in preventing harmful rays from killing us. Our atmosphere also protects us from other harmful rays produced by the sun. We also just happen to be in the right location or the habitable zone in the solar system. This ensures that the temperatures we are exposed to are suitable to life.

I am sure that you are aware that not only the world we live in but the universe that it exists in is quite complex. So complex that even our most brilliant scientists have not been able to decipher all of its mysteries. It is not only complex but incredibly dangerous as well. Every corner of our solar system, galaxy and universe holds untold dangers. This is one of the reasons that there are so few existing worlds with intelligent life. It takes just the right set of circumstances for life to develop on these worlds. One of these criteria that absolutely, positively has to be present is an atmosphere.

I hate to sound like a broken record, but the lack of a protective atmosphere really does make a difference. Chances are that the Earth has the same amount of asteroid collisions as the moon – but you'd never know it. That's because our atmosphere shields us from them. The constant changes on Earth's surface also cover up most of the evidence.

If you want to see what it is like to not have an atmosphere, try living on the moon. Since there is no atmosphere there is not only no air to breathe, there is no water to drink either. You are also exposed to the extreme temperature fluctuations that exist in space. From day to night, the temperature ranges are quite extreme. In the day, it is a balmy 224° Fahrenheit and at night it is a frigid -298° Fahrenheit. Since we do have an atmosphere we do not have to worry about these temperature extremes nor micrometeorites and solar wind irradiation. These come about when the turbulent and frequently relentless conditions that occur on the moon break up deep layers of the crust. This allows the solar wind to sweep up not only the visible gray dust and rock fragments created by this activity, but also invisible fragments of volcanic glass. These extreme conditions make any life on the moon impossible.

You could think of our planet as a really big crib that is protecting us from falling out of bed. Since it provides us with everything that we need to live, we should treat it with more care and love than we do. As I have stated, the atmosphere not only helps to protect us from all but the largest of errant heavenly bodies. They simply burn up from the heat generated by the friction created when asteroids pass through our atmosphere. That is why the moon is full of craters, it has no atmosphere to protect its surface from asteroids and meteorites.

There are many theories as to the origin of life. Some scientists believe we came from asteroids or even comets, while others believe we came from a primordial soup that got its start from electrical charges generated by lightning. Carl Sagan provided an excellent demonstration on how this could take place on his amazing mini-series, the Cosmos which aired on 1980.

One of the reasons that we need to take care of our our world is because there really is nothing suitable for life in our neighborhood. The closest planet for life is many light years away. With our current technology that distance is simply an insurmountable obstacle. We are probably several thousand years away from obtaining the level of technology necessary for interstellar travel. So as I said earlier we better take care of our world.

While I don't believe that we are the cause of global warming, I do believe we are in a cycle that just happens to be one that is involving a warming trend. I also don't believe that our ocean levels are rising. If you don't believe me just take a look at the picture I provided below of Plymouth Rock in Massachusetts.

This rock dates back to 1620. The level of the Atlantic was the same then as it is today. Just a little over 400 years. So what gives?

One of the hottest periods we experienced dates back to the time of the dinosaurs. A more recent time that falls in our recorded history took place during the age of the Egyptian Pharoahs. Neither time involved an industrial revolution. However, this does not mean we are out of the weeds just yet.

A very intelligent man named Jacques Cousteau once said

that if our oceans died, our world would follow within a year. Unfortunately it seems like we are hellbent on doing just that. We are over fishing the oceans, we are killing off our sharks for a tasteless soup and we are polluting the hell out of it as well. This is not the way to care for our greatest treasure, is it? We need to end this trend of mindless and destructive self-gratification. We, as a species give no thought to what the repercussions of our actions are. We just blunder blindly on. I liken our species to a cancerous growth that continues growing unabated in total disregards to boundaries and borders.

The only thing that gives me hope is when I see what kind of beauty our species can create and the totally selfless behavior that we are capable of.

The biggest hurdle we face is ourselves. We have a penchant towards fanaticism. Fanatics are typically singleminded and as a result are intolerant of any views that don't coincide with their own. This intolerance of opposing views and ideas I am afraid will be the cause of our downfall. In just the last few years this trend has worsened. Just ask Alice about going down the rabbit hole. Once you go down it there is little hope of getting out of it.

What we need is smart conservation based on real science not the corrupted crap we call science today. We have to put our planet first not our personal agendas. It makes no sense to kill our planet in an effort to save it. I believe every species has a right to live out their lives on this planet. Just because we are at the top of the food chain doesn't mean that we have the right to destroy the planet or kill off countless lesser species.

Just a side note, there has been a push for electric cars, which started with the hybrid car. Now there is no talk of hybrids but only straight electric cars. Unfortunately our power grids are not robust enough to handle the huge drain that all these electric cars will cause. Where as the hybrid car could charge itself simply by switching to gas when the battery runs low. It would also be an option for travel. The hybrid car could be a good transition to electric cars. Mainly because electric cars are just not where they need to be at this point to totally replace gasoline/diesel fueled vehicles. The same thing happened with digital cameras. It took many years before they were good enough to replace the venerable film camera.

I have a parting thought, are we really the top dog? How easily we were almost overwhelmed by a simple virus. Remember, coronavirus?

This is a parting thought from an essay from The Guardian. It is entitled "None of Our dreams can survive the loss of a planet." By George Monbiot

"With the exception of all-out nuclear war, all the most important issues that confront us are environmental. None of our hopes, none of our dreams, none of our plans and expectations can survive the loss of a habitable planet. And there is scarcely an Earth system that is not now threatened with collapse.

Let's begin with the ground beneath our feet. Soil is a biological structure, created by the organisms that inhabit it. When conditions become hostile to their survival, the structure collapses, and fertile lands turn to dust bowls. The global rate of soil degradation is terrifying. We rely on the soil for 99% of our calories, yet we treat it like dirt.

Ocean ecosystems are in even greater trouble, hammered by a combination of industrial fishing, pollution and acidification, as carbon dioxide dissolves into seawater. Forests, rivers, wetlands, savannahs, the cryosphere (the world's ice and snow): all are being pushed towards the brink.

Above all, climate breakdown is gathering at shocking, unanticipated speed, with disasters occurring at 1.2°C of heating that scientists did not expect until we hit 2 or 3°. Support the Guardian Yet you would scarcely know it. Most of the media, most of the time, either ignores our environmental crisis, downplays it or denies it. The reason is not difficult to discern. Most of the media is owned by corporations or billionaires, who have a major financial interest in sustaining business as usual. To keep the proprietors, shareholders and advertisers happy or, in the case of public sector broadcasters, to keep the government off their backs, the most important issues of all are neglected."

Postcript

I am including this brief note because first, I want total transparency and secondly, I want the reader to be aware of the fact that I have used a great deal of material from the internet to write this book. I did this mainly because I am not an expert on most of the subjects that I have covered in it. I also want the reader to know that I am not making any money from this book. The price that is being charged for this book just covers the fees that Amazon charges to publish it. So if I am not making an money from it, you may ask why I am doing it? The answer is the same one I give my blog patrons. I am doing it to help the public get the most accurate information possible on any given subject. In the case of this book, it is mainly our planet and its environment.

While it is true that the vast majority of the material used in this book was written by other writers, it was collated and crosschecked by me to ensure completeness and accuracy. Where questions have come up regarding the factuality of a particular subject I have included both sides of the argument so that you, the reader can make an informed decision on the matter. In an effort to be as complete as possible, I have covered a great many topics in this book. I hope you have found them to be helpful and informative.

As is the case with any book, the information in it will eventually become outdated. Unfortunately there is not much that I can do about this. It is the nature of the beast. However, I will do my best to keep the material updated in my blog, ***common-sense-in-america.com***.

Appendices

Appendix A--How Many Species Have we Lost Since Mankind First Appeared?

What's the first species humans drove to extinction?

Sometime in the late 1600s, in the lush forests of Mauritius, the very last dodo took its last breath. After centuries of untroubled ferreting in the tropical undergrowth, this species met its untimely end at the hands of humans, who had arrived on the island less than 100 years before. With their penchant for hunting, habitat destruction and the release of invasive species, humans undid millions of years of evolution, and swiftly removed this bird from the face of the Earth.

Since then, the dodo has nestled itself in our conscience as the first prominent example of human-driven extinction. We've also used the dodo to assuage our own guilt: the creature was fat, lazy and unintelligent — and as popular story goes, those traits sealed its inevitable fate.

But in fact, we couldn't be more wrong, said Julian Hume, a paleontologist and research associate with the National History Museum in the United Kingdom. He studies the fossils of extinct species, and has devoted a portion of his career to correcting the dodo's dismal reputation. By digitally modeling the remains of a dodo's skeleton, he's produced a 3D digital reconstruction that draws an altogether different picture of a bird that was faster, more athletic and far brainier than popular culture has led us to believe. "*It was nothing like this big, fat, bulgy thing that was just waddling around. This bird was super adapted to the environment of*

Mauritius," Hume told Live Science. Instead, humans' unrelenting exploitation was the real culprit behind the dodo's untimely death.

But that's not all we've gotten wrong. Despite the commonly held belief, the dodo actually wasn't the first creature that humans drove to extinction — not by a long shot. In fact, humanity was wiping out the world's fauna thousands of years before we set eyes on the dodo. *"There was certainly a lot more going on before and after that event,"* said Hume.

So, if the iconic dodo wasn't the first species we drove to the brink, then which animal gets this disheartening title, instead?

Humans on the move

We've grown accustomed to thinking about human-driven species extinction as a relatively recent trend in our history. Yet, researchers have found convincing palaeontological evidence that dismantles that idea.

"The real problem started when we, as humans, started migrating," Hume said. That starting point is still debated, but most recent estimates suggest that migrations that led to lasting populations of humans spread across the globe began with the movement of hominids — Neanderthals and other ancient human relatives, as well Homo sapiens — out of Africa and southeast Asia, roughly 125,000 years ago. This is where the evidence gets interesting. As humans left their ancestral homes, and over the following tens of thousands of years went on to colonize Eurasia, Oceania, North and South America, the fossil record shows a parallel uptick in the extinction in large-bodied animals — also known as megafauna — across those continents.

"As hominids migrated out of Africa, you see this incredibly regular pattern of extinction," said Felisa Smith, a professor of ecology and evolutionary biology at the University of New Mexico, who studies how animals' body sizes have changed over the course of history. As she and her colleagues explained in a 2018 study published in the journal Science, each time our ancestors set foot in new places, fossil records show that

large-bodied species — the humongous prehistoric relatives of elephants, bears, antelope and other creatures — started going extinct within a few hundred to 1,000 years, at most. Such rapid extinction timescales don't occur at any other point in the last several million years (not since the non-avian dinosaurs were wiped out by an asteroid about 65 million years ago.) "*The only time you see it is when humans are involved, which is really striking,*" Smith said.

Some of those early lost species would seem like fantastical beasts if they roamed Earth today. For example, "*There was an armadillo-like thing called the glyptodon, which was the size of a Volkswagen bus,*" Smith told Live Science. Glyptodons, many equipped with vicious-looking spiked tails, disappeared from the Americas at the end of the last ice age, roughly 12,000 years ago — which is probably connected to the earlier arrival of humans there. The number of gigantic Eurasian cave bears, several hundred pounds heavier than grizzly bears today, went into a steep decline about 40,000 years ago(opens in new tab), around the same time that humans began to spread across their habitat. South America was once home to lumbering giant ground sloths — and humans were also the most likely candidate in their demise, about 11,000 years ago.

What made large animals, in particular, so susceptible to humanity's spread? Megafauna likely represented food, or a threat, to incoming humans. What's more, animals that had never encountered humans before were probably unwary of these strange newcomers migrating into their unspoiled lands, which might have increased their vulnerability to attack. Unlike other smaller animals that breed more rapidly,

An illustration of a short-faced bear defending its territory from a saber-tooth cat during the last ice age. (Image credit: Shutterstock)

megafauna also reproduce more slowly and so have smaller populations compared with other species, Hume explained: "*So if you take out a big section of a population they cannot reproduce quickly enough to build up numbers again.*"

It wasn't just hunting that posed a threat — but also the spread of human-caused fires that would have destroyed swathes of habitat, and increasing competition from humans for food. For instance, it's thought that by preying heavily on the same herbivores, growing numbers of hungry humans helped drive the extinction of the short-faced bear, a gigantic South American species that once stood at over 10 feet (3 meters) tall, and died out roughly 11,000 years ago. Climate change, paired with human impacts like hunting, also proved to be a lethal combination for some megafauna — most famously, mammoths, which went extinct about 10,500 years ago (except for the dwarf woolly mammoth, which survived until about 4,000 years ago on an island off northern Russia). "If you combine climate change with a negative human impact, it's a disaster," said Hume.

An answer?

All of this is to say that humans have systematically wiped out the species around us from almost the beginning of our history. Our migration prompted "*a disaster across the world,*" said Hume. "*We weren't very pleasant.*" Unfortunately, we've continued our ancestors' legacy, with, among thousands of other species, the eradication of Madagascan hippos 1,000 years ago, the loss of moa birds in New Zealand 600 years ago, and the decimation of passenger pigeons 106 years ago. We are also responsible for ongoing extinctions today.

But this still hasn't answered the question of what species went extinct first. And here's the catch: the data on human-driven extinction across the planet is only reliable as far back as about 125,000 years— but that doesn't mean we weren't driving animals to extinction before that in Africa, too. In fact, there's compelling evidence to suggest that before humans migrated out, they unleashed their hunting instincts on species there as well.

Smith's research has revealed that the average body size of African animals 125,000 years ago was only half that of species that were present on other continents around the world. "*Africa is one of the largest continents, so it should have had a mean body size similar to that of the Americas and Eurasia where it was roughly about 100 kilograms [220 lbs.],*" Smith said. "*The fact that it didn't suggests that there had already been an effect of hominids on megafauna in Africa, prior to 125,000 years ago.*"

In essence, because the rest of history tells us that humans are good at dispatching the largest creatures in an ecosystem, we can make a fairly safe assumption that hominids in Africa at the time could have been responsible for extinctions going even further back in time.

Still, there's no way to know for sure what that 'first' species would have been — though Smith takes a wild guess: "It was probably some species in the elephant family. But whether that's palaeomastodon, or stegodon" — the latter being a behemoth with tusks that measured 10 feet (3 meters) long - "*I couldn't tell you.*"

Clues for the future

We may not have a clear answer to that original question - but perhaps the more important one to ask is what humanity's legacy of extinction can teach us about conservation, going into the future.

Past extinctions have revealed that when animals — especially megafauna — disappear, there are profound ecological consequences. Whole landscapes are transformed in the absence of their shaping effects, with changes to vegetation and species diversity. Smith has even published research showing that the decline of global megafauna in past millennia led to dips in the amount of methane they burped out — with potentially transformative consequences for global climate. What's more, when animals disappear, whole rafts of dependent species go down with them.

The iconic dodo presents one such cautionary tale: when the birds died out, so did a Mauritian dung beetle that relied on dodo feces to survive.

Understanding human-driven extinctions of the past can help us figure out what the environmental consequences have been, explained Smith, and how we can limit those in the future by protecting the species that remain. Even the dodo's extinction provides clues that are helping us preserve ecosystems today. Hume is working on a project to catalog pollen spores present in the sediments around dodo fossils, to build up a detailed picture of the lush, palm-fringed forests they once roamed. That's helping conservationists to rewild the island with vegetation that was once there. "We're actually reconstructing the exact species of plants and trees from the environment the dodo was living in, before humans arrived," Hume said.

A bit of paradise was lost when we drove the dodo to extinction — not to mention the thousands of species whose demise came before that. But perhaps with hindsight, and the willingness to learn from our mistakes, some of that can be reclaimed.

-Extinctions have been a natural part of our planet's evolutionary history. More than 99% of the four billion species that have evolved on Earth are now gone.

-At least 900 species have gone extinct in the last five centuries.

-Only a small percentage of species have been evaluated for their extinction risk. This means estimates of species threatened with extinction will be an underestimate of the true number.

-More than 35,000 species have been evaluated to be threatened with extinction today.

-One-quarter of the world's mammals; 1-in-7 bird species; and 40% of amphibians are threatened.

-There have been five mass extinction events in Earth's history: 'The Big

Five'.

-More than 178 of the world's largest species went extinct during the Quaternary Extinction. Overhunting was likely the main driver.

-Extinction rates today are much higher than background rates and rates from previous mass extinctions.

-While many species are in danger, conservation has also saved tens of mammal and bird species from extinction.

Extinctions have been a natural part of the planet's evolutionary history. 99% of the four billion species that have evolved on Earth are now gone. Most species have gone extinct.

But when people ask the question of how many species have gone extinct, they're usually talking about the number of extinctions in recent history. Species that have gone extinct, mainly due to human pressures.

The IUCN Red List has estimated the number of extinctions over the last five centuries. Unfortunately we don't know about everything about all of the world's species over this period, so it's likely that some will have gone extinct without us even knowing they existed in the first place. So this is likely to be an underestimate.

In the chart we see these estimates for different taxonomic groups. It estimates that 900 species have gone extinct since 1500. Our estimates for the better-studied taxonomic groups are likely to be more accurate. This includes 85 mammal; 159 bird; 35 amphibian; and 80 fish species.

To understand the biodiversity problem we need to know how many species are under pressure; where they are; and what the threats are. To do this, the IUCN Red List of Threatened Species evaluates species across the world for their level of extinction risk. It does this evaluation every year, and continues to expand its coverage.

Number of species that have gone extinct since 1500, 2020

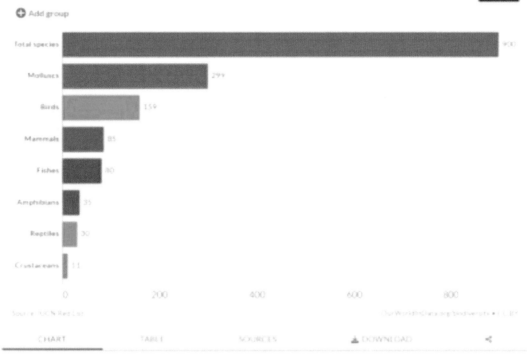

Number of species that have gone extinct since 1500
species · 2020

Group	
Amphibians	35
Animals	778
Arachnids	9
Birds	159
Chromists	0
Corals	0
Crustaceans	11
Fishes	80
Fungi	0
Insects	63
Mammals	85
Molluscs	299
Other animals	7
Plants	122
Reptiles	30
Total species	900

The IUCN has not evaluated all of the world's known species; in fact, in many taxonomic groups it has assessed only a very small percentage. In 2021, it had assessed only 7% of described species. But, this very much varies by taxonomic group. In the chart we see the share of described species in each group that has been assessed for their level of extinction risk. As we'd expect, animals such as birds, mammals, amphibians have seen a much larger share of their species assessed – more than 80%. Only 1% of insects have. And less than 1% of the world's fungi.

The lack of complete coverage of the world's species highlights two important points we need to remember when interpreting the IUCN Red List data:

1. Changes in the number of threatened species over time does not necessarily reflect increasing extinction risks. The IUCN Red List is a project that continues to expand. More and more species are been evaluated every year. In the year 2000, less than 20,000 species had been evaluated. By 2021, 140,000 had. As more species are evaluated, inevitably, more will be listed as being threatened with extinction. This means that tracking the data on the number of species at risk of extinction over time doesn't necessarily reflect an acceleration of extinction threats; a lot is simply explained by an acceleration of the number of species being evaluated. This is why we do not show trends for the number of threatened species over time.

2. The number of threatened species is an underestimate. Since only 7% of described species have been evaluated (for some groups, this is much less) the estimated number of threatened species is likely to be much lower than the actual number. There is inevitably more threatened species within the 93% that have not been evaluated.

We should also define more clearly what threatened with extinction actually means. The IUCN Red List categorize species based on their estimated probability of going extinct within a given period of time. These estimates take into account population size, the rate of change in population size, geographical distribution, and extent of environmental pressures on them. 'Threatened' species is the sum of the following three categories:

-**Critically endangered** species have a probability of extinction higher than 50% in ten years or three generations;

-**Endangered species** have a greater than 20% probability in 20 years or five generations;

-**Vulnerable** have a probability greater than 10% over a century.

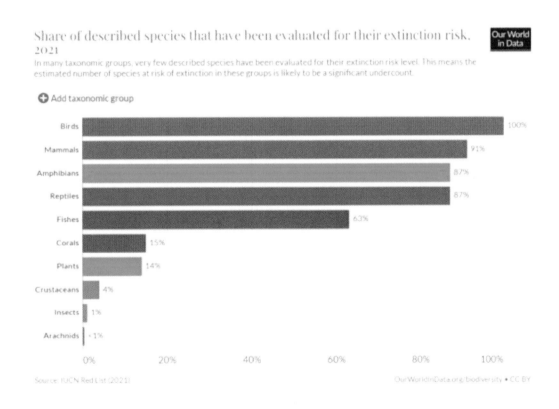

Share of described species that have been evaluated for their extinction risk, 2021

In many taxonomic groups, very few described species have been evaluated for their extinction risk level. This means the estimated number of species at risk of extinction in these groups is likely to be a significant undercount.

Number of species evaluated for their level of extinction risk, 2021

The number of species evaluated for their extinction risk level is a small share of the total number of known species in many taxonomic groups.

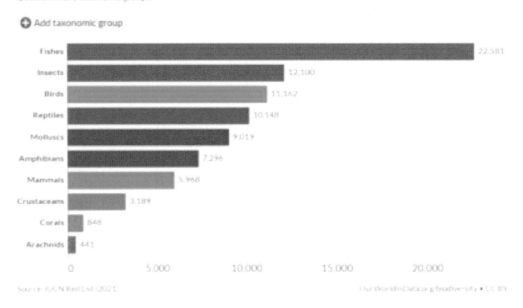

Number of described species

The number of identified and named species, as of 2021. Since many species have not yet been described, this is a large underestimate of the total number of species in the world.

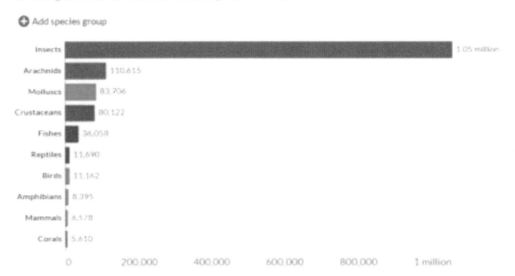

How many species are threatened with extinction?

The IUCN Red List has evaluated 40,084 species across all taxonomic groups to be threatened with extinction in 2021. As we noted earlier, this is a large underestimate of the true number because most species have not been evaluated.

In the chart we see the number of species at risk in each taxonomic group. Since birds, mammals, and amphibians are the most well-studied groups their numbers are the most accurate reflection of the true number. The numbers for understudied groups such as insects, plants and fungi will be a large underestimate.

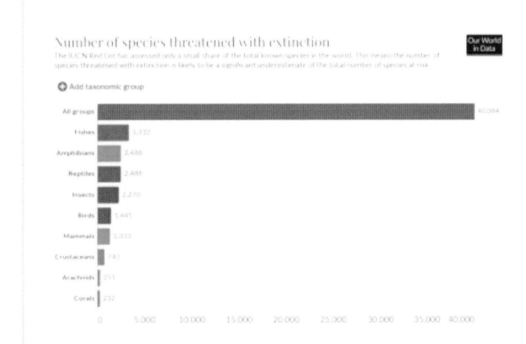

What percentage of species are threatened with extinction?

What share of known species are threatened with extinction? Since the number of species that has been evaluated for their extinction risk is such a small fraction of the total known species, it makes little sense for us to calculate this figure for all species, or for groups that are significantly understudied. It will tell us very little about the actual share of species that are threatened.

But we can calculate it for the well-studied groups. The IUCN Red List provides this figure for groups where at least 80% of described species has been evaluated. These are shown in the chart.

Around one-quarter of the world's mammals; 1-in-7 bird species; and 40% of amphibians are at risk. In more niche taxonomic groups – such as horseshoe crabs and gymnosperms, most species are threatened.

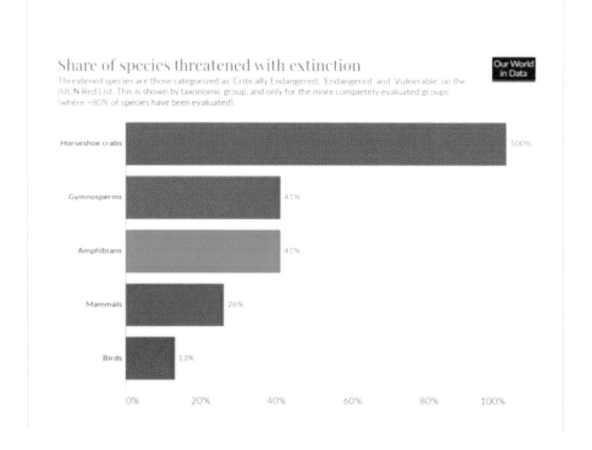

Share of species threatened with extinction

Threatened species are those categorized as 'Critically Endangered', 'Endangered' and 'Vulnerable' on the IUCN Red List. This is shown by taxonomic group, and only for the more completely evaluated groups (where >80% of species have been evaluated).

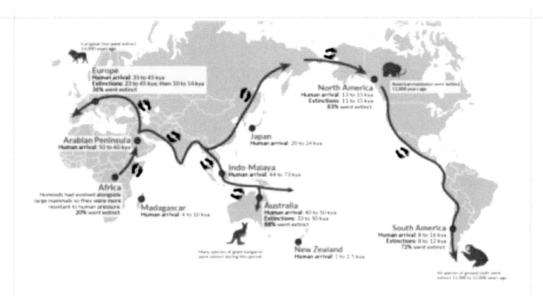

Are we heading for a sixth mass extinction?

Seeing wildlife populations shrink is devastating. But the extinction of an entire species is tragedy on another level. It's not simply a downward trend; it marks a stepwise change. A complex life form that is lost forever.

But extinctions are nothing new. They are a natural part of the planet's evolutionary history. 99% of the four billion species that have evolved on Earth are now gone. Species go extinct, while new ones are formed. That's life. There's a natural background rate to the timing and frequency of extinctions: 10% of species are lost every million years; 30% every 10 million years; and 65% every 100 million years.

What worries ecologists is that extinctions today are happening much faster than nature would predict. This has happened five times in the past: these are defined as mass extinction events and are aptly named the 'Big Five' [we cover them in more detail here]. In each extinction event the world lost more than 75% of its species in a short period of time (here we mean 'short' in its geological sense – less than two million years).

Are we in the midst of another one? Many have warned that we're heading for a sixth mass extinction, this one driven by humans. Is this really true, or are these claims overblown?

How do we know if we're heading for a sixth mass extinction?

Before we can even consider this question we need to define what a 'mass extinction' is. Most people would define it as wiping out all, or most of, the world's wildlife. But there's a technical definition. Extinction is determined by two metrics: magnitude and rate. Magnitude is the percentage of species that have gone extinct. Rate measures how quickly these extinctions happened – the number of extinctions per unit of time. These two metrics are tightly linked, but we need both of them to 'diagnose' a mass extinction. If lots of species go extinct over a very long period of time (let's say, 1 billion years), this is not a mass extinction. The rate is too slow. Similarly, if we lost some species very quickly but in the end it didn't amount to a large percentage of species, this also wouldn't qualify. The magnitude is too low. To be defined as a mass extinction, the planet needs to lose a lot of its species quickly.

In a mass extinction we need to lose more than 75% of species, in a short period of time: around 2 million years. Some mass extinctions happen more quickly than this.

Of course, this is not to say that "only" losing 60% of the world's species is no big deal. Or that extinctions are the only measure of biodiversity we care about – large reductions in wildlife populations can cause just as much disruption to ecosystems as the complete loss of some species. We look at these changes in other parts of our work [see our article on the Living Planet Index]. But here we're going to stick with the official definition of a mass extinction to test whether these claims are true.

There are a few things that make this difficult. The first is just how little we know about the world's species and how they're changing. Some taxonomic groups – such as mammals, birds and amphibians – we know a lot about. We have described and assessed most of their known species. But we know much less about the plants, insects, fungi and reptiles around us. For this reason, mass extinctions are usually assessed for these groups we know most about. This is mostly vertebrates. What we do know is that levels of extinction risk for the small number of plant and invertebrate species that have been assessed is similar to that of vertebrates. This gives us some indication that vertebrates might give us a reasonable proxy for other groups of species.

The second difficulty is understanding modern extinctions in the context of longer timeframes. Mass extinctions can happen over the course of a million years or more. We're looking at extinctions over the course of centuries or even decades. This means we're going to have to make some assumptions or scenarios of what might or could happen in the future.

There are a few metrics researchers can use to tackle this question.

1. Extinctions per million species-years (E/MSY). Using reconstructions in the fossil record, we can calculate how many extinctions typically occur every million years. This is the 'background extinction rate'. To compare this to current rates we can assess recent extinction rates (the proportion of species that went extinct over the past century or two) and predict what proportion this would be over one million species-years.

2. Compare current extinction rates to previous mass extinctions. We can compare calculations of the current E/MSY to background extinction rates (as above). But we can also compare these rates to previous mass extinction events.

3. Calculate the number of years needed for 75% of species to go extinct based on current rates. If this number is less than a few million years, this would fall into 'mass extinction' territory.

Calculate extinction rates for the past 500 years (or 200 years, or 50 years)and ask whether extinction rates during previous periods were as high.

How many species have gone extinct in recent centuries?

An obvious question to ask is how many species have gone extinct already. How close to the 75% 'threshold' are we?

At first glance, it seems like we're pretty far away. Since 1500 around 0.5% to 1% of the world's assessed vertebrates have gone extinct. As we see in the chart, that's around 1.3% of birds; 1.4% of mammals; 0.6% of amphibians; 0.2% of reptiles; and 0.2% of bony fishes. Due to the many measurement issues for these groups – and how our understanding of species has changed in recent centuries – the extinction rates that these predict are likely an underestimate (more on this later).

So, we've lost around 1% of these species. But we should also consider the large number of species that are threatened with extinction. Thankfully we've not lost them yet, but there is a high risk that we do. Species threatened with extinction are defined by the IUCN Red List, and it encompasses several categories:

-**Critically endangered species** have a probability of extinction higher than 50% in ten years or three generations;

-**Endangered species** have a greater than 20% probability in 20 years or five generations;

-**Vulnerable** have a probability greater than 10% over a century.

There's a high chance that many of these species go extinct in the new few decades. If they do, this share of extinct species changes significantly. In the chart we also see the share of species in each group that is threatened with extinction. We would very quickly go from 1% to almost one-quarter of species. We'd be one-third of the way to the '75%' line.

Again, you might think that 1%, or even 25%, is small. At least much smaller than the 75% definition of a mass extinction. But what's important is the speed that this has happened. Previous extinctions happened over the course of a million years or more. We're already far along the curve within only a few centuries, or even decades. We'll see this more clearly later when we compare recent extinction rates to those of the past. But we can quickly understand this from a quick back-of-the-envelope calculation. If it took us 500 years to lose 1% of species, it would take us 37,500 years to lose 75%. Much faster than the million years of previous extinction events. Of course this assumes that future extinctions would continue at the same rate – a big assumption, and one we will come to later. It might even be a conservative one – there might be species that went extinct without us even knowing that they existed at all.

Are recent extinction rates higher than we would expect?

There are two ways to compare recent extinction rates. First, to the natural 'background' rates of extinctions. Second, to the extinction rates of previous mass extinctions.

The research is quite clear that extinction rates over the last few centuries have been much higher than we'd expect. The background rate of extinctions of vertebrates that we would expect is around 0.1 to 1 extinctions per million-species years (E/MSY). In the chart we see the comparison, broken down by their pre- and post-1900 rates.

Modern extinction rates average around 100 E/MSY. This means birds, mammals and amphibians have been going extinct 100 to 1000 times faster than we would expect.

Researchers think this might even be an underestimate. One reason is that some modern species are understudied. Some might have gone extinct before we had the chance to identify them. They will ultimately show up in the fossil record later, but for now, we don't even know that they existed. This might be particularly true for species a century ago when much less resource was put into wildlife research and conservation.

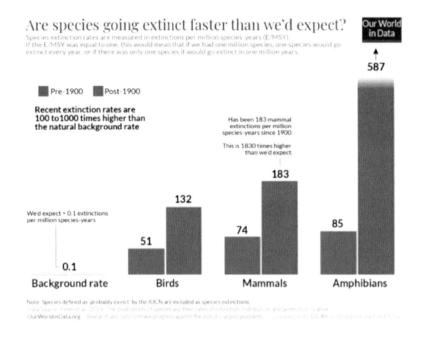

Another key point is that we have many species that are not far from extinction: species that are critically endangered or endangered. There's a high chance that many could go extinct in the coming decades. If they did, extinction rates would increase massively. In another study published in Science, Michael Hoffman and colleagues estimated that 52 species of birds, mammals and amphibians move one category closer to extinction on the IUCN Red List every year. Pimm et al. (2014) estimate that this would give us an extinction rate of 450 E/MSY. Again, 100 to 1000 times higher than the background rate.

How do recent extinction rates compare to previous mass extinctions?

Clearly we're killing off species much faster than would be expected. But does this fall into 'mass extinction' territory? Is it fast enough to be comparable to the 'Big Five'?

One way to answer this is to compare recent extinction rates with rates from previous mass extinctions. Researcher, Malcolm McCallum did this comparison for the Cretaceous-Palogene (K-Pg) mass extinction. This was the event that killed off the dinosaurs around 65 million years ago. In the chart we see the comparison of (non-dinosaur) vertebrate extinction rates during the K-Pg mass extinction to recent rates. This shows how many times faster species are now going extinct compared to then.

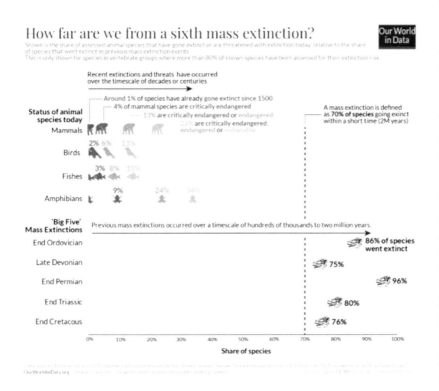

We see clearly that rates since the year 1500 are estimated to be 24 to 81 times faster than the K-Pg event. If we look at even more recent rates, from 1980 onwards, this increases to up to 165 times faster. Again, this might even be understating the pace of current extinctions. We have many species that are threatened with extinction: there is a high probability that many of these species go extinct within the next century. If we were to include species classified as 'threatened' on the IUCN Red List, extinctions would be happening thousands of times faster than the K-Pg extinction.

This makes the point clear: we're not only losing species at a much faster rate than we'd expect, we're losing them tens to thousands of times faster than the rare mass extinction events in Earth's history.

How long would it take for us to reach the sixth mass extinction?

Recent rates of extinction, if they continued, would put us on course for a sixth mass extinction. A final way to check the numbers on this is to estimate how long it would take for us to get there. On our current path, how long before 75% of species went extinct? If this number is less than 2 million years, it would qualify as a mass extinction event.

Earlier we came up with a crude estimate for this number. If it took us 500 years to lose 1% of species, it would take us 37,500 years to lose 75%. That assumes extinctions continue at the average rate over that time. Malcolm McCallum's analysis produced a similar order of magnitude:

54,000 years for vertebrates based on post-1500 extinction rates. Extinction rates have been faster over the past 50 years. So if we take the post-1980 extinction rates, we'd get there even faster: in only 18,000 years.

But again, this doesn't account for the large number of species that are threatened with extinction today. If these species did go extinct soon, our extinction rates would be much higher than the average over the last 500 years. In a study published in Nature, Anthony Barnosky and colleagues looked at the time it would take for 75% of species to go extinct across four scenarios.

1. If all species classified as 'critically endangered' went extinct in the next century;

2. If all species classified as 'threatened' went extinct in the next century;

3. If all species classified as 'critically endangered' went extinct in the next 500 years;

4. If all species classified as 'threatened' went extinct in the next 500 years.

To be clear: these are not predictions of the future. We can think of them as hypotheticals of what could happen if we don't take action to protect the world's threatened species. In each case the assumed extinction rate would be very different, and this has a significant impact on the time needed to cross the 'mass extinction' threshold. The results are shown in the chart.

In the most extreme case, where we lose all of our threatened species in the next 100 years, it would take only 250 to 500 years before 75% of the world's birds, mammals and amphibians went extinct. If only our critically endangered animals went extinct in the next century, this would increase to a few thousand years. If these extinctions happened much slower – over 500 years rather than a century – it'd be around 5,000 to 10,000 years. In any scenario, this would happen much faster than the million year timescale of previous mass extinctions.

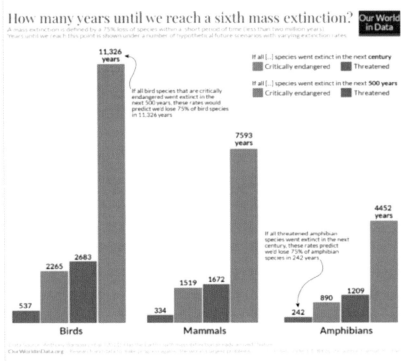

This makes two points very clear. First, extinctions are happening at a rapid rate – up to 100 times faster than the 'Big Five' events that define our planet's history. Current rates do point towards a sixth mass extinction. Second, these are scenarios of what could happen. It doesn't have to be this way.

The good news: we can prevent a sixth mass extinction

There is one thing that sets the sixth mass extinction apart from the previous five. It can be stopped. We can stop it. The 'Big Five' mass extinctions were driven by a cascade of disruptive events – volcanism, ocean acidification, natural swings in climate. There was no one or nothing to hit the brakes and turn things around.

This time it's different. We are the primary driver of these environmental changes: deforestation, climate change, ocean acidification, hunting, and pollution of ecosystems. That's depressing. But is also the best news we could hope for. It means we have the opportunity (and some would argue, the responsibility) to stop it. We can protect the world's threatened species from going extinct; we can slow and reverse deforestation; slow global climate change; and allow natural ecosystems to heal. There are a number of examples of where we have been successful in preventing these extinctions.

The conclusion that we're on course for a sixth mass extinction hinges on the assumption that extinctions will continue at their recent rates. Or, worse, that they will accelerate. Nothing about that is inevitable. To stop it, we need to understand where and why the world's species are going extinct. This is the first step to understanding what we can do to turn things around. This is what our work on Biodiversity aims to achieve.

How many species has conservation saved from extinction?

It's hard to find good news on the state of the world's wildlife. Many predict that we're heading for a sixth mass extinction; the Living Planet Index reports a 68% average decline in wildlife populations since 1970; and we continue to lose the tropical habitats that support our most diverse ecosystems. The United Nations Convention on Biological Diversity set twenty targets – the Aichi Biodiversity Targets – to be achieved by 2020. The world missed all of them. We didn't meet a single one.

Perhaps, then, the loss of biodiversity is unavoidable. Maybe there is nothing we can do to turn things around.

Thankfully there are signs of hope. As we will see, conservation action might have been insufficient to meet our Aichi targets, but it did make a difference. Tens of species were saved through these interventions. There's other evidence that protected areas have retained bird diversity in tropical ecosystems. And each year there are a number of species that move away from the extinction zone on the IUCN Red List.

We need to make sure these stories of success are heard. Of

course, we shouldn't use them to mask the bad news. They definitely don't make up for the large losses in wildlife we're seeing around the world. In fact, the risk here is asymmetric: growth in one wildlife population does not offset a species getting pushed to extinction. A species lost to extinction is a species lost forever. We can't make up for this loss by simply increasing the population of something else. But we can make sure two messages are communicated at the same time.

First, that we're losing our biodiversity at a rapid rate. Second, that it's possible to do something about it. If there was no hope of the second one being true, what would be the point of trying? If our actions really made no difference then why would governments support anymore conservation efforts? No, we need to be vocal about the positives as well as the negatives to make clear that progress is possible. And, importantly, understand what we did right so that we can do more of it.

In this article I want to take a look at some of these positive trends, and better understand how we achieved them.

Pulling animals back from the brink of extinction

For anyone interested in wildlife conservation, losing a species to extinction is a tragedy. Saving a species is surely one of life's greatest successes.

Conservation efforts might have saved tens of beautiful species over the last few decades. The 12th Aichi Target was to 'prevent extinctions of known threatened species'. We might have missed this, but efforts have not been completely in vain.

In a recent study published in Conservation Letters, researchers estimate that between 28 and 48 bird and mammal species would have gone extinct without the conservation efforts implemented when the Convention on Biological Diversity came into force in 1993. 21 to 32 bird species, and 7 to 16 mammal species were pulled back from the brink of extinction. In the last decade alone (from 2010 to 2020), 9 to 18 bird, and 2 to 7 mammal extinctions were prevented. This has preserved hundreds of millions of years of evolutionary history. It prevented the loss of 120 million years of evolutionary history of birds, and 26 million years for mammals.

What this means is that extinction rates over the last two decades would have been at least three to four times faster without conservation efforts.

This does not mean that these species are out-of-danger. In fact, the populations of some of these species is still decreasing. We see this in the chart, which shows how the populations of these bird and mammal species that were expected to have gone extinct are changing. 16% of these bird species, and 13% of the mammal species have gone extinct in the wild, but conservation has allowed them to survive in captivity. Across the critically endangered, endangered and vulnerable categories, 53% of bird and 31% of mammal species have increasing or stable populations. This is positive, but makes clear that many of these species are still in decline. Conservation has only been able to slow these losses down.

This only looks at species on the brink of extinction. Many species in serious but less-threatened categories have been prevented from moving closer to extinction. Around 52 species of mammals, birds and amphibians move one category closer to extinction every year. Without conservation, this number would be 20% higher.

There are more examples. Studies have shown that protected areas have had a positive impact on preserving bird species in tropical forests. These are some of the world's most threatened ecosystems. And while the IUCN Red List usually makes for a depressing read, there are some success stories. This year the European Bison, Europe's largest land mammals, was moved from 'Vulnerable' to 'Near threatened' (meaning it's less threatened with extinction) thanks to continued conservation efforts. We will look at more European success stories later.

Friederike Bolam et al. (2021) looked at what conservation actions were key to saving the mammal and bird species deemed to be destined for extinction.24 For both birds and mammals, legal protection and the growth of protected areas was important. Protected areas are not perfect – there are countless examples of poorly managed areas where populations continue to shrink. We will look at how effective protected areas are in a follow-up article. But, on average, they do make a difference. Clearly these efforts were critical for species that had gone extinct in the wild. Other important factors were controlling the spread of invasive species into new environments; reintroducing old species into environments where they had been previously lost; and restoring natural habitats, such as wetlands and forests.

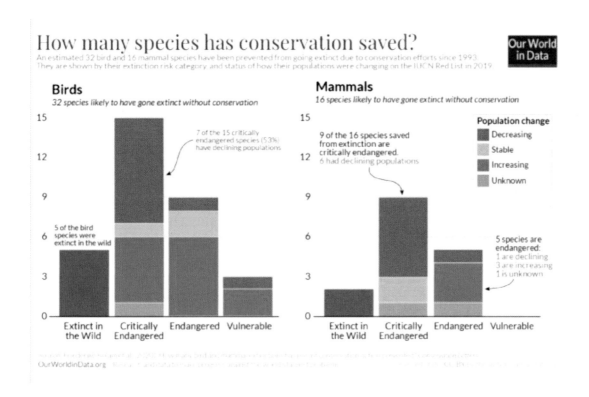

How many species has conservation saved?

An estimated 32 bird and 16 mammal species have been prevented from going extinct due to conservation efforts since 1993. They are shown by their extinction risk category, and status of how their populations were changing on the IUCN Red List in 2019.

Our World in Data

Birds
32 species likely to have gone extinct without conservation

7 of the 15 critically endangered species (53%) have declining populations

5 of the bird species were extinct in the wild

Extinct in the Wild | Critically Endangered | Endangered | Vulnerable

Mammals
16 species likely to have gone extinct without conservation

9 of the 16 species saved from extinction are critically endangered. 6 had declining populations

5 species are endangered:
1 are declining
3 are increasing
1 is unknown

Extinct in the Wild | Critically Endangered | Endangered | Vulnerable

Population change
■ Decreasing
□ Stable
■ Increasing
■ Unknown

OurWorldInData.org

Restoring wildlife populations across Europe

The European Bison might steal the headlines, but there are many good news stories across Europe. Many of the drivers of biodiversity loss – deforestation, overhunting, and habitat loss – are happening in the tropics today. But these same changes also happened across Europe and North America. Only, they happened earlier – centuries ago.

Europe is now trying to restore its lost wildlife and habitats through rewilding programmes. The Zoological Society of London, Birdlife International and European Bird Census Council published a report which details how these efforts are going.25 They looked at how the populations of 18 mammal and 19 of Europe's iconic but endangered bird species had changed over the past 50 years.

Most had seen an overwhelming recovery. Most species saw an increase of more than 100%. Some saw more than 1000% growth. Brown bear populations more than doubled over these 50 years. Wolverine populations doubled in the 1990s alone. The Eurasian lynx increased by 500%. Reintroduction programmes of the Eurasian beaver saw populations increase by 14,000% – a doubling or tripling every decade.

What were the main drivers of this recovery?

Part of Europe's success in restoring wildlife populations in recent decades can be attributed to the fact that their development and harvesting of resources came long ago. My European ancestors had already hunted many species to extinction; expanded agricultural land into existing forest; and built cities, roads and other infrastructure that fragments natural habitats. Only in our very recent past have European countries been able to reverse these trends: reforesting; raising livestock instead of hunting; and now reducing the amount of land we use for agriculture through improved productivity.

But there have also been a number of proactive interventions to restore populations. In the chart here we see the main drivers of recovery across European bird species. At the top of the list is habitat restoration – the re-establishment of wetlands, grasslands, forests and other national habitats. Reintroduction of species has also been key. But protecting existing habitats and species has been equally important. Legal site protections and bans on shooting have been the main recovery drivers of almost as many species.

After millennia of habitat loss and exploitation by humans, wildlife is coming back to Europe. Somewhat ironically, humans have played an important role in this.

While most biodiversity trends point towards a barren future for the planet's wildlife, there are success stories to draw upon. These should not make us complacent, or deflect our attention from the seriousness of these losses. But I think it is important to highlight what we have achieved. Protecting the world's wildlife is not impossible – we've just seen the counter-evidence to this. To commit to wider conservation efforts we need to shout more loudly about these wins. Otherwise policymakers will turn their backs on them and we will lose many beautiful species that we could and should have saved.

Drivers of recovery in European bird populations

The number of European bird species that have seen a significant recovery in their populations in recent decades,categorized by the main driver of their recovery.0 species2 species4 species6 species8 speciesHabitat restoration10 speciesReintroduction9 speciesSite/habitat protection8 speciesProtection from shooting8 speciesCompensation/subsidies6 speciesHabitat shift5 speciesAnti-poisoning campaigns5 speciesSupplementary feeding4 speciesImproved climate3 speciesBan on organochlorines2 speciesControl of problematic species2 species

Wait, Have We Really Wiped Out 60 Percent of Animals?

The findings of a major new report have been widely mischaracterized—although the actual news is still grim.

News networks and social media have been abuzz with the claim that, as The Guardian among others tweeted, "humanity has wiped out 60 percent of animals since 1970"—a stark and staggering figure based on the latest iteration of the WWF's Living Planet report.

But that isn't really what the report showed.

The team behind the Living Planet Index relied on previous studies in which researchers estimated the size of different animal populations, whether through direct counts, camera traps, satellites, or proxies like the presence of nests or tracks. The team collated such estimates for 16,700 populations of mammals, birds, reptiles, amphibians, and fish, across 4,000 species. (Populations here refers to pockets of individuals from a given species that live in distinct geographical areas.)

That covers just 6.4 percent of the 63,000 or so species of vertebrates—that is, back-boned animals—that are thought to exist. To work out how the entire group has fared, the team adjusted its figures to account for any biases in its data. For example, vertebrates in Europe have been more heavily studied than those in South America, and prominently endangered creatures like elephants have been more closely studied (and have been easier to count) than very common ones like pigeons.

Ultimately, they found that from 1970 to 2014, the size of vertebrate populations has declined by 60 percent on average. That is absolutely not the same as saying that humans have culled 60 percent of animals—a distinction that the report's technical supplement explicitly states. "It is not a census of all wildlife but reports how wildlife populations have changed in size," the authors write.

To understand the distinction, imagine you have three populations: 5,000 lions, 500 tigers, and 50 bears. Four decades later, you have just 4,500 lions, 100 tigers, and five bears (oh my). Those three populations have declined by 10 percent, 80 percent, and 90 percent, respectively—which means an average decline of 60 percent. But the total number of actual animals has gone down from 5,550 to 4,605, which is a decline of just 17 percent.

For similar reasons, it's also not right that we have "killed more than half the world's wildlife populations" or that we can be blamed for "wiping out 60 percent of animal species" or that "global wildlife population shrank by 60 percent between 1970 and 2014." All of these things might well be true, but they're all making claims about metrics that were not assessed in the Living Planet Index.

The uncertainties mount when you consider that the 63,000 species of vertebrates are vastly outnumbered by the untold millions of species of invertebrates—spineless creatures like insects, worms, jellyfish, and sponges, which make up the majority of animal life. Their fates are murkier because scientists have collectively spent less time monitoring them. They are harder to study, and draw less attention, than the allegedly more charismatic vertebrates—although plans are afoot to give them their due.

The average 60 percent decline across populations also obscures the fates of individual species. In the hypothetical scenario above, lions are still mostly fine, the tigers are in trouble, and the bears are on the brink of extinction. And of the species covered in the actual Living Planet Index, half are increasing in number, while only half are decreasing. This means that for those that are actually in decline, the outlook is even worse than it first appears.

None of this is to let humanity off the hook. Since prehistory, humans have killed off so many species of mammals that it would take 3 million to 7 million years of evolution for them to evolve an equivalent amount of diversity. At least a third of amphibians face extinction, thanks to climate change, habitat loss, and an apocalyptic killer fungus. Even invertebrates aren't off the hook. There might be fewer data for them, but the data that exist paint an alarming picture of rapidly disappearing insects, even in supposedly pristine forests. Meanwhile, in the oceans, coral reefs are bleaching too quickly to recover: Half of the corals in the Great Barrier Reef have died since 2016. All this evidence points to a period of "biological annihilation" that some have likened to the five great mass extinctions of the past. When the reality is this sensational, there's not much need to sensationalize it even further.

Biodiversity loss: How accurate are the numbers?

Twenty years ago, the Earth Summit in Rio resulted in a Convention on Biological Diversity, now signed by 193 nations, to prevent species loss. But can we tell how many species are becoming extinct?

One statement on the Convention's website claims: "*We are indeed experiencing the greatest wave of extinction since the disappearance of the dinosaurs.*"

While that may (or may not) be true, the next sentence is spuriously precise: "*Every hour three species disappear. Every day up to 150 species are lost.*"

Even putting aside the apparent mathematical error in that claim (on the face of it, if three species are disappearing every hour, 72 would be lost every day) there is an obvious problem in generating any such number. No-one knows how many species exist. And if we don't know a species exists, we won't miss it when it's gone.

"Current estimates of the number of species can vary from, let's say, two million species to over 30 or even 100 million species," says Dr Braulio Dias, executive secretary of the Convention on Biological Diversity. "So we don't have a good estimate to an order of magnitude of precision," he says.

It is possible to count the number of species known to be extinct. The International Union for Conservation of Nature (IUCN) does just that. It has listed 801 animal and plant species (mostly animal) known to have gone extinct since 1500.

But if it's really true that up to 150 species are being lost every day, shouldn't we expect to be able to name more than 801 extinct species in 512 years?

Professor Georgina Mace, who works in the Centre for Population Biology at Imperial College London, says the IUCN's method is helpful but inadequate. "It is never going to get us the answers we need," she says. That's why scientists prefer to use a mathematical model to estimate species loss.

Recently, however, that model has been attacked in the pages of Nature. Professor Stephen Hubbell from the University of California, Los Angeles, says that an error in the model means that it has - for years - over-estimated the rate of species loss.

The model applies something called the *"species to area relationship"* to habitat loss. Put simply, an estimate is made of the number of species in a given area, or habitat - the larger the area, the greater the number of species are said to be in it.

Then the model is worked backwards - the smaller the area, the fewer the species. In other words, if you measure habitat loss, you can use the model

Page 417

to calculate how many species are being lost as that habitat gets smaller.

The problem, says Hubbell, is that the model does not work in reverse. "*The method*," he says, "*when extrapolated backward, doesn't take into account the fact that you need to remove more area to get to the whole range of a species than you need to remove area to find the first individual of a species.*"

Hubbell's point is that if you increase a habitat by, say, five hectares, and your calculations show that you expect there to be five new species in those five hectares, it is wrong to assume that reversing the model, and shrinking your habitat, eliminates five species.

That's because it takes more area to establish extinction - to show that every individual in a species has been eliminated - than it does to discover a new species, which requires coming across just one individual of that species. Hubbell says when corrected the model shows about half as many species going extinct as previously reported.

Unfortunately for scientists trying to measure species loss, the problems don't end there. They also need to calculate the 'background rate' of extinction. If you want to work out the impact of human life on biodiversity, you need to know how many species would have gone extinct anyway without us being here. Mace says that is difficult.

"*Background rates are not constant either,*" she says. "*If you look back through the history of life on Earth, there have been major periods of extinctions. Extinction rates vary a lot.*"

The level of uncertainty faced by researchers in this field means it is perhaps not surprising that no-one can be sure of the scale of species loss. It also means that when a representative of the Convention of Biological Diversity claimed "*every hour three species disappear*" he must have known it was too precise.

But the fact that the precise extinction rate is unknowable does not prove that the problem is imagined.

Page 418

Braulio Dias, executive secretary of the Convention on Biological Diversity, says:

"We know that the drivers behind species loss are mostly increasing - land conversion and degradation, pollution, climate change. And of course the human population is still growing and consumption is growing - and most of that consumption is not sustainable."

Professor Hubbell, too, thinks species loss is a serious issue, even though he believes it has been exaggerated.

There is, though, one other problem faced by anyone who wants to call attention to the issue - the fear that people are inclined to care more about so-called charismatic animals (mostly larger animals which we recognize) than the millions of nameless and microscopic organisms which are also included in species loss models.

Hubbell says we should be at least as concerned about such seemingly unimportant species.

"The proportion of the world's species that are charismatic organisms is really tiny," he says. *"From a biomass point of view, this is a bacterial planet. It's a very parochial view to assume that we should care only about elephants and zebras."*

But if people do care more about charismatic animals than bacteria, which seems likely, then it might prove difficult to get those people to take the issue seriously unless such animals are threatened.

A number of charismatic species, or sub-species, have become extinct in the wild, but have been kept alive in captivity thanks to the efforts of enthusiasts and campaigners.

Others have gone extinct - like the Pyrenean Ibex or the Baiji river dolphin. But compared to the number of species which exist in the world, even taking the lowest estimates of that number, such known cases are very few.

According to IUCN data, for example, only one animal has been definitely identified as having gone extinct since 2000. It was a mollusc.

Past and future decline and extinction of species

One of the largest effects of humans on the natural world has been to raise the rate of extinction of species far above natural levels. This began many thousands of years ago, and as a result the human-caused loss of global biodiversity was already significant before the modern era. Now, the extinction rate is accelerating, biodiversity is in rapid decline, and many ecosystem processes are being degraded or lost.

1. History of human-caused extinctions

The effect of humans on global biodiversity first became significant as modern Homo sapiens migrated from Africa to occupy the other continents. Between about 60,000 and 10,000 years ago, a wave of extinctions of giant animals – mammoths, ground sloths, giant kangaroos, and many others – followed the arrival of people in Eurasia, Australia and the Americas. Probably, these megafauna disappeared because of hunting by humans.

Then, between about 5,000 and 500 years ago people discovered and settled oceanic islands. This resulted in extinction of whatever megafauna lived on those islands, such as New Zealand's moa and Madagascar's giant lemurs and elephant birds. As well, many smaller vertebrates succumbed to the combined pressures of hunting, forest removal, and impacts of alien species transported by voyaging people; presumably there were extinctions of other components of biodiversity as well, but these are not as well known. Because of the remarkable distinctiveness of biodiversity on islands this second wave of extinctions accounted for a great many species. For example, more than 100 endemic mammal species disappeared from the Caribbean islands alone, and human occupation of Pacific Islands resulted in extinction of at least 1,000 bird species, around 10% of all the world's birds.

Since 1500 CE a third and still greater wave of extinction has been growing. This third wave is being driven ultimately by growth of the global human population, increased consumption of natural resources, and globalization. It is affecting a wider range of animals and plants than the preceding two extinction waves, in the oceans as well as on land. Our knowledge of which species have gone extinct since 1500 is collated in the IUCN Red List and is most complete for vertebrates, especially birds, mammals and amphibians: 711 vertebrates are known or presumed extinct since 1500, including 181 birds, 113 mammals and 171 amphibians. We know of almost 600 extinctions each of invertebrates and plants since 1500, but given limited basic knowledge, survey, and assessment of conservation status, the true magnitude of losses in these groups is certain to be far higher.

2. Accelerating extinction rates

The list of known recent extinctions is still only a small fraction of all species on the planet. For example, the tally of bird extinctions since 1500 amounts to 1.6% of all bird species that were living in 1500; the figures for mammals and amphibians are 1.9% and 2.1% respectively. What is more concerning than the raw numbers of extinctions is that they represent a rate of extinction far above pre-human levels. The extinction rate for any group of organisms is expressed as the number of extinctions that would occur each year among a million species (or equivalently, the number that would occur in a century among 10,000 species). Standardizing rates in this way allows comparison of extinction rates in different groups of organisms and time periods. Our best estimates suggest that extinction rates in the recent past have been running 100 or more times faster than in pre-human times, and that the pace of extinction has accelerated over the last few centuries (Figure 1). If this continues, the loss of species will soon amount to a large fraction of all species on the planet.

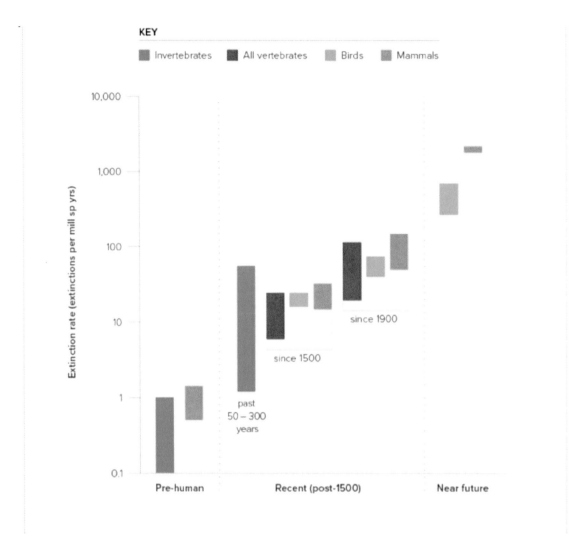

Figure 1. Estimated extinction rates in various animal groups through time, expressed as extinctions per million species per year. The height of each bar represents the range of estimates. Pre-human extinction rates are inferred from the fossil record, recent values from documented extinctions in selected groups, and near-future extinctions are projected from the current rates at which species are transitioning between IUCN categories.

There are two reasons to think that the extinction rate is about to rise still further. The first is that current levels of threat of extinction signal a steep increase in the number of extinctions over the next few decades.
In those groups of plants and animals that have been systematically assessed under IUCN Red List criteria, the proportions classified as threatened with extinction (that is, Critically Endangered, Endangered, or Vulnerable) are typically high, about 25% on average. This figure implies

that a total of approximately one million of the world's species are currently threatened with extinction. Five groups (mammals, birds, amphibians, corals, and cycads) have been comprehensively assessed two or more times since 1980. In all cases the reassessments show an increasing trend in the proportion of species that are threatened.

The most severe category of extinction risk is Critically Endangered. To qualify for this, a species must have some combination of very small total population (250 adults or fewer), extremely restricted distribution (10 km2 or less), and continuing population decline at rates high enough to guarantee extinction within decades. Currently 6,811 species are listed as Critically Endangered (of a total of 120,372 that have been formally assessed, a number still far short of the estimated two million-plus species so far described).

In short, the threat of extinction is now so widespread, and so many species stand on the brink of extinction, it is clear we could be about to lose many more. Even if the future brought nothing worse than the extinction of a significant proportion of all species now listed as Critically Endangered, that would amount to a very large increase in the total number of extinctions since 1500 CE. Because population size is still decreasing in most Critically Endangered species we must consider it likely that many of them will soon be gone.

The near-future rate of extinction depends not just on current levels of threat, but on the speed with which now-threatened species decline all the way to extinction; it depends also on the rate at which species not currently threatened become so, and how quickly they then travel the full path to extinction. These dynamics of extinction risk are unknown for most groups, but they can be described for a few. The best-studied case is the worlds' birds, illustrated in Figure 2.

Between 1988 and 2016 a large cohort of bird species travelled all the way from being Near Threatened (that is, secure, but within sight of one of the markers of Vulnerable) to Critically Endangered (Figure 2). At the same time more than twice as many species joined the ranks of Near Threatened from Least Concern (that is, at minimal risk) and could soon follow the others on the path towards extinction. Another large cohort moved from Least Concern to Vulnerable or Endangered, having crossed the broad territory of Near Threatened in just a few years (Figure 2). The speed of these recent movements from low to high risk suggests that the number of bird extinctions is about to increase much more dramatically than might be suggested by the rather small rise in overall percentage of species listed as threatened (from 12.6% to 13.5% between 1988 and 2016).

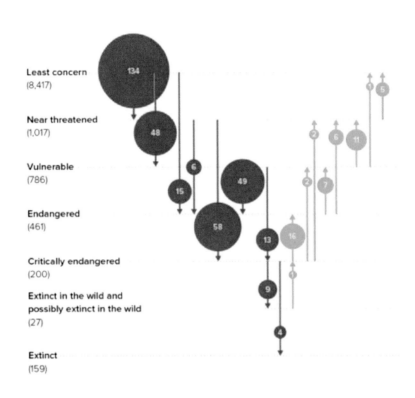

Figure 2. Changes of Red List categories for bird species from 1988 to 2016. Numbers of taxa making each change are shown in the circles. Total birds in each category in 2016 are shown in parentheses; the total for extinctions is the number confirmed since 1500 CE. Data from the IUCN Red List, as compiled by Monroe et al 2019.

Recent studies of birds and mammals have used information like that shown in Figure 2 to estimate transition probabilities between IUCN Red List categories (in both directions, for the better or worse) and forecast rates of extinction over the coming decades. These studies suggest that extinction rates for birds and mammals are about to increase by more than

Page 424

tenfold (Figure 1). Similar accelerations in extinction are likely for other groups that are not as well-known; if anything, the increases could be even greater in many groups of organisms that are given less attention than birds and mammals and so are less likely to be helped by specific conservation actions.

3. Intensifying pressure on biodiversity

The second reason to anticipate a steep rise in extinction is that the forces that caused recent extinctions are as strong as ever. The main direct causes of extinction are loss and degradation of habitats due to human use of land and sea; overexploitation of wild populations; and the impacts on populations and ecological communities of invasive alien species, pollution, and climate change. These direct causes are driven ultimately by demographic, economic and societal factors that increase the pressures that human populations place on biodiversity. Most indicators of the direct and ultimate causes of biodiversity decline show that they are continuing to grow stronger. There have been some improvements—most notably, the expansion of protected areas since 2000 (from 10% to 15% of the land surface of the globe, and 3% to 7% of the oceans) and a recent fall in the (still substantial) global rate of deforestation —but they are too small to offset the general increase in pressure.

There are several other reasons to think that the pressures that have caused extinction in the recent past will have worse effects in the future. Populations of many species are becoming smaller and more geographically restricted, whether or not those species yet qualify as threatened. This makes them more susceptible to threats they might have resisted when abundant and widespread, because for each population affected by some insult such as habitat loss or overexploitation there are fewer others to offset local declines and supply immigrants to replenish losses. Also, the general increase in human impact on nature makes it more likely that remaining natural areas are subject to several different threats at the same time, leading to compounding or synergistic effects with greater total impact.

The future will also bring an increasingly important overlay of global climate change to the long-standing forces of habitat loss, overexploitation, and so on. The most significant effect of climate change may well be to increase the frequency or magnitude of extreme events. These include many that recent experience shows have great potential to damage biodiversity, such as intense tropical cyclones, marine heat waves, and El Niño and La Niña events. Extreme events that affect large areas can force large, abrupt and unexpected declines of many species at one time.

The climate-driven fires that recently burned much of southern Australia supply an illustration of such an extreme event. During the 2019/20 fire season, 97,000 km2 of southern Australian woodlands, forests and associated habitats were burnt by fires of exceptional intensity. The fires caused extreme damage to habitats that typically experience recurrent fires of lower intensity and extent, while consuming other habitats that normally do not burn at all. In the broad region affected by the fires, 243 vertebrate species or subspecies are listed as threatened. Fires overlapped significant portions (>10%) of the ranges of 46 of these threatened vertebrates. Some had most of their habitat burnt, for example 82% for the long-footed potoroo Potorous longipes and 98% for the Kangaroo Island dunnart Sminthopsis griseoventer aitkeni. Another 49 vertebrates not currently listed as threatened had 30% or more of their habitat burned, 100% in the case of Kate's leaf-tailed gecko Saltuarius kateae. It is possible that many currently listed vertebrates will move into more severe threat categories, while re-assessment of previously secure species could see the total number of threatened vertebrates in Australia increase by 14%, as a result of this single event. At this stage there is less complete knowledge of impacts on other species, but rapid appraisals have identified 191 invertebrate and 486 plant species as potentially severely affected.

4. Loss of abundance

The figure of 25% of all species threatened with extinction is one measure of a more general decline of populations of wild species. Analysis of aggregated data on population trends of vertebrates from around the world indicates a general decline in abundance of 68% between 1970 and 2016, due both to extirpation of local populations and reduced numbers in those that remain. Roughly similar trends have occurred in most major regions of the world, in freshwater and dryland ecosystems, and in the oceans as well as on land. There is also growing evidence of widespread decline in the abundance of invertebrates, especially insects. This is best studied in Europe, where it is becoming clear that the abundance and diversity of arthropods is declining even in relatively undisturbed habitats, evidently because of spill-over effects from agricultural land use.

So far, conservation action has had little success in reversing the general decline in abundance of wild species. We have prevented some extinctions; for example, interventions between 1993 and 2020 prevented 21-32 bird and 7-16 mammal extinctions, such that extinction rates in both groups would otherwise have been 2.9-4.2 times higher. This is encouraging, but most improvements have been in moving species out of the Critically Endangered category into Endangered (Figure 2), that is, holding the line against extinction for some of the most severely threatened taxa. Few threatened species have recovered their original distribution and abundance against the much stronger tide running in the other direction (Figure 2).

Image caption: the Critically Endangered orange-bellied parrot Neophema chrysogaster by Tiana Pirtle.

Not all species are being forced into decline; some are becoming more abundant as a result of human disturbance. In general, however, large-bodied and ecologically specialized species are more likely to decline, being replaced by less diverse sets of species that either tolerate disturbance or benefit from it and are capable of invading new or altered habitats. The result of this process is that a great part of the original diversity of nature is being lost from much of the planet. As this happens, ecological communities are being made simpler and some important ecosystem functions are degrading.

5. Species extinction and ecosystem decline

In the places that still have them, very large herbivores such as elephants and rhinos control the structure and pattern of vegetation, promote habitat heterogeneity, limit the extent of wildfire, transport nutrients, and disperse seeds. These various effects combine to promote diversity among smaller animal and plant species; megaherbivores could even influence the climate through alterations to land-surface albedo. The wholesale extinction of mega-herbivores many thousands of years ago damaged ecosystems and diminished biodiversity in ways that are only beginning to be understood. Big predators also sustain biodiversity and stabilize ecosystems by regulating populations of smaller predators and intermediate-sized herbivores.

Among living mammals, amphibians, birds, reptiles and fish, the very largest species continue to be at highest risk of extinction: 59% of living megafauna are threatened, and 70% are decreasing in numbers. The threat of extinction is also exceptionally high among the smallest vertebrates. That is, human impact is deleting the smallest and largest vertebrates, and thereby confining survivors to a narrower size-range than was produced by evolution.

This is one instance of a more widespread phenomenon, in which human impact reduces the diversity and range of traits of organisms in natural assemblages. The general result is a reduction of functional diversity as well as total numbers of species, simplification of ecosystems, and in consequence loss or destabilisation of important ecosystem functions. So, for example in forest and woodland ecosystems the loss of mega-herbivores can result in higher incidence of destructive wildfire; in the oceans the loss of large species is reducing connectivity among ecosystems and thereby making them unstable; and declining diversity of

Page 428

insects diminishes many essential ecosystem functions such as pollination and nutrient re-cycling.

6. Conclusions

Our knowledge of past and future extinction rates makes it clear that the problem of extinction is urgent. The problem has two main components. First, the extinction of species is reducing the total diversity of life on the planet. Although the extinction tally does not yet represent a large proportion of all species, it is substantial and ecologically important. The rate of extinction is rising fast, and on current trends a large fraction of all the world's species could soon be gone. Second, the combination of extinction of some species and declining abundance of many others is causing a general loss of abundance and diversity of wild species and compromising the functioning of ecosystems.

The highest priority for action should be the prevention of extinction, because the extinction of any species is an irredeemable loss. Science-based interventions have a good record in saving species from extinction and recent losses would have been significantly worse without them. The actions that have been most consistently successful are establishment of protected areas, habitat restoration, and intensive management of small populations including reintroduction. The reason that we have not seen more success is primarily that investment in and resourcing of species conservation is in general far too low.

The problem of preventing broader decline of wild species requires more complex solutions, based on retention of large areas of intact habitat together with rewilding of degraded areas, improvements in the sustainability of exploitation of wild populations, development of strategies for reducing the impacts of invasive species at landscape scales, and mitigation of climate change. Accomplishing these changes will require transformations of the relationship of human communities to nature that will depend on the application of science, development of new socio-economic and governance models, and restoration of indigenous knowledge and practices of environmental management.

Resources

livescience.com, "What's the first species humans drove to extinction?" By Emma Bryce; ourworldindata.org, "Extinctions." By Hannah Ritchie and Max Roser; theatlantic.com, "Wait, Have We Really Wiped Out 60 Percent of Animals? The findings of a major new report have been widely mischaracterized—although the actual news is still grim." By Ed Yong; bbc.com, "Biodiversity loss: How accurate are the numbers?" By Richard Knight; royalsociety.org, "Past and future decline and extinction of species." By Christopher N. Johnson;

Appendix B--Real World Examples of Environmental Contamination

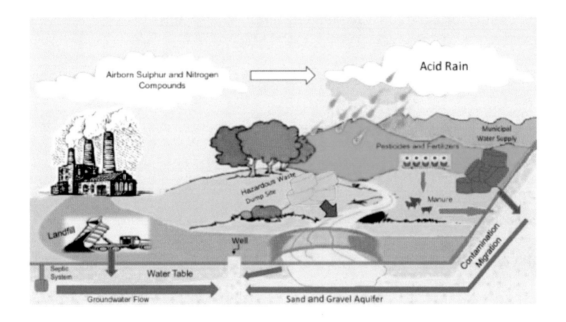

Environmental contaminants are chemicals that accidentally or deliberately enter the environment, often, but not always, as a result of human activities. Some of these contaminants may have been manufactured for industrial use and because they are very stable, thcy do not break down easily.

If released to the environment, these contaminants may enter the food chain. Other environmental contaminants are naturally-occurring chemicals, but industrial activity may increase their mobility or increase the amount available to circulate in the environment, allowing them to enter the food chain at higher levels than would otherwise occur.

A wide variety of environmental contaminants have been detected in foods. These range from metals and "ionic" species like perchlorate to organic (carbon-based) substances, including the so-called "persistent organic pollutants" or POPs (named for their ability to exist in the environment for prolonged periods without breaking down). Legacy POPs such as PCBs have been banned for industrial or agricultural use in Canada for many years, but remain in the food chain. Other POPs have been more recently identified, having been found in the environment and the food chain (for example, brominated flame retardants).

-Lead

-Arsenic

-Bromate

-Brominated Flame Retardants

-Chlorinated Naphthalenes

-Dioxins and Furans

-Mercury

-PCBs

-Perchlorate

-Perfluorinated Chemicals in Food

Oil impacts to the beach environment of Grand Isle, Louisiana. Oil and other chemicals can get into sediments, impacting large coastal areas, threatening human health, and reducing the economic well being of regions that depend on a healthy coastal environment.

Our ocean and coastal areas provide us with a lot – from food, places to boat and swim, and wildlife to enjoy...the list goes on. So when these areas become polluted and unhealthy, it isn't just bad for the environment, it's also bad for us. At NOS, scientists, economists, and other experts are busy monitoring, assessing, and working to clean up contaminants in the environment.

The source

A wide range of chemicals can contaminate our water, land, or air, impacting the environment and our health. Most contaminants enter the environment from industrial and commercial facilities; oil and chemical spills; non-point sources such as roads, parking lots, and storm drains; and wastewater treatment plants and sewage systems. Many hazardous waste sites and industrial facilities have been contaminated for decades and continue to affect the environment.

The impact

Contaminants in the environment can look and smell pretty nasty, but their impacts go beyond just aesthetics. Some pollutants resist breakdown and accumulate in the food chain. These pollutants can be consumed or absorbed by fish and wildlife, which in turn may be eaten by us. Chemicals can also get into sediments, impacting large coastal areas, threatening human health, and reducing the economic well being of regions that depend on a healthy coastal environment.

Evaluation tools

Being able to clean up and restore areas that have been impacted by contaminants requires tools tailored to the needs of specific regions. NOS has developed a range of tools to help coastal communities meet their needs. For example, following the Deepwater Horizon oil spill incident in the Gulf of Mexico, NOAA worked with partners to launch the Environmental Response Management Application Gulf Response, an online mapping tool that delivers environmental resource managers the near-real-time information and data necessary to make informed decisions for environmental response. The site uses the Environmental Response Management Application, a web-based geographic information system platform developed by NOAA and the University of New Hampshire's Coastal Response Research Center. NOS also offers a number of assessment tools and guidance to help coastal decision makers understand the implications of contaminated sediments.

Testing toxicity

Harmful chemical pollution and excess nutrient runoff are serious threats to the coastal environment. NOS scientists are conducting research to help detect and predict how this pollution will impact coastal resources. For example, at the National Centers for Coastal Ocean Science, scientists are evaluating the effects of single contaminants and contaminant mixtures, conducting toxicity-testing with single species, and conducting research in controlled conditions to assess contaminant impacts on biological communities. Scientists are also looking at how environmental and human stressors impact bottlenose dolphin populations.

Responding to contaminants

When contaminants threaten or harm aquatic species, make them unsafe to eat, or degrade their habitat, NOS experts work with partners to evaluate risks and injuries, develop strategies to reduce contaminant loads, and reduce the risk to species. The experts also monitor the effectiveness of cleanup actions and design and implement projects to restore natural resources. At larger waste sites and after oil spills, NOS scientists and economists conduct natural resource damage assessments to determine the nature and extent of harm to natural resources and restoration necessary to bring the resources to a healthier state. NOS works with the parties responsible for the contamination to ensure that injured coastal and marine resources are restored.

Nonpoint pollution

When pollution comes from a source that can't be tied to a specific location, we call it *"nonpoint source pollution."* This kind of pollution occurs when leaking septic tanks or stormwater runoff that has picked up things like sediment, fertilizer, pet waste, or oil drain into streams and rivers that empty into our estuaries and coastal waters. To address this polluted runoff, NOAA and the Environmental Protection Agency jointly administer the Coastal Nonpoint Pollution Control Program. Under the program, all states and territories with approved coastal zone management programs are required to develop and implement coastal programs to reduce the amount of nonpoint source pollution entering our waterways.

Exposure to Environmental Contaminants

What are the trends in human exposure to environmental contaminants?

Importance of Monitoring Human Exposure

Trends in human exposure are important for several reasons:

-Understanding the extent to which human populations are being exposed to environmental contaminants helps identify:

-Contaminants of potential public health concern.

-Population subgroups (e.g., by age, race, ethnicity) who may be disproportionately exposed to contaminants or uniquely vulnerable.

For example, children may have disproportionately greater exposures to environmental contaminants because they drink more water, breathe more air, and eat more food per pound or kilogram of body weight than adults. They may also be more vulnerable to some environmental contaminants at certain stages of development.[1,2]

Tracking the levels of environmental contaminants in a population enables assessment of how exposures to those contaminants are changing in that population over time.

Measures of Human Exposure

Human exposure to environmental contaminants can be measured in the ambient environment (air, water, land), at the point of human contact, or after contaminants have entered the human body through entry portals such as the eyes, skin, stomach, intestines, or lungs.

Different approaches are used to measure or estimate the extent of possible human exposure, each with advantages and disadvantages. These approaches include ambient concentration measurements, exposure modeling, personal monitoring, and biomonitoring.

-**Ambient concentrations:** Measurement of ambient concentrations provides information about how much of a contaminant is present in the environment (air, water, food, or soil), but not how much of the contaminant humans actually come in contact with. In some cases, ambient concentrations may be modeled or estimated rather than measured.

This type of exposure estimate has provided a valuable foundation for many of the regulatory and non-regulatory actions that have been taken to limit exposure to ambient contaminants. Measurements of ambient concentrations of contaminants are presented in Air, Water, and Land indicators, but cannot be directly linked with the biomonitoring indicators presented to address the ROE exposure question.

-**Exposure modeling:** Exposure models estimate exposure by combining information about environmental contaminant concentrations with information about people's activities and locations (e.g., time spent working, exercising outdoors, and sleeping; food consumption) to account for potential contact with contaminants. This approach requires data on contaminant levels where people live, work, and play, as well as knowledge of their day-to-day activities. Exposures can also be modeled to account for the relative toxicity of environmental contaminants within a particular chemical group (e.g., types of pesticides). Exposure indices may be developed to evaluate relative changes in environmental contaminant exposure over time.

-**Personal monitoring:** With personal monitoring, an individual wears a monitoring device during normal day-to-day activities. Personal monitoring provides valuable insights into the source of contaminants to which people are being exposed. It is most commonly used in workplaces.

A challenge with personal monitoring (as with biomonitoring) is ensuring that the extent of sampling is sufficient to be representative of the population being studied. No national-scale personal monitoring data are available.

-**Biomonitoring:** Biomonitoring measures how much of a contaminant—or its metabolite(s) or reaction product(s), referred to as "biomarkers"—are present in the human body. Measurements are most commonly made in blood or urine, but can also be taken from a variety of other body compartments, such as feces, breast milk, hair, nails, and exhaled air, as well as tissues obtained through biopsy or autopsy.

Several environmental contaminants, including heavy metals, some pesticides, and other persistent organic pollutants, can accumulate in the body. Biomonitoring has been used to characterize exposure to lead and some other metals for many years. More recently, advances in biomonitoring have enabled measurement of many other environmental contaminants.

ROE Indicators

The ROE presents one exposure modeling indicator (reported as an exposure index) and seven human biomonitoring indicators to address the question What are the trends in human exposure to environmental contaminants? Pesticide Exposure in Food, Blood Cadmium, Serum

Cotinine, Blood Lead, Blood Mercury, Serum Persistent Organic Pollutants, Urinary Pesticides, and Urinary Phthalates.

Exposure Modeling Indicator

To support dietary risk assessment, EPA models pesticide exposure to food using vetted data sources, tools, and methods. Using this same approach, EPA develops modeled exposure indices, which allow comparison of relative exposure to selected pesticide groups in food to a base year. This integrative approach considers multiple factors that influence exposure to pesticides, including toxicity, measured pesticide residue levels, and food consumption information. The indices reflect when there are exposures to pesticide residues that are more toxic, are more frequently detected at higher concentration, or are present in more highly consumed foods. The index values for each year are relative to the base year and do not directly estimate exposure, risk, or cumulative risk. These index values offer a means to assess relative change in pesticide exposure over time. EPA continues to explore the same types of holistic approaches in evaluating other environmental exposure trends.

Biomonitoring Indicators

By directly measuring environmental contaminants or their metabolites in human fluids or tissues, biomonitoring takes into account the complex set of physiologic and metabolic factors that govern how contaminants are absorbed and distributed within the body.

The biomonitoring indicators (which rely on data from the Centers for Disease Control and Prevention's CDC's National Health and Nutrition Examination Survey EXITEXIT EPA WEBSITE NHANES) provide an overall representation of the levels of selected contaminants, or metabolites of contaminants, in human blood and urine across the U.S. population. These indicators enhance understanding of the extent to which exposure to individual substances has occurred on a national scale. Measurable levels of many of these contaminants appear in at least some subset of the populations tested.

Although ROE biomonitoring indicators show the relative amounts of environmental contaminants in people and in subpopulations over time, by themselves, biomarkers of exposure do not:

-Provide information about the contaminant source.

-Predict whether the presence of the contaminant in the body will result in biological alterations or harmful health effects, either acting alone or in combination with other contaminants.

-Provide information on when, where, and how exposure occurred. For example, lead in children's blood may come from exposure to airborne sources, contaminated water or food, or contaminated soil or dust.

-Explain possible differences among some subpopulations.

Also, there are still many contaminants for which no biomonitoring indicators exist, and others that are simply not feasible to analyze using current technology or data collection methods. These include radon, most criteria air pollutants (e.g., ozone, nitrogen dioxide, carbon monoxide, particulate matter), and biological agents (e.g., molds, certain infectious agents such as bacteria or viruses, dust mites). In many cases, biomonitoring for these contaminants is either cost-prohibitive or not yet technologically feasible.

Biomonitoring methods are constantly evolving, so exposure indicators may be added over time as data become available. For example, as part of its ongoing National Health and Nutrition Examination Survey (NHANES), CDC continues to add environmental contaminants to its biomonitoring efforts. EPA anticipates adding several contaminants to the ROE biomonitoring indicator suite in future years.

Top 25 Brutal Environmental Concerns That You Desperately Need To Know

Our Mother Earth is currently facing a lot of environmental concerns. The environmental problems like global warming, acid rain, air pollution, urban sprawl, waste disposal, ozone layer depletion, water pollution, climate change and many more affect every human, animal, and nation on this planet.

Over the last few decades, the exploitation of our planet and the degradation of our environment has gone up at an alarming rate. As our actions have been not in favor of protecting this planet, we have seen natural disasters striking us more often in the form of flash floods, earthquakes, blizzards, tsunamis, and cyclones.

1. Air Pollution

Pollution of air, water, and soil takes a huge number of years to recover. Industry and engine vehicle fumes are the most obvious toxins. Substantial metals, nitrates, and plastic are poisons in charge of pollution.

While water contamination is brought about by oil slicks, acid rain, and urban sprawl; air contamination is created by different gasses and poisons discharged by businesses and manufacturing plants and burning of fossil fills; soil contamination is majorly created by mechanical waste that takes supplements out of the soil.

2. Water Pollution

Clean drinking water is turning into an uncommon thing. Water is turning into a monetary and political concern as the human populace battles for this need. Waste from industrial and agricultural activities pollute the water that is used by humans, animals, and plants.

3: Soil and Land Pollution

Land pollution simply means degradation of the earth's surface as a result of human activities like mining, littering, deforestation, industrial, construction, and agricultural activities. Land pollution can have a huge environmental impact in the form of air pollution and soil pollution which in turn can have an adverse effect on human health.

4. Climate Change

Climate change is yet another environmental concern that has surfaced in the last couple of decades. Environmental change has different destructive impacts that include, but are not limited to, the melting of polar ice, change in seasons, new sicknesses, and change in the general climate situation.

5. Global Warming

Environmental asset abuse is also an important environmental concern. Fossil fuel utilization brings about the discharge of greenhouse gasses, which causes environmental change. However, individuals are taking endeavors to move to renewable energy sources.

6. Deforestation & Logging

Our woodlands create new oxygen and additionally help in managing temperature and precipitation. At present, timberlands cover 30% of the area, but wooded areas are being lost on a regular basis because people are looking for homes, food, and materials. Deforestation is a huge problem and will just continue to get worse.

7. Increased Carbon Footprint

Temperature increases, like climate change, are the consequence of human practices, including the use of greenhouse gasses. When the atmosphere changes and the heat increases, it can cause a number of problems and start to destroy the world we live in.

8. Genetic Modification

Genetic modification utilizing biotechnology is called genetic engineering. Genetic engineering of food brings about expanded poisons and sicknesses as qualities from a hypersensitive plant can exchange to the target plant. Some of these crops can even be a threat to the world around us, as animals start to ingest the unnatural chemicals and such.

9. Effect on Marine Life

The amount of carbon in the water and the atmosphere is continuing to be a problem in the world around us. The primary effect is on shellfish and microscopic fish, and it has similar effects on osteoporosis in humans.

10. Public Health Issues

The current environmental concerns represent a considerable measure of danger to the well-being of people and creatures. Dirty water is the greatest well-being danger of the world and poses a risk to the health and lifespan of people and animals.

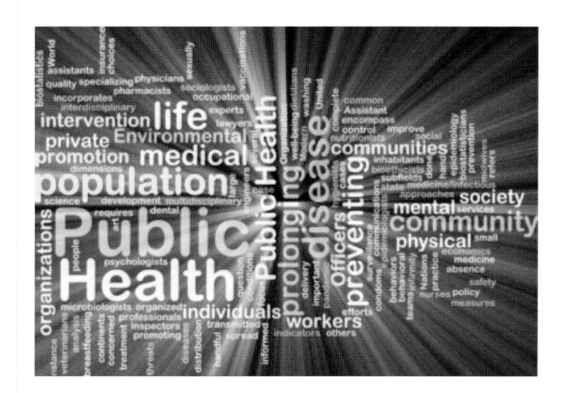

11. Overpopulation

The number of inhabitants on the planet is arriving at unsustainable levels as it confronts a deficiency of assets like water, fuel, and food. Overpopulation is one of the most important environmental concerns.

12: Loss of Biodiversity

Biodiversity is yet another casualty due to the impact of human beings on the environment. It is the result of 3.5 billion years of evolution. Habitat destruction is a major cause of biodiversity loss. Habitat loss is caused by deforestation, overpopulation, pollution, and global warming.

13. Household and Industrial Waste

The overutilization of assets and the formation of plastics are making a worldwide emergency of waste transfer. Developed nations are infamous for creating an unreasonable measure of waste or junk and dumping their waste in the seas and, less created nations.

14. Ozone Layer Depletion

The ozone layer is an undetectable layer of protection around the planet that secures us from the sun's unsafe beams. The depletion of the critical Ozone layer of the air is credited to contamination brought about by Bromide and Chlorine found in Chlorofloro carbons (CFCs). When these poisonous gasses reach the upper parts of the atmosphere, they cause a gap in the ozone layer, the greatest of which is over the Antarctic.

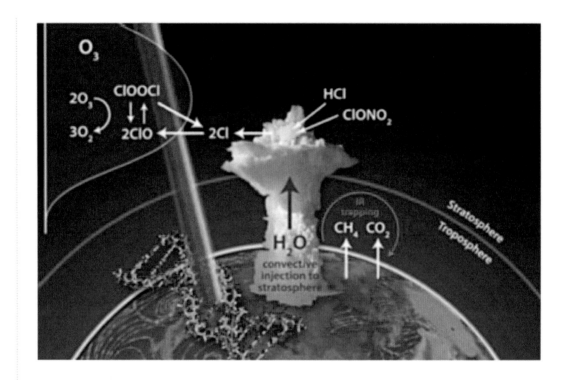

15. Mining

Mining results in the extraction of minerals from the earth's core. These minerals also bring out harmful chemicals from deep inside the earth to the earth's surface. The toxic emissions from mining can cause air, water, and soil pollution.

16: Natural Resource Depletion

Non-renewable resources are limited and will get expired one day. Consumption of fossil fuels at an alarming rate can lead to global warming which can further result in the melting of polar ice caps and an increase in sea levels.

17: Natural Disasters

Natural disasters like earthquakes, floods, tsunamis, cyclones, volcanic eruptions can be unpredictable, devastating, and can cause irreparable damage. They can cause a huge loss of life and property.

18: Nuclear Issues

Radioactive waste is a nuclear fuel that contains radioactive substances and is a by-product of nuclear power generation. The radioactive waste is an environmental concern that is extremely toxic and can have a devastating effect on the lives of the people living nearby, if not disposed of properly. Radioactive waste is considered to be harmful to humans, plants, animals, and the surrounding environment.

19. Loss of Endangered Species

Human overpopulation is prompting the elimination of species and environmental surroundings and the loss of various biomes. Environmental frameworks, which took a huge number of years to come into being, are at risk when any species populace is huge.

20. Acid Rain

Acid rain happens because of the vicinity of specific poisons in the climate. Corrosive downpour might be brought about because of the use of fossil fuels or volcanoes or spoiling vegetation which discharges sulfur dioxide and nitrogen oxides into the air.

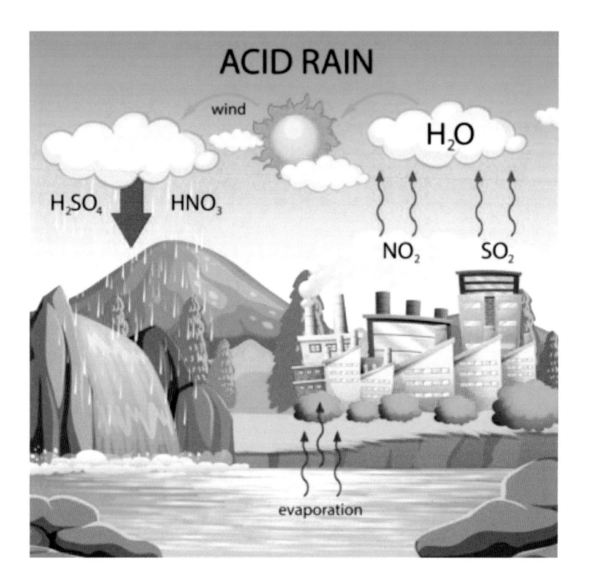

Acid rain happens because of the vicinity of specific poisons in the climate. Corrosive downpour might be brought about because of the use of fossil fuels or volcanoes or spoiling vegetation which discharges sulfur dioxide and nitrogen oxides into the air.

21: Agricultural Pollution

Modern-day agriculture practices make use of chemical products like pesticides and fertilizers to deal with local pests. Some of the chemicals when sprayed do not disappear and in fact, seeps into the ground and thereby harms plants and crops. Also, contaminated water is used for irrigation by farmers due to the disposal of industrial and agricultural waste in local water bodies.

22: Light and Noise Pollution

Noise pollution is another common form of pollution that causes temporary disruption when there is an excessive amount of unpleasant noise. Construction activities, industrialization, an increase in vehicular traffic, lack of urban planning are a few of the causes of noise pollution.

23. Urban Sprawl

Urban sprawl alludes to the relocation of the populace from high thickness urban ranges to low-density provincial zones which bring about the spreading of the city over the more rustic area. Urban sprawl brings about expanded movement, environmental concerns, and well-being concerns.

24: Disposal of Medical Waste

Medical waste is any kind of waste that is produced in large quantities by healthcare centers like hospitals, nursing homes, dental clinics, and is considered to be of a bio-hazardous nature. The waste can include needles, syringes, gloves, tubes, blades, blood, body parts, and many more.

There are a lot of medical waste companies that deal with medical waste disposal and are unique in the waste management industry. They must maintain a fleet of removal vehicles that use especially containment receptacles so that the medical waste is not exposed to the air, or at risk for spilling should there be an accident.

25: Littering and Landfills

Littering simply means disposal of a piece of garbage or debris improperly or at a wrong location usually on the ground instead of disposing them at a trash container or recycling bin. Littering can cause a huge environmental and economic impact in the form of spending millions of dollars to clean the garbage of roads that pollute the clean air.

Landfills, on the other hand, are nothing but huge garbage dumps that make the city look ugly and produce toxic gases that could prove fatal for humans and animals. Landfills are generated due to the large amount of waste that is generated by households, industries, and healthcare centers every day.

Resources

canada.ca, "Environmental Contaminants."; oceanservice.noaa.gov, "Contaminants in the Environment."; epa.gov, "Exposure to Environmental Contaminants: What are the trends in human exposure to environmental contaminants?"; conserve-energy-future.com, "Top 25 Brutal Environmental Concerns That You Desperately Need To Know.";

10d44a0d-2dac-47f0-b49c-b2d27d1729f1R01